Making Grids Work

T0134584

Making Grids Work

Proceedings of the CoreGRID Workshop on
Programming Models
Grid and P2P System Architecture
Grid Systems, Tools and Environments
12-13 June 2007, Heraklion, Crete, Greece

Edited by

Marco Danelutto
University of Pisa
Pisa, Italy

Paraskevi Fragopoulou
Foundation for Research and Technology - Hellas and
Technological Educational Institute of Crete, Heraklion, Greece

Vladimir Getov
University of Westminster
London, UK

 Springer

Editors:
Marco Danelutto
University of Pisa
Pisa, 56127, Italy
marcod@di.unipi.it

Paraskevi Fragopoulou
Foundation for Research and Technology - Hellas (FORTH)
Institute of Computer Science
N. Plastira 100 Vassilika Vouton
GR-700 13 Heraklion, Crete, Greece
fragopou@ics.forth.gr

Department of Applied Informatics and Multimedia
Technological Educational Institute of Crete, Greece

Vladimir Getov
University of Westminster
London, HA1 3TP, UK
V.S.Getov@westminster.ac.uk

ISBN-13: 978-1-4419-4615-7   e-ISBN-13: 978-0-387-78448-9

© 2010 Springer Science+Business Media, LLC.
All rights reserved. This work may not be translated or copied in whole or in part
without the written permission of the publisher (Springer Science+Business Media,
LLC, 233 Spring Street, New York, NY 10013, USA), except for brief excerpts in
connection with reviews or scholarly analysis. Use in connection with any form of
information storage and retrieval, electronic adaptation, computer software, or by
similar or dissimilar methodology now known or hereafter developed is forbidden.
The use in this publication of trade names, trademarks, service marks and similar
terms, even if they are not identified as such, is not to be taken as an expression of
opinion as to whether or not they are subject to proprietary rights.

Printed on acid-free paper.

springer.com

Contents

Preface

Three Institutes of the CoreGRID Network of Excellence organized a common workshop to present and discuss the latest results on Grid and P2P Technologies achieved by the Institute partners as well as the latest developments by researchers outside the CoreGRID community. The three institutes involved are:

- The Institute on *Programming Model*,

- The Institute on *Architectural Issues: Scalability, Dependability, Adaptability*, and

- The Institute on *Grid Systems, Tools, and Environments*.

The aforementioned institutes have a history in organizing joint events – the most recent one being the workshop in Krakow, Poland in June 2006.

The 2007 joint workshop took place at the premises of the Institute of Computer Science, Foundation for Research and Technology-Hellas (FORTH-ICS), Heraklion-Crete, Greece on June 12-13, 2007. The event was organized in two plenary sessions hosting a presentation from the CoreGRID scientific coordinator and three invited speakers, followed by 12 technical sessions hosting the accepted contributions. A total of 42 papers were accepted for presentation among those submitted to the workshop.

The workshop invited speakers presented some of the latest developments in Grid Technology, Semantic Grid, and P2P technology respectively. Their talks focused on ongoing work including some open problems and stimulated interesting discussion among the participants.

The invited speakers and their respective talk titles were the following:

- Dennis Gannon, Indiana University, *"Programming Gateways to the Teragrid"*

- David De Roure, University of Southampton, *"Re- evaluating the Grid"*

- Ann Chervenak, University of Southern California *"Peer-to-peer Approaches to Grid Resource Discovery"*.

All the contributions presented to the workshop have been included in a CoreGRID technical report – TR-0080[1]. The papers presented at the workshop have been submitted to a further formal refereeing process. This volume hosts the selected contributions resulting from this review process.

We wish to thank our hosts from FORTH-ICS for their kind hospitality, the local organization team for providing such superb support, the CoreGRID administrative structure for allowing us to organize the workshop and, in particular, to support the invited speakers, and the entire CoreGRID community for submitting such a large number of interesting and high quality papers and for their enthusiastic participation in the workshop.

Our thanks also go to the European Commission for sponsoring this volume of selected articles from the workshop via the CoreGRID NoE project, grant number 004265.

Marco Danelutto, Paraskevi Fragopoulou, Vladimir Getov

---

[1] Available at http://www.coregrid.net/mambo/content/view/152/292/

Contributing Authors

Marco Aldinucci Istituto di Scienza e Tecnologie dell'Informazione, ISTI-CNR, Pisa, Italy Marco.Aldinucci@isti.cnr.it

Javier Alonso Technical University of Catalonia Barcelona Supercomputing Center, Barcelona,Spain alonso@ac.upc.edu

Cosmin Arad School for Information and Communication Technology (ICT), Royal Institute of Technology (KTH), Stockholm, Sweden icarad@kth.se

Ani Anciaux–Sedrakian Polytechnic University of Catalonia Campus Nord - Modul D6 c/Jordi Girona 1-3 E08034 Barcelona, Spain ani.anciaux@bsc.es

Filipe Araujo CISUC, Department of Informatics Engineering, University of Coimbra, Portugal filipius@dei.uc.pt

Alvaro E. Arenas STFC, Rutherford Appleton Laboratory Chilton, Didcot, UK a.e.arenas@rl.ac.uk

Rosa M. Badia Polytechnic University of Catalonia Campus Nord, Barcelona, Spain rosa.m.badia@bsc.es

Zoltan Balaton MTA SZTAKI Computer and Automation Research Institute of the Hungarian Academy of Sciences Budapest, Hungary balaton@sztaki.hu

Ranieri Baraglia Institute of Information Science and Technologies, CNR, Via Moruzzi 1, 56100 Pisa, Italy ranieri.baraglia@isti.cnr.it

Tomasz Bartynski Institute of Computer Science and ACC CYFRONET AGH University of Science and Technology Al. Mickiewicza 30, 30-059 Krakow, Poland

Alessandro Basso University of Westminster, Harrow School of Computer Science, Watford Road, Harrow HA1 3TP, U.K. bassoa@wmin.ac.uk

Artie Basukoski University of Westminster, Harrow School of Computer Science, Harrow U.K. A.Basukoski02@wmin.ac.uk

Fatiha Bouabache Laboratoire de Recherche en Informatique Universite Paris Sud-XI, Orsay, France fatiha.bouabache@lri.fr

Francoise Baude INRIA Sophia - I3S - CNRS, Universite de Nice Sophia Antipolis, France fbaude@sophia.inria.fr

Shishir Bharathi USC Information Sciences Institute, Marina del Rey, CA, USA shishir@isi.edu

Alexander Bolotov University of Westminster, Harrow School of Computer Science, Harrow, London, U.K. bolotoa@wmin.ac.uk

Hinde Lilia Bouziane INRIA/IRISA, Campus de Beaulieu, 35042 Rennes, France Hinde.Bouziane@inria.fr

Fabienne Boyer INRIA, France fabienne.boyer@inrialpes.fr

Per Brand SICS, Sweden perbrand@sics.se

Marian Bubak Institute of Computer Science, AGH, Krakow, Poland bubak@uci.agh.edu.pl

Sonia Campa Dept. of Computer Science, University of Pisa, Via Buonarroti, 2 - 56127 Pisa, Italy campa@di.unipi.it

Gabriele Capannini ISTI/CNR and Department of Computer Science, University of Pisa, Pisa, Italy gabriele.capanniniimgatisti.cnr.it

Franck Cappello INRIA Futurs/Laboratoire de Recherche en Informatique Universite Paris Sud-XI, Orsay, France fci@lri.fr

Denis Caromel INRIA Sophia Antipolis, CNRS - I3S - University of Nice Sophia-Antipolis, Sophia-Antipolis, France Denis.Caromel@sophia.inria.fr

Ann Chervenak USC Information Sciences Institute, Marina del Rey, CA, USA annc@isi.edu

Maurice Clint School of Computer Science The Queen's University of Belfast Belfast BT7 1NN, U.K. m.clint@qub.ac.uk

Fernando Costa CISUC, Dep Eng Informatica, University of Coimbra, Portugal flcosta@student.dei.uc.pt

Natalia Currle-Linde High Performance Computing Center Stuttgart (HLRS), University of Stuttgart, Stuttgart, Germany linde@hlrs.de

Marco Danelutto Dept. of Computer Science, University of Pisa, Pisa, Italy marcod@di.unipi.it

Patrizio Dazzi ISTI/CNR, Pisa and IMT, Lucca, Italy patrizio.dazzi@isti.cnr.it

David De Roure University of Southampton Electronics and Computer Science Southampton, U.K. dder@ecs.soton.ac.uk

Marios Dikaiakos Department of Computer Science, University of Cyprus, Nicosia, Cyprus mdd@cs.ucy.ac.cy

Patricio Domingues CISUC, Department of Informatics Engineering, University of Coimbra, Portugal luis@dei.uc.pt

Jan Dunnweber Institut fur Informatik, University of Munster, Munster, Germany duennweb@math.uni-muenster.de

Gilles Fedak INRIA Futurs/Laboratoire de Recherche en Informatique Universite Paris Sud-XI, Orsay, France fedak@lri.fr

Joaquim Gabarro Universitat Politecnica de Catalunya ALBCOM Research Group Edifici Ω, Campus Nord Jordi Girona, 1-3, Barcelona, Spain gabarro@lsi.upc.edu

Dennis Gannon Department of Computer Science, Indiana University, Bloomington, USA gannon@cs.indiana.edu

Konstantinos Georgiou University of Patras, CEID, Patras, Greece georgiu@ceid.upatras.gr

Chryssis Georgiou Department of Computer Science, University of Cyprus, Nicosia, Cyprus chryssis@cs.ucy.ac.cy

Vladimir Getov Harrow School of Computer Science, University of Westminster, Harrow, London, U.K. V.S.Getov@westminster.ac.uk

Ali Ghodsi School for Information and Communication Technology (ICT), Royal Institute of Technology (KTH), Stockholm, Sweden

Gabor Gombas MTA SZTAKI Computer and Automation Research Institute of the Hungarian Academy of Sciences, Budapest, Hungary gombasg@sztaki.hu

Sergei Gorlatch Institute for Informatics, University of Munster, Germany gorlatch@math.uni-muenster.de

Carole Goble Department of Computer Science, The University of Manchester, Manchester, U.K. carole.goble@manchester.ac.uk

Tomasz Gubala Institute of Computer Science and ACC CYFRONET AGH University of Science and Technology Al. Krakow, Poland

Thomas Herault INRIA Futurs/Laboratoire de Recherche en Informatique Universite Paris Sud-XI, Orsay, France thomas.herault@lri.fr

Seif Haridi School for Information and Communication Technology (ICT), Royal Institute of Technology (KTH), Stockholm, Sweden seif@kth.se

Joel Hoglund SICS, Sweden joel@sics.se

Stavros Isaiadis Harrow School of Computer Science, University of Westminster, Harrow, London, U.K. S.Isaiadis@westminster.ac.uk

Peter Kacsuk MTA SZTAKI Lab. of Parallel and Distributed Systems, Budapest, Hungary kacsuk@sztaki.hu

Marek Kasztelnik Institute of Computer Science and ACC CYFRONET AGH University of Science and Technology Al. Mickiewicza, Krakow, Poland

Ian Kelley School of Computer Science, Cardiff University, U.K. and Center for Computation Technology Louisiana State University, USA I.R.Kelley@cs.cardiff.ac.uk

Thilo Kielmann Department of Computer Science, Vrije Universiteit, Amsterdam, The Netherlands kielmann@cs.vu.nl

Peter Kilpatrick Computer Science Department, Queen's University of Belfast, Belfast, UK p.kilpatrick@qub.ac.uk

Tamas Kiss School of Informatics, University of Westminster, London, U.K. kisst@wmin.ac.uk

Giorgos Kollias University of Patras, CEID, Patras, Greece gdk@ceid.upatras.gr

Derrick Kondo Laboratoire dŠInformatique de Grenoble INRIA Rhone-Alpes, France dkondo@imag.fr

Domenico Laforenza Istituto di Scienza e Tecnologie dell'Informazione, ISTI-CNR, Pisa, Italy Domenico.Laforenza@isti.cnr.it

Philipp Ludeking University of Munster, Department of Mathematics and Computer Science, Munster, Germany luedeking@uni-muenster.de

Maciej Malawski Institute of Computer Science and ACC CYFRONET AGH University of Science and Technology Al. Mickiewicza, Krakow, Poland malawski@agh.edu.pl

Andre Merzky Department of Computer Science, Vrije Universiteit, Amsterdam, The Netherlands merzky@cs.vu.nl

Piotr Machner Inst. Computer Science, AGH, al. Mickiewicza, Krakow, Poland machner@student.agh.edu.pl

Attila Csaba Marosi MTA SZTAKI Computer and Automation Research Institute of the Hungarian Academy of Sciences Budapest, Hungary

Kyriacos Neocleous Department of Computer Science, University of Cyprus, Nicosia, Cyprus kyriacos@cs.ucy.ac.cy

Harris Papadakis ICS, Foundation for Research and Technology-Hellas, Greece adanar@ics.forth.gr

Ludovic Henrio INRIA Sophia - I3S - CNRS - Universite de Nice Sophia Antipolis, France Ludovic.Henrio@sophia.inria.fr

Paraskevi Fragopoulou ICS, Foundation for Research and Technology-Hellas, Greece fragopou@ics.forth.gr

Noel de Palma INRIA, France noel.depalma@inrialpes.fr

Nikos Parlavantzas INRIA, France nikolaos.parlavantzas@inrialpes.fr

Marco Pasquali ISTI/CNR Pisa Italy IMT, Lucca Institute for Advanced Studies, Lucca, Italy m.pasquali@isti.cnr.it

Jean-Louis Pazat IRISA/INSA, Campus universitaire de Beaulieu, Rennes, France Jean-Louis.Pazat@irisa.fr

Christian Perez INRIA/IRISA, Campus de Beaulieu, Rennes, France Christian.Perez@inria.fr

Josep M. Perez Polytechnic University of Catalonia Campus Nord, Barcelona, Spain josep.m.perez@bsc.es

Stefan Plantikow Zuse Institute Berlin, Takustr. Berlin-Dahlem; and Humboldt-Universität zu Berlin, Rudower Chaussee, Berlin-Adlershof, Germany plantikow@zib.de

Konstantin Popov SICS, Sweden kost@sics.se

Diego Puppin Istituto di Scienza e Tecnologie dell'Informazione, ISTI-CNR, Pisa, Italy and Dept. of Computer Science, University of Pisa, Pisa, Italy Diego.Puppin@isti.cnr.it

Alexander Reinefeld Zuse Institute Berlin, Takustr. Berlin-Dahlem; and Humboldt-Universität zu Berlin, Rudower Chaussee Berlin-Adlershof, Germany ar@zib.de

Nuno Rodrigues Dep. Engenharia Informática, University of Coimbra, Polo II, Coimbra, Portugal Portugal nuno@dei.uc.pt

Roberto Roverso School for Information and Communication Technology (ICT), Royal Institute of Technology (KTH), Stockholm, Sweden roverso@kth.se

Michael Resch High Performance Computing Center Stuttgart (HLRS) University of Stuttgart, Stuttgart, Germany resch@hlrs.de

Laura Ricci Department of Computer Science, University of Pisa, Pisa, Italy ricci@di.unipi.it

Florian Schintke Zuse Intitute Berlin, Berlin-Dahlem, Germany schintke@zib.de

Gheorghe Cosmin Silaghi University of Coimbra, Department of Informatics Engineering Polo II, Coimbra, Portugal gsilaghi@dei.uc.pt

Luis Moura Silva CISUC, Dep Eng Informatica, University of Coimbra, Portugal luis@dei.uc.pt

Ahmad Al-Shishtawy KTH, Sweden ahmadas@kth.se

Gergely Sipos MTA SZTAKI Lab. of Parallel and Distributed Systems, Budapest, Hungary sipos@sztaki.hu

Raul Sirvent Polytechnic University of Catalonia Campus Nord, Barcelona, Spain raul.sirvent@bsc.es

Decio Sousa Dep. Engenharia Informática, University of Coimbra, Polo II, Coimbra, Portugal Portugal decio@dei.uc.pt

Alan Stewart School of Computer Science The Queen's University of Belfast, Belfast, U.K.

Domenico Talia DEIS, University of Calabria, Via P. Bucci, Rende, Italy talia@deis.unical.it

Ian Taylor School of Computer Science, Cardiff University, U.K. and Center for Computation Technology Louisiana State University, USA Ian.J.Taylor@cs.cardiff.ac.uk

A.D. Techiouba ISTI/CNR, Pisa, Italy

Enric Tejedor Universitat Politecnica de Catalunya Barcelona, Spain etejedor@ac.upc.edu

Gabor Terstyanszky School of Informatics, University of Westminster New Cavendish Street, London, U.K. terstyg@wmin.ac.uk

Jeyarajan Thiyagalingam Harrow School of Computer Science, University of Westminster, London, U.K. T.Jeyan@westminster.ac.uk

Nicola Tonellotto Institute of Information Science and Technologies, CNR, Pisa, Italy nicola.tonellotto@isti.cnr.it

Jordi Torres Technical University of Catalonia Barcelona Supercomputing Center, Barcelona,Spain torres@ac.upc.edu

Paolo Trunfio DEIS, University of Calabria, Rende, Italy trunfio@deis.unical.it

Alexandru Tudose School of Informatics, University of Westminster, London, U.K. A.Tudose@student.westminster.ac.uk

Demetris Zeinalipour-Yazti School of Pure and Applied Sciences, Open University of Cyprus, Nicosia, Cyprus zeinalipour@ouc.ac.cy

Wlodzimierz Funika Inst. Computer Science, AGH, Krakow, Poland funika@agh.edu.pl

Wolfgang Ziegler Fraunhofer Institute SCAI, Department for Web-based Applications, Sankt Augustin, Germany wolfgang.ziegler@scai.fraunhofer.de

Corrado Zoccolo Dept. of Computer Science, University of Pisa, Pisa, Italy zoccolo@di.unipi.it

I

COMPONENT PROGRAMMING MODELS

BEHAVIOURAL SKELETONS FOR COMPONENT AUTONOMIC MANAGEMENT ON GRIDS*

Marco Aldinucci, Sonia Campa, Marco Danelutto
Computer Science Department, University of Pisa
Pisa, Italy
{aldinuc, campa, marcod}@di.unipi.it

Patrizio Dazzi, Domenico Laforenza, Nicola Tonellotto
ISTI – CNR
Pisa, Italy
{patrizio.dazzi, domenico.laforenza, nicola.tonellotto}@isti.cnr.it

Peter Kilpatrick
Computer Science Department, Queen's University
Belfast, UK
p.kilpatrick@qub.ac.uk

Abstract   We present behavioural skeletons for the CoreGRID Component Model, which are an abstraction aimed at simplifying the development of GCM-based self-management applications. Behavioural skeletons abstract component self-management in component-based design as design patterns abstract class design in classic OO development. As here we just wish to introduce the behavioural skeleton framework, emphasis is placed on general skeleton structure rather than on their autonomic management policies.

Keywords: components, code adaptivity, autonomic computing, skeletons

*This research is carried out under the FP6 Network of Excellence CoreGRID funded by the European Commission (Contract IST-2002-004265) and the FP6 GridCOMP project partially founded by the European Commission (Contract FP6-034442).

1.   Introduction and Related Work

While developing grid applications neither the target platforms nor their status are fixed, statically or dynamically [12]. This makes application adaptivity an essential feature in order to achieve high performance and to exploit efficiently the available resources [1].

In recent years, several research initiatives exploiting component technology [9] have investigated the possibilities related to component adaptation, i.e. the process of changing the component for use in different contexts. This process can be conceived as either a static or dynamic process.

The basic use of static adaptation covers straightforward but popular methodologies such as *copy-paste* and *OO inheritance*. A more advanced usage covers the case in which adaptation happens at run-time. These systems enable dynamically defined adaptation by allowing adaptations, in the form of code, scripts or rules, to be added, removed or modified at run-time [7]. Among them it is worth distinguishing the systems where all possible adaptation cases have been specified at compile time, but the conditions determining the actual adaptation at any point in time can be dynamically changed [4]. Dynamically adaptable systems rely on a clear separation of concerns between adaptation and application logic. This approach has recently gained increased impetus in the grid community, especially via its formalisation in terms of the *Autonomic Computing* (AC) paradigm [15, 5, 3]. The AC term is emblematic of a vast *hierarchy* of self-governing systems, many of which consist of many interacting, self-governing components that in turn comprise a number of interacting, self-governing components at the next level down [13]. An autonomic component will typically consist of one or more managed components coupled with a single autonomic manager that controls them. To pursue its goal the manager may trigger an adaptation of the managed components to react to a run-time change of application QoS requirements or to the platform status.

In this regard, an assembly of self-managed components implements, via their managers, a distributed algorithm that manages the entire application. Several existing programming frameworks aim to ease this task by providing a set of mechanisms to dynamically install reactive rules within autonomic managers. These rules are typically specified as a collection of when-*event*-if-*cond*-then-*act* clauses, where *event* is raised by the monitoring of internal or external component activity (e.g. the component server interface received a request, and the platform running a component exceeded a threshold load, respectively); *cond* is an expression over internal component attributes (e.g. component life-cycle status); *act* represents an adaptation action (e.g. create, destroy a component, wire, unwire components, notify events to another component's manager). Several programming frameworks implement variants of this general idea, including ASSIST [20, 1], AutoMate [17], SAFRAN [10], and finally the forthcoming CoreGRID Grid Component Model (GCM) [9]. The latter two are derived from a common ancestor, i.e. the Fractal hierarchical component model [16]. All the named frameworks, except SAFRAN, are targeted to distributed applications on grids.

Though such programming frameworks considerably ease the development of an autonomic application for the grid (to various degrees), they rely fully on the application programmer's expertise for the set-up of the management code, which can be quite difficult to write since it may involve the management of black-box components, and, notably, is tailored for the particular component or assembly of them. As a result, the introduction of dynamic adaptivity and self-management might enable the management of grid dynamism and uncertainty aspects but, at the same time, decreases the component reuse potential since it further specialises components with application specific management code.

In this work, we propose *behavioural skeletons* as a novel way to describe autonomic components in the GCM framework. Behavioural skeletons aim to describe recurring patterns of component assemblies that can be (either statically or dynamically) equipped with correct and effective management strategies with respect to a given management goal. Behavioural skeletons help the application designer to 1) design component assemblies that can be effectively reused, and 2) cope with management complexity by providing a component with an explicit context with respect to top-down design (i.e. component nesting).

2.   Grid Component Model

GCM is a hierarchical component model explicitly designed to support component-based autonomic applications in grid contexts. GCM allows component interactions to take place with several distinct mechanisms. In addition to classical "RPC-like" use/provide ports (or client/server interfaces), GCM allows data, stream and event ports to be used in component interaction. Furthermore, collective interaction patterns (communication mechanisms) are also supported. The full specification of GCM can be found in [9].

GCM is therefore assumed to provide several levels of autonomic managers in components, that take care of the non-functional features of the component programs. GCM components thus have two kinds of interfaces: functional and non-functional ones. The functional interfaces host all those ports concerned with implementation of the functional features of the component. The non-functional interfaces host all those ports needed to support the component management activity in the implementation of the non-functional features, i.e. all those features contributing to the efficiency of the component in obtaining the expected (functional) results but not directly involved in result computation. Each GCM component therefore contains an *Autonomic Manager* (AM), interacting with other managers in other components via the component non-functional interfaces. The AM implements the autonomic cycle via a simple program based on the reactive rules described above. In this, the AM leverages on component controllers for the *event* monitoring and the execution of reconfiguration *actions*. In GCM, the latter controller is called the *Autonomic Behaviour Controller* (ABC). This controller exposes server-only non-functional interfaces, which can be accessed either from the AM or an external component that logically surrogates the AM strategy. We call *passive* a GCM component exhibiting just the ABC, whereas we call *active* a GCM component exhibiting both the ABC and the AM.

3.   Describing Adaptive Applications

The architecture of a component-based application is usually described via an ADL (Architecture Description Language) text, which enumerates the components and describes their relationships via the *used-by* relationship. In a hierarchical component model, such as the GCM, the ADL describes also the *implemented-by* relationship, which represents the component nesting.

Typically, the ADL supplies a static vision of an application, which is not fully satisfactory for an application exhibiting autonomic behaviour since it may autonomously change behaviour during its execution[1]. Such change may be of several types:

-   *Component lifecycle.* Components can be started or stopped.

-   *Component relationships.* The used-by and/or implemented-by relationships among components are changed. This may involve component creation/destruction, and component wiring alteration.

-   *Component attributes.* A refinement of the behaviour of some components (which does not involve structural changes) is required, usually over a pre-determined parametric functionality.

In the most general case, an autonomic application may evolve along adaptation steps that involve one or more changes belonging to these three classes. In this regard, the ADL just represents a snapshot of the launch time configuration.

The evolution of a component is driven by its AM, which may request management action with the AM at the next level up in order to deal with management issues it cannot solve locally. Overall, it is a part of a distributed system that cooperatively manages the entire application.

In the general case, the management code executing in the AM of a component depends both on the component's functional behaviour and the goal of

---

[1]However, note that with GCM the ADL provides a hook to accommodate a *behavioural specification*.

the management. The AM should also be able to cooperate with other AMs, which are unknown at design time due to the nature of component-based design. Currently, programming frameworks supporting the AC paradigm (such as the ones mentioned in Sec. 1) just provide mechanisms to implement management code. This approach has several disadvantages, especially when applied to a hierarchical component model:

- The management code is difficult to develop and to test since the context in which it should work may be unknown.

- The management code is tailored to the particular instance of the management elements (inner components), further restricting the component possible reusability.

For this reason, we believe that the "ad-hoc" approach to management code is unfit to be a cornerstone of the GCM component model.

4.   Behavioural Skeletons

Behavioural skeletons aim to abstract parametric paradigms of GCM component assembly, each of them specialised to solve one or more management goals belonging to the classical AC classes, i.e. configuration, optimisation, healing and protection.

Behavioural skeletons represent a specialisation of the algorithmic skeleton concept for component management [5]. Algorithmic skeletons have been traditionally used as a vehicle to provide efficient implementation templates of parallel paradigms. Behavioural skeletons, as algorithmic skeletons, represent patterns of parallel computations (which are expressed in GCM as graphs of components), but in addition they exploit the inherent skeleton semantics to design sound self-management schemes of parallel components.

Due to the hierarchical nature of GCM, behavioural skeletons can be identified with a composite component with no loss of generality (identifying skeletons as particular higher-order components [11]). Since component composition is defined independently from behavioural skeletons, they do not represent the exclusive means of expressing applications, but can be freely mixed with non-skeletal components. In this setting, a behavioural skeleton is a composite component that

- exposes a description of its functional behaviour;

- establishes a parametric orchestration schema of inner components;

- may carry constraints that inner components are required to comply with;

- may carry a number of pre-defined plans aimed at coping with a given self-management goal.

Behavioural skeleton usage helps designers in two main ways: the application designer benefits from a library of skeletons, each of them carrying several pre-defined, efficient self-management strategies; and, the component/application designer is provided with a framework that helps the design of new skeletons and their implementations.

The former task is achieved because (1) skeletons exhibit an explicit higher-order functional semantics, which delimits the skeleton usage and definition domain; and (2) skeletons describe parametric interaction patterns and can be designed in such a way that parameters affect non-functional behaviour but are invariant for functional behaviour.

5.   A Basic Set of Behavioural Skeletons

Here we present a basic set of behavioural skeletons for the sake of exemplification. Despite their simplicity, they cover a significant set of parallel computations in common usage.

One class of behavioural skeletons springs from the idea of *functional replication*. Let us assume the skeletons in this class have two functional interfaces: a one-to-many stream server S, and a many-to-one client stream interface C (see Fig. 1). The skeleton accepts requests on the server interface; and dispatches them to a number of instances of an inner component W, which may propagate results outside the skeleton via C interface. Assume that replicas of W can safely lose their internal state between different calls. For example, the component has just a transient internal state and/or stores persistent data via an external data-base component.

Farm.   A stream of tasks is absorbed by a *unicast* S, each task is computed by one instance of W and sent to C, which collect tasks *from-any*. This skeleton can be equipped with a self-optimising policy because the number of Ws can be dynamically changed in a sound way since they are stateless. The typical QoS goal is to keep a given limit (possibly dynamically changing) of served requests in a given time frame. The AM just checks the average time tasks need to traverse the skeleton, and eventually reacts by creating/destroying instances of Ws, and wiring/unwiring them to/from the interfaces.

Data-Parallel.   A stream of tasks is absorbed by a *scatter* S; each task is split in (possibly overlapping) partitions, which are distributed to replicas of W to be computed. Results are *gathered* and assembled by G in a single item. As in the previous case, the number of Ws can be dynamically changed (between different requests) in a sound way since they are stateless. As in the previous case, the skeleton can be equipped with a self-configuration goal, i.e. resource balancing and tuning (e.g. disk space, load, memory usage), that can be achieved by changing the partition-worker mapping in S (and C, accordingly).

Active-Replication. A stream of tasks is absorbed by a *broadcast* S, which sends identical copies to the Ws. Results are sent to G, which reduces them. This paradigm can be equipped with a self-healing policy because it can deal with Ws that do not answer, produce an approximate or wrong answer by means of a result reduction function (e.g. by means of averaging or voting on results).

The presented behavioural skeletons can be easily adapted to the case that S is a RPC interface. In this case, the C interface can be either a RPC interface or missing. Also, the functional replication idea can be extended to the stateful case by requiring the inner component Ws to expose suitable methods to serialise, read and write the internal state. A suitable manipulation of the serialised state enables the reconfiguration of workers (also in the data-parallel scenario [1]).

In order to achieve self-healing goals some additional requirements on the GCM implementation level should be enforced. They are related to the implementation of GCM mechanisms, such as component membranes and their parts (e.g. interfaces) and messaging system. At the current level of interest, they are primitive mechanisms, in which correctness and robustness should be enforced ex-ante, at least to achieve some of the described management policies.

The process of identification of other skeletons may benefit from the work done within the software engineering community, which identified some common adaptation paradigms, such as *proxies* [18], which may be interposed between interacting components to change their interaction relationships; and dynamic *wrappers* [19]. Both of these can be used for self-protection purposes. For example, a pair of encrypting proxies can be used to secure a communication between components. Wrapping can be used to hide one or more interfaces when a component is deployed into an untrusted platform.

5.1 GCM implementation of Behavioural Skeletons

In terms of the GCM specification [9], a behavioural skeleton is a particular composite component exhibiting an autonomic conformance level strictly greater than one, i.e. a component with passive or active autonomic control. The component exposes pre-defined functional and non-functional client and server interfaces according to the skeleton type; functional interfaces are usually collective and configurable. Since skeletons are fully-fledged GCM components, they can be wired and nested via standard GCM mechanisms. From the implementation viewpoint, a behavioural skeleton is a partially defined composite component, i.e. a component with placeholders, which may be used to instantiate the skeleton. As sketched in Fig. 1, there are three classes of placeholders:

1 The functional interfaces S and C that are GCM membrane controllers.

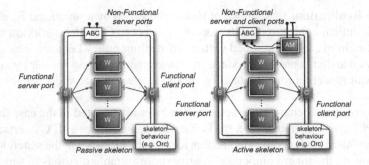

Figure 1. GCM implementation of functional replication. ABC = Autonomic Behaviour Controller, AM = Autonomic Manager, W = Worker component, S = Server interface (one-to-many communication e.g. broadcast, data-parallel scatter, unicast), C = Client interface (many-to-one communication e.g. from-any, data-parallel gather, reduce, select).

    2 The AM that is a particular inner component. It includes the management plan, its goal, and exported non-functional interfaces.

    3 Inner component W, implementing the functional behaviour.

The orchestration of the inner components is implicitly defined by the skeleton type. In order to instantiate the skeleton, placeholders should be filled with suitable entities. Observe that only entities in the former two classes are skeleton specific.

    In addition to a standard composite component, a behavioural skeleton is further characterised by a formal (or semi-formal) description of the component behaviour. This description can be attached to the ADL component definition via the standard GCM ADL hook. In this work we propose a description based on the Orc language, which appears suitable for specification of orchestration in distributed systems [2].

6.   Specifying Skeleton Behaviour

    Autonomic management requires that, during execution of a system, components of the system are replaced by other components, typically having the same functional behaviour but exhibiting different non-functional characteristics. The application programmer must be confident about the behaviour of the replacements with respect to the original. The behavioural skeleton approach proposed supports these requirements in two key ways:

    1 The use of skeletons with its inherent parametrisation permits relatively easy parameter-driven variation of non-functional behaviour while maintaining functional equivalence.

2 The use of Orc to describe component behaviour gives the developer a firm basis on which to compare the properties of alternative realisations in the context of autonomic replacement.

In the following we present an Orc specification of the functional replication example depicted in Fig. 1 followed by several alternative formulations of the client and server interface behaviours. First, a brief overview of the Orc language is presented. A formal description of management plans is not presented here. The skeleton designer can use the description to prove rigorously (manually, at present) that a given management strategy will have predictable or no impact on functional behaviour. The quantitative description of QoS values of a component with respect to a goal, the automatic validation of management plans w.r.t. a given functional behaviour are interesting related topics, which are the subject of ongoing research but outside the scope of the present work.

6.1 The Orc notation

The orchestration language Orc of Misra and Cook [4] is targeted at the description of systems where the challenge lies in organising a set of computations, rather than in the computations themselves. Orc has, as primitive, the notion of a site call, which is intended to represent basic computations. A site, either returns a *single* value or remains silent. Three operators (plus recursion) are provided for the orchestration of site calls:

Sequential composition: $E_1 > x > E_2(x)$ evaluates E_1, receives a result x, calls E_2 with parameter x. If E_1 produces two results, say a and b, then E_2 is evaluated twice, once with argument a and once with argument b. The abbreviation $E_1 \gg E_2$ is used for $E_1 > x > E_2$ when evaluation of E_2 is independent of x.

Parallel composition: $(E_1 \mid E_2)$ evaluates E_1 and E_2 in parallel. Both evaluations may produce replies. Evaluation of the expression returns the merged output streams of E_1 and E_2.

Asymmetric parallel composition: E_1 where $x :\in E_2$ begins evaluation of both E_1 and $x :\in E_2$ in parallel. Expression E_1 may name x in some of its site calls. Evaluation of E_1 may proceed until a dependency on x is encountered; evaluation is then suspended. The first value delivered by E_2 is returned in x; evaluation of E_1 can proceed and the thread E_2 is terminated.

Orc has a number of special sites: "0" never responds; "if b" returns a signal if b is true and remains silent otherwise; "let" always publishes its argument.

Finally, while Orc does not have an explicit concept of "process", processes may be represented as expressions which, typically, name channels that are shared with other expressions. In Orc a channel is represented by a site [4]. *c.put(m)* adds m to the end of the (FIFO) channel and publishes a signal. If the channel is non-empty *c.get* publishes the value at the head and removes it; otherwise the caller of *c.get* suspends until a value is available.

6.2   The Description of Skeletons in Orc

Assume that *data* is sent by an interface S along a number, N, of channels in_i to N workers W_i. Each worker processes its data and sends the result along a channel out_i to interface C (see Fig. 1). The distribution of data by S to the channels may be based on various algorithms depending on the nature of the overall task: see below.

Assume that *data* is a *list* of items to be processed; *#data* is the number of items in *data*; *in* is a *list* of N channels connecting the port S with the workers. *out* is a *list* of N channels connecting the port C with the workers. For a list, l, *head(l)* returns the head of (non-empty) l; *tail(l)* returns the tail of (non-empty) l. Denote by l_i the ith element of the list l. The skeleton system depicted in Fig. 1 may be defined in Orc as follows:

$$system(data, S, G, W, in, out, N) \equiv$$
$$S(data, in) \mid (\mid i : 1 \le i \le N : W_i(in_i, out_i)) \mid C(out)$$
$$W_i(in_i, out_i) \equiv$$
$$in_i.get > tk > process(tk) > r > (out_i.put(r) \mid W_i(in_i, out_i))$$

Server Interface S.   The interface S distributes the *data* in sequence across the channels, *ch*, according to a *distribution* policy that can be substituted by the expression *broadcast, unicast*, or *DP*. The auxiliary expression *next* is used for synchronisation.

$$S(data, ch) \equiv \text{ if } data = [] \gg 0$$
$$\mid \text{ if } data \ne [] \gg distribution(head(data)) \gg S(tail(data), ch))$$

$$next(h_1, \dots, h_N) \equiv \text{ let } 1$$

The *broadcast* sends each item of data to all of the workers.

$$broadcast(item) \equiv next(h_1, \dots, h_N) \text{ where } h_1 :\in ch_1.put(item)$$
$$\dots$$
$$h_N :\in ch_N.put(item)$$

The *unicast* sends each item to a single worker $W_{f(i)}$ where the index i is chosen in a list $[1 \dots N]$. The function f is assumed to be stateful (e.g. successive calls to f can scan the list).

$$unicast(data) \equiv ch_{f(i)}.put(x) \gg \text{ let } 1$$

The *DP* describes the data-parallel scatter. Assume that *#data* is a multiple of N (for simplicity), and the *slice(data,i)* returns the ith slice of *data*, where each slice is of length *#data/N*. The actual definition of "i^{th} slice" may vary, but is abstracted here in the function *slice*. For example, if the first slice corresponds to the first *#data/N* items in *data*, etc. then the distribution is round-robin. In the specification given, the data is divided into N slices and each slice is sent on one of the channels.

$$DP(x) \equiv next(h_1, \ldots, h_N) \text{ where } h_1 :\in ch_1.put(slice(x, 1))$$
$$\ldots$$
$$h_N :\in ch_N.put(slice(x, N))$$

Client interface C. Here interface C receives an item from each worker W_i along channel ch_i and, when it has an item from every worker, applies a *collection* policy. We exemplify here *reduce* and *select* policies.

$$C(ch) \equiv collection(ch) \gg C(ch)$$

The *reduce* function may take an average, select the median, etc. (Note; it is assumed here that all workers supply results; otherwise timeouts could be used to avoid starvation.)

$$collection(ch) \equiv reduce(h_1, \ldots, h_N) \text{ where } h_1 :\in ch_1.get$$
$$\ldots$$
$$h_N :\in ch_N.get$$

Alternatively, the port C may non-deterministically *select* a single data item from one worker and discard the rest.

$$collection(ch) \equiv select(r) \text{ where } r :\in (\mid i : 1 \leq i \leq N : ch_i.get)$$

In all of the presented cases it is easy to verify that the functional behaviour is independent of N, provided W is stateless. Therefore, all management policies that change the value of N do not alter the functional behaviour, and can thus be considered correct.

7.   Conclusion

The challenge of autonomicity in the context of component-based development of grid software is substantial. Building into components autonomic capability typically impairs their reusability. We have proposed behavioural skeletons as a compromise: being skeletons they support reuse, while their parametrisation allows the controlled adaptation needed to achieve dynamic adjustment of QoS while preserving functionality. We have presented a significant set of skeletons, together with their formal Orc functional behaviour description and self-management strategies. We have described how these concepts can be applied and implemented within the GCM. The presented behavioural skeletons have been implemented in GCM-ProActive [6], in the framework of the Grid-COMP project[2] and are currently under experimental evaluation. Preliminary results, not presented in this work, confirm the feasibility of the approach.

---

[2] http://gridcomp.ercim.org, an EU STREP project aimed at providing an open source, reference implementation of the GCM.

References

[1] M. Aldinucci and M. Danelutto. Algorithmic skeletons meeting grids. *Parallel Computing*, 32(7):449–462, 2006. DOI:10.1016/j.parco.2006.04.001.

[2] M. Aldinucci, M. Danelutto, and P. Kilpatrick. Management in distributed systems: a semi-formal approach. In A.-M. Kermarrec, L. Bougé, and T. Priol, editors, *Proc. of 13th Intl. Euro-Par 2007*, LNCS, Rennes, France, Aug. 2007. Springer. To appear.

[3] M. Aldinucci, M. Danelutto, and M. Vanneschi. Autonomic QoS in ASSIST grid-aware components. In B. D. Martino and S. Venticinque, editors, *Proc. of Intl. Euromicro PDP 2006: Parallel Distributed and network-based Processing*, pages 221–230, Montbéliard, France, Feb. 2006. IEEE.

[4] F. Andre, J. Buisson, and J.-L. Pazat. Dynamic adaptation of parallel codes: toward self-adaptable components for the Grid. In *Proc. of the Intl. Workshop on Component Models and Systems for Grid Applications*, CoreGRID series. Springer, Jan. 2005.

[5] A. Andrzejak, A. Reinefeld, F. Schintke, and T. Schütt. On adaptability in grid systems. In *Future Generation Grids*, CoreGRID series. Springer, Nov. 2005.

[6] F. Baude, D. Caromel, and M. Morel. On hierarchical, parallel and distributed components for grid programming. In V. Getov and T. Kielmann, editors, *Proc. of the Intl. Workshop on Component Models and Systems for Grid Applications*, CoreGRID series, pages 97–108, Saint-Malo, France, Jan. 2005. Springer.

[7] J. Bosch. Superimposition: a component adaptation technique. *Information & Software Technology*, 41(5):257–273, 1999.

[8] M. Cole. Bringing skeletons out of the closet: A pragmatic manifesto for skeletal parallel programming. *Parallel Computing*, 30(3):389–406, 2004.

[9] CoreGRID NoE deliverable series, Institute on Programming Model. *Deliverable D.PM.04 – Basic Features of the Grid Component Model (assessed)*, Feb. 2007.

[10] P.-C. David and T. Ledoux. An aspect-oriented approach for developing self-adaptive fractal components. In W. Löwe and M. Südholt, editors, *Proc of the 5th Intl Symposium Software on Composition (SC 2006)*, volume 4089 of *LNCS*, pages 82–97, Vienna, Austria, Mar. 2006. Springer.

[11] S. Gorlatch and J. Dünnweber. From grid middleware to grid applications: Bridging the gap with HOCs. In V. Getov, D. Laforenza, and A. Reinefeld, editors, *Future Generation Grids*, CoreGRID series. Springer, Nov. 2005.

[12] K. Kennedy et al. Toward a framework for preparing and executing adaptive Grid programs. In *Proc. of NSF Next Generation Systems Program Workshop (IPDPS)*, 2002.

[13] J. O. Kephart and D. M. Chess. The vision of autonomic computing. *IEEE Computer*, 36(1):41–50, 2003.

[14] J. Misra and W. R. Cook. Computation orchestration: A basis for a wide-area computing. *Software and Systems Modeling*, 2006. DOI 10.1007/s10270-006-0012-1.

[15] Next Generation GRIDs Expert Group. *NGG3, Future for European Grids: GRIDs and Service Oriented Knowledge Utilities. Vision and Research Directions 2010 and Beyond*, Jan. 2006.

[16] ObjectWeb Consortium. *The Fractal Component Model, Technical Specification*, 2003.

[17] M. Parashar, H. Liu, Z. Li, V. Matossian, C. Schmidt, G. Zhang, and S. Hariri. AutoMate: Enabling autonomic applications on the Grid. *Cluster Computing*, 9(2):161–174, 2006.

[18] S. M. Sadjadi and P. K. McKinley. Transparent self-optimization in existing CORBA applications. In *Proc. of the 1st Intl. Conference on Autonomic Computing (ICAC'04)*, pages 88–95, Washington, DC, USA, 2004. IEEE.

[19] E. Truyen, B. Jfirgensen, W. Joosen, and P. Verbaeten. On interaction refinement in middleware. In J. Bosch, C. Szyperski, and W. Weck, editors, *Proc. of the 5th Intl. Workshop on Component-Oriented Programming*, pages 56–62, 2001.

[20] M. Vanneschi. The programming model of ASSIST, an environment for parallel and distributed portable applications. *Parallel Computing*, 28(12):1709–1732, Dec. 2002.

TOWARDS GCM RE-CONFIGURATION - EXTENDING SPECIFICATION BY NORMS

Alessandro Basso, Alexander Bolotov
University of Westminster
Harrow School of Computer Science
University of Westminster
Watford Road
Harrow HA1 3TP
[bassoa.bolotoa]@wmin.ac.uk

Abstract   We continue investigation of formal specification of Grid Component systems by temporal logics and subsequent application of temporal resolution as a verification technique. This time we enrich the specification language by the ability to capture norms which enables us to formally define a concept of a re-configuration. We aim at integrating a software tool for automated specification as well as verification to ensure a reliable and dynamically re-configurable model.

Keywords: formal specification, formal verification, verification tool, GIDE, deductive reasoning, model checking, deontic logic, re-configuration

1.   Introduction.

Component models enable modular design of software applications that can be easily reused and combined, ensuring greater reliability. This is important in distributed systems where asynchronous components must be taken into consideration, especially when there is need for a dynamic re-configuration. The Grid Component Model (GCM) [12]based on Fractal is the one chosen for our research. In these models, components interact together by being bound through interfaces. However, there is a further need for a method which ensures correct composition and behaviour of components. For the specification of behaviour we can use a rich temporal framework [11] with subsequent application of either model checking or deductive reasoning as a verification technique. Model checking [7], which verifies the properties of the components against the specification, has already been tested in various circumstances, one particular application of this method been tested in [2]. Model checking is a powerful and well established technique allowing to incorporate a number of algorithms and tools to deal even with the famous state explosion problem. However, if applied to a component system, it has one indicative drawback, due to its explorative nature, namely, it cannot consider the environment in which a component system has been developed. At the same time, in building a large scale distributed system, we cannot afford anymore not to take into consideration the entire infrastructure. Deductive methods, on the other hand, can deal with such large systems and furthermore, can be applied to re-configuration scenarios. In our earlier work [1] we applied a specific deductive technique, the temporal resolution method [5] to a simple component model. The complexity of the resolution based verification turned out to be high. The analogous method for the linear-time setting has been recently improved in [8] by the modification of the underlying specification language to obtain a polynomial satisfiability checking complexity. In this paper we propose a new framework for the specification of the re-configuration process: the extension of the temporal specification by the deontic modalities [14]. This enriches the expressive capacities of our formal specification by allowing to represent, additionally, a behaviour protocol.

The paper is organised as follows. In §2 we introduce the architecture and give an informal description of the main concepts: re-configuration (§2.1) and model update (§2.2). Further, in §3 we introduce these concepts formally: in §3.1 we describe the deontic extension of $ECTL^+$ called $ECTL_D^+$, then, in §3.2 define a concept of deontic temporal specification (DTS) and reconfiguration, and in §3.3 provide a specification example. Next, in §4 we describe a resolution based verification technique, introducing new deontic resolution rules and providing an example refutation. Finally, in §5, we give concluding remarks and identify future work.

2. Architecture

We identify three main parts of the architecture: the primitive components, their composition into composite components through the Architecture Description Language (ADL) file and the infrastructure (see Figure 1).

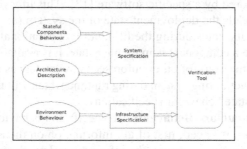

Figure 1. Architecture

The first two are combined to deduce the *stateful component system behaviour* - a high-level behaviour distinct from the one of a single component, which we assume to be already formally verified through other techniques being recently researched. The specification is partially given as an input by the user in the case of primitive components, and partially automatically extrapolated using different sources, such as source code and the ADL file. The infrastructure is specified mainly according to the user's need, and following well defined and accepted constrains such as those for safety, fairness, etc. [15] and in relation to the resources required and services provided. The formal specification derived through this process is a fusion of deontic and computation tree temporal logic, extended from the previous developments in [1], which is a suitable input format for our deductive reasoning tool. The properties to be specified and verified by this techniques are the ones which are not possible to be considered when a system is specified in a static way, this includes but is not limited to: presence of resources and services, availability of distributed components, etc.

In the classical approach to component behaviour specification, the term "behaviour" is referred to the inner component's functionality - if the component is supposed to calculate the factorial, is it doing it correctly? When we consider the stateful component system behaviour instead, we are taking into consideration a different matter: we are looking for those requirements that will make the component "behaving correctly". As a simple example let us consider a parser which checks if all the libraries required by the component are present to calculate the factorial. Furthermore, what happens when we talk about a distributed system, where changes might be needed to be done at runtime? What if we require to replace a component, but the component we want to replace should not be stopped? We have taken into consideration these types of situations while developing a specification procedure. We analyse the life cycle of a component and define its states in a formal way so that they can be used in the system specification. We consider past developments within the GCM and other state aware grid systems [16]to define a set of states to be generated that would monitored by a specific software [13]. This lifecycle is restricted, in fact it only models the deployment state of the system (and, consequently, the transitions of its states during the life), not its operational characteristics. For example, once a component is in running state, it is available. On the other hand, the service may fail for other unforeseen circumstances (hence the need for a component monitoring system during runtime which will report a need for changes into the state behaviour specification).

System/Infrastructure Behaviour. To specify the behaviour of a stateful component system, we need, first of all, information on the architecture and hierarchical components structure, the information flow, the possible requirements, and external requests. It is possible to extrapolate interface and bindings information from the XML based ADL file (as similarly outlined in [16]). This gives us an idea of the flow of the system; the user might need to refine this process, for example to keep significant parameters only or add new parameters. On the other hand, other component's requirements must be taken directly from the component's definitions. Since one of the GridComp functionalities will include a GCM parser to build component models, we will be able to reuse some of the data it will provide to blueprint these requirements, leaving the task to fill in the gaps to a programmer. The infrastructure can represent a general purpose environment based on some common grounds, or a specific one, defined by the programmer. Note that in the former case, infrastructure must, of course, leave room for further expansion and adaptation depending on the programmer's need.

Deontic extension of specification. We develop a specification language based on the fusion of Computation Tree Logic (CTL) and deontic logic to represent the properties of a behaviour protocol of a component system. The requirements of the protocol are understood as norms and specified in terms of deontic modalities, "obligation" and "permission". Note that the introduction of this deontic dimension not only increases the expressiveness of the system capturing the normative nature of the specification but also allows us to approach the reconfiguration problem in a novel way.

2.1   Re-Configuration

We focus our attention on the critical aspect of re-configuration. We begin by clarifying the term re-configuration used in this paper: we refer re-configuration to the process through which a system halts operation under its current source specification and begins operation under a different target specification [17], and more precisely after the deployment has taken place (dynamic reconfiguration). Some examples include the replacement of a software component by the user, or an automated healing process activated by the system itself. In either of these cases we consider the dynamic reconfiguration process as an unforeseen action at development time (known as ad-hoc reconfiguration [3]). When the system is deployed, the verification tool will run continuously and the system will report back the current states for model mapping; if a re-configuration procedure is requested or inconsistency detected, the healing process is triggered. The dynamic re-configuration process works in a circular way [Figure: 2] and it is divided into three major steps detailed below. The approach here is to specify general invariants for the infrastructure and to accept any change to the system, as long as these invariants hold. We assume that the infrastructure has some pre-defined set of norms which define the constraints for the system, in order to ensure system safety, mission success, or other crucial system properties which are critical especially in distributed systems.

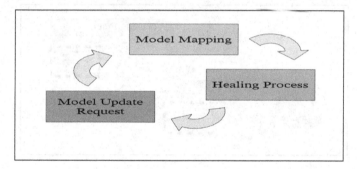

Figure 2. Re-Configuration Cycle

Model update request. A model update request can be triggered by a user's intention to re-configure the system, or by an inconsistency detection from the verification tool. It refers in the model as a change to the behaviour specification and it is constrained by the infrastructure restrictions. For example, the user might want to upgrade a component, but these changes must conform to the limitations set for such component. If the changes themselves are safe for the system, the tool passes to the next step.

Model mapping. For the verification process to understand its current state in the temporal tree, there is a need for a constant 'model mapping'; in other words, a background process needs to be present in order to map the structure of the system into a model tree. This can be easily implemented alongside with a current monitoring system which will keep track of this mapping indicating which parts of the system are currently in which states in the model tree [4].

This process is essential to ensure that no 'past' states are misused by the tool during the healing process.

2.2   Model Update

If the model behaviour needs to be updated according to the new external input parts of the system specification need to be changed. This process is the key to this type of model update architecture and is necessary because, unlike model revision in which the description is simply corrected but the overall system remains unchanged, by updating our specification we are fundamentally changing the system by adding, deleting and replacing states in the model behaviour [9]. Here different types of changes are dealt with in a similar faction, independently from the origin of the update (external user input or self healing process). The behaviour specification is 'extended' to a new type of specification and the verification process is resumed from this point forward [Figure: 3]. This model update process consists of:

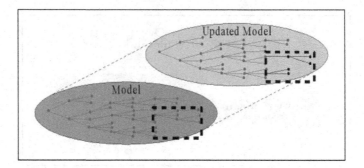

Figure 3.   Model Update

(i) **Norms/Invariant check.** Utilise norms and invariants in the specification for constraints on the set of states to be updated. Here we detect the deontic properties in the specification which could be utilised in the healing process.

(ii) **Compatibility check.** Check if the supplied update to the model conforms with the the set of states to be updated, in other words, the system must check for the presence of the standard bindings of the components, controllers, etc; if so, the model is updated, otherwise, the healing is triggered.

(iii) **Healing process.** Search the tree model for a set of states which conform with the norms and invariants, and is applicable for this set of states. Note that candidate states for such an update in relation for some state s_i, do not have to be in an 'achievable' future of s_i, i.e. do not have to belong to a subtree with the root s_i, but only have to be 'accessible' from the current state according to the norms set by the infrastructure. The candidate set of states (or a more readable parsed version) is reported to the user/developer as a possible solution to the inconsistency detected. (Note that healing is also triggered if there was no supplied update as in the case of inconsistency detection).

3.   Deontic Extension of the Specification Language

In this paper we introduce a new specification formalism, Temporal Deontic Specification (TDS). We assume that the specification of a component model now is either written directly in this new framework of TDS or is initially given in the deontic extension of the logic ECTL$^+$ called ECTL$_D^+$ and then is converted into the TDS. Since the structure of TDS is similar to the SNF$_{CTL}$ we are able to subsequently apply the resolution based verification technique which must be also extended to cope with the normative dimension.

Note that the introduction of this deontic dimension not only increases the expressiveness of the system capturing the normative nature of the specification but also allows us to approach the reconfiguration problem in a novel way.

3.1   ECTL$_D^+$ Syntax and Semantic

In the language of ECTL$_D^+$, where formulae are built from the set, $Prop$, of atomic propositions $p, q, r, \ldots, p_1, q_1, r_1, \ldots, p_n, q_n, r_n, \ldots$, we use the following symbols: classical operators: $\neg, \wedge, \Rightarrow, \vee$; temporal operators: $\square$ – 'always in the future'; $\Diamond$ – 'at sometime in the future'; $\bigcirc$ – 'at the next moment in time'; $\mathcal{U}$ – 'until'; $\mathcal{W}$ – 'unless'; and path quantifiers: $\mathbf{A}$ – 'for any future path; $\mathbf{E}$ – 'for some future path.

For the deontic part we assume a set $Ag = \{a, b, c \ldots\}$ of agents (processes), which we associate with deontic modalities $\mathcal{O}_a(\varphi)$ read as 'φ is obligatory for an agent a' and $\mathcal{P}_a(\varphi)$ read as 'φ is permitted for an agent a'.

In the syntax of ECTL$_D^+$ we distinguish *state* (S) and *path* (P) formulae, such that S are well formed formulae. These classes of formulae are inductively defined below (where C is a formula of classical propositional logic)

$$S ::= C | S \wedge S | S \vee S | S \Rightarrow S | \neg S | \mathbf{A}P | \mathbf{E}P | \mathcal{P}_a S | \mathcal{O}_a S$$
$$P ::= P \wedge P | P \vee P | P \Rightarrow P | \neg P | \square S | \Diamond S | \bigcirc S | S \, \mathcal{U} \, S | S \, \mathcal{W} \, S$$
$$| \square \Diamond S | \Diamond \square S$$

DEFINITION 1 (LITERAL, MODAL LITERAL) *A literal is either p, or $\neg p$ for p is a proposition. A* modal literal *is either $\mathcal{O}_i l$, $\neg \mathcal{O}_i l$, $\mathcal{P}_i l$, $\neg \mathcal{P}_i l$ where l is a literal and $i \in Ag$.*

ECTL$_D^+$ **Semantics.** We first introduce the notation of tree structures, the underlying structures of time assumed for branching-time logics.

DEFINITION 2 *A* tree *is a pair (S, R), where S is a set of states and $R \subseteq S \times S$ is a relation between states of S such that $s_0 \in S$ is a unique root node, i.e.*

there is no state $s_i \in S$ such that $R(s_i, s_0)$; for every $s_i \in S$ there exists $s_j \in S$ such that $R(s_i, s_j)$; for every s_i, s_j, $s_k \in S$, if $R(s_i, s_k)$ and $R(s_j, s_k)$ then $s_i = s_j$.

A *path*, χ_{s_i} is a sequence of states $s_i, s_{i+1}, s_{i+2} \ldots$ such that for all $j \geq i$, $(s_j, s_{j+1}) \in R$. Let χ be a family of all paths of $\mathcal{M}$. A path $\chi_{s_0} \in \chi$ is called a *fullpath*. Let X be a family of all fullpaths of $\mathcal{M}$. Given a path χ_{s_i} and a state $s_j \in \chi_{s_i}$, $(i < j)$ we term a finite subsequence $[s_i, s_j] = s_i, s_{i+1}, \ldots, s_j$ of χ_{s_i} *a prefix* of a path χ_{s_i} and an infinite sub-sequence $s_j, s_{j+1}, s_{j+2} \cdots$ of χ_{s_i} *a suffix* of a path χ_{s_i} abbreviated $Suf(\chi_{s_i}, s_j)$.

Following [11], without loss of generality, we assume that underlying tree models are of at most countable branching.

DEFINITION 3 (TOTAL COUNTABLE ω-TREE) *A countable ω-tree, τ_ω, is a tree (S, R) with the family of all fullpaths, X, which satisfies the following conditions: each fullpath is isomorphic to natural numbers; every state $s_m \in S$ has a countable number of successors; X is R-generable [11], i.e. for every state $s_m \in S$, there exists $\chi_n \in X$ such that $s_m \in \chi_n$, and for every sequence $\chi_n = s_0, s_1, s_2 \ldots$ the following is true: $\chi_n \in X$ if, and only if, for every m $(1 \leq m)$, $R(s_m, s_{m+1})$.*

Since in ω trees fullpaths are isomorphic to natural numbers, in the rest of the paper we will abbreviate the relation R as $\leq$.

Next, for the interpretation of deontic operators, we introduce a binary agent accessibility relation.

DEFINITION 4 (DEONTIC ACCESSIBILITY RELATION) *Given a countable total tree $\tau_\omega = (S, \leq)$, a binary agent accessibility relation $D_i \subseteq S \times S$, for each agent $i \in Ag$, satisfies the following properties: it is serial (for any $k \in S$, there exists $l \in S$ such that $D_i(k, l)$), transitive (for any $k, l, m \in S$, if $D_i(k, l)$ and $D_i(l, m)$ then $D_i(k, m)$), and Euclidian (for any $k, l, m \in S$, if $D_i(k, l)$ and $D_i(k, m)$ then $D_i(l, m)$).*

Let $(S, \leq)$ be a total countable ω-tree with a root s_0 defined as in Def 3, X be a set of all fullpaths, $L : S \times Prop \longrightarrow \{\textbf{true}, \textbf{false}\}$ be an interpretation function mapping atomic propositional symbols to truth values at each state, and every $R_i \subseteq S \times S$ $(i \in 1, \ldots, n)$ be an agent accessibility relation defined as in Def 4. Now a model structure for interpretation of ECTL_D^+ formulae is $\mathcal{M} = \langle S, \leq, s_0, X, L, D_1, \ldots, D_n \rangle$.

Reminding that since the underlying tree structures are R-generable, they are suffix, fusion and limit closed [11], in Figure 4 we define a relation '$\models$', which evaluates well-formed ECTL_D^+ formulae at a state s_m in a model $\mathcal{M}$.

DEFINITION 5 (SATISFIABILITY) *A well-formed ECTL_D^+ formula, B, is satisfiable if, and only if, there exists a model $\mathcal{M}$ such that $\langle \mathcal{M}, s_0 \rangle \models B$.*

$\langle \mathcal{M}, s_m \rangle$	$\models p$	iff	$p \in L(s_m)$, for $p \in Prop$
$\langle \mathcal{M}, s_m \rangle$	$\models \mathbf{A}B$	iff	for each $\chi_{s_m}, \langle \mathcal{M}, \chi_{s_m} \rangle \models B$
$\langle \mathcal{M}, s_m \rangle$	$\models \mathbf{E}B$	iff	there exists χ_{s_m} such that
			$\langle \mathcal{M}, \chi_{s_m} \rangle \models B$
$\langle \mathcal{M}, \chi_{s_m} \rangle$	$\models A$	iff	$\langle \mathcal{M}, s_m \rangle \models A$, for state formula A
$\langle \mathcal{M}, \chi_{s_m} \rangle$	$\models \square B$	iff	for each $s_n \in \chi_{s_m}$, if $m \leq n$ then
			$\langle \mathcal{M}, Suf(\chi_{s_m}, s_n) \rangle \models B$
$\langle \mathcal{M}, \chi_{s_m} \rangle$	$\models \bigcirc B$	iff	$\langle \mathcal{M}, Suf(\chi_{s_m}, s_{m+1}) \rangle \models B$
$\langle \mathcal{M}, \chi_{s_m} \rangle$	$\models A \mathcal{U} B$	iff	there exists $s_n \in \chi_{s_m}$ such that $m \leq n$
			and $\langle \mathcal{M}, Suf(\chi_{s_m}, s_n) \rangle \models B$
			and for each $s_k \in \chi_{s_m}$, if $m \leq k < n$
			then $\langle \mathcal{M}, Suf(\chi_{s_m}, s_k) \rangle \models A$
$\langle \mathcal{M}, \chi_{s_m} \rangle$	$\models A \mathcal{W} B$	iff	$\langle \mathcal{M}, \chi_{s_m} \rangle \models \square A$ or $\langle \mathcal{M}, \chi_{s_m} \rangle \models A \mathcal{U} B$
$\langle \mathcal{M}, s_m \rangle$	$\models \mathcal{O}_a B$	iff	for each $s_n \in S$, if $D_a(m, n)$ then
			$\langle \mathcal{M}, s_n \rangle \models B$
$\langle \mathcal{M}, s_m \rangle$	$\models \mathcal{P}_a B$	iff	there exists $s_n \in S$, such that $D_a(m, n)$
			and $\langle \mathcal{M}, s_n \rangle \models B$

Figure 4. ECTL$_D^+$ semantics

DEFINITION 6 (VALIDITY) *A well-formed* ECTL$_D^+$ *formula, B, is valid if, and only if, it is satisfied in every possible model.*

3.2 Reconfiguration formalisation

To define a concept of propositional deontic temporal specification we extend a normal form defined for the logic ECTL$^+$, SNF$_{CTL}$, which was developed in [5–6]. Recall that the core idea of the normal form is to extract from a given formula the following three types of constraints. *Initial constraints* represent information relevant to the initial moment of time, the root of a tree. *Step constraints* of the form indicate what will happen at the successor state(s) given that some conditions are satisfied 'now'. Finally, *sometime constraints* keep track on any eventuality, again, given that some conditions are satisfied 'now'.

The SNF$_{CTL}^D$ language is obtained from the ECTL$_D^+$ language by omitting the $\mathcal{U}$ and $\mathcal{W}$ operators, and adding classically defined constants **true** and **false**, and a new operator, **start** ('at the initial moment of time') defined as $\langle \mathcal{M}, s_i \rangle \models$ **start** iff $i = 0$.

Similarly to SNF$_{CTL}$, we incorporate the language for indices which is based on the set of terms IND $= \{\langle f \rangle, \langle g \rangle, \langle h \rangle, \langle LC(f) \rangle, \langle LC(g) \rangle, \langle LC(h) \rangle \ldots \}$, where f, g, h ... denote constants. Thus, $\mathbf{E}A_{\langle f \rangle}$ means that A holds on some path labelled as $\langle f \rangle$. All formulae of SNF$_{CTL}$ of the type $P \Rightarrow \mathbf{E} \bigcirc Q$ or

$P \Rightarrow \mathbf{E}\Diamond Q$, where Q is a purely classical expression, are labelled with some index.

DEFINITION 7 (DEONTIC TEMPORAL SPECIFICATION - DTS) *DTS is a tuple $\langle In, St, Ev, N, Lit \rangle$ where In is the set of initial constraints, St is the set of step constraints, Ev is the set of eventuality constraints, N is a set of normative expressions, and Lit is the set of literal constraints, i.e. formulae that are globally true. The structure of these constraints called* clauses, *is defined below where each α_i, β_m, γ or l_e is a literal,* **true** *or* **false**, *d_e is either a literal or a modal literal involving the $\mathcal{O}$ or $\mathcal{P}$ operators, and $\langle \mathrm{ind} \rangle \in$ IND is some index.*

$$\mathbf{start} \Rightarrow \bigvee_{i=1}^{k} \beta_i \qquad \text{(In)}$$

$$\bigwedge_{i=1}^{k} \alpha_i \Rightarrow \mathbf{A}\bigcirc [\bigvee_{m=1}^{n} \beta_m] \qquad \text{(St A)}$$

$$\bigwedge_{i=1}^{k} \alpha_i \Rightarrow \mathbf{E}\bigcirc [\bigvee_{m=1}^{n} \beta_m]_{\langle \mathrm{ind} \rangle} \qquad \text{(St E)}$$

$$\bigwedge_{i=1}^{k} \alpha_i \Rightarrow \mathbf{A}\Diamond\gamma \qquad \text{(Ev A)}$$

$$\bigwedge_{i=1}^{k} \alpha_i \Rightarrow \mathbf{E}\Diamond\gamma_{\langle \mathrm{LC(ind)} \rangle} \qquad \text{(Ev E)}$$

$$\mathbf{true} \Rightarrow \bigvee_{e=1}^{n} d_e \qquad \text{(D)}$$

$$\mathbf{true} \Rightarrow \bigvee_{e=1}^{n} l_e \qquad \text{(Lit)}$$

In order to give a formalisation of the reconfiguration process we adapt the approach given in [17] extending it to the usage of norms. We assume that we are given a set of specification properties, S_i be the start state and S_j the end state of the system, a set of norms, N, and a set of invariants I. We can define a reconfiguration, $\mathcal{R}$, to be applicable when the following conditions holds:
- $\mathcal{R}$ commences when the initial state S_i is not operating anymore and finishes before the last state to be updated, S_j, becomes compliant with the system.
- S_j is the appropriate choice for the target specification at some point during $\mathcal{R}$.
- Time for $\mathcal{R}$ is less or equal than the time for the transition from S_i to S_j.
- The transition invariant(s), I, holds during $\mathcal{R}$.
- The norms, N, for S_j are true at the time when $\mathcal{R}$ finishes.
- The lifetime of $\mathcal{R}$ bounded by any two occurrences of the same specification.

The conditions for reconfigurations can be considered as a set of restriction, which when true allow for the model to be simply replaced. The reconfiguration conditions above give a clear indication to which states in the model can be changed and when, while the temporal specification sets the conditions for the change and defines the acceptable states which will replace the current ones.

3.3   Example Specification

Let us consider an example specification in which we use of norms for reconfiguration, and where a component is requested to be updated.

Let r represent a property that a core component is bound to the system (one that should be always available and should not be 'touched'), and let q be a new upgraded version of this core component. Now the expression $\mathbf{A}\square(r \Rightarrow \mathcal{O}_i \neg q)$ stands for the obligation of not binding this new component once r is present.

Assume that the system received a request for the permission to eventually bind q. In the table below we summarise these conditions of the component system and their representations in the language of TDS (note that w is a new (auxiliary) proposition introduced to achieve the required form of DTS clauses).

Conditions of the System	Constraints of DTS
Invariant Property r	$\mathbf{A}\Box((\mathbf{start} \Rightarrow r) \land (r \Rightarrow \mathbf{A}\bigcirc r))$
Obligation of not binding new component q	$\mathbf{A}\Box(r \Rightarrow \mathcal{O}_i\neg q)$
A request for the permission to eventually bind q	$\mathbf{A}\Box((r \Rightarrow \mathbf{E}\Diamond w) \land (w \Rightarrow \mathcal{P}_i q))$

4. Resolution Based Verification Technique

We first update the set of resolution rules developed for SNF_{CTL} [6] by new resolution rules capturing the deontic constraints. However, due to the lack of space, here we present only those rules that will be involved into an example of the refutation.

$DRES$	$SRES$	$TRES$
$\mathbf{true} \Rightarrow D \lor \mathcal{O}_i l$	$A \Rightarrow \mathbf{A}\bigcirc(l \lor D)$	$A \Rightarrow \mathbf{A}\Box l$
$\mathbf{true} \Rightarrow D' \lor \mathcal{P}_i\neg l$	$B \Rightarrow \mathbf{A}\bigcirc(\neg l \lor E)$	$B \Rightarrow \mathbf{E}\Diamond l_{(f)}$
$\mathbf{true} \Rightarrow D \lor D'$	$A \land B \Rightarrow \mathbf{A}\bigcirc(D \lor E)$	$B \Rightarrow \mathbf{E}(\neg A \mathcal{W} l)_{(f)}$

Resolution Example Here we present a resolution refutation for the set of clauses of TDS obtained for the component system analysed in the previous section.

	TDS			$Proof$	
1.	$\mathbf{start} \Rightarrow r$		6.	$\mathbf{true} \Rightarrow \neg r \lor \mathcal{O}_i\neg q$	*from 3*
2.	$r \Rightarrow \mathbf{A}\bigcirc r$		7.	$\mathbf{true} \Rightarrow \neg w \lor \mathcal{P}_i q$	*from 5*
3.	$r \Rightarrow \mathcal{O}_i\neg q$		8.	$\mathbf{true} \Rightarrow \neg r \lor \neg w$	$DRES, 6, 7$
4.	$r \Rightarrow \mathbf{E}\Diamond w_{(f)}$		9.	$\mathbf{start} \Rightarrow \neg r \lor \neg w$	*temporising*, 8
5.	$w \Rightarrow \mathcal{P}_i q$		10.	$\mathbf{true} \Rightarrow \mathbf{A}\bigcirc(\neg r \lor \neg w)$	*temporising*, 8
			11.	$r \Rightarrow \mathbf{A}\bigcirc w$	$SRES, 2, 10$
			12.	$r \Rightarrow \neg r \mathcal{W} w$	$TRES, 2, 11, 4$
			13.	$r \Rightarrow w \lor \neg r$	$\mathcal{W}$ *removal*, 12
			14.	$\mathbf{start} \Rightarrow \neg r \lor w$	$\mathcal{W}$ *removal*, 12
			15.	$\mathbf{start} \Rightarrow \mathbf{false}$	$SRES, 1, 9, 14$

Here the reconfiguration request is rejected, hence no changes to the model.

5. Conclusions

The need for a safe and reliable way to reconfigure systems, especially distributed, resource depending and long running systems, has led to the need for a formal way to describe and verify them before risking to take some action. In this paper we have given a definition for dynamic reconfiguration and a formal way to specify the behaviour of a component model and its infrastructure. Furthermore we have demonstrated how we can apply this formal specification to model update techniques that conform to the definition of dynamic reconfiguration given. The method introduced can also be used to prevent inconsistency and suggest corrections to the system in a static and/or dynamic environment. Indeed, if the verification technique discovers inconsistencies in the configuration then the 'healing' process is triggered: the process of "re-configuring" of the computation tree model that conforms the protocol. To ensure the consistency we must supply the system with internal 'clocks' which is needed to synchronise the states that belong to different branches of the computation tree. We are planning to eventually embed all these features in a prototype plug-in for the GridComp GIDE and test it on case studies proposed by industry partners.

References

[1] A. Basso, A. Bolotov, A. Basukoski, V. Getov, L. Henrio and M. Urbanski. Specification and Verification of Reconfiguration Protocols in Grid Component Systems. In *Proceedings of the 3rd IEEE Conference On Intelligent Systems IS-200*, 2006, IEEE.

[2] T. Barros and L. Henrio and E. Madelaine. Verification of Distributed Hierarchical Components. In *Proc. of the International Workshop on Formal Aspects of Component Software (FACS'05)*. Electronic Notes in Theor. Computer Sci. 160. pp. 41-55 (ENTCS), 2005.

[3] Batista, T., Joolia, A. and Coulson, G. Managing Dynamic Reconfiguration in Component-based Systems Proceedings of the European Workshop on Software Architectures, June, 2005, Springer-Velag LNCS series, Vol 3527, pp 1-18.

[4] F. Baude and D. Caromel and F. Huet and L. Mestre and J. Vayssi Interactive and Descriptor-Based Deployment of Object-Oriented Grid Applications HPDC '02: Proceedings of the 11 th IEEE International Symposium on High Performance Distributed Computing HPDC-11 p. 93, IEEE Computer Society.

[5] A. Bolotov. *Clausal Resolution for Branching-Time Temporal Logic*. PhD thesis, Department of Computing and Mathematics, The Manchester Metropolitan University, 2000.

[6] A. Bolotov and M. Fisher. A Clausal Resolution Method for CTL Branching Time Temporal Logic. *Journal of Experimental and Theoretical Artificial Intelligence.*, 11:77–93, 1999.

[7] E. M. Clarke, A. Fehnker, S. Jha and H. Veith. Temporal Logic Model Checking., Handbook of Networked and Embedded Control Systems, 2005, pages 539-558.

[8] C. Dixon, M. Fisher, and B. Konev. Tractable Temporal Reasoning. In *Proceedings of the Twentieth International Joint Conference on Artificial Intelligence (IJCAI-07)*, pages 318-323, January 6-12th 2007.

[9] T. Eiter and G. Gottlob. On the complexity of propositional knowledge base revision, updates, and counterfactuals. PODS '92: Proceedings of the eleventh ACM SIGACT-SIGMOD-SIGART symposium, p261-273, 1992.

[10] M. Endler. A language for implementing generic dynamic reconfigurations of distributed programs. In Proceedings of the 12th Brazilian Symposium on Computer Networks, pages 175-187, 1994.

[11] E. A. Emerson. Temporal and Modal Logic. In J. van Leeuwen, editor, *Handbook of Theoretical Computer Science: Volume B, Formal Models and Semantics.*, pages 996–1072. Elsevier, 1990.

[12] GCM program committee Basic Features of the Grid Component Model Deliverable D.PM.04, CoreGRID, March 2007.

[13] V. Getov, A. Basukoski, J. Thiyagalingam, Y. Yulai and Y. Wu Grid programming with COMPonents : an advanced component platform for an effective invisible grid GRIDComp Technical Report, July 2007

[14] A. Lomuscio and B. Wozna. A complete and decidable axiomatisation for deontic interpreted systems. In *DEON*, volume 4048 of *Lecture Notes in Computer Science*, pages 238–254. Springer, 2006.

[15] Z. Manna and A. Pnueli. Temporal Specification and Verification of Reactive Modules. Weizmann Institute of Science Technical Report, March 1992

[16] S. Schaefer. CDDLM - Component Model In proceeding to the Open Grid Forum, March 2006

[17] Elisabeth A. Strunk and John C. Knight. Assured Reconfiguration of Embedded Real-Time Software. DSN '04: Proceedings of the 2004 International Conference on Dependable Systems and Networks (DSN'04), 2004, p. 367, IEEE Computer Society.

A FLEXIBLE MODEL AND IMPLEMENTATION OF COMPONENT CONTROLLERS

Francoise Baude, Denis Caromel, Ludovic Henrio and Paul Naoumenko
INRIA Sophia - I3S - CNRS - Universite de Nice Sophia Antipolis
{fbaude,dcaromel,lhenrio, pnaoumen}@sophia.inria.fr

Abstract   The GCM (Grid Component Model) is a component model that is being defined by the CoreGRID institute on Programming Models; it is based on the Fractal component model. It is intended at overcoming the insufficiencies of the existing component systems when it comes to Grid computing. Its main characteristics are: hierarchical composition, structured communications with support for asynchrony, support for deployment, functional and non-functional (NF) adaptivity, and autonomicity. As in the Fractal component model, the GCM distinguishes *controllers* which implement NF concerns and are gathered in a *membrane* from the functional content of the component.

This article presents a refinement of the Fractal/GCM model and an API for adopting a component design of the component membranes, as suggested by the GCM specification. The objective of this framework is to provide support for both adaptivity and autonomicity of the component control part. In the design of the model refinement and the API for NF components, we also take into account hierarchical composition and distribution of the membrane, which is crucial in the GCM. Our approach is flexible because it allows "classical" controllers implemented by usual objects to coexist with highly dynamic and reconfigurable controllers implemented as components.

Keywords: GCM, component control, separation of concerns, autonomicity.

1.   Introduction

Components running in dynamically changing execution environments need
to adapt to these environments. In Fractal [3] and GCM (Grid Component
Model) [4] component models, adaptation mechanisms are triggered by the non-
functional (NF) part of the components. This NF part, called the *membrane*,
is composed of *controllers* that implement NF concerns. Interactions with
execution environments may require complex relationships between controllers.
In this work we focus on the adaptability of the *membrane*. Examples include
changing communication protocols, updating security policies, or taking into
account new runtime environments in case of mobile components. Adaptability
implies that evolutions of the execution environments have to be detected and
acted upon, and may also imply interactions with the environment and with
other components for realizing the adaptation.

We want to provide tools for adapting controllers. This means that these
tools have to manage (re)configuration of controllers inside the membrane and
the interactions of the membrane with membranes of other components. For
this, we provide a model and an implementation, using a standard component-
oriented approach for both the application (functional) level and the control (NF)
level. Having a component-oriented approach for the non-functional aspects
also allows them to benefit from the structure, hierarchy and encapsulation
provided by a component-oriented approach.

In this paper, we propose to design NF concerns as compositions of components as suggested in the GCM proposal. Our general objective is to allow
controllers implemented as components to be directly plugged in a component
membrane. These controllers take advantage of the properties of component
systems like *reconfigurability*, i.e. changing of the contained components and
their bindings. This allows components to be dynamically adapted in order to
suit changing environmental conditions. Indeed, among others, we aim at a
component platform appropriate for *autonomic Grid applications*; those applications aim to ensure some quality of services and other NF features without
being geared by an external entity.

In this paper we provide a twofold contribution: first, refinements of the Frac-
tal/GCM model concerning the structure of a membrane; second, a definition
and an implementation of an API that allows GCM membranes to be themselves
composed of components, possibly distributed. Both for efficiency and for flexibility reasons, we provide an implementation where controllers can either be
classical objects or full components that could even be distributed. We believe
that this high level of flexibility is a great advantage of this approach over the
existing ones [8, 7]. Our model refinements also provide a better structure for
the membrane and a better decoupling between the membrane and its externals.
Finally, our approach gives the necessary tools for membrane reconfiguration,

providing flexibility and evolution abilities. The API we present can be split in three parts:

- Methods dedicated to component instantiation: they allow the specification of a NF type of a component, and the instantiation of NF components;

- Methods for the *management of the membrane*: they consist in managing the content, introspecting , and managing the life-cycle of the membrane. Those methods are proposed as an extension of the Fractal component model, and consequently of the GCM;

- An optional set of methods allowing *direct operations on the components that compose the membrane*: they allow introspection, bindings and life-cycle management of the components inside the membrane, as would be possible using the Fractal API extended with the previously mentioned methods. They take into consideration the distributed nature of the GCM.

This paper is organized as follows. Section 2 presents refinements of the Fractal/GCM model and the API for (re)configuring the membrane; then Section 3 presents the implementation of the API, using GCM/ProActive; Section 4 presents the related work; finally Section 5 concludes.

2.   Componentizing Component Controllers

After an example motivating our approach, this section describes the structure of the membrane and primitives for creating and manipulating NF components. Indeed, the purpose of our approach is to design the management of the application as a component system; that is why we want to adopt a GCM design for the NF part of a component. Consequently, like any GCM component, the ones inside the membrane can be distributed. Thanks to such a design, NF requests can be triggered by external (NF) components in a much more structured way. For autonomicity purposes, reconfigurations can be triggered by controllers belonging to the membrane itself.

2.1   Motivating Example

Here we present a simple example that shows the advantages of componentizing controllers of GCM components. In our example, we are considering a naive solution for securing communications of a composite component. As described in Figure 1, secure communications are implemented by three components inside the membrane: Interceptor, Decrypt, and Alert. The scenario of the example is the following: the composite component receives encrypted messages on its server functional interface. The goal is to decrypt those messages. First, the incoming messages are intercepted by the Interceptor component. It forwards all the intercepted communications to Decrypt, which can be an off-the-shelf component (written by cryptography specialists) implementing a

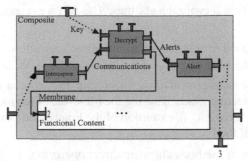

Figure 1.   Example: architecture of a naive solution for secure communications

specific decryption algorithm. The Decrypt component receives a key for decryption through the non-functional server interface of the composite (interface number 1 on the figure). If it successfully decrypts the message, the Decrypt component sends it to the internal functional components, using the functional internal client interface (2). If a problem during decryption occurs, the Decrypt component sends a message to the Alert component. The Alert component is charge to decide on how to react when a decryption fails. For example, it can contact the sender (using the non-functional client interface – 3) and ask it to send the message again. Another security policy would be to contact a "trust and reputation" authority to signal a suspicious behaviour of the sender. The Alert component is implemented by a developer who knows the security policy of the system. In this example, we have three well-identified components, with clear functionalities and connected through well-defined interfaces. Thus, we can dynamically replace the Decrypt component by another one, implementing a different decryption algorithm. Also, for changing the security policy of the system, we can dynamically replace the Alert component and change its connexions. Compared to a classical implementation of secure communications (for example with objects), using components brings to the membrane a better structure and reconfiguration possibilities. To summarize, componentizing the membrane in this example provides dynamic adaptability and reconfiguration; but also re-usability and composition from off-the-shelf components.

2.2   A Structure for Componentized Membranes

Figure 2 shows the structure we suggest for the component membrane. The membrane (in gray) consists of one object controller and two component controllers, the component controllers are connected together and with the outside of the membrane by different bindings. For the moment, we do not specify whether components are localized with the membrane, or distributed.

Before defining an API for managing components inside the membrane, the definition of the membrane given by the GCM specification needs some refinements. Those refinements, discussed in this section, provide more details

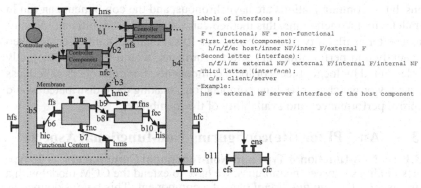

Figure 2.   New structure for the membrane of Fractal/GCM components

about the structure a membrane can adopt. Figure 2 represents the structure of
a membrane and gives a summary of the different kinds of interface roles and
bindings a GCM component can provide. As stated in the GCM specification,
NF interfaces are not only those specified in the Fractal specification, which are
only external server ones. Indeed, in order to be able to compose NF aspects,
the GCM requires the NF interfaces to share the same specification as the
functional ones: role, cardinality, and contingency. For example, in GCM, client
NF interfaces allow for the composition of NF aspects and reconfigurations
at the NF level. Our model is also flexible, as all server NF interfaces can be
implemented by both objects or components controllers.

All the interfaces showed in Figure 2 give the membrane a better structure
and enforce decoupling between the membrane and its externals. For example,
to connect *nfc* with *fns*, our model adds an additional stage: we have first to
perform binding *b3*, and then binding *b9*. This avoids *nfc* to be strongly coupled
with *fns*: to connect *nfc* to another *fns*, only binding *b9* has to be changed.

In Figure 2, some of the links are represented with dashed arrows. Those
links are not real bindings but "alias" bindings (e.g. b3); the source interface is
the alias and it is "merged" with the destination interface. These bindings are
similar to the export/import bindings existing in Fractal (b6, b10) except that no
interception of the communications on these bindings is allowed.

Performance Issues   While componentizing the membrane clearly improves
its programmability and its capacity to evolve, one can wonder what happens
to performance. First, as our design choice allows object controllers, one can
always keep the efficiency of crucial controllers by keeping them as objects.
Second, the overhead for using components instead of objects is very low if the
controllers components are local, and are negligible compared to the communication time, for example. Finally, if controllers components are distributed,
then there can be a significant overhead induced by the remote communica-

tions, but if communications are asynchronous, and the component can run in parallel with the membrane, this method can also induce a significant speedup, and a better availability of the membrane. To summarize, controllers invoked frequently and performing very short treatments, would be more efficiently implemented by local objects or local components. For controllers called less frequently or which involve long computations, making them distributed would improve performances and availability of the membrane.

2.3   An API for (Re)configuring Non-functional Aspects

2.3.1   Non-functional Type and Non-functional Components.   To type check bindings between membranes, we have to extend the GCM model with a new concept: the *non functional type* of a component. This type is defined as the union of the types of NF interfaces the membrane exposes. To specify the NF type of a component, we propose to overload the Fractal newFcInstance method (the one to create functional components) as follows:

```
public Component newFcInstance(Type fType,Type nfType,
                    any contentDesc, any controllerDesc);
```

In this method, nfType represents the NF type of the component; it can be specified by hand. Of course the standard Fractal type factory has to be extended in order to support all possible roles of NF interfaces.

The NF type can also be specified within a configuration file: the controller descriptor argument (controllerDesc) can be a file written in Architecture Description Language (ADL) containing the whole description of the NF system as we will suggest in Section 3.2.

Components inside the membrane are *non-functional components*. They are similar to functional ones. However, their purpose is different because they deal with NF aspects of the *host component*. Thus, in order to enforce separation of concerns, we restrict the interactions between functional and NF components. For example, a NF component cannot be included inside the functional content of a composite. Inversely, a functional component cannot be added inside a membrane. As a consequence, direct bindings between functional interfaces of NF and functional components are forbidden.

To create NF components, we extend the common Fractal factories (generic factory and ADL factory). For generic factory, we add a method named newNFcInstance that creates this new kind of components:

```
public Component newNFcInstance(Type fType,Type nfType,
                    any contentDesc, any controllerDesc);
```

Parameters of this method are identical to its functional equivalent and NF components are created the same way as functional ones. To create NF

```
public void addNFSubComponent(Component component) throws
    IllegalContentException;
public void removeNFSubComponent(Component component) throws
    IllegalContentException, IllegalLifeCycleException,
    NoSuchComponentException;
public Component[] getNFcSubComponents();
public Component getNFcSubComponent(string name) throws
    NoSuchComponentException;
public void setControllerObject(string itf, any controllerclass)
    throws NoSuchInterfaceException;
public void startMembrane() throws IllegalLifeCycleException;
public void stopMembrane() throws IllegalLifeCycleException;
%\end{lstlisting}
```

Figure 3.   General purpose methods defined in MembraneController interface

components using Fractal ADL[2], developers need to modify or add some of
the modules within the factory. These modules depend on the implementation
of the newNFcInstance method and on the Fractal/GCM implementation.

2.3.2   General Purpose API.   To manipulate components inside membranes, we introduce primitives to perform basic operations like adding, removing or getting a reference on a NF component. We also need to perform
calls on well-known Fractal controllers (*life-cycle controller*, *binding controller*,
...) of these components. So, we extend Fractal/GCM specification by adding
a new controller called *membrane controller*. As we want it to manage all
the controllers, it is the only mandatory controller that has to belong to any
membrane. It allows the manual composition of membranes by adding the
desired controllers. The methods presented in Figure 3 are included in the
MembraneController interface; they are the core of the API and are sufficient
to perform all the basic manipulations inside the membrane. They add, remove,
or get a reference on a NF component. They also allow the management of
object controllers and membrane's life-cycle. Referring to Fractal, this core API
implements a subset of the behavior of the life-cycle and content controllers
specific to the membrane. This core API can be included in any Fractal/GCM
implementation. Reconfigurations of NF components inside the membrane are
performed by calling standard Fractal controllers. The general purpose API
defines the following methods:

- addNFSubComponent(Component component): adds the NF component
  given as argument to the membrane;

- removeNFSubComponent(Component component): removes the specified component from the membrane;

```
public void bindNFc(String clientItf, String serverItf) throws
   NoSuchInterfaceException, IllegalLifeCycleException,
   IllegalBindingException, NoSuchComponentException;
public void bindNFc(String clientItf, Object serverItf) throws
   NoSuchInterfaceException, IllegalLifeCycleException,
   IllegalBindingException, NoSuchComponentException;
public void unbindNFc(String clientItf) throws
NoSuchInterfaceException,
   IllegalLifeCycleException, llegalBindingException,
   NoSuchComponentException;
public String[] listNFc(String component) throws
NoSuchComponentException; public Object lookupNFc(String itfname)
throws NoSuchInterfaceException,
   NoSuchComponentException;
public void startNFc(String component) throws IllegalLifeCycleException,
   NoSuchComponentException;
public void stopNFc(String component) throws
IllegalLifeCycleException, NoSuchComponentException; public String
getNFcState(String component) throws NoSuchComponentException;
```

Figure 4.   Distribution specific methods implemented by MembraneController

- getNFcSubComponents(): returns an array containing all the NF components;
- getNFcSubComponent(string name): returns the specified NF component, the string argument is the name of the component;
- setControllerObject(string itf, any controllerclass): sets re-
  places an existing controller object inside the membrane. Itf specifies the
  name of the control interface which has to be implemented by the controller
  class, given as second parameter. Replacing a controller object at runtime
  provides a very basic adaptivity of the membrane;
- startMembrane(): starts the membrane, i.e. allows NF calls on the host
  component to be served. This method can adopt a recursive behavior, by
  starting the life-cycle of each NF component inside the membrane;
- stopMembrane(): Stops the membrane, i.e. prevents NF calls on the host
  component from being served except the ones on the membrane controller.
  This method can adopt a recursive behavior, by stopping the life-cycle of
  each NF component.

2.3.3   Distribution-specific API.   Considering the distribution aspect of
the GCM, we provide an extension to the core API. As usual in distributed
programming paradigms, GCM objects/components can be accessed locally
or remotely. Remote references are accessible everywhere, while local references are accessible only in a restricted address space. When returning a local
object/component outside its address space, there are two alternatives: create

a remote reference on this entity; or make a copy of it. When considering a copy of a NF local component, the NF calls are not consistent. If an invocation on getNFcSubComponent(string name) returns a copy of the specified NF component, calls performed on this copy will not be performed on the "real" NF component inside the membrane. Figure 4 defines a set of methods that solves this problem. As copies of local components result in inconsistent behavior, the alternative we adopt is to address NF components by their names instead of their references. These methods allow to make calls on the binding controller and on the life-cycle controller of NF components that are hosted by the component membrane. Currently, they don't take into account the hierarchical aspect of local NF components.

Somehow this new API can be considered as higher level operations compared to the API of Figure 3. Indeed, they address the NF components and call their controllers at once. For example, here is the Java code that binds two components inside the membrane using the general purpose API. It binds the interface "i1" of the component "nfComp1" inside the membrane to the interface "i2" of the component "nfComp2". Suppose mc is a reference to the *MembraneController* of the host component.

```
Component nfComp1=mc.getNFcSubComponent("nfComp1");
Component nfComp2=mc.getNFcSubComponent("nfComp2");
Fractal.getBindingController(nfComp1).
        bindFc("i1",nfComp2.getFcInterface("i2"));
```

But, if the code above is executed by an entity outside the membrane and "nfComp1" is a passive component; then it is not the component "nfComp1" inside the membrane that is bound to "nfComp2" but a copy of it. Using the API of Figure 4, this binding can be realized by the following code, that binds the component "nfComp1" correctly, regardless of whether it is active or passive

```
mc.bindNFc("nfComp1.i1","nfComp2.i2");
```

Similarly to the example above, all the methods of Figure 4 result in calls on well-known Fractal controllers. Interfaces are represented as strings of the form *component.interface*, where *component* is the name of the inner component and *interface* is the name of its client or server interface. We use the name "membrane" to represent the membrane of the host component, e.g. membrane.i1 is the NF interface i1 of the host component; in this case *interface* is the name of an interface from the NF type. For example, bindNFc(string, string) allows to perform the bindings: *b1, b2, b4, b3, b9, b7* and *b5* of Figure 2.

The two parts of our API (Figures 3 and 4) can be included in two separate interfaces. Then developers can choose to implement one or both of these interfaces inside each component.

3.   Implementation and Ongoing Work

3.1   Context

The ProActive library is a middleware for Grid computing, written in Java, based on activities, with asynchronous communications and providing a deployment framework. A GCM/ProActive component is instantiated by an activity, i.e. an active object, some passive objects, together with a request queue and a single thread. Because the smallest unit of composition is an activity, GCM/ProActive may be considered as a *coarse-grained* implementation of the Fractal/GCM component model w.r.t. the Julia or the AOKell implementations, where the smallest unit of composition is a (passive) object. A reference implementation of the GCM is being implemented over ProActive, it follows its programming model, especially concerning remote objects/components (called *active objects/components*) and local objects/components (called *passive objects/components*).

3.2   Current Limitations and Future Work

Currently, we have implemented in GCM/ProActive the structure proposed in the previous sections with most of the suggested interfaces and API. Our `MembraneController` is able to manage NF active components and passive objects as controllers. One of the strong points of our implementation is that membranes can consist of both passive objects and active components.

We review below the current status of the implementation and the main limitations that have to be addressed in the future.

Support Passive Components We do not support passive components for the moment. We will investigate on strategies to include also passive NF components. The idea consists in reusing components from existing frameworks (e.g. Julia or AOKell).

Describing the membrane by an ADL For the moment, the only way to instantiate NF components inside the membrane is programmatically: first create a NF component with the `newNFcInstance` method, second add and bind the NF components thanks to invocations on the membrane controller. These operations can be performed either by an external entity (e.g. another component or the framework that instantiates the host component) or by an autonomic controller inside the membrane. In addition to this manual method, we want the developer to be able to describe whole membrane in a separate file, given as last argument of the `newFcInstance` method. This way, the membrane can be designed separately from the functional content.

Considering the membrane as a composite component eases its description with its set of interfaces, objects and internal components; it also allows us to describe the membrane in an (extended) ADL language. External functional interfaces of this composite correspond to both internal and external NF interfaces of the host component. Then membrane's description can be referenced as the controllers description inside the functional ADL. This ADL "composite view" is only necessary at design time: when the membrane is actually created, the composite component should be "dissolved" inside its host component, i.e. the host component will be the parent of the functional and NF components. This avoids unnecessary intermediate interfaces, and having to deal with the "membrane's membrane". In Figure 5, the membrane is a composite drawn with a dashed border line which does not exist at runtime.

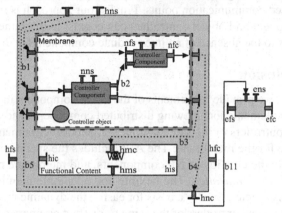

Figure 5.   The membrane is designed as a composite component

4.   Related Work

First of all, our approach for adaptivity has the great advantage to allow the usage of many related works. Indeed, by using a component-based approach for the design and implementation of controllers, we can also apply existing knowledge on self-adaptativity at the application level (e.g., [5]) to the NF level.

Other research teams have also proposed to provide a component-based model for the implementation of membranes. Control microcomponents from the Asbaco project [7] are specific components using a control API different from Fractal's, and requiring a specific ADL language (because microcomponents are injected following an aspect oriented approach).

AOKell [8–9] proposes a component-based approach using the Fractal API for engineering membranes, but their controller components cannot be distributed, neither collaborate with object controllers. Moreover, the membrane is necessarily designed and executed as a composite component entailing one additional level of indirection for requests toward the membrane components. Recently, Julia's Fractal implementation moved towards components in the membrane; their approach is similar to the one of AOKell.

In [6], the authors also advocate the componentization of the membranes in order to enable the dynamic choice between various implementations of the same technical service according to the runtime context of a Fractal component.

Our approach has some differences with the ones cited above. We provide more details about the structure of a membrane. The first useful concept is the NF type: it helps to decide at runtime which NF interfaces will be exposed by the membrane and to type-check NF bindings. Moreover, new roles have been introduced for NF interfaces. This helps developers to have more control over NF bindings and to design the membrane separately from the functional content with well defined communication points. Finally, our approach is more flexible, because component and object controllers can coexist in the same membrane, partially thanks to the absence of an intermediate component for the membrane.

5.   Conclusion

In this paper, we provide refinements of the GCM component model, an API, and a partial implementation allowing distributed components and local objects to coexist as controllers of the same membrane. Model refinements provide a better structure for the membrane. The API includes the specification of component NF type, the creation of NF components, and membrane management with the *MembraneController*. The flexible and adaptable membrane design presented in this article provides a basis for easing the dynamic management of interactions between controllers of the same or distinct components. Including the future work presented in Section 3.2, we plan to experiment some autonomic adaptation scenarios. Thanks to these scenarios, we will evaluate the capability of the membrane to orchestrate two kinds of reconfigurations: reconfiguration of the functional inner component system, following the idea of hierarchical autonomic decision paths [1]; and reconfiguration of the membrane itself when the adaptation is related to NF properties of the host component.

References

[1] M. Aldinucci, C. Bertolli, S. Campa, M. Coppola, M. Vanneschi, and C. Zoccolo. Auto-
     nomic Grid Components: the GCM Proposal and Self-optimising ASSIST Components.
     In *Joint Workshop on HPC Grid programming Environments and Components and Com-
     ponent and Framework Technology in High-Performance and Scientific Computing at
     HPDC'15*, June 2006.

[2] E. Bruneton. Fractal ADL Tutorial http://fractal.objectweb.org/tutorials/
     adl/index.html. Technical report, ObjectWeb Consortium, March 2004.

[3] E. Bruneton, T.Coupaye, and J. Stefani. The Fractal Component Model http://fractal.
     objectweb.org/specification/index.html. Technical report, ObjectWeb Consor-
     tium, February 2004.

[4] CoreGRID Programming Model Virtual Institute. Basic features of the grid component
     model (assessed), 2006. Deliverable D.PM.04, CoreGRID, Programming Model Institute.

[5] P. David and T. Ledoux. Towards a framework for self-adaptive component-based applications. In J.-B. Stefani, I. Demeure, and D. Hagimont, editors, *Proceedings of Distributed Applications and Interoperable Systems 2003, the 4th IFIP WG6.1 International Conference, DAIS 2003*, volume 2893 of *Lecture Notes in Computer Science*, pages 1–14, Paris, Nov. 2003. Federated Conferences, Springer-Verlag.

[6] C. Herault, S. Nemchenko, and S. Lecomte. A Component-Based Transactional Service, Including Advanced Transactional Models. In *Advanced Distributed Systems: 5th International School and Symposium, ISSADS 2005, Revised Selected Papers*, number 3563 in LNCS, 2005.

[7] V. Mencl and T. Bures. Microcomponent-based component controllers: A foundation for component aspects. In *APSEC*. IEEE Computer Society, Dec. 2005.

[8] L. Seinturier, N. Pessemier, and T. Coupaye. AOKell: an Aspect-Oriented Implementation of the Fractal Specifications, 2005. http://www.lifl.fr/~seinturi/aokell/javadoc/overview.html.

[9] L. Seinturier, N. Pessemier, L. Duchien, and T. Coupaye. A component model engineered with components and aspects. In *Proceedings of the 9th International SIGSOFT Symposium on Component-Based Software Engineering (CBSE'06)*, Lecture Notes in Computer Science. Springer, June 2006.

ANALYSIS OF COMPONENT MODEL EXTENSIONS TO SUPPORT THE GRICOL LANGUAGE

Hinde Bouziane[1], Natalia Currle-Linde[2], Christian Perez[1] and Michael Resch[2]

(1) INRIA/IRISA, Rennes, France

{Hinde.Bouziane,Christian.Perez}@inria.fr

(2) High Performance Computing Center Stuttgart (HLRS),
University of Stuttgart, Stuttgart, Germany

{linde,resch}@hlrs.de

Abstract

Nowadays, programming grid applications is still a major challenge. Several systems, tools and environments have appeared to allow end-users to describe applications without dealing with the complexity of the grid infrastructure. An application description in such environments is done through high level languages such as the Grid Concurrent Language (GRICOL). Independently of the application domain, this language enables the description of highly complex scientific experiments. While such a high level language is offered to end-users, the question of how to implement it is raised. The contribution of this paper is to analyze the support of a GRICOL application within component models, in particular the support of its temporal composition represented by a control flow construction.

Keywords: programming model, software component, programming language, control-flow, data-flow, GriCoL.

1.   Introduction

The development of grid technologies provides technical possibilities for dealing with compute-intensive applications. As a consequence, scientists and engineers are producing an increasing number of complex applications which make use of distributed grid resources. However, the existing grid services do not allow scientists to design complex applications on a high level of organization. Hence, an integrated system is needed for describing applications with a high level of abstraction so that it is not required to have a knowledge of the specific features of the grid.

In our view, a language for programming experiments must fulfill the following requirements: a) it must be of maximum simplicity (easy to understand and use); b) it must provide maximum execution efficiency (parallelism) and c) it must exploit full capabilities of supercomputer applications and to build from them more complex constructions. GRICOL is an example of such a language.

While high level programming languages are offered to end-users, the issue is about the way to implement them. To handle underlying grid applications, software component technology appears to be a promising approach. This technology has been expanded through the appearance of several component models like CCA [5], CCM [11], DARWIN [9], FRACTAL [6], GCM [10], GRID.IT [3] or SCA [1]. They tend today to facilitate the design of large scale scientific applications and to reduce the complexity of their building process.

The contribution of this paper is to analyze – and to reduce – the gap that exists between GRICOL and existing software component models in general. Being from CoreGRID, GCM is of particular interest. This gap is present due to the fact that existing component models are only based on spatial composition while GRICOL offers temporal composition. The long term goal is to define a common component model for all the software layers as sought by the CoreGRID Institute on Grid Systems, Tools, and Environments.

Section 2 presents GRICOL while Section 3 analyzes the missing features of existing component models. Section 4 presents our approach to extend component models with temporal composition. Section 5 discusses how our proposal fills the gap to support GRICOL. Finally Section 6 concludes the paper.

2.   Grid Concurrent Language

GRICOL [7] is a parallel language for programming complex compute- and data-intensive tasks without being tied to a specific application domain. It is a graphical-based language in which the main elements are blocks and modules. These elements have a defined internal structure and interact with each other through defined interfaces. They allow wrapping functionalities in order to utilize the capacities of supercomputer applications and to enable interactions with other language elements and structures. Program codes, which may be generated in any language, are wrapped in a standard language capsule.

In addition, GRICOL is a multi-tiered language. The multi-tiered model of organization enables the user, when describing the experiment, to concentrate primarily on the common logic of the experiment program, and subsequently on the description of the individual fragments of the program. GRICOL has a two-layer model for the description of the experiment and an additional sub-layer for the description of the repository of the experiment. The top level of the experiment program, the control flow level, is intended for the description of the logical stages of the experiment. The main elements of this level are blocks and connection lines. The lower level, the data flow level, provides a detailed description of components at the top level. The main elements of the data flow level are program modules and database areas. The repository sub-layer provides a common description of the database. The remainder of this section presents an overview of the main GRICOL layers.

2.1   Control flow level

To describe the logic of the experiment, the control flow level offers different types of blocks: solver, condition, merge/synchro and message blocks. A solver block is composed of nodes of data processing. It represents applications which use numerical methods of modeling. The control blocks are either nodes of data analysis or nodes for the synchronization of data computation processes. They evaluate results and then choose a path for further experiment development. Another important language element on the control flow level is the connection line. Connection lines indicate the sequence of execution of blocks in the experiment. There are two mechanisms of interaction between blocks: batch and pipeline. If the connection line is red (solid) in color, control is passed to the next block only after all runs in the previous block have finished (batch). If the connection line is blue (dashed) in color, control is transferred to the next block after each computation of an individual data set has been completed (pipeline).

Figure 1(a) shows an example of an experiment program at the control flow level. The start-block begins a parallel operation in solver blocks B.01 and B.02. After execution of B.02, processes begin in solver blocks B.03 and B.04. Each data set which has been computed in B.04 is evaluated in control block B.05. The data sets meeting specified criterion are selected for further computation. These operations are repeated until all data sets from the output of B.04 have been evaluated. The data sets selected in this way are synchronized by a merge/synchronize block with the corresponding data sets of the other inputs of B.06. The final computation takes place in solver block B.07.

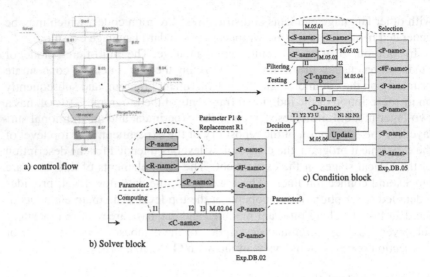

a) control flow

b) Solver block

c) Condition block

Figure 1.   Example of an experiment program.

2.2   Data flow level

A typical example of a solver block program is a modeling program which cyclically computes a large number of input data sets. The solver block consists of computation, replacement, parameterization modules and a database (Figure 1(b)). Computation modules are functional programs which organize and execute data processing on grid resources. Parameterization modules are modules which generate parameter values. These values are transferred to computation modules. The generation of parameter values takes place according to rules specified by the user, either as mathematical formula or a list of parameter values. Replacement modules are modules for remote parameterizations. A more detailed description of the working of the modules is given in [7].

A typical control block program carries out an iterative analysis of the data sets from previous steps of the experiment and selects either the direction for the further development of the experiment or examines whether the input data sets are ready for further computation, and subsequently synchronizes their further processing. The condition block on Figure 1(c) consists of selecting, filtering, testing, decision and updating modules, as well as a database. The selecting and updating modules are used for the interaction between modules and the database. A filtering module is used for additional selection of the input data taken from the experiment database with the help of the selecting module. Testing modules are programs which carry out a comparative analysis of input data sets and check if the data arrays are in accordance with given criteria or not. Depending on the logical evaluation by the testing module, the decision module makes possible to rename, re-index the input data sets, and to write them in the database as long as they meet the conditions.

The remainder of this paper proposes a component based implementation of GRICOL. The next section studies how the different levels of GRICOL can be mapped on a component based composition.

3. Analysis of mapping GRICOL to component models

In order to analyze the support of a GRICOL application within existing component models, let us split the analysis into several steps regarding the principles used to compose such an application:

- **Black boxes.** When composing a GRICOL application at the control or data flow levels, blocks and modules are black boxes for which only external links have to be specified. Therefore, blocks and modules can be straightforwardly mapped to software components with ports.
- **Hierarchical composition.** This is illustrated by the composition of blocks at a higher level and composition of modules at a lower level. Such a hierarchical composition is already allowed by component models, like FRACTAL or GCM.
- **Repository.** This is a storage space where data are read or written. This space is accessed from all experiment blocks and forms a global memory. It can be of several natures depending on the resources environment that is used. For instance, it can be a database or a distributed shared space. This memory can be logically encapsulated inside a component and the access to stored data can be done through getting/setting operations. It is also possible to use our proposed approach [4] to allow transparent data sharing between components. The proposed solution is based on the addition of a new family of ports named data ports. The proposal illustrates also the use of a grid data-sharing service.
- **Data flow composition.** This describes data availability constraints to perform a computation (solver block) or a decision (condition block). The building process of a data flow specifies also the way of accessing data (through parameterized, replacement, etc. modules). A communication between modules, which are considered as components, is based on a request-reply principle. Such a principle can be mapped to a *getting* operation with the profile *DataType get()*. Therefore, it is straightforward to associate such an operation to a classical component port. As the user specifies the name of input and output data of a module, these names can be used to identify associated ports.
- **Control flow composition.** This is the relevant type of composition that motivates the present work. It specifies the time dependency between blocks. That means, it builds the sequence (possibly conditional sequences) of the execution of blocks. As far as we know, such a temporal composition is not offered by existing component models. In fact, according to supported communication

types, only spatial composition is available. Such a communication can be either
1) a remote method invocation (CCM, CCA or FRACTAL); 2) a message passing
(DARWIN); 3) an event (CCM) or 3) a data streaming (GRID.IT). With these
communication types, a control flow composition can be simulated by explicit
coordination of the global application execution. However, this is done by the
programmer inside the application code. This solution may lead to a complex
code, especially for large applications with parallel computations. Hence, we
propose an extension of component models to overcome such a limitation.

4.   Towards a component model with temporal composition

The aim of the present work is to give an overview of our approach that
enables component models to easily support temporal composition. This work
is not restricted to support the specific case of GRICOL, but it is generalized to
the support of workflow based compositions.

A workflow composition [12] is based on a control flow eventually coupled
with a data flow composition. That means, a control flow may be driven by some
data availability at the same level of composition. Several concepts are used in
a workflow context: tasks, task's input and output data availability constraints
and control flow patterns like sequence, synchronization or condition.

As component models, workflow management systems like Triana [2] or
P-GRADE [9] aim to support large scale scientific applications. Nevertheless,
in order to support simply and efficiently multiple programming paradigms
inside one application, it may be suitable to have both spatial and temporal
composition within a same model.

This section presents how workflow concepts can be introduced in a component based application. Only sequence for control flow patterns are specified
in this paper. We assume that other patterns are implicitly supported inside
components. We also use a CCM based formalism to present our proposal. That
assumes a component to have a framework and a user view of a defined port.
The user view is either external (composition interfaces) or internal (interfaces
accessible from functional implementation).

4.1   Temporal ports model

In addition to classical (spatial) ports, we define another family of ports,
called temporal ports. A temporal port is associated to a data type and can be of
two kinds: *input* port, associated to an input data type, or *output* port, associated
to an output data type. The right part of Figure 2 shows a definition example
of the *A* component ports. These ports are implemented by the interfaces
represented on the left of Figure 2. First, the internal view of the *A* ports
allows the component's implementation to retrieve (or set) an input (or output)

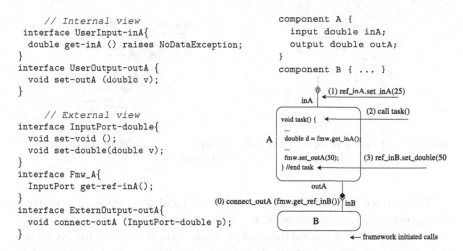

Figure 2.   Example of interfaces offered to the programmer by temporal ports and their usage.

data from (or on) the *inA* (or *outA*) port. Second, the external view defines a *connect-outA(..)* operation to connect *outA* to a given *p* port with a compatible data type. The *InputPort-double* interface associated to *p* allows its data to be set to a given value. Finally, the *set-void* operation is defined for special use cases, as will be explained below. It sets the port's data to a *void* value. We assume also that a user can specify a *void* type to define a temporal port.

4.2   Task model

The second concept introduced is a component *task*. A task is a predefined operation with the profile: *void task()*. It is implemented by the user and is automatically called by the framework. The start of this operation is constrained by data reception on the component's input ports. During the execution of the task, the programmer can get and/or set input and output data values thanks to the internal view of temporal ports. When the *task()* operation is terminated, the framework checks if each output data was set by the user, otherwise the data is marked with a special flag *novalue*. After that, no marked data are sent on connected ports. Figure 2 gives an overview of the task model at work.

However, a programmer may want to produce more than one result on its *output* ports. In this case, it is at the responsibility of the programmer to notify the framework about the end of the generation of a set of output data. This notification is done through an operation *output-ready()* implemented by the framework. Therefore, when this operation is called, the framework performs the described checking and sending processes. Symmetrically, we defined the operation *input-wait()* to ask for getting multiple values on *input* ports.

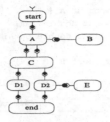
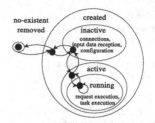

Figure 3.   Example of an assembly with   *Figure 4.*   Overview of the runtime life cycle
spatial and temporal compositions.   of a component.

As described here, temporal ports and task model seem to be close to data
stream usage. To avoid confusion, it is relevant to note that proposed concepts
are implicated in a temporal dimension, while it is not the case for events or
data streams. A component can define such spatial ports as well as temporal
ports, but only temporal ports direct the temporal behavior of an assembly.

4.3   Composition model

Within our proposal, an application can be based on spatial, temporal or
spatial and temporal compositions. The introduction of temporal ports has
no impact on a purely spatial composition, so the paper focuses on the use
of temporal ports. Figure 3 illustrates a coupled use of spatial and temporal
composition. The relevant property of such an assembly is that a control flow is
expressed. In fact, according to Section 4.1 and Section 4.2, a user can order
the execution of all tasks. For example, the connection of the output ports of
the *A* component to the input ports of the *C* component describes the fact that
an execution of *C*'s task follows an execution of *A*'s task.

However, to build a control flow, a start point must be determined. It is why
we defined a particular type of component named *start*. This component is
assumed to be provided by the framework and to be responsible for triggering
task executions on connected components. We defined also a component named
end for explicit specification of the end point of a task execution sequence in the
control flow. Therefore, from the start point of the control flow, if a sequence
reaches an instance of the *end* component or a component without output ports,
then the task of this component forms the end point of the sequence.

4.4   Runtime life cycle model

In existing component models, a component instance has a life state which
may evolve before and during an application execution. In our proposal, we
specified the following states: non-existent, created, inactive, active, running
and removed. The temporal composition model has a relevant impact on the

specification of these states. This section presents the main states. All states and state transitions are represented in Figure 4.

• **Created.** This defines the state when a component is instantiated. Three creation processes are specified depending on the temporal composition of an application. The creation can be static, *lazy* dynamic or *pre-lazy* dynamic. A *static* instantiation is done before execution time, typically at the deployment step. A *lazy* dynamic instantiation however, is done once the control flow reaches the use of this instance, while *pre-lazy* instantiation may be done before.

• **Active.** This determines the fact that a component instance is well connected and configured. An instance is said to be configured when its functional state is determined, for instance by setting attribute variables. When a component is active, its provided functionality can be safely used. In our proposal, *input* ports have a relevant role in the activation process. In fact, in addition to determine a task's inputs, *input* ports can be used for dynamic configuration purposes. Therefore, we defined the following rule: if a component instance has at least one *input* port, then, in addition to be connected and configured, this instance is activated once input data on connected *input* ports are received.

• **Removed.** this state may be automatically reached once the component is no longer attainable by the control flow during the execution, making it useless.

To summarize, each of the specified task, temporal port and life cycle models has a strong relation with each other. They provide facilities to coordinate an application execution and to express its dynamic evolution at the assembly level.

5.   Model instantiation on the control flow level of GRICOL

Now that a temporal composition model is proposed, let us present how a GRICOL control flow can be instantiated in our proposal.

GRICOL defines two types of control connections: serial and pipeline connections. Independently of the type, a GRICOL connection can be mapped to a connection of an *output* port to an *input* one. As there is no data flow specification at the control flow level, the port types can be simply set to *void*. Now, depending on the control connection type, the behavior of two connected blocks, *A* and *B* for instance, is different. For a serial connection, *A*'s task waits the end of its all computation processes before a *void* data is sent on its *output* port. For a pipeline connection however, *A*'s task can notify the framework about the end of a computation through the *output-ready()* operation (Section 4.2). *B*'s task can react to the end of one *A*'s computation through the *input-wait()* operation. It can be noted that, contrarily to GRICOL, we do not distinguish the connection type at the assembly level. This is not a limitation, as GRICOL imposes such a distinction for automatic functional code generation.

6.   Conclusion

Through the Grid Concurrent Language, this paper exposed missing features in existing component models regarding the support of workflow applications. As an attempt to overcome this limitation, we presented an overview of our ongoing work on the support of temporal composition within a component assembly model. In particular, we presented how a component model can be extended to enable an assembly to express a control flow coupled with a data flow composition. That was possible thanks to an additional family of ports, named temporal ports. Only the specification of general principles was presented. The next step is to provide a complete specification and its instantiation on existing component models.

References

[1] Service Component Architecture Specifications. http://www.osoa.org/.

[2] The Triana Project. http://www.trianacode.org.

[3] M. Aldinucci, S. Campa, M. Coppola, M. Danelutto, D. Laforenza, D. Puppin, L. Scarponi, M. Vanneschi, and C. Zoccolo. Components for high performance Grid programming in the Grid.it project. In *Proc. of the Workshop on Component Models and Systems for Grid Applications (June 2004, Saint Malo, France)*. Springer, January 2005.

[4] G. Antoniu, H.L. Bouziane, L. Breuil, M. Jan, and C. Pérez. Enabling transparent data sharing in component models. In *6th IEEE International Symposium on Cluster Computing and the Grid (CCGRID)*, pages 430–433, Singapore, May 2006.

[5] D.E. Bernholdt, B.A. Allan, R. Armstrong, F. Bertrand, K. Chiu, T.L. Dahlgren, K. Damevski, W.R. Elwasif, T.G. W. Epperly, M. Govindaraju, D.S. Katz, J.A. Kohl, M. Krishnan, G. Kumfert, J.W. Larson, S. Lefantzi, M.J. Lewis, A.D. Malony, L.C. McInnes, J. Nieplocha, B. Norris, S.G. Parker, J. Ray, S. Shende, T.L. Windus, and S. Zhou. A component architecture for high-performance scientific computing. *Int. Journal of High Performance Computing Applications*, November 2005. ACTS Collection special issue.

[6] E. Bruneton, T. Coupaye, and J.B. Stefani. Recursive and dynamic software composition with sharing. In *Seventh International Workshop on Component-Oriented Programming (WCOP02)*, Malaga, Spain, June 2002.

[7] N. Currle-Linde, F. Boes, and M. Resch. GriCoL: A Language for Scientific Grids. In *Proceedings of the 2nd IEEE International Conference on e-Science and Grid Computing*, Amsterdam, Netherlands, 2006.

[8] R. Lovas, G. Dozsa, P. Kacsuk, N. Podhorszki, and D. Drotos. Workflow support for complex grid applications: Integrated and portal solutions. In *Proceedings of the 2nd European Across Grids Conference*, pages 129–138, Nicosia, Cyprus, 2004.

[9] J. Magee, N. Dulay, and J. Kramer. A Constructive Development Environment for Parallel and Distributed Programs. In *Proceedings of the International Workshop on Configurable Distributed Systems*, pages 4–14, Pittsburgh, US, March 1994.

[10] Partners of the CoreGrid WP3 institute. Proposals for a grid component model. Technical report, February 2006. D.PM.02.

[11] OMG. CORBA component model, v4.0. Document formal/2006-04-01, April 2006.

[12] W.M.P van der Aalst, A.H.M. ter Hofstede, B. Kiepuszewski, and A.P. Barros. Workflow patterns. *Distributed and Parallel Databases*, 14(3):5–51, July 2003.

II

RESOURCE DISCOVERY AND SCHEDULING

PEER-TO-PEER APPROACHES
TO GRID RESOURCE DISCOVERY

Ann Chervenak and Shishir Bharathi
USC Information Sciences Institute,
Marina del Rey, CA, USA
annc@isi.edu
shishir@isi.edu

Abstract   Peer-to-peer organization of Grid resource discovery services would have several desirable features, including high scalability, high reliability, self-organization and self-healing. In this paper, we describe challenges in applying P2P techniques to Grid services. These include the choice of overlay configuration and varying security requirements for Grid and P2P environments. We present the design and implementation of two peer-to-peer Grid resource discovery services: an unstructured peer-to-peer information service and a structured peer-to-peer replica location service. We discuss the design tradeoffs, performance and scalability of these two systems as well as related work and ongoing challenges for applying P2P techniques to Grid discovery services.

Keywords: peer-to-peer, resource discovery

1.   Introduction

In distributed Grid computing environments, several types of services are needed for discovery of resources. For example, many Grids include information services that aggregate general information about Grid resources, such as the availability and current load of computational and storage resources. Other Grid resource discovery services may be more specialized, for example, metadata services that allow discovery of data items based on descriptive attributes and replica location services that allow discovery of replicated data items.

Currently, most services for resource discovery in Grids are query-based index services. These services may be centralized or distributed, and they consist of one or more indexes that aggregate information about resources. Since centralized indexes represent a single point of failure in the Grid environment, it is often desirable to distribute resource discovery services. Typical Grid resource discovery services are distributed using a hierarchical structure.

These resource discovery services have several common characteristics. A front end for each service typically provides a query interface for clients. This query interface may be general or specialized, with APIs that are specific to the type of resource information stored in the service and that support common queries. The back end for these services typically includes a database that stores resource information. Each resource discovery service responds to client queries by identifying resources that match desired properties specified in the queries. These resource discovery services must be scalable, both in terms of holding large amounts of resource information and supporting high query rates. These services also need to be highly available and fault tolerant.

To achieve these properties, Grid resource discovery services are typically organized as hierarchies, where the top nodes represent starting points for queries. These top nodes aggregate or replicate information from one or more lower-level services and support queries on the aggregated information. Redundancy is built into the hierarchy for increased scalability and fault tolerance.

As Grids grow larger, the number of distributed resources is also increasing. It is challenging to organize resource discovery services into efficient hierarchies that avoid the creation of cycles and ensure that nodes do not become hot spots. Resource discovery services also require efficient flow of information in the hierarchy and keeping that information as fresh as possible. Providing these features complicates the design of distributed resource discovery services.

In recent years, there has been much research in peer-to-peer (P2P) systems, in which the nodes of a system act as peers that create an overlay network to exchange information. Peer-to-peer systems have several desirable properties, including high scalability and reliability and the capability of self-healing the P2P overlay when nodes fail or join the network [1-3]. Several researchers have observed that P2P and Grid paradigms have several goals in common [4] [5], and some P2P Grid services have been developed [6-8].

In this paper, we describe the challenges and advantages of applying peer-to-peer techniques to Grid resource discovery services. We describe two examples, a Grid information service and a Grid replica location service, to which we applied these techniques.

The remainder of this paper is organized as follows. The next section describes existing approaches to providing resource discovery in Grids. This is followed by an overview of peer-to-peer technologies and a discussion of challenges in applying these techniques to Grids. We describe our unstructured P2P information service and structured P2P replica location service. Finally, we discuss related work and conclude with a description of ongoing challenges in merging P2P and Grid technologies.

2. Existing Grid Resource Discovery Services

Three general categories of resource discovery services are currently provided in Grid environments. These include information services that aggregate information about the state of grid resources, replica location services that specialize in information about the locations of replicated data items, and metadata services, which provide registration and discovery for descriptive attributes of data sets. In this section, we give several examples of existing Grid resource discovery systems.

2.1 Information Services: The GT4 Index Service

Applications running in the Grid need efficient access to information about resources and services. This information can have a considerable impact on scheduling decisions, replica selection, and planning for workflow execution. Information about available resources and their characteristics is typically collected by information services and served to applications via query/response or publish/subscribe interfaces. Czaj-kowski et al. [9] discuss several issues that affect the design of Grid Information Services. Requirements include aggregating information from multiple types of services and processing different types of queries across the information. Clients may query for explicitly named resources or make attribute-based queries, such as requesting nodes with a certain amount of computational power. Query results may include information about the proximity of resources or the duration for which the information is valid.

One example of a Grid information service is the Monitoring and Discovery System (MDS) Index Service, which is part of the Globus Toolkit Version 4 (GT4). The Index Service collects, aggregates and publishes information from other Grid services.

   An Index Service collects information from a variety of sources called aggre-
gator sources that can collect information using three methods: querying the
state of Grid resources; subscribing to resource state and collecting information
when notifications are received; or running executables that test the state of
resources and collecting the output.

   Figure 1 shows the example of a two level hierarchy of MDS4 Index Services.
GT4 Index Services lower in the hierarchy periodically push a subset of their
information to one or more index services higher up in the hierarchy.

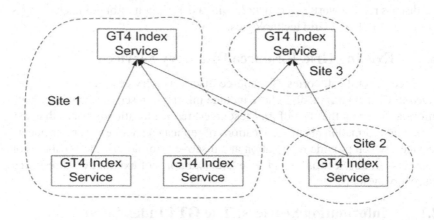

Figure 1.   Example of a hierarchical configuration of GT4 Index

   In a simple hierarchical configuration (Figure 1), indexes at the top of the
hierarchy subscribe to the state of local index services and replicate their information. Clients can query a top level index and immediately obtain query
results. This approach of replicating information in top level index services is
often taken in small grids.

   Alternatively, each local index can publish a summary of its information,
and the top level index can subscribe to these summaries and publish them.
Query results from top level indexes are essentially pointers to the complete
information stored at local indexes. The client then queries local indexes until
it obtains the required information. This approach is appropriate for larger
grids where it might not be possible for a single top level index to replicate
all information from local indexes. This scheme also distributes the query
processing load. A top level index performs simpler queries on summary
information, while local indexes perform more complex queries.

2.2 Replica Location Services

A Replica Location Service (RLS) provides functionality to register and discover data replicas. When a user creates a new replica of a data object, the user also registers the existence of the replica in the RLS by creating an association between a logical name for the data item and the physical location of the replica. An RLS client discovers data replicas by querying the catalog based on logical identifiers for data, physical locations or user-defined attributes associated with logical or physical names. In earlier work, Chervenak et al. [10] proposed a parameterized RLS framework that allows users to deploy a range of replica location services that make tradeoffs with respect to consistency, space overhead, reliability, update costs, and query costs by varying six system design parameters. A Replica Location Service implementation based on this framework is available in the Globus Toolkit Versions 3 and 4. We have demonstrated that this RLS implementation provides good performance and scalability [11].

The Replica Location Service design consists of two components. Local Replica Catalogs (LRCs) maintain consistent information about logical-to-target mappings on a site or storage system, where the target of the mapping is usually the physical file name of the replica. Replica Location Indexes (RLIs) aggregate information about mappings contained in one or more LRCs. The RLI contains mappings from logical names to one or more LRCs that in turn contain logical-to-target mappings for those names. The RLS achieves reliability and load balancing by deploying multiple and possibly redundant RLIs in a hierarchical, distributed index. An example RLS deployment is shown in Figure 2.

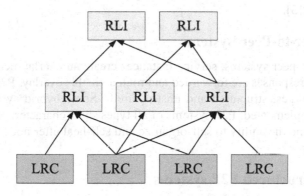

Figure 2. Distributed Replica Location Service

2.3   Metadata Services

Metadata is information that describes data sets. Metadata services allow scientists to record information about the creation, transformation, meaning and quality of data items and to discover data items based on these descriptive attributes. In the past, scientists have largely relied on ad hoc methods (descriptive file and directory names, lab notebooks, etc.) to record information about data items. However, these methods do not scale to terabyte and petabyte data sets consisting of millions of data items. Extensible, reliable, high performance Grid services are required to support registration and query of metadata information.

Some physical level metadata relate to characteristics of data objects, such as their size, access permissions, owners and modification information. Replication metadata information, such as that stored in an RLS, describes the relationship between logical data identifiers and one or more physical instances of the data. Other metadata attributes describe the contents of data items, allowing the data to be interpreted. This descriptive metadata may conform to an ontology agreed upon by an application community. A special case of descriptive metadata is provenance information, which records how data items are created and transformed.

Many metadata services are centralized, because many applications require a high degree of consistency for metadata information. This consistency is needed because accurate identification of data items is essential for correct analysis of experimental and simulation results. These services can also be distributed in wide area Grid environments if more relaxed consistency can be tolerated by applications.

Examples of Grid metadata services include the Metadata Catalog Service [12, 13] and the MCAT metadata catalog for the Storage Resource Broker project [14, 15].

3.   Peer-to-Peer Systems

In peer-to-peer systems, service instances create an overlay network, and queries and responses are forwarded and routed via this overlay. P2P overlays are of two types, structured and unstructured. Some hybrid systems have also been implemented. P2P systems of all types share characteristics of high scalability and the ability to self-organize and self-heal after node failures in the P2P network.

3.1   Structured P2P systems

A structured peer-to-peer overlay typically uses a mechanism such as a distributed hash table to deterministically identify the node on which a particular <key, value> pair will be stored and retrieved. Thus, structured P2P approaches are usually concerned with locating resources that can be named or identified by keys [4]. Therefore, a structured P2P approach may be particularly well-suited to Grid resource discovery services such as replica location services or metadata services, where clients query for information associated with a globally unique logical or physical data identifier. A structured approach may be less appropriate for general Grid information services, where queries for information about resources may not be associated with unique resource identifiers.

There has been extensive research in structured P2P approaches to information services. Chord [1], Pastry [16], and CAN [3] are based on distributed hash table (DHT) techniques. A significant advantage of DHT-based structured P2P systems is that they provide strong bounds on query and update performance.

Recent systems [17] also allow attribute-based searches of complex information such as RDF [18] using structured approaches. Cheema et al. [8] developed a strategy for searches on multiple machine attributes on a structured P2P network by representing resources as overlapping arcs on a DHT ring.

3.2   Unstructured P2P Systems

An unstructured P2P usually does not impose any constraints on links between nodes in the system. Whereas in DHT based structured overlays, nodes peer only with other nodes that are ŞcloseŤ in the identifier space, in unstructured overlays, the choice of neighbors to peer with is less restrictive and is often probabilistic or randomized.

Unstructured overlays do not create associations between nodes and links in the system and the information stored in those nodes. By contrast, DHT based P2P systems require that the information being stored can be converted into a <key, value> format so that it can be forwarded to the node that manages the corresponding key. Some publish subscribe systems create overlay tree networks where each node forwards information along a specified link to propagate information from publishers to subscribers. In contrast, unstructured P2P systems do not require that information adhere to a particular format or be tied to the structure of the overlay. Information is usually stored only at the node where it was generated or replicated in a probabilistic manner. Query-response pathways are also not well defined. Queries are propagated in the system using flooding based algorithms, and responses are routed back on the same path as the queries.

Napster [19], Gnutella [20] and Kazaa [21] are among the well known unstructured P2P file sharing systems. P2P technologies have been successful in these file sharing applications by allowing peers to host content, discover content on other peers, and download that content.

These systems have been popular in the Internet community despite known disadvantages such as the vulnerability of central indexes in Napster [22] and the high network loads imposed by GnutellaŠs flooding algorithms [23]. Optimizations of unstructured systems have been developed based on file and query distributions and on the use of replication and caching.

Unstructured peer-to-peer networks cannot provide the same guarantees provided by structured overlays regarding the number of hops taken by a query message to reach a node that can answer the query, nor can unstructured systems guarantee that results will be returned if they exist in the network. The time-to-live field in the message dictates how far the message travels in the network, so the message may not reach all nodes. Applications built on top of such systems must be capable of dealing with these issues as they do with other failure modes.

3.3   Challenges in Applying P2P Techniques to Grid Resource Discovery

While the convergence of peer-to-peer and Grid systems has long been predicted, challenges remain in incorporating P2P techniques into production Grid services.

One issue is the possible performance penalty of submitting a query to a wide area peer-to-peer network versus submitting the query to a specialized resource discovery service that maintains locality for related information. Resolving queries in a P2P overlay may require multiple network hops. Structured P2P networks, in particular, may distribute resource information widely in the overlay, since the distribution is based on the hashed values of keys. This distribution maintains a balance among the nodes in the overlay for the number of mappings stored at each node, but the locality of related resource information may be lost. By contrast, existing Grid resource discovery services often support locality of related information. For example, in a typical Replica Location Service, all mappings associated with files on a storage system are likely to be stored in the same local catalog, so queries for files in a logical collection that are co-located may be satisfied by a single local catalog. Similarly, existing Grid information services tend to aggregate information about all the resources at a site in a single index service.

Security issues also tend to be more of a concern in Grid environments than in Internet file sharing applications. In Grids, access to resources and to information about resources may need to be controlled. Authentication of users as well as authorization decisions on discovery and access operations may be required. By contrast, in file sharing P2P networks, typically any node can query all other nodes to discover and download files, and any node can host content and make it available to other nodes. We need a security model that allows Grid resource discovery services to use peer-to-peer overlays safely.

There are additional practical challenges for applying P2P techniques to Grid systems. It has taken several years for Grid resource discovery services to become sufficiently scalable and stable to support the requirements of Grid systems. To support the higher scalability possible with P2P networks, we need to further improve existing Grid services to support better service configuration and dynamic deployment.

4. Applying Unstructured P2P Techniques to a Grid Information Service

Next, we illustrate many of the issues we have identified for applying P2P techniques to Grid resource discovery services by describing the design of a P2P information service [7].

In our design, modified GT4 Indexes called P2P Indexes organize themselves into an unstructured P2P overlay network. Queries from a user to any index in the P2P system may be forwarded to other indexes, and query results are routed back to the user. Our system differs from other P2P-based resource discovery services [1-3, 8, 17] that use nodes in the overlay network to store and replicate resource information. We use the P2P network only for self-organization and query forwarding among P2P indexes, which are optimized to store resource information and perform associated queries. We do not replicate information via the overlay because resource information may change quickly and therefore cannot be replicated easily. Each P2PIndex in our system can also be accessed as a typical GT4 Index service without having to go through the P2P overlay. In summary, our approach separates the routing of queries in the P2P overlay from the storage and retrieval of information.

In the following sections, we describe several design issues for this system, including our use of an unstructured overlay network, two performance optimizations, and a multi-tier security model that facilitates the integration of P2P and Grid services.

4.1 Unstructured P2P Overlay Network

We use an unstructured overlay network for the peer-to-peer GT4 Index service. Unstructured networks are easy to build and support different optimizations of the overlay at different regions in the network, such as higher connectivity between certain nodes and locality-based modifications to the topology. Most previous work in unstructured P2P networks has been in the areas of file sharing or data storage systems rather than in information services. Unstructured P2P networks are well-suited for information services like MDS4 that store arbitrary XML rather than information with a fixed schema. By contrast, a DHT-based structured P2P overlay would need to generate hash keys on values in every entry in the information service.

Our design differs from these approaches in that we do not make assumptions about the distribution of queries or rely upon replication or caching. We assume that our P2P Index Services are updated via an out-of-band mechanism and that only queries are propagated via the unstructured overlay.

Another reason we chose an unstructured overlay is that many structured systems implicitly assume that all nodes in the system can store data originating at other nodes. This may not be the case in Grids, where nodes may belong to different administrative domains. Policy restrictions may prevent nodes from storing information generated at other sites. By contrast, nodes in unstructured P2P networks are not required to store information generated at other nodes. If information is replicated via the overlay, each node may choose not to store information originating at other nodes without affecting message forwarding and routing.

4.2   Performance Optimizations

In an unstructured P2P system, the use of a flooding algorithm introduces the problem of exponential growth in the number of messages sent in the network. We discuss two optimizations that are designed to improve the performance of our system.

Since information is not replicated via the P2P framework, query results are not cached at intermediate nodes. However, a node could cache the queries themselves and note which of its peers responded to each query. In a query caching scheme similar to the learning-based strategy described by Iamnitchi et al. [4], a node forwards a query to peers that responded to that query in the past. We implement a scheme called query caching with probabilistic forwarding, where each node deterministically forwards a query message to all the peers specified in the cache that responded to the query in the past and also probabilistically forwards the query to other peers. This may identify nodes that have been recently updated and can now respond to the query.

Queries to an information service usually belong to two broad categories: general attribute-based queries (e.g., Şwhich sites are running GridFTP servers?Ť) and specific queries for resources (e.g., Şwhat is the URL for the GridFTP server on node X?Ť). General queries are used to gather information, possibly to aid in scheduling decisions, and therefore the client expects multiple responses. Such queries will be forwarded to several nodes in the network (depending on time-to-live, max-hops, etc.), even if other nodes have already responded. These general queries may be optimized by forwarding the query in the network before each node evaluates the query on its own contents. Using this early forwarding scheme, each node can evaluate the query in parallel.

For more specific queries, the client expects a single response. In this scenario, early forwarding may increase the number of messages being sent in the network, so it may be better to evaluate the query locally first before forwarding it to peers.

Ideally, an application should be able to provide hints about whether a query is general or specific to the P2P framework as part of the message. Each node could use this information to make better routing choices.

4.3 Security Model

Next, we describe a security model for the use of peer-to-peer techniques with Grid services.

Our model is based on the observation that grid applications are not usually standalone applications. Whereas in file sharing applications such as KaZaA and Gnutella, the P2P overlay is used for indexing and looking up file information as well as the transfer of data, in grid applications this functionality is achieved via several distinct grid services. In our model, different policies are used to control access to different services and resources. The P2P Index Service provides information about resources but not access to those resources, and therefore it enforces only those policies related to retrieving information. Policies related to accessing the resources themselves (submitting jobs, retrieving files, etc.) are enforced by the services that provide that access.

This model can also be extended with a further level of indirection, to only forward queries in the P2P layer but not route back the query response. Instead, pointers are returned to those nodes that have the required information. The user then interacts directly with those nodes to get the query responses, using the security mechanisms required at those nodes.

Certain grids may choose to adopt a relaxed security model by allowing unauthenticated users to query for resource information and enforcing authentication and authorization only when the resources are accessed.

4.4 Implementation and Performance

Figure 3 illustrates the implementation of the P2P Index service. The original Globus Toolkit Version 4 (GT4) Index Service implementation is based on the Web Services Resource Framework (WS-RF) standards [24]. This standard allows state to be associated with Grid services as resource properties.

The GT4 Index Service is a WS-Resource that operates on a stateful IndexServiceResource. In our implementation, the P2P Index Service operates on a P2PIndexServiceResource that is composed of an IndexServiceResource and a P2PResource, as illustrated in Figure 3. The P2PResource component is responsible for creating and maintaining the P2P overlay and for forwarding and routing messages in the network. The P2PResource component maintains a list of its peers identified by their endpoint references and a cache of the messages it has seen identified by their message IDs. It also maintains a routing table that stores the identity of the peer to which responses to each message must be routed.

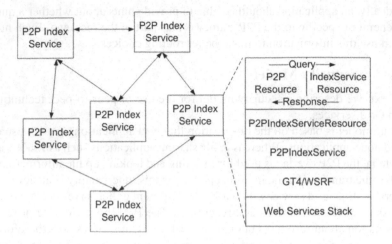

Figure 3.   The P2P Index Service

The P2P Index Services in the Grid organize themselves into an unstructured P2P system using an approach similar to those used in file sharing applications. The message format and the message forwarding algorithm used in our system are similar to those used in Gnutella-like systems [20].

Queries from a user are forwarded to other P2P indexes, and the results of processing queries at these indexes are routed back to the user via the unstructured P2P overlay.

We also implemented query caching with probabilistic forwarding in our system. Each node contains a configuration parameter that controls the probability with which a query is forwarded to a peer that did not respond to the same query earlier. Setting this parameter to 0 is equivalent to enabling a pure query caching scheme where queries are forwarded only to the peers that are listed in the cache. Setting this parameter to 1 is equivalent to disabling the cache, since in that case all queries are forwarded to all peers.

Finally, we implemented the early forwarding scheme described above. A node configuration parameter determines whether that node checks for application hints in the message and uses those hints to decide whether to perform early forwarding to other nodes.

Performance measurements of the P2P Index Service [7] showed that using the P2P layer adds a small and constant overhead to operations on the Index Service and that providing a distributed P2P index allowed significant scalability improvements compared to a single Index Service.

5. Applying Structured P2P Techniques to Grid Replica Location Services

In earlier work [6, 25], we implemented and evaluated a structured peer-to-peer version of the Globus Replica Location Service. The goal of this work was to take advantage of P2P techniques for more flexible organization of RLS servers. In the RLS system currently supported in the Globus Toolkit, each RLS deployment is statically configured. If a Replica Location Index service fails, the Local Replica Catalogs that send state updates to those index services have to be manually redirected. Using peer-to-peer techniques to self-organize networks of RLS index services should provide more automated and flexible membership management, which is desirable for larger RLS deployments and dynamic environments where servers frequently join and leave the system.

For our implementation, we implemented a structured peer-to-peer network among the Replica Location Index (RLI) nodes that contain logical-name, LRC mappings. This design is consistent with the security model we have already described, where we assume that resource discovery at the P2P RLI level has less strict security requirements. Access to the logical-name, target-name mappings in the Local Replica Catalog and to physical files requires stricter security.

In the P2P RLS, we replicate mappings among the P2P RLI nodes, unlike in the information service described in the last section. We are able to use a structured overlay because it is easier to hash on logical names in the RLS than on arbitrary XML content in information services. In addition, replica mappings tend to be much less dynamic than resource information.

In our design, a peer-to-peer RLS server consists of an unchanged Local Replica Catalog (LRC) that maintains consistent logical-name, target-name mappings and a Peer-to-Peer Replica Location Index node (P-RLI) that maintains logical-name, LRC mappings. The P2P RLS design uses a Chord overlay network [1] to self-organize P-RLI servers. Chord is a distributed hash table that supports scalable key insertion and lookup. Each node has log (N) neighbors in a network of N nodes. A key is stored on its successor node, the first node with ID equal to or greater than key. Key insertion and lookup are achieved in log (N) hops. Our implementation uses the Chord algorithm to store mappings of logical names to LRC sites. It generates a Chord key for each logical name by applying the SHA1 hash function and stores the logical-name, LRC mappings for that logical name on the P-RLI successor node.

When a P-RLI node receives a query for LRC(s) that store mappings for a logical name, it directly answers the query if it contains the corresponding logical-name, LRC mapping(s). Otherwise, the P-RLI node routes query to the root node that contains those mappings via the structured overlay network.

After receiving a list of local replica catalogs from the P-RLI network, the client queries LRCs directly for mappings from logical names to replica locations.

We implemented a prototype of the P2P Replica Location Service that extends the RLS implementation in Globus Toolkit Versoin 3.0. The P-RLI server implements the Chord protocol operations, including join, update, query, and find successor operations, as well as operations for joining and stabilizing the structured overlay. The Chord protocols are implemented on top of the RLS remote procedure call layer.

We measured the performance of our P2P RLS system with up to 15 nodes and verified that query and update latencies increase at rate of O(logN) with size of overlay network, as expected. We also simulated the performance of larger P-RLS networks. Finally, we demonstrated the advantages of replicating mappings on multiple nodes, which results in a more even distribution of mappings among nodes and improved load balancing for popular mappings.

6.   Related Work

Earlier, we discussed related work on peer-to-peer systems. Here, we focus specifically on related work in Grid resource discovery services.

6.1   P2P Grid Resource Discovery Services

Two systems closely relate to our P2P information and replica location services: the GLARE system and another P2P replica location service.

Like our system, GLARE [26] uses the GT4 Index Service to discover sites in the Grid. However, unlike our approach, GLARE indexes exchange information with each other, organize themselves into peer groups and build a super-peer overlay.

Ripeanu et. al [27] constructed a peer-to-peer overlay network of Replica Location Services. Unlike our P2P RLS system, which uses a structured overlay to forward queries to a node that can answer an LFN query, in this scheme, each node distributes a digest of all LFNs registered at that node to all other nodes in the overlay. Thus, each node maintains a compressed image of the global system. When a client queries a node for a particular LFN mapping, the node first checks its locally stored mappings and answers the query, if possible. If not, the node checks its locally stored digests that summarize the contents of remote nodes. Finally, if the node finds a remote node that matches the LFN, it contacts that node to obtain the mappings.

6.2   Grid Information Systems

There have been several efforts to design efficient, reliable and scalable monitoring and information services for large scale distributed systems.

The previous version of the Globus Monitoring and Discovery Service (MDS2) [9] is a hierarchical design. Information Providers push resource information into Grid Resource Information Services which then push that information to Grid Index Information Services.

The MonALISA system [28], or Monitoring Agents using a Large Integrated Services Architecture, consists of autonomous, self-describing agent subsystems that collect and process different types of information in a coordinated fashion. The network servers hosting agent based services are connected via a P2P network.

The Relational-Grid Monitoring Architecture (R-GMA [29]) is a monitoring framework in which all published monitoring information appears as if it were resident in a single, large, relational database.

Other Grid information services include Nagios [30], Ganglia [31] and Hawkeye [32].

6.3   Replica Location and Metadata Services

The European DataGrid project implemented a different Replica Location Service based on the RLS Framework [10] that was used as part of their replica management architecture [33].

Several Grid systems merge replica and metadata management. These include the Storage Resource Broker [15], the Grid DataFarm [34], and the gLite [35] systems that register and discover replicas using a metadata catalog. These systems differ from the Globus Replica Location Service in several ways: they use a centralized catalog for replica registration and discovery; this catalog also contains logical metadata information that describes the content of data files, which is deliberately kept separate in our system; and these systems use these metadata catalogs to maintain consistency among replicas.

7.   Conclusion

We have argued that a peer-to-peer organization of resource discovery services would have several desirable features including high scalability, high reliability, self-organization and self-healing. We described the design and implementation of an unstructured P2P Information Service based on the GT4 Index Service that separates the routing of queries from data sharing in the overlay. We also presented a structured P2P Replica Location Service that replicates mappings in the overlay.

Challenging issues remain for applying P2P techniques to Grid resource discovery issues. First, the choice of structured versus unstructured overlays is likely to have a significant impact on the performance of queries for related information. For the P2P Information Service, we opted to use an unstructured overlay to maintain locality of related information in individual Index Services.

However, in general, resolving queries in a P2P overlay may require multiple network hops, which may increase query latency.

Second, we discussed security issues that differ for Grid and traditional internet file sharing applications. Grid environments tend to have stricter requirements for authentication and authorization. We proposed a model that allows looser security at the resource discovery level of the architecture, with stricter security enforced for access to resources themselves. The widespread applicability of this model to Grid applications and services still needs to be evaluated.

Finally, practical issues remain for applying P2P techniques to existing Grid services. To support a highly-scalable P2P network of resource discovery services, each of these services must be easy to configure and deploy. Substantial improvements are needed in existing resource discovery services to support this more dynamic service deployment scenario.

Acknowledgments

This research was supported in part by DOE Cooperative Agreements DE-FC02-01ER25449 and DE-FC02-01ER25453 and by the National Science Foundation under the grant OCI 0534027.

References

[1] I. Stoica, R. Morris, D. Karger, F. Kaashoek, and H. Balakrishnan, "Chord: A Scalable Peer-To-Peer Lookup Service for Internet Applications," presented at ACM SIGCOMM, 2001.

[2] B. Y. Zhao, J. D. Kubiatowicz, and A. D. Joseph, "Tapestry: An infrastructure for fault-resilient wide-area location and routing," U.C. Berkeley, Berkeley Technical Report UCB-CSD-01-1141, April 2001 2001.

[3] S. Ratnasamy, P. Francis, M. Handley, R. Karp, and S. Shenker, "A Scalable Content-Addressable Network," presented at ACM SIGCOMM, 2001.

[4] A. Iamnitchi, I. Foster, D. Nurmi, "A Peer-to-Peer Approach to Resource Discovery in Grid Environments," presented at Eleventh IEEE Int'l Symposium High Performance Distributed Computing (HPDC-11), Edinburgh, Scotland, 2002.

[5] I. Foster and A. Iamnitchi, "On Death, Taxes, and the Convergence of Peer-to-Peer and Grid Computing," presented at Int'l Workshop on Peer-to-Peer Systems (IPTPS'03), Berkeley, CA, USA, 2003.

[6] M. Cai, A. Chervenak, M. Frank, "A Peer-to-Peer Replica Location Service Based on a Distributed Hash Table," presented at SC2004 Conference, Pittsburgh, PA, 2004.

[7] S. Bharathi and A. Chervenak, "Design of a Scalable Peer-to-Peer Information System Using the GT4 Index Service," presented at Seventh IEEE International Symposium on Cluster Computing and the Grid (CCGrid 2007), Rio de Janeiro, Brazil, 2007.

[8] A. S. Cheema, M. Muhammad, and I. Gupta, "Peer-to-Peer Discovery of Computational Resources for Grid Applications," Proceedings of 6th IEEE/ACM International Workshop on Grid Computing (Grid 2005), pp. 179-185, 2005.

[9] K. Czajkowski, S. Fitzgerald, I. Foster, C. Kesselman, "Grid Information Services for Distributed Resource Sharing," presented at Tenth IEEE International Symposium on High-Performance Distributed Computing (HPDC-10), 2001.

[10] A. Chervenak, E. Deelman, I. Foster, L. Guy, W. Hoschek, A. Iamnitchi, C. Kesselman, P. Kunst, M. Ripeanu, B, Schwartzkopf, H, Stockinger, K. Stockinger, B. Tierney, "Giggle: A Framework for Constructing Sclable Replica Location Services," presented at SC2002 Conference, Baltimore, MD, 2002.

[11] A. L. Chervenak, N. Palavalli, S. Bharathi, C. Kesselman, R. Schwartzkopf, "Performance and Scalability of a Replica Location Service," presented at Thirteenth IEEE Int'l Symposium High Performance Distributed Computing (HPDC-13), Honolulu, HI, 2004.

[12] G. Singh, Shishir Bharathi, Ann Chervenak, Ewa Deelman, Carl Kesselman, Mary Manohar, Sonal Pail, Laura Pearlman, "A Metadata Catalog Service for Data Intensive Applications," presented at SC2003, 2003.

[13] E. Deelman, Gurmeet Singh, Malcolm P. Atkinson, Ann Chervenak, Neil P. Chue Hong, Carl Kesselman, Sonal Patil, Laura Pearlman, Mei-Hui Su, "Grid-Based Metadata Services," presented at 16th International Conference on Scientific and Statistical Database Management, 2004.

[14] SRB Project, "MCAT - A Meta Information Catalog (Version 1.1), http://www.npaci.edu/DICE/SRB/mcat.html."

[15] A. Rajasekar, M. Wan, R. Moore, W. Schroeder, G. Kremenek, A. Jagatheesan, C. Cowart, B. Zhu, S. Y. Chen, and R. Olschanowsky, "Storage Resource Broker-Managing Distributed Data in a Grid," Computer Society of India Journal, Special Issue on SAN, vol. 33(4), pp. 42-54, 2003.

[16] A. Rowstron, P. Druschel., "Pastry: Scalable, distributed object location and routing for large-scale peer-to-peer systems," presented at International Conference on Distributed Systems Platforms (Middleware), 2001.

[17] M. Cai, Martin Frank, "RDFPeers: A Scalable Distributed RDF Repository based on A Structured Peer-to-Peer Network," presented at 13th International World Wide Web Conference(WWW2004), New York, NY, 2004.

[18] F. Manola and E. Miller, "Resource Description Framework (RDF) Primer, http://www.w3.org/TR/2004/REC-rdf-primer-20040210/," 2004.

[19] "Napster, http://www.napster.com."

[20] Y. Chawathe, S. Ratnasamy, L. Breslau, N. Lanham, and S. Shenker, "Making Gnutella-like P2P Systems Scalable," presented at ACM SIGCOMM 2003, Karlsruhe, Germany, 2003.

[21] J. Liang, R. Kumar, and K. W. Ross, "The KaZaA Overlay: A Measurement Study," Computer Networks Journal (Elsevier), 2005.

[22] A. Crespo, et al., "Routing Indices for Peer-to-peer systems," presented at ICDCS, 2002.

[23] J. Ritter, "Why Gnutella canŠt scale, no really...," 2001," Preprint http://www. darkridge. com/jpr5/doc/gnutella. html.

[24] K. Czajkowski, D. F. Ferguson, I. Foster, J. Frey, S. Graham, I. Sedukhin, D. Snelling, S. Tuecke, and W. Vambenepe, "The WS-resource framework. Version 1.0., http://www-106.ibm.com/developerworks/library/ws-resource/ws-wsrf.pdf," 2004.

[25] A. L. Chervenak and M. Cai, "Applying Peer-to-Peer Techniques to Grid Replica Location Services," Journal of Grid Computing, vol. 4, pp. 49-69, 2006.

[26] M. Siddiqui, et al., "GLARE: A Grid Activity Registration, Deployment and Provisioning Framework," presented at SC 2005, Seattle.

[27] M. Ripeanu, Ian Foster, "A Decentralized, Adaptive, Replica Location Mechanism," presented at 11th IEEE International Symposium on High Performance Distributed Computing (HPDC-11), Edinburgh, Scotland, 2002.

[28] "MonALISA: MONitoring Agents using a Large Integrated Services Architecture, http://monalisa.cacr.caltech.edu/monalisa.htm," 2006.

[29] A. Cooke, A.Gray, L. Ma, W. Nutt, J. Magowan, P. Taylor, R. Byrom, L. Field, S. Hicks, and J. Leake, "R-GMA: An Information Integration System for Grid Monitoring," presented at Proceedings of the 11th International Conference on Cooperative Information Systems, 2003.

[30] "Nagios, http://www.nagios.org/ ", 2006.

[31] M. L. Massie, Brent N. Chun, and David E. Culler., "The Ganglia Distributed Monitoring System: Design, Implementation, and Experience," Parallel Computing, vol. 30, 2004.

[32] Condor Project, "Hawkeye: A Monitoring and Management Tool for Distributed Systems, http://www.cs.wisc.edu/condor/hawkeye/," 2007.

[33] D. Cameron, J. Casey, L. Guy, P. Kunszt, S. Lemaitre, G. McCance, H. Stockinger, K. Stockinger, G. Andronico, and W. Bell, "Replica Management in the European DataGrid Project," Journal of Grid Computing, vol. 2, pp. 341-351, 2004.

[34] O. Tatebe, S. Sekiguchi, Y. Morita, S. Matsuoka, and N. Soda, "Worldwide Fast File Replication on Grid Datafarm," presented at Computing in High Energy and Nuclear Physics (CHEP03), La Jolla, CA, USA, 2003.

[35] P. Kunszt, P. Badino, A. Frohner, G. McCance, K. Nienartowicz, R. Rocha, and D. Rodrigues, "Data Storage, Access and Catalogs in gLite," presented at Local to Global Data Interoperability-Challenges and Technologies, 2005.

GRID SUPERSCALAR AND JOB MAPPING ON THE RELIABLE GRID RESOURCES

Ani Anciaux–Sedrakian, Rosa M. Badia, Raul Sirvent and Josep M. Pérez
Polytechnic University of Catalonia
Campus Nord - Modul D6 c/Jordi Girona 1-3 E08034 Barcelona, Spain
ani.anciaux@bsc.es
rosa.m.badia@bsc.es
raul.sirvent@bsc.es
josep.m.perez@bsc.es

Thilo Kielmann and Andre Merzky
Vrije Universiteit
De Boelelaan 1081A 1081HV Amsterdam, The Netherlands
kielmann@cs.vu.nl
andre@merzky.net

Abstract   The dynamic nature of grid computing environment requires some predictions regarding resource reliability and application performance. In such environments, avoiding resource failures is as important as the overall application performance. The aim of this work is to identify the most available, least-loaded and fastest resources for running an application. We describe a strategy for mapping the application jobs on the grid resources using GRID superscalar [8] and GAT [1].

Keywords: reliability, high performance computing, superscalar, application toolkit

1.   Introduction

The number of applications that use grid computing systems are relatively limited. One of the blocking reasons is difficulty of their development. This is due to the intrinsic complexity of the programming interface in one hand and heterogeneity and dynamicity of grid environments on the other hand. The aim of this paper is to cope with complexity of grid applications development. In this context, we address two main issues: (i) the choice of computation resources for the application to obtain a robust and efficient execution, and (ii) the co-existence of distinct underlying middleware on the grid.

The first part of this work presents an approach to select compute resources by combining performance criteria (like computation and data transfer capacity) with predicted resource reliability. A grid environment offers a large numbers of similar or equivalent resources that grid users can select and use for their workflow applications. These resources may provide the same functionality, but offer different QoS properties. A workflow QoS constraint includes five dimensions: time, cost, quality, reliability and security [11]. The basic performance measurement is time (the first dimension), representing the total time required for completing the execution of a workflow. The second dimension represents the cost of workflows execution[1]. Quality refers to the measurement related to the quality of the output of workflow execution. Reliability is related to the probability of failures for execution of workflows. Finally, security refers to confidentiality of the execution of workflow jobs and the trustworthiness of resources (in [2] some studies in this field are represented).

This work is not only focused on the reliability dimension, in order to minimize failures, but also considers the time dimension. Mapping the applications jobs onto the most appropriate resources is a multi-criterial process and not always the performance is an issue but also reliability. Resources manually chosen by grid users may be the most powerful ones, but are not always the most reliable ones. The problem is how to map the jobs onto suitable resources, in order to minimize the probability of failure for execution of workflows. Workflow execution failures can occur for the following reasons: variation in the execution environment configuration, non-availability of required services or software components, overloaded resource conditions, system running out of memory, and errors in computational and network fabric components. Therefore, the natural way to maximize the reliability will be examining theses parameters which are relatively the potential reason of faults and avoiding them.

The second part of this paper shows how to provide a Grid programming environment that is both high-level and platform-independent. In general, grid

---

[1]It includes the cost related to the managing of workflow systems and usage charge of Grid resources for processing workflow jobs.

applications are restricted to one specific grid middleware package. Therefore, submitting unmodified existing application codes to remote grid resources may be faltering, since the desired middleware may not available in that remote resource. This runs contrary to the vary nature of grids, which imply a heterogencous environment in which applications must run. In order to be effective, a grid application must be able to run in any environment in which it finds itself. Ideally grid applications would discover required grid services at run time, and use them as needed, independent of the particular interfaces used by the application programmer. To reach this goal, using a middleware which assume the platform-independent feature can solve this complexity of application development.

The remainder of this article is organized as follows: Section 2 describes how to select reliable and efficient resources. Section 3 first describes GRID superscalar, then reviews the implementation and integration of the proposed reliability strategy in GRID superscalar and at the end shows how to make GRID superscalar a platform independent runtime system. In section 4 some early experiments are presented. Finally section 5 concludes the paper.

2. Resource selection

Due to the variability in grid-computing environments, it is difficult to assume resources reliability: both load and availability of heterogeneous grid resources varies dynamically. As applications can have a wide variety of characteristics and requirements, there is no single best solution for mapping workflows onto known reliable resources for all workflow applications. This section describes a strategy to find the most reliable resources while also minimizing the overall application completion time, i.e. by maximizing jobs performance and/or minimizing communications time, in respect to the application characteristics.

Our approach for solving this problem starts with retrieving the information from available resources. This information may be requested before workflow execution starts, in order to help users take the right decision while choosing the appropriate resources. The proposed strategy, composed of two steps, is based on the ranking of the resources: in the first step, called trust-driven step, parameters related to the potential source of faults are collected. The resources are then ranked with respect to their ability to guarantee the maximum level of reliability. Ranking allows increasing the overall reliability of application execution. In the second step, called performance-driven step, the ranking of each resource is revisited by taking the performance criteria (computation power and data transfer capacity) into account. This compromise between reliability and performance leads to increase computation robustness and to decrease overall execution time. These two steps, which are done before execution, are described more in detail in the following part.

2.1   Trust-driven step

In the trust-driven step, some information and hardware requirements for the resources are retrieved, such as the availability of the resources, its trustfulness and the available amount of memory. Part of this information is stored in a database, in order to have a historical trace of resources state. This database can be located anywhere in the grid. The collected information is used for helping the users to find an appropriate resource where their jobs will most likely not fail. All this information may be gathered and stored either independently and/or before running the application. Obviously, the database could become more affluent if more information is retrieved about the hardware requirements.

During the trust-driven step, the availability of resources is computed first. It shows resource accessibility across an IP network. Let r_i denotes the ith grid resource, na_i^j the number of times when the resource r_i was not available at the moment j and ta_i^j the total number of attempts to verify the resource availability. The availability of resources is defined as:

$$availability(r_i) = 1 - na_i^{j+1}/ta_i^{j+1} \tag{1}$$
$$na_i^{j+1} = na_i^j + dbna_i \ \ and \ \ ta_i^{j+1} = ta_i^j + dbta_i \tag{2}$$

Where $dbna_i$ and $dbta_i$ (in equation 2) is the information stored previously on the database. After the availability calculation, the database is updated; the new value of na_i^{j+1} and ta_i^{j+1} will be stored ($dbna_i = na_i^{j+1}$ and $dbta_i = ta_i^{j+1}$).

Afterwards, information concerning the resource trustfulness is collected. Trustfulness is evaluated by parameters which may generate some faults during the execution. In particular, we take into account resources dropping (i.e. job crashing during the execution due to the sudden unavailability of resource), execution environment variations, job manager failures (i.e. system cancel the job) and network failure (i.e. packets loss between resources). In this part of trust-driven step, a value (called distrust value) is assigned to each resource. The distrust value increases when the assigned resource does not meet the computation requirement and the job fails (due to the one of the mentioned parameters). For example, when a job has crashed during the execution, the distrust value of that resource will be increased. We consider that all the resources are trustable from the start (their background is blank). However in the course of the time the background of each resource will be evaluated and will confirm if its trustfulness is always maintained or not. Consequently, the resources with the lower distrust value are better matched for the components (workflow jobs) of the application. The trustfulness of resources is defined as below in equation 3.

$$distrust(r_i) = trv_i^{j+1} = trv_i^j + dbtrv_i \qquad (3)$$

Where trv_i^{j+1} represents the distrust value of ith resource at the $j + 1$ moment and $dbtrv_i$ is the distrust value of the resource r_i stored previously on the database.

At this point, resources are sorted with respect to the level of reliability they offer (using availability and trustfulness metrics). After all, the sorted resources will be qualified, by taking into consideration the amount of memory, which the application requires for the execution. The necessary amount of physical memory is computed using estimation on the number and the size of input, output and temporary files. Hence in order to avoid restarting the application, we first authenticated the most available and trustfulness resources, then we identified the resources with the available amount of physical memory. Once the reliability of resources is assumed known, a rank value is evaluated to each eligible resource: rrank (r_i). The resources with the smallest rrank value are the least reliable ones.

if $(\text{rrank}(r_i) < \text{rrank}(r_j)) \rightarrow r_i$ is less reliable than r_j

2.2 Performance-driven step

In the second step (performance-driven step), the challenge consists in selecting the eligible resources among the reliable ones, in order to obtain a high level of efficiency for the application. Therefore we need to choose the fastest and least-loaded resources where the data movement cost between resources[2] is the least.

Let $R = r_1, r_2, \ldots, r_n$ denotes the set of qualified grid resources and $T = t_1, t_2, \ldots, t_m$ designates the set of jobs running in the grid resources. The performance of jth job (t_j) running in these eligible resources may be estimated by the following equation (equation number 4). It takes into consideration three crucial parameters having an impact on performance.

$$Time(t_j) = \mu \times ET(t_j, r_i) + \gamma \times FTT(t_j, r_i) + \delta(t_j, r_i) \qquad (4)$$

The first parameter, $ET(t_j, r_i)$, presents the time required for completing the jth job on the resource r_i. This time take into consideration the processor speed and memory access pattern.

The second parameter, $FTT(t_j, r_i)$, presents the spent time for transferring required data for running the jth job in the resource r_i. The effectiveness of this

---

[2]The data movement cost between master and the remote hosts contributes plainly to the overall execution time.

parameter may be evaluated in two ways: either by using the time to transfer the required data for the job t_j; or by the considering the time of a round trip (source to target r_i) of packets on the network. In the first case this amount may calculate in the following way : $FTT(t_j, r_i) = L(r_j) + vol(t_j)/B(r_j)$ where $vol(t_j)$ presents the amount of the required data for t_j. $L(r_j)$ and B(r_j) present respectively the latency and bandwidth of network estimated via NWS [16] or netperf[3]. In the second case this amount may estimate by using ping program which transfers some data in bytes.

Finally, the last parameter δ (r_i) describes queue waiting time which can increase the overall execution time of an application[4], which prompts a more detailed study. In order to retrieve the information regarding the application waiting time in a queue, we use the approach proposed in Delphoi [7] which implements an appropriate strategy to predict this waiting time. The application waiting time may in general depend on both the application size (i.e., the number of hosts required to run it) and the queue load. For this reason, the proposed strategy forecasts three categories (fully used and normally used and empty queue), where each of them uses three classes of application sizes, small (1 to 4 hosts), medium (5 to 16 hosts), and large (17 or more hosts). By taking application size and queue load into account, an average waiting time can be predicted before running the application, allowing to determine the least loaded queue at the runtime. This parameter helps the user to claim a resource with small estimated response times.

In the equation number 4, both γ and μ weighted parameters are specified to give more importance to data transfer time or to the job execution time, depending on the respective application requirement.

Hence, in order to find the resources ensuring the least data transfer time , in this step, information such as processor speed, network related characteristic (the ping program outputs, network latency and bandwidth) and charge of resources is retrieved.

Once the execution time is estimated, another rank value is assigned to each resource called prank (r_i) which expresses the power of each resource. In this case the resource r_i is more powerful when its prank value is bigger, i.e. when its estimated execution time for the job is smaller.

if $(\text{prank}(r_i) < \text{prank}(r_j)) \rightarrow r_i$ is less powerful than r_j

The major issue now is to find the most powerful resource among the most reliable ones, as the most reliable resources are not necessarily the most powerful ones. The proposed policy is designed to find a compromise between these two metrics. For this purpose, we give another rank value to the resources

---

[3]http://www.netperf.org/netperf/NetperfPage.html
[4]In the case of a cluster of workstations, δ (r_i) is replaced by the resource load.

called grank (r_i). This value is a weighted linear combination of rrank (r_i) and prank (r_i) computed as follows, where α and β are the weights, which can be customized by the users (reflecting the application requirements) to give more importance to one over the other:

$$grank(r_i) = \alpha.rrank(r_i) + \beta.prank(r_i) \qquad (5)$$

As a result, the resource with the highest grank will be relatively the most powerful and the most reliable resource, in respect to the user and application requirements. Hence, the performance-derived step allows identifying the reliable resources, which will be able to finish the job in the least time.

3.   GRID superscalar: a middleware independent system allowing resource prediction

The previously described strategy, which tries to find the reliable and powerful resources, is integrated in the GRID superscalar system. This section first describes briefly GRID superscalar, then explains the implementation of reliability strategy in this system using Grid Application Toolkit (GAT) [1] and argues the choice of this toolkit. The integration of this solution in GRID superscalar will help users to take the right decision while choosing the appropriate resources before application execution starts.

3.1   GRID superscalar

The GRID superscalar [8], which could be considered as a workflow system, is a framework mainly composed of a programming interface, a deployment center and a run-time system. It runs actually on top of Globus [12] Toolkit, Ninf-G [13] and ssh/scp. GRID superscalar programming environment requires the following functions in the main program: GS-On() and GS-Off() functions are provided for initialization and finalization of the run-time. GS-Open(), GS-Close(), GS-FOpen() and GS-FClose() for handling files. GS-Barrier() function has been defined to allow the programmers to wait till all grid jobs finish. The user specifies the functions (jobs), which are desired to be executed in a remote server in the grid, via an IDL file. For each of these functions, the type and nature (input, output or input/output) of the parameters must be specified. The deployment center is a Java-based Graphical User Interface, which implements the grid resource management and application configuration. It handles early failure detection, transfers the source code to the remote machines, and generates some additional source code files required for the master and the worker parts (using the gsstubgen tool). It compiles the main program on the localhost, and the worker programs on the remote hosts, and finally generates the configuration files needed at run-time. The run-time library is able to detect job dependencies, builds a job graph, which enables to discover the inherent parallelism of the sequential application, and performs concurrent job submission. Techniques such as file renaming, file locality, disk sharing, checkpointing constraints specification are applied to increase the application performance.

3.2   Resource selection on GRID superscalar

As presented in section 2, the information such as the availability and the trustfulness of resources, the resource load and the amount of physical memory, the consistency of retrieved information, etc. is required for the proposed schema.

Some of this information like the amount of physical memory or the resource load is retrieved via the Mercury Monitoring System[5][15]. Another part of this information like the network latency and bandwidth may be estimated by some tools like NWS or netperf.

A large part of resource trustfulness is computed within GRID superscalar. GRID superscalar detects if any of the worker jobs fails due to an internal error, or because it has been killed for any reason. It is important to mention that the application and the user related failures(such as forgetting to run grid-proxy-init) are not considered in the trustfulness parameter. Besides, the resource trustfulness concerning the network failure may detect via ping program to verify the packets loss between resources.

All the information regarding the remote resources can be computed using any remote job submission system[6]. Once the information is computed, the local host collects them. Thereafter, part of this information is stored in a database[7], which allows to generate the historic trace of previously computed information. When all the information is retrieved, then the resources are sorted using the equation number 5.

Both the necessary information retrieval and the reliability strategy implementation are integrated in deployment center of GRID superscalar. This later permits to realize the proposed prediction scheme for reliable resources selection, by using application performance information (computation and data transfer capacity).

---

[5]The Mercury Monitoring System is a general-purpose grid monitoring system developed by the GridLab project. It supports the monitoring of machines, grid services and running applications. Mercury features a flexible, modular design that makes it easy to adapt Mercury for various monitoring requirements.
[6]Like job submission system in GAT, Globus or Unicore Toolkits
[7]For this purpose, the "Advert Management" service in Grid Application Toolkit offers us the possibility of storing and retrieving information, which is kept persistent throughout multiple and independent executions if GRID superscalar: this service allows each resource to maintain its own advertisements.

3.3 Middleware independent grid programming environment

In order to have our mechanism running in a larger number of grid environments, we use Grid Application Toolkit for the implementation of our prediction strategy. GAT provides a glue layer which maps the API function calls executed by an application to the corresponding grid middleware functionality. GAT was developed by the EC-funded GridLab project. It provides a simple and stable API to various grid environments (like Globus, Unicore [20] , ssh, GridLab services [21]).

Moreover, in order to have a both high-level and platform-independent grid programming environment which allows resource prediction, we implement GRID superscalar (runs actually on top of Globus Toolkit) on top of GAT.

GRID superscalar realization requires mainly the following GAT functionalities: file management, remote job submission and job state notification. File management deals with the access management of files on remote grid storage resources (like copying, moving and deleting file instances). Remote job submission permits starting and controlling jobs running on remote grid resources. Finally job state notification examines the state (initial, scheduled, running and stopped) of remote jobs. Implementing both the prediction mechanism and GRID superscalar's runtime system using GAT, allows sustaining a both high-level and platform-independent grid programming environment.

4. Experimentation

The objective of this section is to show some results of our implementation. We first present the utilized platform, and then the result of several experiments. The presented experimentations are done on the DAS2 testbed. DAS-2 is a wide-area distributed computer situated at five Dutch Universities in the Netherlands. It consists of 200 Dual Pentium-III nodes with 1 GB Random Access Memory. The Vrije Universiteit's cluster, containing 72 nodes, is the largest cluster, the other clusters consist of 32 nodes.

The following tables show the retrieved information for 4 cluster of DAS2. The first column in both tables contains the cluster names. The second column contains the availability of resources and the third one the trustfulness of them. The fourth and fifth columns show the total amount of physical and swap memory (in KB) in the system. Please note that a part of the capacity presented for physical memory is used by the operating system, the application, etc. Finally the last column shows the file transfer time (in sec) between the master and the respective workers. In table 2, the second column presents the job size running on the workers, and the third column shows the queueing waiting time (in sec). For the sake of clarity we illustrate just the waiting time for the small jobs.

Table 1.   Retrieval information regarding the reliability and performance of three workers.

worker	availability	distrust	memory	swap	file transfer time
fs1.das2.liacs.nl	1.00	0.0	1540592	2096472	11.0
fs0.das2.cs.vu.nl	0.88	5.0	1540592	2096472	11.2
fs3.das2.ewi.tudelft.nl	0.61	6.0	1026584	2096472	11.1
fs2.das2.nikhef.nl	0.79	7.0	1540592	2096472	11.3

Table 2.   Queuing waiting time for three workers.

worker	job size	queue wait time
fs1.das2.liacs.nl	small	12 sec
fs0.das2.cs.vu.nl	small	10 sec
fs3.das2.ewi.tudelft.nl	small	80 sec
fs2.das2.nikhef.nl	small	135 sec

The information presented in table 1 indicates that for those jobs which need less than 32 processors, fs1.das2.liacs.nl worker is the most appropriate and reliable resource. In the case where the jobs need more than 32 processors, obligatory fs0.das2.cs.vu.nl worker (the only cluster with 72 processors) will be chosen. Regarding the application requirements user can give more importance to the reliability or the execution time. In this case, by taking into account the information presented in table two, worker fs1.das2.liacs.nl may be chosen if the reliability parameter is more important. In the opposite case, when the execution time is more important fs0.das2.cs.vu.nl worker may be chosen. To realize the experimentations, we use three different kinds of applications: matrix multiplication, cholesky factorization of matrices and fastdnaml computation to estimate the phylogenetic trees of sequences.

In order to evaluate the effectiveness of proposed reliability strategy we use fastdnaml application which uses a large sequence as input (its execution takes quiet long time). In the first case the most reliable resources in DAS2 are chosen. Therefore we use fs0.das2.cs.vu.nl cluster situated in Amsterdam as master and fs1.das2.liacs.nl cluster located in Liden as worker (we use 4 processors of this cluster). The execution of this application is completed successfully and takes 5149,55 sec. In the second case instead of fs1.das2.liacs.nl we choose fs2.das2.nikhef.nl situated in Amsterdam university as worker (we use also 4 processors of this cluster). This cluster is less reliable and our application is failed after 4038,01 sec, due to sudden unavailability of this cluster. This means that we lost 78,41% of the time for completing this execution, by choosing a less reliable resource.

Table 3. GRID superscalar on top of Globus and GAT.

application	master	worker	using GAT	using Globus
matrix multiplication	fs0.das2.cs.vu.nl	fs1.das2.liacs.nl	252,12 sec	174,25 sec
cholesky factorization	fs0.das2.cs.vu.nl	fs1.das2.liacs.nl	575,30 sec	348,02 sec
fastdnaml	fs0.das2.cs.vu.nl	fs1.das2.liacs.nl	5149,55 sec	3947,25 sec

We developed a version of GRID superscalar based on GAT. In order to evaluate the performance of GRID superscalar on top of GAT and on top of Globus, we used the three types of application that we presented. The results are presented in table 3. We notice that GAT reduces the applications performance. The performance decreases around 30% in the case of matrix multiplication, 40% in the case of Cholesky factorization and 28% in the case of fastdnaml. This is due to the non functionality of pre staging and post staging of files in the used GRAM adaptors in one hand and the lack of clustering file copying in gridftp adaptors on the other hand.

Further work should perform similar experiments in a heterogeneous environment, where the selection of reliable and efficient resources is more critical.

5. Conclusion

Distributed environments, and in particular grids, are inherently unreliable. Frequent failures of their components and applications make development difficult, especially to the scientists who are not necessarily grid experts. This paper first presents a mechanism, which allows to run the application jobs on the most reliable and most powerful resources, in respect to the application requirements. Our described system gathers all the necessary characteristics about resources. Thanks to the collected information, our system finds and chooses the most suitable and adequate resource for each of the jobs. This paper also shows how to obtain a high-level and platform-independent, grid programming environment. It proposes to combine GRID superscalar runtime system with GAT, taking advantage of their respective properties. In this way GRID superscalar may run across various Grid middleware systems such as various versions of Globus, Unicore or ssh/scp.

References

[1] G. Allen, K. Davis, T. Goodale, A. Hutanu, H. Kaiser, T. Kielmann, A. Merzky, R. van Nieuwpoort, A. Reinefeld, F. Schintke, T. Schütt, E. Seidel, B. Ullmer. *The Grid*

Application Toolkit: Towards Generic and Easy Application Programming Interfaces for the Grid. In the proceeding of the IEEE, vol. 93(3):534-550, 2005.

[2] G. Allen, D. Angulo, T. Goodale, T. Kielmann, A. Merzky, J. Nabrzysky, J. Pukacki, M. Russell, T. Radke, E. Seidel, J. Shalf, I. Taylor. *GridLab: Enabling Applications on the Grid.* In proceeding of Grid Computing - GRID 2002 : Third International Workshop, 39-45, 2002.

[3] I. Foster and C. Kesselman. *Globus: A Metacomputing Infrastructure Toolkit.* In International Journal of Supercomputer Applications, vol. 11(2):115-128, 1997.

[4] V. Huber *UNICORE: A Grid Computing Environment for Distributed and Parallel Computing.* In Proceedings of 6th Internatioanl Conference on Parallel Computing Technologies (PaCT-2001), Springer, LNCS 2127, 258-266, 2001.

[5] S. Hwang and C. Kesselman. *Grid Workflow: A Flexible Failure Handling Framework for the Grid.* In the proceeding of 12th IEEE International Symposium on High Performance Distributed Computing, 126Ű137, 2003.

[6] G. Gombás, C. Attila Marosi and Z. Balaton. *Grid Application Monitoring and Debugging Using the Mercury Monitoring System.* In Advances in Grid Computing–EGC 2005, vol. 3470:193-199, 2005.

[7] J. Maassen, R. V. Van Nieuwpoort, T. Kielmann, K. Verstoep. *Middleware Adaptation with the Delphoi Service.* In Concurrency and Computation: Practice and Experience, vol. 18(13):1659-1679 , 2006.

[8] R. Sirvent, J. M. Pérez, R. M. Badia, J. Labarta. *Automatic Grid workflow based on imperative programming languages.* In Concurrency and Computation: Practice and Experience, vol. 18(10):1169-1186, 2006.

[9] Y. Tanaka, H. Nakada, S. Sekiguchi, T. Suzumura, and S. Matsuoka. *Ninf-G: A Reference Implementation of RPC-based Programming Middleware for Grid Computing.* In Journal of Grid Computing, vol. 1(1):41-51, 2003.

[10] R.Wolski, N. Spring, and J. Hayes. *The NetworkWeather Service: A Distributed Resource Performance Forecasting Service for Metacomputing.* In Journal of Future Generation Computing Systems,vol 15(5-6):757-768, 1999.

[11] J. Yu and R. Buyya. *Taxonomy of Scientific Workflow Systems for Grid Computing.* In Sigmod Record, vol. 34(3):44-49, 2005.

[12] S. Zhao and V. Lo. *Result Verification and Trust-based Scheduling in Open Peer-to-Peer Cycle Sharing Systems.* In IEEE Fifth International Conference on Peer-to-Peer Systems, 2005.

DESIGN AND IMPLEMENTATION OF A HYBRID P2P-BASED GRID RESOURCE DISCOVERY SYSTEM

Harris Papadakis
Foundation for Research and Technology-Hellas, Institute of Computer Science, Greece
adanar@ics.forth.gr

Paolo Trunfio, Domenico Talia
DEIS, University of Calabria, Italy
trunfio@deis.unical.it
talia@deis.unical.it

Paraskevi Fragopoulou*
Foundation for Research and Technology-Hellas, Institute of Computer Science, Greece
fragopou@ics.forth.gr

Abstract   Peer-to-peer (P2P) computing is recognized as one of most prominent paradigms to achieve scalability in key components of Grid systems. One of these components is resource discovery, whose duty is to provide system-wide up-to-date information about resources, a task inherently limited in scalability. Unlike typical P2P systems, Grid systems manage not only static resources, but also resources whose characteristics change dynamically over time. To cope with this scenario, recent P2P-based Grid resource discovery systems employ a combination of Distributed Hash Tables (DHTs) to manage static resources, and unstructured (i.e., broadcast-like) search techniques for dynamic resources. In this paper we elaborate on this approach by designing and implementing a Grid resource discovery system that employs a dynamic querying algorithm over a structured DHT-based overlay. The system has been fully implemented and deployed on the Grid'5000 platform for testing and evaluation. The experimental performance results demonstrate the efficiency of the implemented system, both in terms of number of messages and time needed to complete the search.

Keywords: resource discovery, peer-to-peer, distributed hash tables.

*With the Department of Applied Informatics and Multimedia, Technological Educational Institute of Crete, Greece.

1.   Introduction

To achieve their envisioned global-scale deployment, Grid systems need to be scalable. Peer-to-peer (P2P) techniques are widely viewed as one of the prominent ways to reach the desired scalability. Resource discovery is one of the most important functionalities of a Grid system and, at the same time, one of the most difficult to scale. Indeed, the duty of a resource discovery system (such as the Globus MDS [1]) is to provide system-wide up-to-date information, a task which has inherently limited scalability. To add to the challenge, Grid resource discovery systems need to manage not only static resources, but also resources whose characteristics change dynamically over time, making the design critical.

Recent work [2] proposed a framework that combines the use of Distributed Hash Tables (DHTs) to search static Grid resources, and an unstructured P2P search algorithm to locate dynamic resources. Differently from standard unstructured protocols, such framework searches for dynamic resources by using a "dynamic querying" algorithm, which exploits a DHT structure to distribute queries across nodes without generating redundant messages.

In this paper we elaborate on such an approach by designing and implementing a hybrid P2P-based Grid resource discovery system that supports both static and dynamic information retrieval, and push and pull models. Like recent unstructured systems, our system is based on a two-tier approach, with peers divided in two categories (*Superpeers* and *Peers*) based on the level of service they can provide. Following this approach, each Superpeer acts as a server for a number of regular Peers, while Superpeers connect to each other in a P2P fashion at a higher level [3]. Unlike unstructured systems, we organize Superpeers using a DHT-based system, namely Chord [4] and its implementation Open Chord [5].

The search for static information is performed in a structured-like fashion, while dynamic information search is performed in an efficient unstructured-like fashion tailored to the DHT structure. Thus, the proposed system is hybrid in more than one aspect. The two-tier approach couples the completely decentralized P2P paradigm with a limited degree of centrality to reduce the effort of providing a global view of the system resources. In addition, our system couples the structured topology with a brodcast-like mechanism reminiscent of unstructured systems to locate dynamic information. The support for both a push and a pull approach to resource discovery allows for a trade-off between message cost for resource discovery and staleness of provided information.

The system has been fully implemented and deployed on the Grid'5000 platform [6] for testing and evaluation. The experimental performance results presented in this paper demonstrate the efficiency of the implemented system, both in terms of number of messages and time needed to complete the search.

The remainder of the paper is organized as follows. Section 2 discusses related work on P2P-based resource discovery. Section 3 presents the system design, and describes the algorithm of dynamic querying implemented by the system. Section 4 discusses the implementation of the system and its evaluation on the Grid'5000 platform. Finally, Section 5 conclude the paper.

2.   Related work

P2P-based resource discovery systems allow nodes participating in the system to share both the storage load and the query load. In addition, they provide a robust communication overlay. P2P-based Grid resource discovery mechanisms that appear in the literature can be divided into two categories: structured and unstructured [7]. Most proposed systems depend on a structured P2P underlying layer. A structured system however assumes that all pieces of information are stored in an orderly fashion according to their values in a DHT. This is the reason structured systems support efficient resource discovery. However, apart from static resources, Grids include dynamic resources whose values change over time. Whenever the value of a resource attribute stored in a structured system changes, it needs to be republished. If this occurs too often, the cost of republishing becomes prohibitively high.

Flooding is supported by those P2P-based Grid resource discovery systems that follow the unstructured approach. Flooding, however, can generate a large volume of traffic if not carefully deployed, due to the duplicate messages generated during this process. Several P2P-based Grid resource discovery algorithms appear in the literature, trying to alleviate the excessive volume of traffic produced during flooding [8]. One of the first alternatives proposed was random walks. Each node forwards each query it receives to a single neighboring node chosen at random, a method that generates very little traffic but suffers from reduced network coverage and long response time. As an alternative, multiple random walks have been proposed, where the querying node starts simultaneously k parallel random walkers. Although compared to a single random walk this method has better behavior, it still suffers from low network coverage and long response time compared to flooding.

Hybrid methods that combine flooding with random walks have been proposed in [9]. Schemes like Directed Breadth First Search (DBFS) forward queries only to those peers that have provided results to past requests, under the assumption that they will continue to do so. Interest-based schemes aim to cluster together peers with similar content, under the assumption that those peers are better suited to serve each other needs. In another family of algorithms, query messages are forwarded selectively to part of a node neighbors based on predefined criteria or statistical information. For example, each node selects the first k highest capacity nodes or the k connections with the smallest latency to forward new queries [10]. A somewhat different approach named forwarding indices builds a structure that resembles a routing table at each node [11]. This structure stores the number of responses returned through each neighbor on each one of a preselected list of topics. Other techniques include query caching, or the incorporation of semantic information in the network [12–13].

An approach that has been used to make resource location in unstructured P2P systems more efficient is the partitioning of the overlay network into subnetworks using content characterization methods. A different subnetwork is formed per content category. Each subnetwork connects all peers that possess files belonging to the corresponding category. A system that exploits this approach is the Semantic Overlay Networks (SONs) [12]. SONs use a semantic categorization of music files based on the music genre they belong to. The main drawback of this method is the semantic categorization of the content. An approach that overcomes this semantic categorization method has been proposed in [13].

A controlled flooding mechanism, known as "dynamic querying," has been proposed to reduce the number of messages generated by unstructured P2P systems [14]. In this paper a dynamic querying-like approach is implemented and evaluated. The method exploits the benefits of dynamic querying over the overlay network of a DHT-based P2P system to eliminate duplicate messages, thus reducing significantly the total number of messages generated by every search. The dynamic querying algorithm implemented in our framework is described in the next section.

3.   System design

The proposed system is based on a two-tier architecture in which nodes belong either to the category of *Peers* or *Superpeers*, based on the level of service they can offer. Most participants act as normal Peers, while the high-bandwidth participants act as Superpeers. Superpeers participate normally in the P2P overlay and also act on behalf of Peers, which participate in the system indirectly by connecting to Superpeers. There are several reasons for this "stretching" of the P2P system definition, which dictates that all participants have equal roles and responsibilities. The first one is to improve the scalability of the system by exploiting the heterogeneity of participating nodes. This essentially means that more work can be assigned to those participants that can handle it, while at the same time removing most of the workload from the less capable peers. In addition, Peers can provide their corresponding Superpeer with static information about the resources they manage. Thus, when a Superpeer receives a query, it can forward the query only to those Peers whose resources match the static criteria. The Peers will then reply with any local resource information that also matches the dynamic part of the query.

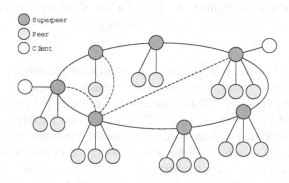

Figure 1.   The architecture of the proposed system. Dashed lines indicate the fingers nodes in the Chord overlay.

While such two-tier approach is widely implemented by unstructured P2P systems, in our framework we organize Superpeers using Chord [4], a well known DHT-based system. There are two main reasons for this. The first one is that the Chord structure can be used to quickly resolve queries based on static information. The second reason is that the structure of Chord allows to distribute a query to all nodes in the overlay avoiding redundant (i.e., duplicate) messages. In particular, we implemented an algorithm for "dynamic querying" over a DHT, described in Section 3.1. Such algorithm allows to distribute the query to as many nodes as it is required to locate the desired information, instead of flooding the entire network for every query. This means that the cost of the lookup is further reduced, depending on the amount of matching resources that exist in the system and the number of the results required by the user.

The architecture of the system is schematically represented in Figure 1. Four types of components are defined:

- *Superpeers*: The main components of the system. They are organized in a Chord network and implement the dynamic querying algorithm. Each one is responsible for a number of Peers.

- *Peers*: Provide information about the resources they manage. The information is provided to the corresponding Superpeer following either a *push* or *pull* model (see below).

- *Clients*: Connect to a Superpeer and issue queries on behalf of a user, also managing the delivery of query responses to the user.

- *Cache Servers*: The entry-points for Peers and Superpeers to the network (not shown in the figure). They hold a list of the most recently joined Superpeers and return a subset of that list to any requestor.

As mentioned above, our system provides support for both push and pull models for the dissemination of resource information (especially regarding the dynamic information). This approach is similar to the one used in the Monitoring and Discovery System (MDS) of Globus Toolkit 2, where the various GRIS modules register themselves (and their static information) to a GIIS module [1]. Each GRIS has the autonomy to decide whether it will periodically push the dynamic information to its corresponding GIIS (*push model*), or it will wait for the GIIS to query each of its registered GRISs for that information, when needed (*pull model*). In our system, each Peer can be configured to send to its Superpeer its static information only, or to periodically send up-to-date copies of its dynamic information.

Notice that, while Figure 1 shows only one Superpeer overlay, the system can be extended to include multiple overlays, one for each type of static resource information, as proposed in [15]. This will greatly reduce the number of Superpeers contacted during a dynamic query lookup.

In the remainder of this section we briefly describe the algorithm of dynamic querying over a DHT as it has been implemented in our system.

3.1   Querying dynamic resources

Dynamic querying [14] is a technique used in unstructured P2P networks to reduce the traffic generated by the search process. The query initiator starts the search by sending the query to a few of its neighbors and with a small Time-to-Live (TTL). The main goal of this first phase is to estimate the popularity of the resource to be located. If such an attempt does not produce a sufficient number of results, the search initiator sends the query towards the next neighbor with a new TTL. Such TTL is calculated taking into account both the desired number of results, and the resource popularity estimated during the previous phase. This process is repeated until the expected number of results is received, or until all the neighbors have been queried.

The algorithm of dynamic querying over a DHT, as outlined in [2], uses a combination of the dynamic querying approach with an algorithm for efficient broadcast over DHTs proposed in [16], which allows to perform a broadcast operation with minimal cost in a Chord-based P2P network. In a network of N nodes, a broadcast message originating at an arbitrary node reaches all other nodes after exactly $N - 1$ messages, with $logN$ steps. In order to explain how dynamic querying over a DHT works, we first recall the algorithm of broadcast over DHTs.

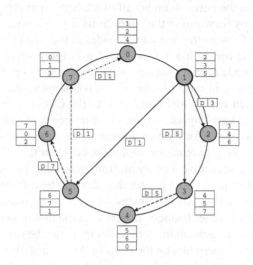

Figure 2. An example of broadcast over a Chord DHT.

Broadcast over a DHT. Let us consider a fully populated Chord ring with $N = 2^m$ nodes and an m-bit identifier space. Each Chord node x has a finger table, with fingers pointing to nodes $x + 2^{i-1}$, where $i = 1...m$. Each of these m nodes, in turn, has its fingers pointing to other m nodes in the same way. The broadcast initiator node sends the query to all nodes in its finger table, and in turn, these nodes do the same with nodes in their finger tables. In this way, all nodes are reached in m steps. Since the same node may be pointed to by multiple fingers, the following strategy is used to avoid redundant messages. Each message sent by a node contains a "limit" argument, which is used to restrict the forwarding space of the receiving node. The "limit" argument of a message sent to the node pointed to by finger i is finger $i + 1$. Figure 2 gives an example of such Chord ring with $m = 3$ (eight nodes, three-bit identifier space and finger tables with three entries). In this example, *Node 1* initiates the broadcast of a data item D. The "limit" is sent together with the data item. Three steps of communication between nodes are shown with solid, dashed, and dashed-dotted lines. *Node 1* reaches all other nodes via $N - 1 = 7$ messages within $m = 3$ steps. The same procedure applies to Chord rings with $N < 2^m$ (i.e., not fully populated rings). In this case, the number of distinct fingers of each node is likely to be $logN$, on the average.

Dynamic querying over a DHT. In brief, the algorithm of dynamic querying over a DHT works as follows. The initiator node (that is, the Superpeer that submits the query to the network on behalf of a Client) starts by processing the query locally, and by forwarding the query to its first n unique fingers. These fingers will in turn forward the query to all nodes in the portions of the network they are responsible for, following the broadcast algorithm described above. When a Superpeer node receives a query, it checks for local resources matching the query criteria and, in case of match, it sends a query hit directly to the initiator node, which will in turn forward it to the Client. After sending the query to its first n unique fingers, the algorithm proceeds iteratively as follows.

First, the initiator waits for a given amount of time, which is the estimated time needed by the query to reach the farthest node under the nth unique finger, plus the time needed to receive a query hit from that node. Then, if the number of received query hits is equal or greater than the number of query hits desired by the Client, the initiator node terminates. Otherwise, it continues the search by sending the query to other k unique fingers after the first n ones. The value of k is chosen by calculating the number of nodes that must be contacted to obtain the desired number of query hits on the basis of the estimated popularity of the resource, which is in turn calculated as the ratio between the current number of received query hits and the estimated number of nodes reached through the first n unique fingers (which is likely to be 2^n [4]).

The iterative procedure above is repeated until the desired number of query hits is obtained, or there are no more fingers to contact. Note that, if the resource popularity is properly estimated on the first iteration, two iterations - including the first one - are sufficient to obtain the desired number of query hits.

4.   Implementation and evaluation

We implemented the system using Java. Basically, each one of the system components (Superpeer, Peer, Client, and Cache Server) has been implemented as a separate Java application that can be installed independently from the other components. TCP sockets have been used to let the system components communicate with each other.

For building the Superpeer overlay we used Open Chord, an implementation of the Chord algorithm by the University of Bamberg [5]. Open Chord provides an API that enables the use of a Chord DHT within Java applications. However, that API provided only methods for joining/leaving a Chord network and inserting/removing keys from it. In order to perform dynamic querying over the overlay, we extended the Open Chord API by adding the functionality to send arbitrary messages between nodes in the system. Such send operation is asynchronous, since the controlled broadcast performed by dynamic querying is executed in a Breadth-First-Search rather than a Depth-First-Search fashion. In addition, we added a functionality that allows a developer to access the (sorted) finger table of Chord, as needed by the dynamic querying algorithm.

In the implementation of the dynamic querying algorithm, the number of unique fingers contacted during the first iteration is set to 6. As the number of nodes reachable through n distinct fingers is likely to be 2^n (see Section 3.1), the number of Superpeers contacted during the first iteration is $2^6 = 64$ on the average.

While queries are distributed using the Chord overlay, results are sent directly to the query initiator. That is, if a Peer contains resources that match the query criteria, it issues a query hit message directly to the Superpeer that initiated the dynamic querying (i.e., the Superpeer to which the Client that issued the query is connected). That Superpeer will in turn forward the query hits over its open socket with the Client, as they arrive.

4.1 Experimental results

In this section we discuss the performance of the proposed resource discovery system in a real Grid scenario. We focused on the efficiency of the system in terms of number of messages and time needed to complete a search. For our experiments we used the Grid'5000 testbed, a highly reconfigurable, controllable and easy to monitor Grid platform gathering nine sites geographically distributed in France and featuring a total of 5000 CPUs [6]. Grid'5000 is an ideal testbed for our experiments, since not only it allowed us to test the system in a real Grid platform, but it also contains sites from all of France, which more closely matches the environment of a global-scale Grid.

We used several hosts from four Grid'5000 sites (Rennes, Sophia, Nancy, and Orsay) for a total of 410 nodes across six clusters of those sites. Each host was used to execute a number of independent Peer and Superpeer applications. In order to distribute the load across sites, Peers and Superpeers have been uniformly distributed across nodes. Thus, given the number of available nodes, N, and chosen the overall number of Superpeers, S, and the average number of Peers connected to each Superpeer, P, we executed an average number of S/N Superpeers and $P \times (S/N)$ Peers on each node.

Each Peer and Superpeer entered the system at random times. It was, thus, quite unlikely for a Superpeer to have in its finger table Superpeers running on the same host, or for a Peer to connect to a Superpeer in the same machine. We then initiated several Clients, each of which submitted the same batch of queries, each one having search criteria with a different probability to match resources in the network. Given a query, we define the probability of match, p, as the ratio between the total number of resources that match the query criteria, and the total number of Peers in the network. When submitting the query, each Client specifies the desired number of query hits R, i.e., the number of resources to be located that match the query criteria.

We measured two performance parameters:

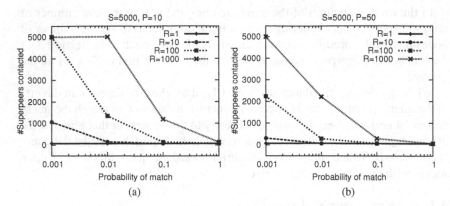

Figure 3.   Number of Superpeers contacted to perform queries with different probabilities of match and different numbers of required results (R), in two network scenarios: (a) S=5000, P=10; (b) S=5000, P=50.

- The number of Superpeers contacted by each query.

- The time required by each query hit to reach the Client.

Notice that the first parameter corresponds to the number of messages generated by the algorithm of dynamic querying over the DHT. For the second parameter, a significant value is the time required by the Rth query hit to reach the Client (where R is the desired number of results), since it represents the amount of time needed to reach the goal of the search.

The experiments have been performed in two network scenarios: 1) $S = 5000$ and $P = 10$; 2) $S = 5000$ and $P = 50$. For each network scenario we submitted queries with four different probabilities of match ($p = 0.001, 0.01, 0.1,$ and 1.0) and four numbers of required query hits ($R = 1, 10, 100,$ and 1000), and for all these queries we measured both the number of Superpeers contacted and the time required by each query hit to reach the Client.

Figure 3 shows the number of Superpeers contacted during the various experiments. The search of one resource ($R = 1$) in both scenarios (Figure 3a and Figure 3b) generates an average of 68.4 messages, which is close to the average number of Superpeers reachable through the first 6 fingers. In most experiments, in fact, at least one Peer responded with a query hit during the first iteration of the search.

For higher values of R, the number of Superpeers contacted depends significantly on the value of p. This is because for small values of p the first iteration does not produce enough results, and so at least another iteration must be performed. Let us consider, for example, the case of $R = 10$ in the network with $P = 10$ (Figure 3a). When $p = 0.01$, an average of 147 Superpeers are contacted indicating that 7 fingers have been queried on the mean (6 of which during the first iteration). When $p = 0.001$, an average of 1067 Superpeers are contacted, corresponding to 10 fingers. Similar behavior applies to the network with $P = 50$ and for other values of R.

As shown in Figure 3a and Figure 3b, in some cases all 5000 Superpeers are contacted during the search. This happens when the algorithm, on the basis of the estimated popularity of the resource, calculates that all remaining fingers must be contacted to obtain the desired number of results. This, obviously, will or will not lead to success based on the actual presence of enough matching resources in the network. In every case, the number of messages is bound to the number of Superpeers, without redundancy.

Figure 4 shows the time needed to receive the query hits in some of the experiments described above. For space limitations, we show only the results of searches with $R = 100$ and $R = 1000$ for various values of p. For some values of p, the search did not succeed to find the desired number of resources, because they were not available. For example, with $p = 0.001$, it is impossible to find 1000 resources when $S = 5000$ and $P = 10$. That's why Figure 4a reports only results for $p = 0.01, 0.1,$ and 1.0. The same applies to Figure 4c and Figure 4d.

For all values of R, in both network scenarios, the time needed to receive the Rth query hit was in the order of few hundreds milliseconds. As expected, comparing the results for a given value of P and R (for example Figure 4b) we note that times increase as p decreases. Moreover, lines for higher values of p are more flat, indicating that all query hits arrive in a small time interval. This happens because for high values of p the search is completed in only one iteration, and so there is not the additional delay of a new round of search. When a second iteration of search is performed (as for $p = 0.001$ in Figure 4b), the line shows two trends: the first part with few results arriving at different times from the first 6 fingers, the second part, more flat, with several results arriving in a more close time sequence.

Comparing the arrival times of query hits for the same values of R but different values of P (for example, Figure 4a vs Figure 4b), we find that a higher value of P leads to reduced times for any value of p. This is due to the higher number of Peers - and thus matching resources - that are reached during the first iteration of dynamic querying when P is higher. Such result confirms that the two tier-approach leads to reduced search time when there is a good proportion between the number of Superpeers and Peers in the system.

As a final remark, all the experimental results presented above demonstrate the efficiency of the implemented system. The dynamic querying algorithm was able to limit and control the number of messages generated by the search in function of the probability of match and the number of desired results, while its coupling with the two-tier architecture allowed to ensure very low search times in all the experimental scenarios.

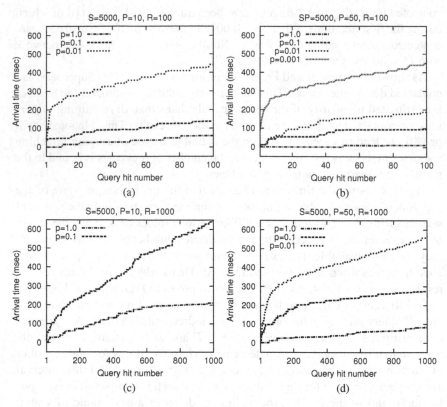

Figure 4.   Time to receive query hits under different probabilities of match, in four scenarios:
(a) P=10, R=100; (b) P=50, R=100; (c) P=10, R=1000; (d) P=50, R=1000. In all cases S=5000.
The values on the x-axis represent the arrival numbers of the received query hits. The values on
the y-axis are the times needed to receive the various query hits after the query submission.

5.   Conclusions

We designed and implemented a Grid resource discovery system that combines the flexibility of unstructured P2P systems and protocols, such as the
two-tier architecture and the dynamic querying approach, with the efficiency of
structured DHT-based systems like Chord.

The performance of the implemented system has been evaluated in a real Grid
environment using the Grid'5000 testbed. The experimental results presented in
the paper demonstrated the efficiency of the algorithm of dynamic querying over
a DHT to control the number of messages generated by the resource discovery
tasks, and its coupling with the two-tier architecture ensured very low search
delays in all experimental scenarios.

Acknowledgement

We would like to thank the Grid'5000 team for allowing us to use their platform for experimenting our system. This research work is carried out under the EU FP6 Network of Excellence CoreGRID (Contract IST-2002-004265).

References

[1] Globus MDS. http://www.globus.org/toolkit/mds.

[2] D. Talia, P. Trunfio, J. Zeng. Peer-to-Peer Models for Resource Discovery in Large-scale Grids: A Scalable Architecture. VECPAR'06, Rio de Janeiro, Brazil, 2006.

[3] B. Yang, H. Garcia-Molina. Designing a Super-peer Network. Int. Conf. on Data Engineering (ICDE 2003), Bangalore, India, 2003.

[4] I. Stoica, R. Morris, D. Karger, M. F. Kaashoek, H. Balakrishnan. Chord: A Scalable Peer-to-peer Lookup Service for Internet Applications. ACM SIGCOMM'01, San Diego, USA, 2001.

[5] Open Chord. http://open-chord.sourceforge.net.

[6] Grid'5000. http://www.grid5000.fr.

[7] P. Trunfio, D. Talia, H. Papadakis, P. Fragopoulou, M. Mordacchini, M. Pennanen, K. Popov, V. Vlassov, S. Haridi. Peer-to-Peer resource discovery in Grids: Models and systems. Future Generation Computer Systems, vol. 23, n. 7, 2007.

[8] Q. Lv, P. Cao, E. Cohen, K. Li, S. Shenker. Search and Replication in Unstructured Peer-to-Peer Networks. Int. Conf. on Supercomputing (SC 2002), Baltimore, USA, 2002.

[9] C. Gkantsidis, M. Mihail, A. Saberi. Hybrid Search Schemes for Unstructured Peer-to-Peer Networks. IEEE INFOCOM 2005, Miami, USA, 2005.

[10] D. Tsoumakos, N. Roussopoulos. A Comparison of Peer-to-Peer Search Methods. Int. Workshop on the Web and Databases (WebDB 2003), San Diego, USA, 2003.

[11] A. Crespo, H. Garcia-Molina. Routing Indices for Peer-to-peer Systems. Int. Conf. on Distributed Computing Systems (ICDCS'02), Vienna, Austria, 2002.

[12] A. Crespo, H. Garcia Molina. Semantic Overlay Networks for P2P Systems. Int. Conf. on Agents and Peer-to-Peer Computing (AP2PC 2004), New York, USA, 2004.

[13] K. Sripanidkulchai, B. Maggs, H. Zhang. Efficient Content Location using Interest-based Locality in Peer-to-Peer Systems. IEEE INFOCOM 2003, San Franciso, USA, 2003.

[14] A. A. Fisk. Gnutella Dynamic Query Protocol v0.1. http://www.the-gdf.org/wiki/index.php?title=Dynamic-Querying.

[15] H. Papadakis, P. Fragopoulou, E. P. Markatos, M. Dikaiakos, A. Lambrinidis. Divide et Impera: Partitioning Unstructured Peer-to-Peer Systems to Improve Resource Location. 2nd CoreGRID Integration Workshop, Krakow, Poland, 2006.

[16] S. El-Ansary, L. Alima, P. Brand, S. Haridi. Efficient Broadcast in Structured P2P Networks. 2nd Int. Workshop on Peer-to-Peer Systems (IPTPS'03), Berkeley, USA, 2003.

BACKFILLING STRATEGIES FOR SCHEDULING STREAMS OF JOBS ON COMPUTATIONAL FARMS

R. Baraglia*, G. Capannini*°, M. Pasquali*•
D. Puppin*, L. Ricci°, A.D. Techiouba*

* *ISTI/CNR – Pisa – Italy*
• *IMT, Lucca Institute for Advanced Studies – Lucca – Italy*
° *Department of Computer Science – University of Pisa – Italy*
{r.baraglia, g.capannini, m.pasquali, d.puppin}@isti.cnr.it – ricci@di.unipi.it

Abstract   This paper presents a set of strategies for scheduling a stream of batch jobs on the machines of a heterogeneous computational farm. Our proposal is based on a flexible backfilling, which schedules jobs according to a priority assigned to each job submitted for execution. Priority values are computed as a result of a set of heuristics whose main goal is to improve resources utilization and to meet the job QoS requirements. The heuristics consider job deadlines, estimated execution time and aging of the jobs in the scheduling queue. Furthermore, the set of software licenses required by a job is also considered. The different proposals have been compared through simulations. Performance figures show the applicability of our approach.

Keywords: scheduling, resource management, quality of service

1.   Introduction

In this paper we propose a set of strategies for scheduling a stream of batch jobs on the machines of a heterogeneous computational farm. A computational farm can integrate hw/sw heterogeneous resources such as workstations, parallel systems, servers, storage arrays, and software licenses. In such an environment, users should submit their computational requests without necessarily knowing on which computational resources these will be executed. A fruitful exploitation of a computational farm requires scheduling algorithms able to efficiently and effectively allocate the user jobs on the computational resources [7].

Our proposal is based on the backfilling technique [2], which has been initially introduced for scheduling streams of jobs on parallel supercomputers.

Backfilling has been originally introduced to extend the *First Come First Served* (*FCFS*) approach in order to increase the efficiency of the resource usage. Backfilling improves resource utilization by allowing the first job J of the queue to reserve resources that are not available and by evaluating the possible execution of successive jobs in the submission queue. These jobs can be executed if and only if they do not exploit the resources reserved by J or their execution terminates within the *shadow time*, i.e. the time where all the reserved resources become available. This scheduling strategy requires the knowledge of an estimation of the execution time of any job.

In this paper we propose a set of extensions to the original backfilling introduced to support heterogeneity. The basic idea of our approach is to assign a priority to each job in the submission queue by considering both the optimization of the usage of the system resources and a set of QoS requirements of the jobs. Job priorities are computed at each scheduling event, i.e. at a job submission and at a job ending, by using a set of heuristics.

For instance, our solution supports job deadlines by dynamically increasing the priority of a job when its deadline is approaching, and by minimizing the priority of a job when its deadline is exceeded. Furthermore, it also takes into account the type of resources required by each job. We have considered, for instance, the set of software licenses required for the execution of each job. In a heterogeneous environment, some software licenses may require a specific operating system or may be installed on a specific machine only. Furthermore, a maximum number of copies of a software license, which can be simultaneously utilized, is often defined. This value is generally smaller than the number of machines of the computational farm. In this case the license requirements of the jobs must be considered in the scheduling process in order to optimize the usage of such resources. Our scheduler detects critical licenses, i.e. licenses whose number of concurrently usable copies is smaller than the number of copies required by the jobs in the submission queue, and assigns to each job a priority proportional to the amount of critical licenses it requires. Since jobs requiring a large number of critical licenses release them after their termination, they should be executed as soon as possible in order to let the scheduler to define more flexible scheduling plans. Other heuristics reducing job starvation and improving job response time are defined as well.

We have developed two different extensions of the original backfilling algorithm. In the first one, the maximum priority is always assigned to the first job in the queue. Furthermore, this job may reserve all the unavailable resources it needs and the reservation is preserved even if a higher priority job is submitted. The other jobs in the submission queue are ordered according to their priority and are considered by the scheduler according to the standard backfilling algorithm. As in backfilling, this strategy prevents starvation.

According to the second extension the job J with the highest priority is able to make resource reservation, but such reservation may be canceled if a job with a higher priority is submitted or if the priority of a previously submitted job is updated and exceeds that of J. In this way another job may be moved to the first position of the queue.

We have developed an event driven ad-hoc simulator to evaluate the different versions of the proposed schedulers.

Section **??** reviews some proposals based on backfilling. In Section 3, we describe the target architecture considered, while Section 4 introduces the heuristics designed to compute the job priorities. These heuristics are described in sections 5 and 6. Section 7 shows experimental results. Finally, Section 8 describes conclusions and future works.

2. Related Work

First Come First Served (FCFS) is one of the simplest approach to job scheduling [9]. FCFS schedules jobs according to their submission order and checks the availability of the resources required by each job. If all the resources required by a job J are available, J is immediately scheduled for the execution, otherwise it is queued. Every job submitted while J is waiting for the execution is queued, even if the resources it requires are available. Despite its simplicity, this approach presents several advantages. FCFS does not require an estimation of job execution times and their implementation is straightforward. Furthermore, it guarantees that the response time of a job J, i.e. the time elapsed between the submission time of the job and its termination time, does not depend on the execution times of the jobs submitted later. On the other hand, this fairness property can imply a low utilization of the system resources, because a submitted job cannot be executed until previous submitted jobs are scheduled.

The main goal of the *backfilling approach* is to improve FCFS by increasing the utilization of the system resources and by decreasing the average waiting time of the job in the queue of the scheduler [10]. Different variants of the basic backfilling approach have been proposed.

The *Conservative Backfilling* approach allows each job to reserve the resources it needs, when it is inserted into the job queue [10]. A job may be executed before those previously submitted, if its execution does not violate the reservations made by such jobs. This strategy improves system usage by allowing jobs requiring a few available resources for a short time to overtake longer jobs in the queue. This way, the order of submission may be violated only if overtaking jobs do not delay the execution of jobs submitted earlier.

In a popular variant of backfilling, the *EASY (Extensible Argonne Scheduling system)* scheduler [3] [5] [1], developed for the IBM SP2 supercomputer, only the first job in the submission queue is allowed to reserve the resources it needs.

This approach is more "aggressive" because it increases resource utilization, even if jobs could be delayed by others submitted later.

Most backfilling strategies consider jobs candidate both for execution and for backfilling according to a FCFS strategy. An alternative solution is introduced in *Flexible Backfilling*. Here, jobs are prioritized according to some policy. In [6] a backfilling solution combines three kind of priorities, an administrative, a user and a scheduler priority. The first two priority classes give to the administrators and to the users respectively, the possibility to favor a class of jobs. The scheduler priority is introduced to guarantee that no job is starved.

Currently, several of these algorithms are exploited in commercial and open source job schedulers [8], such as Maui scheduler [8] [4], and Portable Batch System [11]. However, none of these schedulers deal with an entire range of system constraints and user requirements.

3.   The System Model

The target architecture considered in this paper is a large computational farm, where each machine may be mono-processor or multi-processor. Each machine is characterized by its computational power and executes jobs using the Space-Sharing (SS) policy. In SS, the set of processors in a machine is partitioned and each partition is assigned to the exclusive use of a job. All the jobs are considered not preemptable.

Even if the proposed backfilling algorithms do not look for the best matching among jobs and machines, the machines of the farm are ordered according to their computational power in order to exploit the most powerful first. This strategy does not balance the computational load, but favors the response time of the jobs. We suppose that a set of software licenses may be activated on the machines of the computational farm. Each license may be activated on a subset of the machines of the computational farm, for instance, because the license requires a specific operating system or a specific CPU. Furthermore, the number of software licenses of a specific type is generally smaller than the number of machines on which they may be activated. These are *floating* licenses because they are activated on the proper machines according to the job requests. On the other hand, *non-floating* licenses are permanently bound on a specific machine, and they can be considered like any other attributes characterizing that machine. Each job requires a set of software licenses for its execution and may be executed only on the subset of machines where all the required licenses may be activated. Each submitted job is characterized by its estimated execution time and may specify a deadline for its execution.

4. Heuristics

This section defines a set of heuristics to assign priorities to submitted jobs. The main goal of this assignment is to fulfill a set of users and system administrator QoS requirements. Users may require, for instance, the compliance with job deadlines, while the goal of the system administrator is to optimize the use of the system resources. The value of the priority $P(J)$ assigned to each job J is the weighted sum of the values computed by each heuristics. This value may be dynamically modified at each scheduling session. We have defined the following heuristics: *Minimal Requirements, Aging, Deadline, Licenses,* and *Response*.

The Minimal Requirements heuristics fixes the associations among jobs and machines. It selects a set of machines that has the computational requirements suitable to perform a job. In our study, we considered only the following requirements: number of processors and sw licenses activable on a machine.

The goal of the Aging heuristics is to avoid job starvation. For this reason higher scores are assigned to those jobs, which have been present in the queue for a longer time. The value of the priority assigned to job J is increased as follow:

$$
\begin{aligned}
P(J)+ &= age\text{-}factor \cdot age(J) \\
age(J) &= wall\text{-}clock - submit(J)
\end{aligned}
\tag{1}
$$

where $age\text{-}factor$ is a multiplicative factor set by an administrator according to the adopted system management policies, $wall\text{-}clock$ is the value of the system wall-clock when the heuristics is computed, and $submit(J)$ is the time when the job is submitted to the scheduler.

The main goal of the Deadline heuristics is to maximize the number of jobs, which terminates their execution within their deadline. It requires a job estimation execution time in order to evaluate its completion times, with respect to the current wall-clock. The heuristics assigns a minimal value to any job whose deadline is far from its estimated termination time. When the distance between the completion time and the deadline is smaller than a threshold value, the score assigned to the job is increased in inverse proportion with respect to the distance. The threshold value may be tuned according to the importance assigned by the scheduler to this heuristics. Finally, if the job goes over its deadline before it is scheduled, its score is set to 0. As said before, a job is scheduled on the first available most powerful machine. Since, jobs with a closer deadline receive higher priority, this strategy should improve the number of jobs executed within their deadline. Let $ex\text{-}execution(J)$ be the estimated execution time of job J, and $dline(J)$ the deadline for the execution of J. Let us define

$$
\begin{aligned}
t_e(J) &= ex\text{-}execution(J) + wall\text{-}clock \\
over\text{-}ex\text{-}t(J) &= k \cdot ex\text{-}execution(J) \quad \textbf{with } k > 1 \\
t_s(J) &= dline(J) - over\text{-}ex\text{-}t(J) \\
\alpha(J) &= (max - min)/over\text{-}ex\text{-}t(J)
\end{aligned}
\tag{2}
$$

where $t_e(J)$ denotes the job estimated termination time with respect to the current wall-clock, $over\text{-}ex\text{-}t(J)$ denotes an overestimation of the estimated execution time of job J, and $t_s(J)$ denotes the time corresponding to the threshold value of the distance from the deadline. $\alpha(J)$ is the growing factor computed as the ratio between the predefined range of assignable scores and $over\text{-}ex\text{-}t(J)$. The value $P(J)$ is increased by the Deadline heuristics according to the following formula:

$$
P(J) + = \begin{cases}
min & \textbf{if } t_e(J) < t_s(J) \\
min + \alpha(J) \cdot (t_e(J) - t_s(J)) & \textbf{if } t_s(J) \le t_e(J) \le dline(J) \\
0 & \textbf{if } t_e(J) > dline(J)
\end{cases}
$$

The Licenses heuristics assigns a higher score to jobs requiring a larger amount of critical resources. The rationale is that when these jobs end their execution, a set of licenses may become non critical and the scheduler is able to compute more flexible scheduling plans. Let us define

$$
\begin{aligned}
\rho(l) &= requests(l)/total(l) \\
l_c(J) &= \{l \in \textbf{\textit{licenses required by J}} : \rho(l) > 1\} \\
l_{\bar{c}}(J) &= \{l \in \textbf{\textit{licenses required by J}} : \rho(l) \le 1\}
\end{aligned}
\tag{3}
$$

$P(J)$ is increased according to this formula:

$$
P(J) + = \sum_{l \in l_{\bar{c}}} \rho(l) + d \cdot \sum_{l \in l_c} \rho(l)
$$

where $d = max\{|\cup_{\forall J}\, l_{\bar{c}}(J)|, 1\}$.

Eventually, the Wait Minimization heuristics favors jobs with the shortest estimated execution time. The rationale is that shorter jobs are executed as soon as possible in order to release the resources they have reserved and to improve the average waiting time of the jobs in the scheduling queue. Let $priority\text{-}boost\text{-}value$ be the factor set by an administrator according to system management policies and $min\text{-}ex\text{-}t = min\{ex\text{-}execution(J) : J \in queue\}$, the value of $P(J)$ is increased by the heuristics as follows:

$$
P(J) + = priority\text{-}boost\text{-}value \cdot \frac{min\text{-}ex\text{-}t}{ex\text{-}execution(J)}
$$

5. The BF-UNMOD Scheduler

BF-UNMOD implements a Flexible Backfilling strategy by assigning the highest priority to the first job in the queue, and by ordering the remaining jobs according to the priority assigned by the heuristics introduced in the previous section. The first job of the queue preserves the highest priority until its execution starts, while the rest of the queue is reordered at each scheduling event. Like Easy Backfilling, BF-UNMOD adopts an "aggressive" strategy by enabling reservations for the first job in the queue only. The algorithm exploits priorities to improve job QoS and efficiency in the usage of the system resources. For instance, the priority of jobs approaching their deadline is increased at each scheduling session. By increasing the priority of jobs exploiting critical licenses, *BF-UNMOD* increases efficiency.

6. The BF-MOD Scheduler

BF-MOD differs from BF-UNMOD because it preserves the reservation until a job with a higher priority is submitted. When a job J reaches the first position within the queue, it is allowed to reserve the resources it needs. Further, jobs are ordered according to their priority and they can be used for backfilling. At the next scheduling event, the reservation made by J is preserved if and only if BF-MOD assigns the highest priority to J. Otherwise, another job with the highest priority is allowed to reserve resources. Suppose, for instance, that a job with a forthcoming deadline is submitted. BF-MOD schedules this job as soon as possible by canceling the reservations of the first job in the queue at the next scheduling event. On the other way, the prediction of the starting execution time of a job is more difficult. A simple way to avoid job starvation is to increase the weight computed by the Aging heuristics.

7. Experimental Results

In this section, we present the evaluation conducted to investigate the effectiveness of the scheduling solutions carried out by the proposed schedulers. The evaluation was conducted by simulations using different streams of jobs, which inter-arrival times are generated according to a negative exponential distribution with a different parameter. To conduct our evaluation we developed an event driven ad-hoc simulator. For each simulation, we randomly generated a stream of jobs, a set of licenses and a set of machines whose parameters were generated according to a uniform distribution in the ranges:

- Job Estimated execution time [500 ÷ 3000].

- Job Deadline Margin [30 ÷ 250].

- Number CPUs [1 ÷ 8] required by a job or available on a machine.

- License Ratio [50% ÷ 70%] is the maximum number of concurrently usable copies of a sw license.

- License Suitability [90%] is the probability that a sw license is usable on a machine.

- License Needs [30%] is the probability that a job needs a sw license.

- Number of jobs without deadline 30%.

Tests were conducted by simulating a cluster of 100 machines, 20 sw licenses, 1000 jobs, and using five job streams generated with average job inter-arrival time fixed equal to 4, 6, 12, 24 and 48 simulator time unit. Each stream leads to a different system workload (computed as the sum of the number of jobs ready to be executed and the number of the jobs in execution), through a simulation run. The closer job inter-arrival time is, the higher the contention in the system is. To obtain stable values each simulation was repeated 20 times with different job attributes values. To evaluate the schedules carried out by BF-MOD and BF-UNMOD, we have considered the following metrics:

- *System Usage.* This measures the efficiency of the system, and it is defined as follows:

$$System\text{-}Usage = \frac{\sharp CPU\text{-}in\text{-}use}{min(\sharp total\text{-}CPUs, \sharp jobs\text{-}in\text{-}system)}$$

   where $\sharp CPU\text{-}in\text{-}use$ is the number of active CPUs, $\sharp total\text{-}CPUs$ is the available total number of CPUs, and $\sharp jobs\text{-}in\text{-}system$ sums the number of waiting jobs and those in execution.

- *License Usage.* This measures the efficient exploitation of the sw licenses. It is computed as the *System Usage* metric, in which $\sharp CPU\text{-}in\text{-}use$ is replaced with $\sharp Licenses\text{-}in\text{-}use$, $\sharp total\text{-}CPUs$ with $\sharp available\text{-}Licenses$ and $\sharp jobs\text{-}in\text{-}system$ with $\sharp licenses\text{-}requested\text{-}by\text{-}jobs$.

- *Out Deadline.* This measures the number of jobs executed without respecting their deadline. This does not include jobs, which must not be executed within a given deadline.

- *Slow Down.* This metric is the Average of the Slow Down of the analyzed jobs ($E[SlowDown(J)]$). It shows how the system load delays the execution of jobs, it is computed according to the following expressions:

   - $SlowDown(J) = \frac{Tw_J + Texec_J}{Texec_J}$
   - $SlowDown = E[SlowDown(J)]$

where $SlowDown(J)$ is the Slow Down of the job J, Tw_J is the time spent by J in queue, and $Texec_J$ is the execution time of J.

We have compared BF-MOD and BF-UNMOD with FCFS and BF-FCFS, which is an implementation of *EASY* backfilling. The implementation of these versions of backfilling differ with respect to classical algorithms because of the target architecture which is a heterogeneous one, rather than a homogeneous multiprocessor machine. As a consequence, jobs considered by our algorithms may require different sw/hw resources, like licenses. The original backfilling algorithms have been modified to consider all these resources when defining a scheduling plan.

In Figures 1, 2 and 3, the results obtained for the different strategies with respect to the metrics previously defined are compared. Figure 1 shows the percentage of the jobs executed do not respecting their deadline. It can be seen that BF-MOD and BF-UNMOD obtain better results in each test. When the available computational power is able to maintain low the system contention (i.e. for 24, 48 average job inter-arrival times), the use of backfilling technique leads to a higher system usage, which permits to improve the percentage of the jobs that are executed respecting their deadline. On the other hand, when the system contention is higher (i.e. for 4, 6, 12 average job inter-arrival times) the exploitation of the job priority leads to better results. Figure 2 shows the percentage of system usage. It can be seen that the backfilling technique leads to a better system usage, in particular when the system contention is higher.

Figure 3 shows the slow down trend through simulation runs. It can be seen that the backfilling technique is able to drastically reduce the average job waiting time.

Table 1 shows the percentage of both the sw license usage and the number of jobs executed out of their deadline, by changing the License Ratio parameter.

The first part of Table 1 shows that to assign higher priorities to jobs requiring a higher number of critical sw licenses leads to an improvement only when the sw licenses contention is high. When the sw licenses contention decreases the proposed schedulers lead to worse results. This occurs because jobs requiring a fewer number of critical licenses, but with a closer deadline, receive higher priorities delaying the execution of jobs requiring a higher number of sw licenses but with a far deadline.

The second part of Table 1 shows that, when the contention on sw license increases, the scheduler obtains a higher number of jobs executed respecting their deadlines, by changing the reservation for the first queued job at each scheduling event.

The experimental results show the applicability of the proposed strategy. Both BF-UNMOD and BF-MOD outperforms FCFS and BF-FCFS in terms of system usage and number of jobs that are executed respecting their deadline.

% License Usage				
License Ratio	FCFS	BF fcfs	BF unmod	BF mod
30%-50%	55.7	78.5	80.5	79.7
40%-60%	52.1	76.1	75.5	76.3
50%-70%	49.5	74.8	72.2	72.4
% Tardily Jobs				
License Ratio	FCFS	BF fcfs	BF unmod	BF mod
30%-50%	95.6	78.9	74.5	73.5
40%-60%	95.5	74.8	69.4	69.0
50%-70%	95.5	74.6	66.2	66.2

Table 1.   Percentage of used licenses and relative percentage of the jobs executed that do not respect their deadline.

The differences are considerable for each analyzed job inter-arrival times. In case of high inter-arrival times, i.e. when the scheduling phase is less critical, BF-FCFS shows a performance similar to our proposed strategies. BF-UNMOD and BF-MOD do not improve the slow down over BF-FCFS, which does a good scheduling plan w.r.t. standard FCFS. In the analyzed cases, BF-UNMOD and BF-MOD behaves in the same way. This means that the simpler approach followed by BF-UNMOD is sufficient for the task at end. We are investigating this issue.

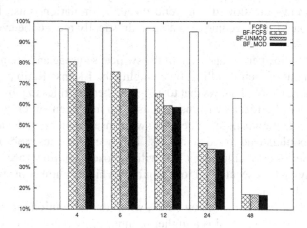

Figure 1.   Percentage of the jobs executed that do not respect their deadline varying the job inter-arrival time.

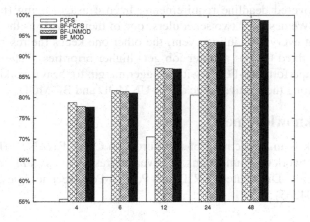

Figure 2. Percentage of used system hw resources varying the job inter-arrival time.

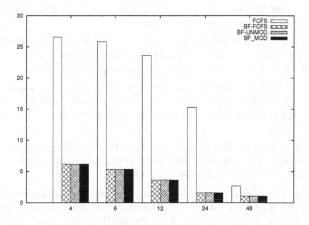

Figure 3. Slow Down trend varying the job inter-arrival time.

8. Conclusion and Future Work

In this work, we presented a set of extensions to the Backfilling Scheduling algorithm, designed to allow scheduling over heterogeneous resources. Our

BF-MOD and BF-UNMOD strategies extend Flexible Backfilling, by utilizing a variety of heuristics to re-assign priorities to queued jobs. Our proposed heuristics covered deadline requirements, license usage, aging (to prevent starvation). We designed two schedulers: one of them reassigns the priorities of all jobs at every scheduling event, the other one keeps the reservation of the first job fixed (unless another job gets higher priorities). The proposed strategies outperform BF-FCFS, with a bigger margin for heavy workloads. We are investigating the relative value of BF-UNMOD and BF-MOD.

9.   Acknowledgment

This work is in the activity of the European CoreGRID NoE (European Research Network on Foundations, Software Infrastructures and Applications for Large Scale, Distributed, GRID and Peer-to-Peer Technologies, contract IST-2002-004265)

References

[1] D. Talby, D.G. Feitelson, *"Supporting Priorities and Improving Utilization of the IBM SP using slack based backfilling"*, in 13-th Parallel Processing Symposium,pp. 513-517, April 1999.

[2] D. Tsafrir, Y. Etsion, D.G. Feitelson, *"Backfilling Using System-Generated Predictions Rather than User Runtime Estimates"*, IEEE Transactions on Parallel and Distributed Systems, vol.18, n. 6, pp. 789-803, June 2006.

[3] D. Lifka, *"The ANL/IBM SP scheduling system"*, in 1st Workshop on Job Scheduling Strategies for Parallel Processing (JSSPP), D.G. Feitelson and L. Rudolph (eds.), pp. 295-303, Springer-Verlag, Apr 1995. Lect. Notes Comput. Sci. vol. 949.

[4] D. Jackson, Q. Snell, and M. Clement, *"Core algorithms of the Maui scheduler"*, in 7th Workshop on Job Scheduling Strategies for Parallel Processing (JSSPP), D.G. Feitelson and L. Rudolph (eds.), pp. 87-102, Springer-Verlag, Jun 2001. Lect. Notes Comput. Sci. vol. 2221.

[5] A.W. Mu'alem and D.G. Feitelson, *"Utilization, Predictability, Workloads and User Runtime Estimates in Scheduling the IBM SP2 with Backfilling"*, IEEE Trans. Parallel and Distributed Systems 12(6), pp. 529-543, Jun 2001.

[6] S-H. Chiang, A. Arpaci-Dusseau, M.K. Vernon, *"The impact of more accurate requested runtimes on production job scheduling performance"*, in Job Scheduling Strategies for Parallel Processing, D.G. Feitelson, L. Rudolph, and U. Schwiegelshohn (eds.), pp. 103-127, Springer Verlag, LNCS, vol. 2537, 2002.

[7] I. Foster, C. Kesselman, *"The Grid: Blueprint for a new Computing Infrastructure"*, (2nd edition), Morgan Kaufmann Publishers, 1999.

[8] Y. Etsion, D. Tsafrir, *"A Short Survey of Commercial Cluster Batch Schedulers"*, Technical Report 2005-13, School of Computer Science and Engineering, The Hebrew University of Jerusalem, May 2005.

[9] U. Schwiegelshohn and R. Yahyapour, *"Analysis of first-come-first-serve parallel job scheduling"*, in SODA '98: Proceedings of the ninth annual ACM-SIAM symposium on

Discrete algorithms, Philadelphia, PA, USA, 1998. Society for Industrial and Applied Mathematics.

[10] D.G. Feitelson, L. Rudolph, and U. Schwiegelshohn, *"Parallel job scheduling - a status report"*, June 2004.

[11] R. Henderson and D. Tweten. *"Portable batch system: External reference specification"*, Technical report, NASA Ames Research Center, 1996.

III

DEVELOPMENT AND RUNTIME
ENVIRONMENTS

COMPONENT-BASED DEVELOPMENT ENVIRONMENT FOR GRID SYSTEMS: DESIGN AND IMPLEMENTATION *

Artie Basukoski, Vladimir Getov, Jeyarajan Thiyagalingam, Stavros Isaiadis
Harrow School of Computer Science
University of Westminster
Watford Road, Northwick Park
Harrow, London HA1 3TP, U.K.
A.Basukoski02@westminster.ac.uk
V.S.Getov@westminster.ac.uk
T.Jeyarajan@westminster.ac.uk
S.Isaiadis@westminster.ac.uk

Abstract   Component-oriented development is a software design method which enables users to build large scale Grid systems by integrating independent and possibly distributed software modules (components), via well defined interfaces, into higher level components. The main benefit from such an approach is improved productivity. Firstly, due to abstracting away network level functionalities, thus reducing the technical demands on the developer. Secondly, by combining components into higher level components, component libraries can be built up incrementally and made available for reuse. In this paper, we share our initial experiences in designing and developing an integrated development environment for Grids to support component-oriented development, deployment, monitoring, and steering of large-scale Grid applications. The development platform, which is tightly integrated with Eclipse software framework, was designed to empower the developer with all the tools necessary to compose, deploy, monitor, and steer Grid applications. We also discuss the overall functionality, design aspects, and initial implementation issues.

Keywords: component-oriented development, grid platform, integrated development environment, eclipse

---

*This research work has been partially supported by the GridCOMP and CoreGRID projects funded by the European Commission.

1.   Introduction

Grid systems have become tightly integrated as an indispensable part of the computing community for solving problems in different domains. Computational Grids offer remarkable benefits for solving a given problem, especially in connection with performance and resources. Although the main focus is about the runtime performance, the actual investment in terms of time includes both the execution time and the time for software development. This implies that the development experience has a direct impact on the "time-to-solution" cycle.

The software development can be simplified by following a component-oriented paradigm [2], where faster development is achieved through higher levels of abstraction. Although there exists substantial amount of ground work in facilitating the design and the utilisation of modern Grid systems, rarely do any of them offer a unified and integrated solution with the support of full-fledged component-oriented development. It has been recognized, however, that component technologies and their associated tools become very attractive for building complex Grid applications [8]. Indeed, when constructing distributed programs from separate software components, the ability for rapid composition and the support for dynamic properties at runtime may bring substantial reductions to the "time-to-solution" cycle.

In this paper, we discuss our initial experiences in developing a component-based Grid integrated development environment (GIDE). The environment is designed based on the model-driven approach using standard software tools for both development and integration within the Eclipse framework [4]. This essentially means that the platform will be hosted as part of the Eclipse framework, enabling developers to leverage the benefits of both the Eclipse and GIDE environments.

Our Grid IDE offers extensive support for component-oriented development and for post-development functionalities covering deployment, monitoring, and steering. In essence, the environment offers full support for different user groups of Grid – developers, application users and data-centre operators. In supporting the development, we embrace the Grid Component Model (GCM) [14], which, unlike other component models, truly supports various aspects of Grids, in terms of programming – heterogeneity and dynamicity.

The paper is organized as follows: Section 2 provides an overview of related work while Section 3 discusses requirements arising from different user groups. The architectural design of the GIDE is presented in Section 4. Finally, Section 5 concludes outlining some directions for future work.

2. Related Work

Providing support for Grid applications has been a major focus of many different projects. However, notable differences exist based on the target user group being addressed.

Friese et al. [6] discuss a set of Eclipse-based development tools for Grids, based on the model-driven approach. Their approach is to support the development through Unified Modelling by providing a well separated model mapping layer. In essence, their approach relies on two different layers where the top-level layer provides the model information while the underlying layer provides the correct mapping for the underlying platform. Their tool set covers the automation of this mapping between the layers. Once developed through the appropriate model, applications can be monitored, deployed and maintained through the tool set. This is in contrast to our approach, where we rely on a well-specified Grid component model and a strict software engineering approach. Further, although both their work and our work rely on the Eclipse platform for providing rich functionality, our work is more user friendly and more developer-oriented through permitting visual composition of applications. However, the target user group covers the same group as ours.

The Grid Engine (GriDE) and sub projects thereof from Sun Microsystems [15] provide substantial support for development. This, however, in contrast to our work, is entirely targeted towards work-flow based applications without any explicit notion of components. The underlying platform is Netbeans [11].

The Web Tools Platform project [16] of Eclipse also aims at providing support for Grid applications from within Eclipse. However, the main support is through wizards for creating Java web services or variants without any clear support for Grid-specific issues.

The g-eclipse [7] project provides an integrated workbench in a similar manner to us. Its main focus is on what we refer to as steering and provides tools for monitoring Grid resources, job creation, deployment and inspection. There is however, no support for graphical composition.

In addition to all these, there are other projects that [9, 3] offer support for developing Grid applications. However, it is not uncommon to see that the majority of them do not offer well-specified and clear support for any Grid-specific component models.

3. An Overview of Requirements

The Grid IDE is aimed at supporting a number of different user groups. We can classify the user groups as follows:

Application Developers: Application developers require support for developing Grid applications through graphical composition as well as having to support source-code based development. This approach aligns with industrial efforts in building applications through graphical composition [4]. However, providing support for developing Grid applications poses additional requirements, including support for Grid component models and composite components, and the complexities of deploying these components over distributed systems. Additional tools are necessary to enable deployment, monitoring of both component status and resource, and steering of components to maximise resource utilisation.

Application Users: The GIDE should facilitate the deployment of applications and subsequently, the monitoring of deployed applications. The monitoring process provides a set of opportunities for concerned users to monitor their running application in real-time. This functionality is also shared with the application developers who need such facilities to test the application during development.

Data Centre Operators: Data centres have high turnover rates. Hence there is a need for a design that would facilitate fast handovers and enable other operators to assist newcomers in coming to terms with the applications quickly. In order to achieve this we intend to deliver a standalone application as a Rich Client Platform (RCP) application, which provides the key functionalities that would be required by a data centre. These features are arranged within the deployment, monitoring, and steering perspectives. Also, personalisation of views should be limited as far as possible, so that a uniform design is visible to all operators in order to enhance handover and communication.

The following is an overview of the key requirements considered for each user group during the design of the GIDE.

1 Provide a Grid IDE for programmers and composers.

   The main goal is to produce an integrated programming and composing GUI. It should provide the developer with graphical tools to develop both normal code and legacy code into primitive components, as well as tools for assembling existing Grid components into larger composite components. Additional support tools should also be provided, such as tools to search for suitable components, and tools to finalise the configuration of the application before execution.

2 Provide tools for the deployment of a given Grid component configuration or application.

   The main goal is to develop a component launcher tool that enables the developer to simply point to a component and execute. Of course the launcher will need to associate a deployment descriptor with each launched component. In addition this tool must provide monitoring at execution. This can be achieved via a components execution monitor tool, capable of monitoring the runtime dynamics of set of components, such as location, memory, status, etc.

3 Provide a Grid IDE for data-centre operators.

A simplified tool for installing, monitoring and mapping necessary component code to available resources. The tool must support steering, for installing, removing, and re-installing new versions of component code. It must also provide tools for the monitoring of resources. These include usage level of resources required for execution of component based code, as well as external services the components might need to execute.

4. Design of the GIDE

Our vision for the GIDE design is to provide the developer with a single environment for the development pipeline. As can be seen from Figure 1 this includes graphical composition, deployment, monitoring and steering of grid based applications.

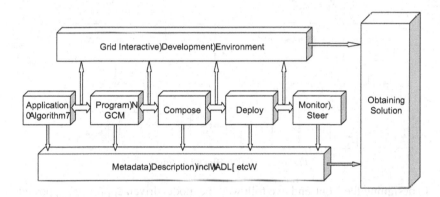

Figure 1. Component-Based Program Development Pipeline

Our philosophy is to restrict the programmer as little as possible, and enable the developer full access to all levels of the language hierarchy. By language hierarchy we mean that the developer will be capable of switching between developing graphically via a Component Model view, and coding directly in a suitable computer language using some middleware API. Given that the underlying component model for our platform is GCM we selected Java and Eclipse as the development platform. This enables the maximum integration with the ProActive library [12], which is the GRID middleware for this reference implementation. Eclipse is also well known for its extensibility via the development of suitable plugins and hence provides a seamless path from code to component model in a uniform development platform. This ensures that the target user groups can benefit from a richer set of functionalities [6].

In addition to this, deployment, monitoring and steering are also being developed as plug-ins. Some monitoring capability is already present in the Interactive Control and Debugging of Distribution (IC2D) application [1] which provides graphical monitoring of Active Objects. This needs to be extended in order to enable the deployment and monitoring of components. The main advantage of relying on this plug-in-based approach is that specific features could be activated (plugged-in) on demand. Figure 2 gives a block diagram representation of the GIDE design.

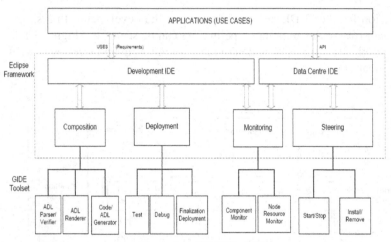

Figure 2.   GIDE Block Diagram

In designing the front-end, we followed the model driven approach supported by the Eclipse platform. In the case of composition, our model is the final output from the IDE — composition. The underlying architecture of the IDE relies on this model for the functionalities. The model is well supported by a front end based on the Graphical Editing Framework (GEF) [5] and inherited features from GEF, such as event handlers.

4.1   Composition

The composition process is enabled via a fully interactive environment. The underpinning feature which enables such interactivity is the event driven approach. Eclipse acts as the host platform to our environment. The Graphical Editing Framework, GMF-Runtime, and Eclipse facilitate handling of different events within the environment. These events are captured by the host platform through a message loop processed by the Eclipse, which are then routed to the dedicated event handlers or providers of the environment. These event handlers or providers are linked to the underlying model so that the changes are reflected upon editing

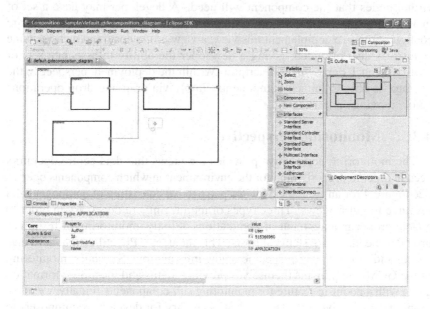

Figure 3. Component Composition Perspective

A prototype has been completed for the Composition perspective (see Figure 3). The central area focuses the user on the graphical composition view which provides the developer with a palette of available components that can be dragged and dropped on the composition canvas. Components can also be imported from existing Architecture Description Language (ADL) files and stored in the component palette. ADL files conform to the GCM-specification for describing compositions such as in [2]. Components can then be resized and moved, modified and stored. Connections between the interfaces can be drawn directly between the components using the connection tool. Composition is achieved by drawing a membrane around a group of components and defining interfaces. The developer is able to switch between the graphical view, and a view of the fractal description of the component as an ADL file. The ADL file can then be exported and used for deployment.

4.2   Deployment Perspective

This perspective consists of views needed for application deployment. The main view is of a deployment descriptor editor to map physical hosts to virtual nodes. Deployment descriptors are used to associate components with virtual nodes. Virtual nodes are included in ADL files to specify the number of virtual nodes that the component will need. A developer may have a set of these deployment descriptors to be used for deployment to different hardware configurations. To complement this view, a view of the hosts and their resource statuses is also provided, giving a developer the ability to associate sets of hosts with each deployment descriptor. Within the deployment perspective the operator is able to launch components simply via drag-and-drop operations before moving on to steering.

4.3   Monitoring Perspective

The monitoring perspective provides the views that data centre operators need in order to properly monitor the environment in which components operate. See Figure 4 for an example Monitor perspective consisting of component and resource monitor views. Three types of monitoring are necessary in order to enable proper management of applications. Firstly, monitoring of resources provides the hardware status of hosts. This includes CPU utilization, hard disk space, and other platform specific status information. Secondly, monitoring of the GCM components themselves provides status and location information along with a zoom-in feature for monitoring sub-components. Finally, we allow monitoring of active objects, which is necessary for developers/composers to debug and monitor applications during the development phase.

4.4   Steering Perspective

More useful for data centre operators, the aim of the steering perspective is to provide views to enable the operator to start, stop and relocate components. Building on the monitoring and host views, it has as its main focus a component monitoring view. This view graphically shows the components location and their status. An additional view shows the geography and resource availability of the hosts, virtual nodes, as well as the components that are running on them. Based on these views, the operator has the facility to start, stop or move components from one virtual node to another while monitoring their status to ensure correct execution.

5.   Conclusions and Future Work

We have outlined our approach in designing and implementing a component-based development environment for Grid, targeting different user groups. Our

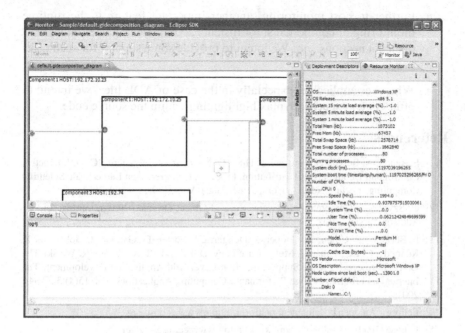

Figure 4.   Monitor Perspective

environment utilises some existing work and is based on the Eclipse framework. The environment follows both the model- and event-driven approaches and offers better support for different user groups. We have implemented a prototype where the underlying component model is GCM. The prototype provides support for composition and monitoring of component-based applications. The IDE provides seamless support for both high level graphical composition, and low level source code access of the resulting compositions. This approach facilitates debugging, and does not restrict advanced users by forcing them to solve all issues via composition for cases where it may not be the most appropriate solution.

Future work:

- While the GIDE currently supports the automatic generation of ADL files through an export facility, generating Java skeleton source files for components is an essential feature.

- There are plans to include a live composition validation feature, which will inform the developer when there is an error in the current composition through non-intrusive visual means (e.g. a red/green flag on the Composition perspective).

■ Further to host monitoring, another important feature is the runtime monitoring of components, for instance, component queue status, load, open connections, etc. We intent to provide some support for such tasks in a feature version.

■ Wherever applicable, especially in the case of ADL files, we intend to offer context-specific syntax highlighting within the source code.

References

[1] F. Baude, A. Bergel, D. Caromel, F. Huet, O. Nano, and J. Vayssiere. IC2D: Interactive Control and Debugging of Distribution, Proc. Int. Conference on Large-Scale Scientific Computing, Lecture Notes in Computer Science, Vol. 2179:193–200, 2001.

[2] C. Szyperski. Component Software: Beyond Object-Oriented Programming, 2nd ed. Addison-Wesley, 2002.

[3] F. Berman, A. Chien, K. Cooper, J. Dongarra, I. Foster, D. Gannon, L. Johnsson, K. Kennedy, C. Kesselman, J. Mellor-Crummey, D. Reed, L. Torczon, and R. Wolski The GrADS Project: Software Support for High-Level Grid Application Development. The International Journal of High Performance Computing Applications, Vol. 15(4):327–344, 2001.

[4] Eclipse - An open development platform. http://www.eclipse.org.

[5] Eclipse Graphical Editing Framework. http://www.eclipse.org/gef/

[6] T. Friese, M. Smith, and B. Freisleben. Grid Development Tools for Eclipse. Eclipse Technology eXchange Workshop eTX at ECOOP. 2006.

[7] g-Eclipse Project. http://www.geclipse.org/

[8] V. Getov, G. von Laszewski, M. Philippsen, and I. Foster. Multiparadigm Communications in Java for Grid Computing. Communications of the ACM, Vol. 44(10):118–125, 2001.

[9] GMT Project. http://www.eclipse.org/gmt/

[10] Model Driven Architecture. http://www.omg.org/mda.

[11] Netbeans IDE. http://www.netbeans.org/.

[12] ProActive Java Grid Middleware. http://www-sop.inria.fr/oasis/proactive/

[13] The Fractal Project. http://fractal.objectweb.org/

[14] Proposal for a Grid Component Model. CoreGRID Deliverable, D.PM.002, 2005.

[15] S. See, J. Song, L. Peng, A. Stoelwinder, and H.K. Neo. GriDE: A Grid-Enabled Development Environment, Proc. Int. Workshop on Grid and Cooperative Computing, Part I, Lecture Notes in Computer Science, Vol. 3032:495–502, 2003.

[16] Web Tools Platform Project. http://www.eclipse.org/webtools/

GRID-ENABLING A PROBLEM SOLVING ENVIRONMENT: IMPLEMENTATION AND EVERYDAY USE

Konstantinos Georgiou, Giorgos Kollias* and Efstratios Gallopoulos
University of Patras, CEID, 26500, Patras, Greece
[georgiu@,gdk@hpclab.,stratis@]ceid.upatras.gr

Abstract   We describe a simple, yet powerful API for accessing and using Grid resources from within Jylab, a novel, extensible scientific computing workbench consisting of a suite of open-source Java libraries scriptable through a Jython interpreter. The API provides a Java-based, Python-scriptable interactive environment and aims to simplify Grid application development and use. We demonstrate the utilization of the API in the context of an application from Internet algorithmics, specifically creating an index of crawled Web pages and using it for link-based ranking calculations (PageRank) and search queries.

Keywords: problem solving environment, internet algorithmics, PageRank, python programming language

---

*Also Research Academic Computer Technology Institute, RACTI. Partly supported by GRID-APP project of Hellenic General Secreteriat of Research and Technology (GSRT)

1.   Introduction

The Grid [10] is an important program execution platform, especially for
the scientific community. Quite abstractly it resembles batch systems of past
decades when jobs were "submitted to run" on the powerful computational
resources of the day. Today, there is a multitude of physical, software and
application resources that are available, sitting remotely and distributed, and
the Grid system mediates in their management and orchestration. Nevertheless,
it is common knowledge that a lot remains to be done to bring the level of this
mediation at a level that would be satisfactory for the average user, who is well
versed in an application area but is not an expert in the modes and languages of
interaction with the various components of the Grid.

A command line interface (CLI) to Grid services facilitates some tasks.
Often, however, researchers want to seamlessly integrate Grid services into
their working environment, which frequently consists of an interactive scripting
system (e.g. MATLAB, Mathematica, Scilab, Octave, Python). To meet these
challenges, we present a package for accessing and using the Grid infrastructure.
It is implemented in Python and uses ideas drawn from projects like Geodise
[5, 9] and Ganga [3], for building simple abstractions for the four fundamental
Grid user activities, namely Grid access, information retrieval, job submission
and data management. This package is incorporated in Jylab [6, 13], an
extensible scientific computing workbench consisting of a suite of open-source
Java libraries scriptable via a Jython interpreter. The idea is to allow Jylab
users to delegate jobs to the Grid and then collect and analyze output without
leaving the comfort of an interactive environment. We demonstrate the value
and simplicity of our package by building an application consisting of a set of
Python scripts building an index of crawled Web pages to be used for ranking
calculations (PageRank) and search queries. Some of them are scheduled for
execution on Grid resources while less demanding ones are executed locally.
In any case they are composed and coordinated under a common environment,
Jylab, thus making Grid application development a lot easier.

Our application heavily interacts with the Web, but is assigned to Grid
nodes thus saving bandwidth for network connection at user's site, where
applications are actually launched. Consists of a set of rudimentary crawlers,
packaged as Grid jobs and building link structures. These structures are merged
and expressed in adjacency matrix form to be subsequently used in ranking
calculations performed mainly on Grid nodes. Some of these calculations are
repeated for several parameter values, benefitting from the fact that "parameter-
sweep" type computations are lend themselves well for the Grid platform.

Section 2 presents the proposed API, which actually wraps CLI Grid middleware commands. We refer to this as 'Grid-enabling' the environment and
distinguish it from 'Grid-ifying', that is a method for installing it -on the fly-

to the worker node (WN) to execute the submitted job, present in Section 3. Section 4 describes our application consisting of jobs to be executed on the Grid (mainly producing crawl indices) as well as components used to analyze them locally. Section 5 discusses some of our conclusions and future plans.

2. Grid-enabling Jylab

In wrapping Grid commands we set as a goal to abstract away submitter's location, thus providing a common API for Grid interaction for users either at a user interface (UI) or at a computer connectable to a UI (e.g. laptop at home or on the move). Since we did not want to demand the installation of a separate ssh client, we integrated its functionality into Jylab in the form of Ganymed [4], which is a pure Java library implementing SSH-2 protocol. In what follows, actual API calls are used for stressing the simplicity of our approach.

A user 'enters the Grid' at the Jylab prompt, effectively generating a limited-lifetime proxy certificate, by issuing a login() command, using its virtual organisation as parameter (there is a dual command logout() for destroying his proxy). At this point a Grid object is generated in the background which inspects whether Jylab is used from a UI or not.

This decides the specific Executor object to be used for forwarding commands during the session. Both local (user at UI) and remote (user elsewhere) Executors are defined. A remote Executor executes a command over an SSH session (note that many such sessions can be multiplexed over a single SSH connection also represented in a special class). Typically three streams (stdin, stdout, stderr) are associated with the process corresponding to command execution and the Executor should capture all these and monitor data available over them. We used a multithreading approach for their inspection in order to avoid blocking the application for indefinite time intervals.

Commands typically belong to Grid CLI. Wrapping at this level, rather than at the C or Java API level gives maximum flexibility (various Grid middleware CLI wrappers can be constructed all sharing common notation; currently typical gLite commands have been wrapped) and is comparatively simple to implement: Captured streams from processes executing the commands can be used for their communication to the Jylab environment. Output streams follow certain patterns and regular expressions can isolate useful info (e.g. the ID of a submitted job).

After entering the Grid a user usually wants to get information either on jobs already executing (jobs()) or other generic info concerning Grid infrastructrure or his credentials (info()). He may also request moving files either into the Grid (upload()) or out of it (download()), removing them (remove()) or replicate some files across multiple storage elements (SEs) for enforcing a good degree of proximity of his data to actual computation node if compute element (CE) has to be chosen arbitrarily (replicate()). Also Grid file catalog (LFC) commands are wrapped (e.g. `listdir()`). A general guide is to use -if possible-function names from the corresponding standard Python os module.

Apart from functions, our Jylab Grid interface also comes with a user visible class Job, perhaps the most important of our software entities. It has methods with self-explanatory methods like `submit()`, `cancel()`, `status()`, `getOutput()`, `readFile()`; a typical use of this class is depicted in Fig. 1.

```
from jylab.grid import *
# entering the grid
login(<vo>)
# submitting a job
job = Job()
job.vo = <vo>
job.inputsandbox = ['/path/to/file1','/path/to/file2',
                    '/path/to/file3']
job.outputsandbox = ['outfile1'.'outfile2']
job.arguments = "file1 10"
job.submit()
job.status()
job.getOupout()
job.readFile("std.out")
```

Figure 1.   Using Job class

3.   Grid-ifying Jylab

As described previously, Jylab can be used as a transparent environment for accessing Grid functionality: Initiating and terminating Grid sessions, describing and submitting jobs as well as extracting information on Grid infrastructure and managing data files are seamlessly supported in Jylab through a minimal but powerful function/class API. The user keeps working in a familiar workbench abstracting Grid functions into conveniently named notations.

However a Grid job is executed at WNs and Jylab is probably not available. So one might argue that it cannot be the runtime environment for our application. In other words, when developing Grid software, Jylab should not be an option and so some of the advantages it could offer in terms of homogeneity are lost.

Fortunately, this misfortune turns to be accidental and a remedy is available: Jylab consists of open source components (typically Java libraries scriptable through Python scripts) and an emerging API organizing components' namespaces under a well defined hierarchy. So part of the solution would be a flexible repackaging of these components; then, in a preprocessing stage, a Jylab Grid job could assemble its runtime environment 'on the fly', by downloading and installing Jylab on the currently executing WN - not known beforehand. Loosely inspired by `portage` package management system, we implemented a simple abstraction of a package (module `jylabme.py`) for each component supporting at minimum the following methods:

- `wget()` locally retrieves open source archives from Web repositories.

- `adapt()` adapts the archive for Jylab (usually discarding some of its content and repackaging).

- `upload()` (copies and) registers repackaged archive with a Grid location.

- `download()` downloads component files from a Grid location.

- `install()` installs the packages -typically to a WN- usually by extracting downloaded archives.

Containing module is coded in standard Python (available at all sites) and since it actually assembles Jylab runtime environment, it should be considered as the entry point for all Jylab applications executing at Grid nodes. It imports `gridme.py` module: this is a lightweight wrapper (also coded in standard Python) of commonly used Grid commands, with names identical to the ones chosen in `jylab.grid`, however aiming at Grid-application interactions only at bootstrap time.

The application starts execution just after the assembly is complete and is typically implemented as a series of Jylab scripts. In practice bootstrap lasts < 10 secs, to be amortized by 'application proper' execution time, with archives replicated at nearby SEs. Note that neither version dependency or Jylab persistency mechanism is included in our abstraction since needed packages are considered already known at submission time and local Unix accounts at WNs are dynamically assigned to Grid users. A high-level model of this approach is depicted in Fig. 2.

4.   Applying the API: An Internet application on the Grid

In what follows we demonstrate the feasibility of running a bandwidth-costly Internet application over Grid nodes. In particular we argue that the Grid can be used for operating high-performance, on-demand crawlers, collecting and indexing specific parts of the Web. Crawled data can be used in serving search queries or drive further analysis using well established methods from Internet algorithmics. As a result, we obtain significant savings in network bandwidth and computational resources at the submitter's site: multiple crawling/indexing jobs can be submitted in parallel and costly numerical linear algebra calculations can be delegated to Grid nodes.

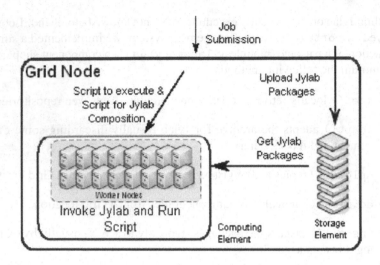

Figure 2.   A high-level view of Grid-ifying Jylab

We stress the fact that all computations are expressed in Python, often described as 'executable pseudocode' due to its flexibility. Mature Java frameworks are utilized, however without making it necessary to switch to Java coding; even Grid-interactions are wrapped in Python modules as presented earlier. The fact that only a single (interactive) syntax has to be learnt helps the practitioner in focusing on his application rather on the peculiarities of assembling heterogeneous software stacks. On the other hand, performance hotspots can always be coded and compiled in Java; note, however, that in a Grid application like ours, perhaps the most decisive bottleneck becomes the network itself, only remotely followed by the cost of crossing middleware layers, but both these factors lie well beyond ordinary user's control. Although geared towards stressing the convenience of our proposed Grid API, this application serves yet another purpose: The user not only analyzes and uses a dataset but also collects and builds it on-demand. So not only data processing but also data compilation is *personalized*.

Our application consists of two phases: Grid phase (crawling, indexing, part of data analysis; executing at Grid nodes, realized as Grid jobs) and Local phase (visualization, part of data analysis, searching; executing at user's machine).

4.1   Grid phase

The main component for the crawling/indexing phase executed at Grid nodes is Nutch. Nutch [7–8] is an open source search engine able to operate at the local filesystem, an intranet or even at the entire Web scale providing advanced crawling, indexing and searching functionality. It typically manages three data

structures, organized in separate directories under the search engine's data top
folder by default.

The *Web database* hosts link information on the Web graph being crawled;
both nodes and edges of the graph structure are included (respectively implemented by page and link entities). Each *set of segments* contains pages fetched
and indexed in a single iteration of the crawl process. Finally the *index* merges
segments' indices with duplicates deleted; it is actually the inverted index of all
the documents already retrieved. Its operation follows a well defined pattern:
A Web database is created (if not already existing) and initialized with a set of
URLs. These URLs (a fetchlist) drive crawlers (fetchers) that download content
into a segment(directory); links extracted from these pages update the Web
database and a new fetchlist is generated and assigned to fetchers to populate a
fresh segment in a generate/fetch/update iterative loop, exited only when crawl
depth is reached. Then segments are indexed and resulting indices are suitably
merged in a single index to be subsequently used in searching. This phase
mainly involves the execution of Jylab scripts, so a Jylab gridification step as
previously described is necessary; required packages are however ensured to
have already been uploaded to a neighboring SE (relative to the desirable target
CE) and so the download-install time at the WN is minimized (a few seconds).
The main part of our application follows, effectively executing

- `crawl(urls, depth)`, with `urls` a list of seed URLs and `depth` our
  crawl's depth; this function wraps Nutch functionality in a most convenient way, and

- a handful of commands for archiving crawl data produced at WN (crawl
  archive) and uploading it to a Grid storage location (lfn)

Our application can also be instructed to print timing, environment, etc information to stdout; as stdout is captured and returned to submitter, this was a very
handy monitoring tool for us (after all *our* output is safely stored at a SE by job's
finish time). Note that each such crawl/indexing job has only three parameters,
`(urls, depth, lfn)` and so many job instances of this type can be easily
generated and scheduled to Grid resources; a Nutch specific configuration file
can alternatively fine-tune many aspects of the procedure.

4.2   Local phase

Grid phase produces a crawl archive. This archive can be downloaded locally
and used in at least two scenaria. We can use Nutch's Web application, suitably
hosted in a servlet container (e.g. `apache tomcat`) to perform search queries
on the crawl archive (Fig. 3, left). The Web interface is similar to the one
offered by commercial search engines. It even has some unique features, such
as a facility explaining the score for each hit together with a ranking of the

containing document among other metadata(Fig. 3, right). Hit scores are
computed through a dot-product between document and query vectors (in a
Vector Space Model for IR) as documented e.g. in [2]. Also for a document
$boost = score * \ln(e + inlinks)$ and $score$ is PageRank-like value attained
by running LinkAnalysisTool in Nutch (by default disabled for relatively
small scale crawls like ours, $score = 1.0$). Note that ranking algorithms used
by commercial search engines are highly proprietary and accessing them is out
of the question. Searching in Jylab, however, can be performed interactively by

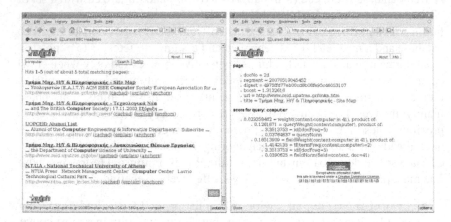

Figure 3.   Nutch search engine. The results of a query submitted to the web interface of Nutch
search engine are shown; the underlying information index has been collected by running Nutch
(crawling/indexing phase) over Grid nodes (left). Metadata and internal algorithm details for
ranking calculations; of interest to data-mining researchers (right).

means of a Nutch API. Using this facility, we also reconstructed the crawled
graph structure from Web database in a form suitable for Jung.

Jung [15] is a framework for the analysis and visualization of network data.
At minimum, it provides constructors for vertices, edges and graphs of various
types, organized in a well engineered class hierarchy. Arbitrary user data can
be attached to these objects, predicates filtering out graph structural elements
or constraining a graph composition can be defined and event handling actions
be registered. Also a collection of algorithms is included for ranking graph
elements, detecting similarity (clustering) or structural equivalence (block-
modelling) between them, calculating graph topology measures, generating
synthetic networks and transforming. It also features a visualization system
composed of layout, drawing area and renderer objects: A renderer paints
vertices and edges of a graph into a drawing area using element locations calculated by the respective layout. Various standard graph formats are supported for
importing/exporting graph data into this framework.

We have integrated Jung's visualization and ranking capabilities in a convenient interface (Fig. 4). Link structure from Grid-produced crawls can be explored interactively. Mouse clicks on nodes trigger small reports on the respective page: url, immediate neighbors and ranking scores calculated by PageRank [16, 14] and HITS [12] algorithms are produced. Such analysis could be delegated to the Grid phase for large graphs; Jung provides graph to sparse matrix converters and linear algebra algorithms can readily be applied to the resulting matrix objects [1]. Note, however, that in the specific examples presented here, the resulting graphs are small enough to be locally ranked almost instantly. Note that this integration can be implemented in less than 100 lines of Python code in Jylab! PageRank calculations in particular are packaged into functions parameterized by teleportation parameter α, permitting fast sweeps of PageRank evolution under variations of α for the intranet scale crawls of our examples.

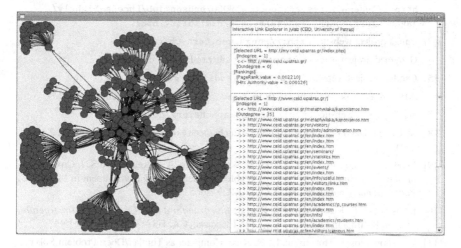

Figure 4. Integrating Jung's visualization and ranking capabilities in a convenient interface

5. Conclusions and future work

Easy to use APIs are critical for the rapid prototyping and development of Grid applications. We presented such an API tightly integrated with Jylab, an interactive scientific workbench, flexible enough to be easily deployable on Grid nodes and thus serve as the runtime platform for Grid applications (available for download at [6]). The application we described collects, indexes and analyzes Web pages using Grid resources but also provides collected data archives for subsequent local analysis and visualization. Parts of the analysis model Web data as matrix objects and can readily exploit well known numerical linear algebra algorithms. We concluded from our experiments that the Grid API contributes toward code simplicity and readability. We anticipate that it will facilitate harvesting and harnessing network and computational resources in order to create suitable Grid platform utilization scenaria. In the context of Internet algorithmics that is a major thrust of our applications research, we envisage a system in which Web accessible material could be dynamically collected, its content analyzed, and results used to steer subsequent data collection-analysis cycles, all within the Grid. User-friendly integration with existing Problem Solving Environments [11] and well established computing practices will be key features of this effort.

References

[1] Colt Java class library website. `http://dsd.lbl.gov/~hoschek/colt/`.

[2] Documentation for `org.apache.lucene.search.Similarity` class. `http://lucene.zones.apache.org:8080/hudson/job/Lucene-Nightly/javadoc/org/apache/lucene/search/Similarity.html`.

[3] Ganga project website. `http://ganga.web.cern.ch/ganga/`.

[4] Ganymed project website. `http://www.ganymed.ethz.ch/ssh2/`.

[5] Geodise project website. `http://www.geodise.org/`.

[6] Jylab project wiki site. `http://scgroup4.ceid.upatras.gr:10080/trac/`.

[7] Nutch project website. `http://lucene.apache.org/nutch/`.

[8] M. Cafarella and D. Cutting. Building Nutch: Open Source Search. *ACM Queue*, 2, April 2004.

[9] M. H. Eres, G. E. Pound, Z. Jiao, J. L. Wason, F. Xu, A. J. Keane, and S. J. Cox. Implementation and utilisation of a Grid-enabled problem solving environment in MATLAB. *Future Gener. Comput. Syst.*, 21(6):920–929, 2005.

[10] I. Foster and C. Kesselman. *The Grid 2: Blueprint for a New Computing Infrastructure*. Morgan Kaufmann Publishers Inc., San Francisco, CA, USA, 2003.

[11] E. Gallopoulos, E. Houstis, and J. R. Rice. Computer as Thinker/Doer: Problem-Solving Environments for Computational Science. *IEEE Comput. Sci. Eng.*, 1(2):11–23, 1994.

[12] J.M. Kleinberg. Authoritative Sources in a Hyperlinked Environment. *J. ACM*, 46:604–632, 1999.

[13] G. Kollias and E. Gallopoulos. Jylab: A System for Portable Scientific Computing over Distributed Platforms. In *2nd IEEE Int'l. Conf. on e-Science and Grid Computing(e-Science 2006): Session on Innovative and Collaborative Problem Solving*, Amsterdam, December 2006. IEEE.

[14] A.N. Langville and C.D. Meyer. *Google's Pagerank and Beyond: The Science of Search Engine Rankings*. Princeton University, 2006.

[15] J. O' Madadhain, D. Fisher, P. Smyth, S. White, and YB Boey. Analysis and visualization of network data using JUNG. *Journal of Statistical Software*, 2005.

[16] L. Page, S. Brin, R. Motwani, and T. Winograd. The PageRank Citation Ranking: Bringing Order to the Web. Technical report, Stanford University, 1998.

A COMPONENT-BASED INTEGRATED TOOLKIT

Enric Tejedor and Rosa M. Badia
Universitat Politecnica de Catalunya
Barcelona, Spain
etejedor@ac.upc.edu
rosab@ac.upc.edu

Thilo Kielmann
Vrije Universiteit
Amsterdam, The Netherlands
kielmann@cs.vu.nl

Vladimir Getov
University of Westminster
London, UK
V.S.Getov@westminster.ac.uk

Abstract   This paper presents the Integrated Toolkit, a framework which enables the easy development of Grid-unaware applications. While keeping the Grid transparent to the programmer, the Integrated Toolkit tries to optimize the performance of such applications by exploiting their inherent concurrency when executing them on the Grid. The Integrated Toolkit is designed to follow the Grid Component Model (GCM) and is therefore formed by several components, each one encapsulating a given functionality identified in the GRID superscalar runtime.

Currently, a first functional prototype of the Integrated Toolkit is under development. On the one hand, we have chosen ProActive as the GCM implementation and, on the other, we have used JavaGAT as a uniform interface to abstract from the underlying Grid middleware when performing job submission and file transfer operations. Thus far, we have tested our prototype with several simple applications, showing that they maintain the same behaviour as if they were executed locally and sequentially.

Keywords: Integrated Toolkit, components, Grid Component Model, Grid-unaware applications, concurrency exploitation, performance optimization.

1.   Introduction

This paper focuses on the specification and design of the *Integrated Toolkit*: a framework which enables the easy development of Grid-unaware applications (those to which the Grid is transparent but that are able to exploit its resources). The Integrated Toolkit is mainly formed by an *interface* and a *runtime*. The former should give support to different programming languages, graphical tools and portals, and should provide the application with a small set of API methods. The latter should provide the following features:

- The Grid remains as transparent as possible to the application. The user is only required to select the tasks to be executed on the Grid and to use few API methods.

- Performance optimization of the application by exploiting its inherent concurrency. The possible parallelism is checked at task level, automatically deciding which tasks can be run at every moment. The most suitable applications for the Integrated Toolkit are those with coarse-grain tasks.

- Task scheduling and resource selection taking into account task requirements and performance issues.

This paper is organized as follows. We begin by proposing a design for the Integrated Toolkit in Section 2. Then, using a simple example, we give some usage and operation details of a first Integrated Toolkit prototype in Section 3. After that, we present some preliminary tests of the prototype in Section 4. Finally, we describe some related work in Section 5 before the conclusions and future work of Section 6.

2.   A GCM-based design of the Integrated Toolkit

This document proposes an Integrated Toolkit based on the Grid Component Model (GCM) [1], a component model intended for the Grid which takes the Fractal specification [2] as reference. Therefore, the Integrated Toolkit runtime is defined as a set of Fractal components, each of them in charge of a given functionality. The design, inspired on the GRID superscalar framework [3], comprises the following components:

- *Task Analyser* (TA): receives incoming tasks and detects their precedence, building a *task dependency graph*. It implements the interface used by the application to submit tasks: when such a request arrives, it looks for data dependencies between the new task and all previous ones. When a task has all its dependencies solved, the TA sends it to the Task Scheduler.

- *Task Scheduler* (TS): decides where to execute the dependency-free tasks received from the TA. This decision is made accordingly to a certain *scheduling algorithm* and taking into account three information sources: first, the available Grid resources and their capabilities; second, a set of user-defined constraints for the task; and third, the location of the data required by the task. The scheduling strategy could also be changed on demand, thanks to the dynamic and reconfigurable features of GCM.

- *Job Manager* (JM): in charge of *job submission and monitoring*. It receives the scheduled tasks from the TS and delegates the necessary file transfers to the File Manager. When the transfers for a task are completed, it transforms the task into a Grid job in order to submit it for execution on the Grid, and then controls the proper completion of the job. It could implement some kind of fault-tolerance mechanism in response to a job failure.

- *File Manager* (FM): takes care of all the operations where files are involved, being able to work with both logical and physical files. It is a composite component which encompasses the *File Information Provider* (FIP) and the *File Transfer Manager* (FTM) components. The former gathers all information related with files: what kind of file accesses have been done, which versions of each file exist and where they are located. The latter is the component that actually transfers the files from one host to another; it also informs the FIP about the new location of files.

3. Usage and operation example of the Integrated Toolkit

Taking the design presented in Section 2 as reference, we are working on a first Integrated Toolkit prototype. Regarding the implementation choices, we took Java as the programming language and ProActive 3.2 and JavaGAT 1.6 as the base technologies.

ProActive [5] is a Java Grid middleware library for parallel and distributed computing. Among some other features, it provides an implementation of the Fractal specification with some extensions, thus contributing to the development of GCM. Hence, our Integrated Toolkit is in fact formed by ProActive components and benefits from the following GCM properties: hierarchical composition, separation between functional and non-functional interfaces, synchronous and asynchronous communications, collective interactions between components and ADL-based description of the component structure.

JavaGAT is the Java version of the Grid Application Toolkit [5], which is a generic and flexible API for accessing Grid services from application codes, portals and data management systems. The calls to the GAT API are redirected to specific adaptors which contact the Grid services, thus offering a uniform interface to numerous types of Grid middleware. Our Integrated Toolkit uses JavaGAT for job submission and file transfer operations.

The following subsections explain, through a simple example, how to write an application that uses the Integrated Toolkit and which call sequences between subcomponents take place when executing it.

3.1   Original code of the sample application

Consider a Java application which generates random numbers and cumulatively sums them (from now on, we will call it *Sum*). Figure 1 shows its main code.

```
initialize(f1);
for (int i = 0; i < 2; i++) {
    genRandom(f2);
    add(f1, f2);  // f1 <- f1 + f2
}
print(f2);
```

Figure 1.   Original code of Sum. All method parameters (f1, f2) are file names. After putting a zero value in f1 (initialize), random numbers are generated (genRandom) and then added to the accumulated sum stored in f1 (add).

3.2   Selecting the tasks and inserting API method calls

In order to make the application use the Integrated Toolkit, the programmer is only required to write a Java interface declaring the tasks that will be executed on the Grid and to use few API methods.

```
public interface SumItf {
    @MethodConstraints(operatingSystemType = "Linux")
    void genRandom(
        @ParamMetadata(type = Type.FILE, direction = Direction.OUT)
        String f
    );
    @MethodConstraints(processorArch = "Intel", processorSpeed = 1.8f)
    void add(
        @ParamMetadata(type = Type.FILE, direction = Direction.INOUT)
        String f1,
        @ParamMetadata(type = Type.FILE, direction = Direction.IN)
        String f2
    );
}
```

Figure 2.   Annotated interface for Sum

Concerning the interface, Java annotations [11] must be used to specify some metadata about the tasks. On the one hand, it is mandatory to state, for each parameter of a task, its type (currently, we only support the file type) and its direction (IN, OUT or INOUT). On the other, the programmer can also impose the constraints that a given resource must fulfil to execute a certain task (regarding, for instance, the operating system or the architectural characteristics) Figure 2 corresponds to the interface of Sum, containing the mentioned metadata.

Regarding the API, it offers methods to start and stop the Integrated Toolkit, request the execution of tasks and open files to work with them locally. Figure 3 shows the final code of Sum, resulting from the inclusion of API calls. Currently, the programmer has to deal with all these methods but, in the future, we will implement a mechanism to free (totally or partially) the application developers from that duty; for that purpose, some possible alternatives could be a source-to-source compiler, a code generation tool or a modified Java class loader.

```
initialize(f1);
IntegratedToolkit it = new IntegratedToolkitImpl("Sum");
it.startIT();
ITExecution itExe = (ITExecution)it;
for (int i = 0; i < 2; i++) {
    itExe.executeTask("genRandom", 1,
                    f2, ParamType.FILE_T, ParamDirection.OUT);
    itExe.executeTask("add", 2,
                    f1, ParamType.FILE_T, ParamDirection.INOUT,
                    f2, ParamType.FILE_T, ParamDirection.IN);
}
String finalF2 = it.openFile(f2, OpenMode.READ);
print(finalF2);
it.stopIT(true);
```

Figure 3. Code of Sum with calls to the Integrated Toolkit API

3.3 Internal processes and communications

This section describes the main internal processes of the Integrated Toolkit which are triggered when executing the Sum application, that is, what each subcomponent does, which communications take place between subcomponents and in which order.

3.3.1 Initialization. After being deployed and started, the components must be initialized. For that purpose, the Integrated Toolkit has a multicast interface which transforms a single initialization invocation on the runtime into a list of invocations and forwards them to all the subcomponents.

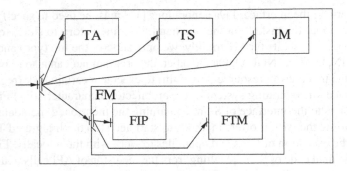

Figure 4. Initialization of the Integrated Toolkit

3.3.2   Task analysis, scheduling and job submission. When the initialization phase finishes, the task processing can begin. As said in Section 2, the TA is the component which receives task execution requests from the application. In the case of Sum, a total of 4 tasks will be issued (2 per iteration).

The TA registers the file accesses of a task with the help of the FIP, which keeps track of the file versions that are eventually created: whenever a task writes a file it creates a new version of that file, and this new version is assigned a renaming. Then, the TA discovers the dependencies between the task and all previous ones, thanks to a structure where it stores the last writer task for each file. The current Integrated Toolkit only considers file dependencies, while in future versions other kinds of data (scalars, arrays, etc.) will be taken into account.

The task dependency graph for Sum is the one depicted in Figure 5. The dependencies represented with dashed lines are automatically removed by means of the renaming technique, so that only RaW ones remain.

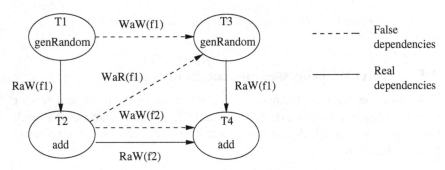

Figure 5. Task dependency graph of the Sum application

Tasks with no dependencies pass to the next step: the scheduling. According to the graph of Sum, the first suitable tasks are T1 and T3: they can be run in parallel on the Grid. When receiving these tasks from the TA, the TS decides, following a certain scheduling algorithm, the destination hosts where they will be executed. Currently only a FIFO algorithm is implemented, though more complex ones will be added in the future to try, for instance, to reduce the execution and transfer times.

Once the scheduling is done, the TS communicates its decision to the JM. For a given task, the latter requests all the necessary file transfers to the FTM, which invokes the JavaGAT API to actually perform them. When all the input files of the task are in the destination host, the JM transforms the task into a GAT job, submits it to the Grid and subscribes to its state change notifications.

3.3.3   Task completion.   Whenever a callback which informs about the end of a job is received, the JM notifies the TS of that fact. At its turn, the TS forwards the notification for the corresponding task to the TA. If the task has finished successfully, the TA removes the edges to all its successors from the graph and searches for newly dependency-free tasks to send for scheduling; otherwise, an error is thrown (see Section 3.3.6 for further details about error situations). For instance, in the case of Sum, T2 sees how all its dependencies are solved after T1 ends.

3.3.4   Opening a file.   The Integrated Toolkit interface also offers a method to work with a file on the user's local machine. A call to openFile in a given point of the application makes the API perform the following actions: first, it registers the file access by invoking the FIP; second, if the open call is for reading or appending, it requests to the TA to be notified when the last writer task of the file ends; third, also for read and append modes, it makes the last version of the file be transferred to the local host of the user by contacting the FTM; finally, it returns the file name of this version, so that the application can open the necessary I/O streams.

3.3.5   End of the application.   When the application reaches a stopIT call, the API makes it block until three events take place: first, the completion of all the tasks created until that moment; second, the transfer to the user's local host of all the result files, that is, the final version of each of the files accessed by the application; third, the deletion of all intermediate file versions, which will not be used anymore. The first event is notified by the TA, and the two last ones are triggered by the FTM.

Furthermore, the stopIT method allows to specify whether the Integrated Toolkit must finish definitely or not. In the first case, all the subcomponents are stopped, cleaned and killed, while in the second one they are just stopped, so that they can be restarted later and accept new task execution requests.

3.3.6   Error handling.   During the execution of the application, the Integrated Toolkit runtime can experience errors of different kinds: a job submission that has failed, a problem with a file transfer, an exception in some point of the code, etc. Unfortunately, managing an error produced inside the Integrated Toolkit while it is working is not a trivial issue. Since all its subcomponents are interconnected and communicate constantly, a failure in one of them could impede the overall system to work properly. The general response to such a situation should be to stop the components as quickly as possible; however, there are a couple of points that must be considered when facing an error.

On the one hand, the components that form the Integrated Toolkit cannot be stopped in any arbitrary order because they have data dependencies. A dependency between two components A and B appears when A invokes a synchronous method on B and waits for its result. The problem arises if B is stopped before it can serve the request from A; in that case, A would remain blocked waiting for the result of the call and it could never serve the stop control request[1].

If one invokes the stop method of the Integrated Toolkit life-cycle controller (stopFc, see [2]) the call is forwarded to all the hierarchy of components in an *a priori* unknown order. Nevertheless, the synchronous calls between subcomponents lead to the dependencies shown in Figure 6, and such dependencies impose a stop order that must be respected; otherwise, we could experience a deadlock. One solution could be to redefine the Integrated Toolkit life-cycle controller to ensure that the subcomponents are stopped in an adequate order, specifically the following one: TA, TS, JM, FTM, FIP.

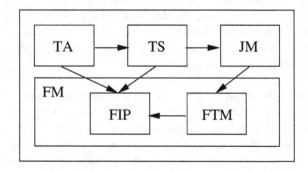

Figure 6.   Data dependencies between Integrated Toolkit subcomponents

On the other hand, it is not enough to stop the subcomponents when an error appears, because that suspends their internal communications but does not

---

[1]This theoretical behaviour has only been checked with ProActive components, therefore it might differ for other implementations of the Fractal/GCM model.

finish the ongoing operations on the Grid. Consequently, a cleaning process must begin after stopping the subcomponents, and it includes two main actions: first, canceling the submitted jobs and unregistering for their state notifications; second, avoiding the beginning of new transfers (the JavaGAT API does not allow to cancel a transfer in progress[2]). This postprocessing can be done by means of a custom controller, contacted by the life-cycle controller when the component is stopped.

The methodology to face an error that has been explained above is probably the best one, but currently it cannot be applied efficiently in practice. To stop the components as fast as possible, the stopFc invocation should be placed in the head of each subcomponent request queue, so that it could be served next. However, ProActive does not allow to give higher priority to control requests for the time being; it is certainly possible to examine the whole queue each time a request is going to be served (searching for an eventual stop call), but that would clearly lead to a poor performance. Therefore, trying to stop the Integrated Toolkit while in operation would take a while, and during this time the system is doing useless work and could behave unpredictably.

The currently adopted solution aims to minimize the time between the error and the finalization of the system, while informing the user of what has exactly happened. Whenever an abnormal situation occurs, the component that detects it tells the Integrated Toolkit API about it. Then, the API invokes a multicast immediate service[3] that is forwarded to every component and that performs the necessary cleanup. After that, without actually stopping the components, a kill method is invoked on the Integrated Toolkit in order to destroy all the component structure. Lastly, the error message is returned to the user.

4. Preliminary tests

Our prototype is still in the test phase. Thus far, some preliminary tests have been performed. The objective of these tests was not to obtain performance measures, but to show that applications which benefit from the Integrated Toolkit maintain the same behaviour as if they were executed locally and sequentially. Concerning the GAT adaptors, we used the local, Globus Pre-WS and SSH ones for job submission, and the local, GridFTP and SSH ones for file transfer.

Following subsections describe some of the chosen applications and which functionalities of the Integrated Toolkit we wanted to test in each one.

---

[2]The JavaGAT API methods to perform file transfers are synchronous and block the thread that invokes them until the transfer is finished.

[3]ProActive immediate services permit to run a method of a component server interface without having to wait in the request queue. The execution takes place immediately and in parallel with the normal services of the component.

4.1   Matrix multiplication

The *Matmul* application multiplies two matrices. It takes as input the matrices divided in blocks, which are themselves smaller matrices of doubles. Tasks work with blocks, which are stored in files. In our tests, we varied both the number of blocks of the input matrices and the number of elements in each block. More blocks implies more tasks, and larger blocks means tasks which are more coarse-grained.

We began with Matmul to perform a general and simple test of the Integrated Toolkit. The results showed that its main functionalities were performing well. The following points were checked: component deployment, start and stop; task creation, analysis and scheduling; file version management and transfer; job submission and monitoring.

4.2   Cholesky decomposition

The *Cholesky* application decomposes a symmetric positive-definite matrix (A) into a lower triangular matrix (L) and its transpose (U). As Matmul, all matrices are divided in blocks, which are taken by tasks as their unit of work.

With Cholesky we wanted to take the task analysis and scheduling tests a step further. Concerning the analysis, Cholesky generates a highly connected dependency graph, which represents a much more challenging test for the TA. Regarding the scheduling, there are five types of task (that is, five different methods to execute remotely) on which to impose particular constraints, and that allows to check if they are actually scheduled on the resource/s whose capabilities match their constraints.

The results were satisfactory, demonstrating that the Integrated Toolkit is able to manage applications with complex dependencies and to schedule their tasks respecting the required constraints.

4.3   Counter increment

The Counter application performs several increments on the integer value contained in a file. Some of the increments are spawned as remote tasks, and some of them are executed locally.

The objective of this application was to test the openFile method, since it must be called before a local increment in order to get the right file version. The method was invoked alternatively with the write-only access mode to replace the value of the counter and with the read-write one to increment it; in the case of the latter, the file needs to be transferred to the user's local host, while with the former it is not necessary thanks to the renaming technique.

The results showed that the counter was properly incremented both in the local and remote ways, and its final value was the expected one.

5. Related work

Other approaches that enable the programming of parallel applications for computational Grids are Satin, HOCs and ASSIST. Satin [6] is a Java based programming model for the Grid which allows to explicitly express divide-and-conquer parallelism. It uses marker interfaces to indicate that certain method invocations need to be considered for potentially parallel (spawned) execution. Moreover, synchronization is also explicitly marked to wait for the results of an invocation. HOCs [7] is a component-oriented approach based on a master-worker schema. Higher-Order Components (HOCs) express recurring patterns of parallelism that are provided to the user as program building blocks, pre-packaged with distributed implementations. ASSIST [8] is a programming environment aimed at providing parallel programmers with user-friendly, efficient, portable, fast ways of implementing parallel applications. It includes a skeleton based parallel programming language and a set of compiling tools and runtime libraries.

Besides, there exist several systems that permit workflow definition and execution on Grids, for instance P-GRADE and SEGL. P-GRADE [9] is a general purpose, workflow-oriented computational Grid portal. It offers a high-level, graphical workflow development system and an execution environment for various Grids. SEGL [10] allows to define complex workflows which can be executed in a Grid environment, and supports the dynamic generation of parameter sets. It also makes possible the execution of sets of independent tasks of interdependent jobs which can turn either synchronously or asynchronously on heterogeneous systems.

6. Conclusions and future work

We have proposed a componentised design of the Integrated Toolkit, a framework which facilitates the development of Grid-unaware applications and which can also provide Grid-aware ones with some functionalities. After that, we have presented a first implementation of the Integrated Toolkit through an example, explaining how to write a simple application that uses the Integrated Toolkit and which internal processes are triggered in order to execute it. Finally, we have shown that the Integrated Toolkit prototype has been able to run several sample applications on the Grid.

Furthermore, thanks to the componentised nature of the design presented in Section 2, we believe that the Integrated Toolkit could also offer an alternative to develop Grid-aware applications, which could use the runtime as a whole or deploy solely specific subcomponents. For instance, a programmer interested in adding a scheduling functionality to an application could choose to deploy only the TS subcomponent, binding its interfaces to the ones of the application components.

Forthcoming phases of this project will:

- Extend and improve the functionalities of the Integrated Toolkit subcomponents. Some of the envisaged features are: fault-tolerance mechanisms for job submission and file transfer, new scheduling algorithms, checkpointing of tasks to avoid resuming the application from scratch in case of failure, dependency analysis which takes into account different data types (not only files but also scalars and arrays), identification of the critical path in the task dependency graph, and so on.

- Study the possible bottlenecks in our component design. Synchronous calls cause waiting times that could be partly avoided if the data dependencies are minimized. Moreover, too frequent communications between components could also degrade the performance of the system.

- Implement controllers to steer the behaviour of the Integrated Toolkit. These controllers could serve to modify certain parameters (such as the scheduling algorithm used), change the overall structure (add/remove/ bind/unbind components), manage the persistence of the application (in relation to the checkpointing and fault recovery mechanism), etc.

References

[1] Proposals for a Grid Component Model, CoreGRID Deliverable D.PM.02, 2006.

[2] Fractal specification, http://fractal.objectweb.org/specification/index.html

[3] R. M. Badia, Jesús Labarta, Raul Sirvent, Josep M. Perez, Jose M. Cela and Rogeli Grima. *Programming Grid Applications with GRID superscalar*. Journal of GRID Computing, Vol. 1 Issue 2. Pages: 151-170, June 2003.

[4] ProActive, http://www-sop.inria.fr/oasis/proactive/

[5] Grid Application Toolkit, http://www.gridlab.org/gat/

[6] Rob van Nieuwpoort, Jason Maassen, Thilo Kielmann and Henri E. Bal. *Satin: Simple and Efficient Java-based Grid Programming*. Scalable Computing: Practice and Experience, 6(3):19-32, September 2005.

[7] Sergei Gorlatch and Jan Dunnweber. *From Grid Middleware to Grid Applications: Bridging the Gap with HOCs*. In Future Generation Grids, Springer Verlag, 2005.

[8] Marco Aldinucci, Massimo Coppola, Marco Danelutto, Marco Vanneschi and Corrado Zoccolo. *ASSIST as a Research Framework for High-performance Grid Programming Environments*. In Jose C. Cunha and Omer F. Rana, editors, Grid Computing: Software environments and Tools. Springer-Verlag, 2004.

[9] P-GRADE portal, http://www.lpds.sztaki.hu/pgportal/

[10] Natalia Currle-Linde, Uwe Kuester, Michael M. Resch, Benedetto Risio. *Science Experimental Grid Laboratory (SEGL) Dynamical Parameter Study in Distributed Systems*. In proceedings of the 2005 International Conference on Parallel Computing (ParCo 2005), pp 49-56, Malaga, Spain.

[11] Java annotations, http://java.sun.com/j2se/1.5.0/docs/guide/language/annotations.html

[12] Design of the Integrated Toolkit with Supporting Mediator Components, CoreGRID Deliverable D.STE.05, 2006.

THE ROLE OF OVERLAY SERVICES IN A SELF-MANAGING FRAMEWORK FOR DYNAMIC VIRTUAL ORGANIZATIONS

Per Brand, Joel Hoglund and Konstantin Popov
SICS, Sweden
{perbrand,joel,kost}@sics.se

Noel de Palma, Fabienne Boyer and Nikos Parlavantzas
INRIA, France
{noel.depalma,fabienne.boyer,nikolaos.parlavantzas}@inrialpes.fr

Vladimir Vlassov and Ahmad Al-Shishtawy
KTH, Sweden
{vladv,ahmadas}@kth.se

Abstract   We combine and extend recent results in autonomic computing and structured peer-to-peer to build an infrastructure for constructing and managing dynamic virtual organizations. The paper focuses on the middle layer of the proposed infrastructure, in-between the Niche overlay system on the bottom, and an architecture-based management system based on Jade on the top. The middle layer, the overlay services, are responsible for all sensing and actuation carried out by the VO management. We describe in detail the API of the resource and component overlay services both on the management node and the nodes hosting resources. We present a simple use case demonstrating resource discovery, initial deployment, self-configuration as a result of resource availability change, self-healing, self-tuning and self-protection. The advantages of the design are 1) the overlay services are in themselves self-managing, and sensor/actuation services they provide are robust, 2) management can be dealt with declaratively and at a high-level, and 3) the overlay services provide good scalability in dynamic VOs.

Keywords: autonomic computing, peer-to-peer, overlay services

1.   Introduction

The context of this work is the effort to combine, integrate and extend recent results in autonomic computing with structured peer-to-peer systems. The ultimate goal is to build an infrastructure for constructing and managing dynamic collaborative virtual organizations (VOs) for resource sharing. This paper focuses on the middle layer of this infrastructure, a number of vital VO-management services. We outline the design of these *overlay services*, and describe in detail two of them. We also briefly show how these services interface with high-level management functions and the underlying structured peer-to-peer system.

We target Internet-based VOs characterized by high levels of dynamism along two dimensions. Firstly, the identities of the individual members and resources available to the VO is continuously changing. Secondly, the number/amount of resources and members also changes in time.

Self-management (or autonomic computing) is actively pursued as human system administration is expensive, error-prone, and often non-optimal. There is a considerable body of work in this area, and some progress has been made. In VOs with high rates of dynamism self-management becomes crucial.

The focus in this paper is on management aspects of component-based (distributed) applications/services running within a VO. The application needs to be maintained in the context of dynamic VOs where the individual resources being used by the application components leave the system, as more suitable resources enter the system, as loads change, as resource fail, etc.

The paper is organized as follows. First we introduce our three-layered architecture and its role in VO management, and describe its layers focusing on the overlay services. We then present a simple use case, involving deploying an application and instrumenting appropriate self-* policies. The use case concentrates on the interaction between the overlay services and the management logic. Finally, we relate to other work and conclude.

2.   Architecture

Within the framework set by VO policy, members provide resources and services to the VO. VO management monitors, aggregates, presents and controls these resources and services to/for the VO members. Services are also created within the VO making use of the aggregated resources.

One of the tasks of VO management, and the focus of this paper, is deploying and managing applications that make use of aggregated computation and/or storage facilities. Managing these applications, presented to members as services, in the face of dynamism will require frequent management interventions.

Our infrastructure for managing dynamic VOs can be split into three layers. The *topmost* layer, the management policy/logic layer, consists of high-level management functions and tools. This let VO managers set appropriate policies for applications and services that are run in the VO. This includes aspects of application configuration, healing, and tuning, as well as policies that prioritize between applications/services upon resource contention. The *bottommost* layer is a self-organizing overlay network called Niche that connects all machines/resources in the VO. Niche is based on a DHT, and includes a publish/subscribe service. The *middle* layer, the overlay services are the focus of this paper. They provide VO management services such as discovery, resource monitoring, member monitoring, and deployment of components.

2.1   Management Logic

Our approach to self-management for dynamic VOs is the architecture-based control one and based on earlier work on the Fractal component model and the Jade management system [6]. Our system has one or more manager components that are continuously monitoring (through sensors) and controlling (via actuators) the VO in a feedback loop in accordance with high-level policies/goals and system administration input. Self-management includes self-healing, self-tuning, self-configuration, and self-protection.

The control approach of management distinguishing between three aspects of management:

Sensing: the ability to sense or observe the state of system and system elements. In general observation may be active (triggered by the observer) or passive (triggered by the element).

Actuation: the ability to control and affect the system elements.

Decision: the logic that given knowledge of the system elements (provided by sensing) decides on actions (done by actuation) to ensure proper operation of the system. This ranges from simple rules to sophisticated AI techniques.

An architecture description language (ADL) is used to specify declaratively the initial deployment and simple self-configuration and self-healing behaviours of the system. Architectures are specified in terms of components and bindings. Component descriptions include requirements and preferences for resources necessary for deployment of the component. Component descriptions state also component properties crucial for management logic, such as whether the component's state can be extracted into a data structure.

Other self-* behaviours are specified in terms of events and handlers and abstractions thereof. Events reflect status changes in the VO, such as availability of resources, and status changes of application components, such as failures. Event handlers evaluate the status of the application and the environment and can replace, add and remove application components and bindings.

The high-level ADL descriptions are compiled into the low-level management logic assembler that utilizes the VO-management overlay services. While the

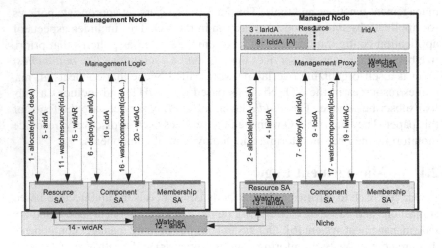

Figure 1.   System Architecture and the Use Case.

ADL descriptions refer to architecture-level notions, the assembler code works with mutable references to low-level entities such as resource and component handlers, entity and VO status watchers, and stateful event handlers.

2.2   Overlay Services

The overlay services are primarily sensor and actuation services (SA in Figure 1). They also provide the infrastructure for delegation of management logic. All nodes in the system are known to the SA services and are part of the same overlay. When nodes enter or leave the system they join/leave the overlay. When resources join/leave the system they report this to their local overlay proxy, an action that may lead to a management action as some management rule is triggered. Resources are also monitored for failures. An actuating command such as deploying a component on a given resource is issued on a management node and will eventually reach a correct managed node, where the deployment is triggered using the managed node API.

The figure on the left shows the system architecture at management nodes. The management logic senses and actuates through the three overlay services through well-specified management APIs.

1. Resource sensor and actuator service
2. Component/service sensor and actuator service
3. Member sensor and actuator service

The three services are reflected in three front-end subsystems that perform only a small amount of computation, packaging and bookkeeping. Communication with other nodes takes place exclusively in the Niche layer.

The figure on the right shows the system architecture at managed nodes. The Management Proxy component interacts with the three overlay services through the services' managed node API interfaces. The proxy interacts with resources and components allocated/located on the local machine on behalf of the VO. The interface between the management proxy and the overlay services is used in particular for 1) notifications of resources joining and leaving the VO as the owning members withdraws and add resources to the VO and 2) components communicating via bindings with other components currently residing on remote nodes. A physical node may be both manager and managed.

3. Niche

Overlay services described in this paper exploit the Distributed K-ary System (DKS) [1, 3] middleware and its extension called Niche. DKS has a circular identifier space, similarly to Chord [16]. Each node is responsible for Ids in the interval between its own Id and the Id of its predecessor. A message sent to a DKS Id is received by the node responsible for that Id. DKS provides broadcast and multicast [2, 8]. DKS allows to build a data storage layer on top of it, where every DKS node keeps data items with Ids it is responsible for.

DKS self-organizes itself as nodes join, leave and fail. DKS overlay can notify the data storage layer about changes of responsibility of nodes, so that the nodes can transfer the data items accordingly. Symmetric replication [10] can be used to distribute replicas among DKS nodes, enabling concurrent requests improving efficiency and fault-tolerance.

Niche extends the DKS and provides in particular the *set of network references* abstraction, SNR hereafter. A SNR keeps a set of references to abstract entities. Individual references in a SNR can be accessed by their SNR-specific Ids. References to entities can be updated. SNR assumes that clients that receive out-of-date references as a result of a concurrent read operation can recognize the problem. For example, if the entity represents a component that is relocated to another node, an attempt to access the previous location of the component will result with an `out-of-date reference` error. Concurrent reads and updates can be also controlled with a conditional update operation that proceeds only if the reference supplied as an additional parameter is equal to the reference currently held in the SNR.

A SNR also monitors the status of its entities and can notify clients that are subscribed to entity status updates. SNR entities can communicate their status to SNR, either by status polling by the SNR or by asynchronous messages sent to SNR. SNR failure monitoring of resources is polling-based, using the existing DKS functionality.

SNRs are implemented as items in a data storage layer atop of DKS. Each SNR set element contains the reference Id and the reference itself. A SNR contains also a possibly empty set of references to Niche entities that are subscribed for reference status updates. This set of subscriptions is shared by all references in the SNR. SNRs are stored on Niche nodes responsible for their set Ids. SNRs are reliable and scalable using symmetric replication: whenever a DKS node discovers that it became responsible for a SNR it has no data for, it contacts one of other SNR replicas.

4.   Overlay Services

The elements of the management logic assembler can be divided into categories based on their place in the management feedback loop.

Events: Sensing is realized through events.

Sensor installation: This instruments the sensing, which can be seen as publish directives. Discovery operations and watchers belong here, where management asks the overlay services to find resources (active sensing) or monitor specific entities (passive sensing), respectively. Information on entities will only be available if there are watchers installed.

Triggers: This is an actuating part of the management logic whereby a command is sent to a specific entity or groups of entities.

Activation of event handlers: Activating an event handler may be seen as a subscription. Event handlers can be created and/or stopped. For one event there may be more than one event handler, which may be triggered in arbitrary order.

4.1   Management API

In the following section the management API is described in an abstract form. We describe the more important functions of the resource and component overlay services and all operations used in the use case section.

We use VO-wide identifiers for resources, components, watchers, bindings and groups. Futures are used to simplify data-flow dependencies. When created, a future represents an unknown value which will be instantiated, which allows waiting for that value. For most futures a failure indication is a possible value. Futures are identified by a capital F in the variable name.

Sensor Installation	`wid:discoverResource(req, compare, tCompare, currentRes)`
	`widF:watchComponent(cid, compParam, compare, tCompare)`
	`widF:watchResource(rid, resParam, compare, tCompare)`
	`stopWatcher(wid)`

These instructions install sensors which will continuously report about resources matching given requirements or component and resource changes specified by parameters. For a sensor to report a change, the change has to be significant, as calculated by the given `compare`-function, and a threshold function `tCompare` that determines if a resource is sufficiently better than `curRes`.

Triggers
```
aridF:allocate(rid, specification)
boolF:deallocate(arid)
cidF:deploy(component, arid)
fcidF:passivate(cidA)
fcidF:checkpoint(cidA)
boolF:start(cid)
gcidF:group(listOfComponentIds)
boolF:addToGroup(gid, cid)
bidF:bind(cid, gcid, bindDescSource, bindDescDestination, type)
boolF:unbind(bid)
rid:oneShotResourceDiscover(req, compare)
```

The deploy trigger is overloaded. The argument can be code, a checkpoint, url, etc. The data associated with passivation is stored in Niche under `fcidF`. Bindings are assumed to be unidirectional and asynchronous. If needed, binding descriptions for the sending and delivering side give additional information to connect the components.

Events
```
resourceReport(wid, oldState, newState)
componentReport(wid, componentParam, oldValue, newValue)
discoveryReport(wid, rid, resourceDescription)
```

Resource and component report correspond to watch subscriptions, while discovery report corresponds to `discoverResource` subscriptions. They are generated if the change has triggered the initially given threshold function.

Event Handlers
```
upon event eventName(wid, es) with <attributes> do
activateEventHandler(rule, wid, initAttributes)
passivateEventHandler(rule, wid)
```

The event handler is triggered by an exact match on both the event name, and the value of the id, `wid`. Es represents parameters given in the event, attributes represents parameters given when instantiating the event handler.

4.2   Managed Node Side API

The managed node side of the API works with local ids. The sensor and actuator services will do the conversion between local and global ids.

Downcalls, Initiated by Management Proxy Layer
```
resourceJoin(lrid, description)
resourceLeave(lrid)
resourceChange(lrid)
componentChange(lcid, description)
send(lbid, Object)
```

The information generated by resource join can trigger resourceReport(s) or be found through `discoverResource` calls. The `leave` and `change` calls

generates resource and component reports, if there are subscribers. Send is used
when component make calls on established bindings.

Upcalls Initiated by Overlay Services

```
result:allocate(lrid, description)
result:deallocate(lrid)
lcid:deploy(lrid, componentDescription)
bool:undeploy(lcid)
data:passivate(lcid)
lbid:bind(lcid, description)
bool:unbind(lbid)
lwid:watchComponent(lcid, eventDescriptions)
state:pollComponentState(lcid)
deliver(lbid, Object)
```

The allocate operation might consume the entire resource or just a part, in
which case a new `rid` is given for the allocated part, while the old `rid` refers
to the free remainder. The deallocate operation might return an instruction to
merge two chunks of a previously split resource, or they might remain split.

5.   Use Case

We demonstrate the use of the management overlay services with an application that consists of a single master component and multiple worker components.
The master divides a computational task into independent subtasks, delivers
each subtask to a random worker for processing taking advantage of the *any*
type of bindings, and collects and collates the results.

5.1   ADL Specification

```
definition MasterWorkerApplication
component Master
  content = MasterImpl;
  resourceSpecs requirements = "OS=Linux and MemorySize>4GB", preferences = "MemorySize";
  componentAttributes stateful,serializeable;
component Workers
  content = WorkerImpl;
  cardinality = 3;
  resourceSpecs requirements = "CPUSpeed>3GHz", preferences = "CPUSpeed";
  componentAttributes stateless;
binding B1
  client = Master.OutputInterface; server = Worker.InputInterface; type = any
```

A tool maps the ADL description to manager assembly code. This code
contains invocations to the overlay services via the management API, as shown
in Section 5.2. The binding element of type *any* causes the invocations to be
delivered to a single, random group member.

The management code for self-configuration and self-healing does not change
the application's architecture, and can therefore be generated from the same
ADL specification automatically (see for example Section 5.3). For the master
component, the `componentAttributes` field states that the component is
stateful and therefore its state must be moved when the component is relocated,
and that it is serializable meaning that the state can be actually saved into a data
structure, as needed by e.g. the checkpointing code.

Self-tuning involves adjusting the number of workers when their load changes. The application ADL contains the policy `self-tuning-workers` describing this behaviour. The `ComponentStateChange` event specification causes setting up a watcher for a specific parameter of a source component using a given threshold value. The handler `ManageGroupWithLimits` changes the number of components in the `Workers` group such that the load moves into the region specified by `low` and `high` parameters.

```
policy self-tuning-workers
    event = ComponentStateChange(source=Workers, componentParam="Load", threshold="100")
    handler = ManageGroupWithLimits(target=Workers, low="1000", high="2000")
```

5.2   Initial Deployment

The following sections of management assembler code are produced automatically from the ADL descriptions. Waits are implicit; futures used as input parameters block calls until instantiated. Error-handling is omitted. The execution of the code is illustrated in Figure 1.

```
ridA:oneShotResourceDiscover(reqA, compare)
% + similarly for 3 B resources => ridB[1-3]
desA := specifications(preferenceA, ridA)
% specifications produces a description of how much of the resource is to be allocated
aridA:allocate(ridA, desA)
cidA:deploy(A, aridA)
% + similarly for 3 B components => cidB[1-3], initialNumberOfComponents = 3
gid:group([cidB[1],cidB[2],cidB[3]])
bid:bind(cidA,gid, BDesA,BDesB, one-to-any-binding)
widAR:watchResource(aridA, [used->fail, used->leaving], any, any)
% 'any' indicates that all changes of declared types should be reported, no filtering
activateEventHandler(self-config-leave, widAR, [bid, cidA, aridA, gid])
widA:discoverResource(reqA, compare, tCompare, ridA)
activateEventHandler(self-config-join, widA, [bid, cidA, aridA, gid]
% do periodic check-pointing to enable self-healing for A:
timeGenerate(checkPoint(cidA), timeInterval)
activateEventHandler(checkpointing, id)
activateEventHandler(self-healing, widAR, [...])
activateEventHandler(self-tuning, widB[X], [...])
```

5.3   Self-* Rules

The rules are active until stopped, so they may be fired many times. Parameter names are left out when they are understandable from the context.

Self-Configuration

```
upon event discoveryReport(wid, newrid, RDes) with <bid, cidA, aridA, gid, preferencesA> do
    % the system reports a better resource match - newrid - for component A, move it there
    boolF:unbind(bid)
    fcid:passivate(cidA)
    boolF:deallocate(aridA)
    aridA:allocate(rid, specification(prefA, RDes))
    cidA:deploy(pcid, aridA)
    bid:bind(cidA, gid)

upon event resourceReport(widA, from, to) with <bid, cidA, aridA, gid, ...> do
    if from==used && to==leaving then % resource is leaving, find new & move component there
```

```
newRidA:oneShotResourceDiscover(reqA, compare)
boolF:unbind(bid)
pcid:passivate(cidA)
boolF:deallocate(aridA)
aridA:allocate(newRidA, specification(preferencesA, newRidA))
cidA:deploy(pcid, aridA)
bid:bind(cidA, gid)
```

Note that the `aridA` and other attributes are reset at rule termination so the rule can be fired again.

Self-healing

```
upon event resourceReport(widA, from, to) with <...> do
  if from==used && to==failed then
    % resource failed, find new & restore checkpointed component there
    newRidA:oneShotResourceDiscover(reqA, compare)
    aridA:allocate(newRidA, specification(prefA, desc))
    cidA:deploy(fcidA, aridA) % "frozen"cidA from periodic checkpoint
    bid:bind(cidA, gid)
```

Self-Tuning

```
upon event componentReport(widB[X], load, oldLoad, newLoad) with <gid, ...> do
  if loadMeasure(load[1..NoB]) > HighLimit then
    % load is high, deploy one more B-component
    newRidB:oneShotResourceDiscover(reqB, compare)
    newAridB:allocate(newRidB, specifications(prefB, desc)
    newCidB:deploy(B, newAridB)
    addToGroup(newCidB, gid)
    noB:=noB+1
    update(load[])
  elseif loadMeasure(load[1..NoB]) < LowLimit then
    if noB > initialNumberOfComponents then  % load is low, one B-component can be removed
      deallocate(lowestLoad(widB[]))
      noB:=noB-1
      update(load[])
```

6.   Related Work

Niche builds on a state-of-the-art overlay, DKS. A good survey of overlays and comparisons with DKS can be found in [9].

Several P2P-based publish/subscribe systems have been developed, for both structured e.g. [7, 17] and unstructured e.g. [12] P2P networks. To our best knowledge, structured pub/sub systems do not provide a robust and scalable event-notification mechanism (with high delivery guarantees) that could tolerate churn in highly dynamic Grids. However some of the resent unstructured pub/sub systems [4–5] are scalable and can handle churn.

There is a considerable industrial and academic interest in self-* systems. Some approaches, e.g. [14, 11], rely on P2P to support some of self-* aspects in Grid. Our work aims at utilizing P2P to provide support for all self-* aspects in Grid component-based applications.

The AutoMate project [15] proposes the Accord [13] programming framework to deal with challenges of dynamism, scale, heterogeneity and uncertainty in Grid environments. The Accord's approach for self-management is similar to our approach. Accord is based on the concept of autonomic element that represents self-manageable entities. Self-management is guided by behaviour and interaction rules. The Accord framework provides support for run-time composition of elements and run-time injection of rules. We believe AutoMate's self-* rules can be implemented using our framework. Our work, however, does not stipulate a specific programming model and can be used to provide self-* management support for legacy applications.

The benefits of overlay-based middleware to support complex, heterogeneous, self-configuring Grid applications has been recognized in GridKit [11]. GridKit provides resource discovery and management services, and interaction services. However, GridKit does not provide specific services for component management, and did not address all of the self-* issues.

7. Discussion and Conclusions

In our architecture the overlay services form the middle layer of an infrastructure for the management of dynamic VOs. They are responsible for all sensing and actuation necessary for self-management of VO applications. As the overlay services are based on a DHT, we have been leveraging results in the area, and been able to provide services that are both self-managing internally and robust. The fact that the overlay services are self-managing simplifies making the robust VO management.

Dynamic VOs are characterized by high rates of churn so that there is risk of overwhelming the management with a flood of status information and the need to take corrective actions. This might exceed bandwidth, storage and computing limitations and complicate dealing with management nodes' failures. This is ameliorated by the following properties of the overlay services. First, the overlay services are available to all nodes in the VO and therefore support replication of management nodes. Second, overlay services can accommodate sensing abstractions that can aggregate churn events and therefore hide them from other elements of the management. Handling abstractions inside the overlay make for fewer messages arriving at the management node, fewer messages overall in the system, and lower latencies. Third, overlay services support intelligent and dynamic delegation of management logic between nodes in the VO. Placing management elements near or together with the components themselves can optimize performance and overhead of self-management, and simplify making the self-management robust on its own.

This is work in progress, to date a number of overlay service functions have been designed, and some of these have been implemented.

Acknowledgments This research is supported by the European project Grid4All and the CoreGrid Network of Excellence.

References

[1] Distributed k-ary system (dks). http://dks.sics.se/.

[2] L. Onana Alima, A. Ghodsi, P. Brand, and S. Haridi. Multicast in DKS(N,k,f) overlay networks. In *Proc. of the 7th Int. Conf. on Principles of Dist. Systems*. Springer, 2003.

[3] L.O. Alima, S. El-Ansary, P. Brand, and S. Haridi. DKS(N,k,f): A family of low communication, scalable and fault-tolerant infrastructures for P2P applications. In *3rd IEEE Int. Symp. on Cluster Computing and the Grid*, pages 344–350. IEEE, 2003.

[4] R. Baldoni, R. Beraldi, L. Querzoni, and A. Virgillito. Efficient Publish/Subscribe through a Self-Organizing Broker Overlay and its Application to SIENA. *The Computer Journal*, 50(4):444–459, 7 2007.

[5] Silvia Bianchi, Pascal Felber, and Maria Gradinariu. Content-based publish/subscribe using distributed r-trees. In *Euro-Par*, pages 537–548, 2007.

[6] Bouchenak *et al.* Architecture-based autonomous repair management: An application to J2EE clusters. In *Proceedings of the 24th IEEE Symp. on Reliable Distributed Systems*. IEEE, 2005.

[7] M. Castro, P. Druschel, A. Kermarrec, and A. Rowstron. SCRIBE: A large-scale and decentralized application-level multicast infrastructure. *IEEE Journal on Selected Areas in Communications (JSAC)*, 20(8):1489–1499, 2002.

[8] S. El-Ansary, L. Onana Alima, P. Brand, and S. Haridi. Efficient broadcast in structured P2P networks. In *Proc. 2nd Int. Workshop On Peer-To-Peer Systems*. Springer, 2003.

[9] A. Ghodsi. *Distributed k-ary System: Algorithms for Distributed Hash Tables*. PhD thesis, Royal Institute of Technology (KTH), 2006.

[10] A. Ghodsi, L. Onana Alima, and S. Haridi. Symmetric replication for structured peer-to-peer systems. In *Proceedings of The 3rd Int. Workshop on Databases, Information Systems and P2P Computing*, Trondheim, Norway, 2005.

[11] Grace *et al.* GRIDKIT: Pluggable overlay networks for grid computing. In *Proc. Distributed Objects and Applications (DOA'04)*, volume LNCS 3291. Springer, 2004.

[12] A. Gupta, O. Sahin, D. Agrawal, and A. El Abbadi. Meghdoot: content-based publish/subscribe over P2P networks. In *Proceedings of the 5th ACM/IFIP/USENIX Int. Conf. on Middleware*, pages 254–273. Springer, 2004.

[13] H. Liu and M. Parashar. Accord: A programming framework for autonomic applications. *IEEE Transactions on Systems, Man and Cybernetics*, 36(3):341–352, 2006.

[14] Mayer *et al.* ICENI: An integrated Grid middleware to support E-Science. In *Proceedings of the Workshop on Component Models and Systems for Grid Applications*, CoreGRID series, pages 109–124. Springer, 2005.

[15] M. Parashar, Z. Li, H. Liu, V. Matossian, and C. Schmidt. Enabling autonomic grid applications: Requirements, models and infrastructure. In *Proceedings of the Conf. on Self-Star Properties in Complex Information Systems*, volume LNCS 3460. Springer, 2005.

[16] I. Stoica, R. Morris, D. Karger, M.F. Kaashoek, and H. Balakrishnan. Chord: A scalable peer-to-peer lookup service for internet applications. In *Proceedings of the ACM SIGCOMM '01 Conference*, pages 149–160, San Diego, CA, August 2001.

[17] S. Voulgaris, E. Rivière, A.-M. Kermarrec, and M. van Steen. Sub-2-Sub: Self-organizing content-based publish subscribe for dynamic large scale collaborative networks. Technical Report RR-5772, INRIA, December 2005.

CARRYING THE CRASH-ONLY SOFTWARE CONCEPT TO THE LEGACY APPLICATION SERVERS

Javier Alonso and Jordi Torres
Technical University of Catalonia
Barcelona Supercomputing Center,
Barcelona,Spain
alonso@ac.upc.edu
torres@ac.upc.edu

Luis Silva
University of Coimbra
CISUC, Portugal
luis@dei.uc.pt

Abstract   In the last few years, high-availability on internet services has become a main goal for the academia and industry. We all know how complex and heterogeneous Internet service systems are and how sensitive to suffer from transient failures or even crashes also. Because developing systems that are guaranteed to never crash and never suffer transient or intermittent failures seems an impractical and unfeasible business, there is a need to develop mechanisms that can suffer crashes and transient failures as if they were a clean shutdown. Behind this idea, the creators of the crash-only software concept proposed a new design strategy in order to get crash-safe and fast recovery systems by defining a list of laws which are needed in order to achieve that goal. However, their proposals are focused on new systems design. For this reason, we will discuss how to develop crash-safe and masked fast self-recovery legacy systems following the ideas behind the crash-only software concept. In our work, we have focused on legacy application servers because they are a more sensitive piece of the internet services' big puzzle.

Keywords: crash-only software, legacy software, self-recovery, self-healing, automatic recovery

1.   Introduction

High-availability has become one of the main success characteristics for every company engaged in e-business and e-commerce since every company wants their internet services running 24x7 to maximize their revenue. For all internet service companies, high-availability is of paramount importance because unavailability time means potential revenue losses. In recent history, there have been famous internet service outages, resulting in big revenue losses and a bad image for service companies' owners. In general terms, [1] calculates that the cost of downtime per hour can go from 100k for online stores up to 6 million dollars for online brokerage services. One of the most important cases occurred in April 1999, when e-Bay suffered a 24-hours outage. In that time, it was calculated that e-Bay lost around 5 billion dollars in revenue and stock value [4]. This type of failures and similar outages, like the 15 minutes Goggle Outage in 2005 can also affect the customer loyalty and investor confidence [5], resulting in a potential loss of revenue.

Unfortunately, system outages and application failures do occur, provoking crashes.

We can classify the bugs in two big sets of them: permanent failures and transient failures.

The first subset refers to bugs that can be solved in development processes because they're easy to reproduce. However, the second type of failures, also known as Heisenbugs [3] are difficult to fix because they're difficult to reproduce because they depend on the timing of external events and often the best way to skip them is to simply restart the application, the application server or even the whole physical or virtual machine.

We have focused on this second type of bug.

Internet services are complex and dynamic environments where there are lots of components interacting with each other. This type of environments are sensitive to transient failures; however, a simple restart to solve possible failures and crashes may not be enough to solve them and indeed, if we apply blind restarts, internet services can suffer application data inconsistency problems. This happens because while we restart the internet service, the volatile state of user sessions needed for future interactions between the application and the user to achieve a successful communication is lost, also displaying the restart process to end users as a failure or a crash.

As it seems that it is unfeasible to build systems that are guaranteed to never crash or suffer transient failures, G. Candea and A. Fox proposed the crash-only software concept [7]. The crash-only software is based on the idea of designing software systems that handle failures by simply restarting them without attempting any sophisticated recovery. Since, some authors have proposed the idea of developing new Internet services using the concept of crash-only software. The crash-only concept can be seen like a generalization of the transaction model taken from the data storage world. The crash-only system failures have similar effects over the data storage systems. However, what happens with the recently designed and deployed internet services, usually made-up by cooperative legacy servers?

In this paper, we discuss the possibility to migrate the crash-only software concept to these legacy servers for internet services. We focus on application servers because traditionally, these servers have the business logical of the applications and are more sensitive to the transient failures or potential crashes.

As an example, we expose the classical online flight ticket store. We have a multi-tier application environment made-up by one web server for static web pages, an application server for business logical and a database server for storing all ticket flight information.

We can define the session in this environment as the process in between the user logs-in and finally, logs-out. During this process the user can search for flights, add some of them to his/her shopping basket and pay for them. If there was a crash during the session process, the more sensitive point of the multi-tier application would be the application server, because the web server only manages static information and database servers have their traditional after crash recovery systems. The application servers have the responsibility to manage the session state. This session state is needed for the session's success because the session state contains information useful to the session's subsequent states. For this reason, if there was a crash in a legacy application server, a simple and blind restart could be dangerous to the consistency of the business logic state.

Due to the crash-only constraints we restrict our proposal to application servers with external session state storage, which meets crash-only laws like SSM [8] or Postgres database system [15].

This paper's main goal is to migrate the ideas proposed by authors of the crash-only concept to the current legacy application servers and put them to practice in order to obtain a "crash-safe" and "fast" recovery system.

The second goal of our proposal is to hide any possible crash from the end-users improving the crash-only software concept which achieves crash-safe and fast recovery systems although it doesn't avoid the occasional unavailability time, as it was shown through the Microreboot technique [6]. The rest of the paper follows as: Section 2 presents the crash-only software properties. Section 3 discusses the viability of crash-only software characteristics on legacy application servers' environments. Section 4 presents our proposal architecture to achieve our two principal goals and section. Section 5 concludes this paper.

2.   Crash-only Software

The crash-only concept is based on the idea that all systems can suffer transient failures and crashes thus it'd be useful to develop systems that could overcome a potential crash or transient failure. Furthermore, normally the system crash recovery time is lower than the time needed to apply a clean reboot using the tools provided by the application itself. Table 1 illustrates this reasoning.

System	Clean Reboot	Crash Reboot
RedHat 8 (with ext3fs)	104 sec	75 sec
JBoss 3.0 application server	47 sec	39 sec
Windows XP	61 sec	48 sec

Table 1.   Table obtained from [7]

The reason for this phenomenon is the desire to improve the system performance. The systems usually store potential non-volatile information on volatile devices, like RAM, to be faster and obtain higher performance. For this reason, before a system can be rebooted, all this information has to be saved on non-volatile devices like hard disks to maintain data consistency. However, in the case of a crash reboot all this information is lost and potential inconsistency state may result after reboot.

Based on these potential problems, crash-only software is software where a crash behaves as a clean reboot. Every crash-only system has to be made of crash-only components and every crash-only component has only one way to stop - by crashing the component- and only one way to start the component: applying a recovery process. To obtain crash-only components, authors defined five properties that the component has to include:

(a). *All important non-volatile state is managed by dedicated state stores.* The application becomes a stateless client of the session state stores, which helps and simplifies the recovery process after a crash. Of course, this session state store has to be crash-only, otherwise the problem has just moved down to the other place.

(b). *Components have externally enforced boundaries.* All components have to be isolated from the rest of the components to avoid that one faulty component may provoke another fault on another component. There are different and potential ways to isolate components. One of the most successful ways for isolating components which has become popular in the last few years is virtualization [16].

(c). *All interactions between components have a timeout.* Any communication between components has to have a timeout. If no response is received after that time, the caller can assume that the callee is failing and the caller can start a crash and recovery process for the component failing.

(d). *All resources are leased.* The resources cannot be coupled up indefinitely thus it is necessary to either guarantee the resources be free after a limited time or the component using the resources crashes.

(e). *Requests are entirely self-describing.* It is needed that all requests are entirely self-describing to make the recovery process easier. After a crash, the system can continue from where the previous instance left off. It is necessary to know the time to live (TTL) of the request and the indempotency property.

Trying to describe in fine detail all philosophy of Crash-only software in this paper would be out of scope. In order to obtain more information, we recommend you visit the ROC project [2] and the website [17] and other authors' papers around this concept.

3. Crash-only and masking failure Architecture for Legacy Application Servers

Our architecture is focused on a determinate set of application servers: application servers with external session state storage. The reason is because we cannot force an application server to manage their internal session objects to external storage without changing the code. We want to propose a solution which avoids modifying the legacy application server code because this can be a titanic work or even impossible if the software is also closed.

The architecture is made-up by three main components: the Requests Handler (RH), the Storage Management Proxy (SMP) and the Recovery Manager (RM) as shown in figure 1.

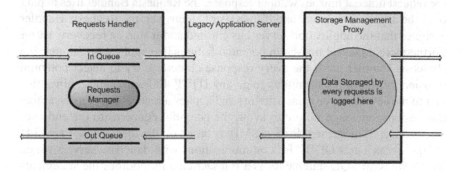

Figure 1.   Basic Architecture diagram

The Requests Handler has the responsibility to capture all HTTP requests that are sent to the application server from a potential end-user or a web server. Two queues and one requests manager form the RH. There is one requests queue, a responses queue, and a requests manager to manage and synchronize them.

When a new request is sent to the application server, RH handles the request and copies the request to the requests queue and then the request is redirected to the application server without any modification. When the application server sends a response to the end-user or web server, the Requests Handler captures the response and copies the response to the response queue and redirects the response without changes to the end-user.

To achieve this behavior the Requests Handler has to work in the same network domain as the application server and has to be configured to work in a promiscuous mode, and by using the application server IP it can capture all the application server requests and discard all not relevant requests (e.g. non-HTTP requests). Capturing the response is quite more complicated because, the Request Manager has to save all IP sources from all requests without response in the requests queue and any packet sent by the application server to one of the IP's from the requests queues will be captured. When the response is captured, the request associated to the response is removed from the queue. We are based on the idea that the requests and responses can be joined if we understand that the requests from one end-user are sequential and the responses too, for this reason, using the source IP of the request and the destination IP of the response can be enough to join one response with its request.

The Requests Handler has more important tasks other than only preserving a copy to know what in-flight requests are there in the application server. It has also the responsibility of detecting potential failures (transient failures and crashes).

Based on the idea proposed by [7] and [11], every time that one request is sent to the application server from the Requests Handler, a timeout is activated. If the request timeout finishes without response, the Requests Handler tries to ping over the application server and if there isn't an answer, the Requests Handler assumes that the application server has crashed and it starts a recovery action. Furthermore, to detect fine-grain potential failures like application failures, the Requests Handler reads the every response content to try to detect potential transient or intermittent failures (e.g. any HTTP 400 error) and notifies this fact to the developers or administrators and applies a recovery action discarding the response message failure to avoid the potential concerns to the end-user. The Storage Management Proxy (SMP) is based on the idea proposed in [14]. [14]proposes a new ODBC for communications with data base servers which understands all SQL statements as a transaction and modifies the statements syntax to achieve a successful behavior. This ODBC is integrated in Phoenix APP [10], to achieve a system with crash-safe processes.

We have simplified the idea proposed in [14]. Our system only stores information of the communications between the application server and any data storage device (database servers or session state storage). The information obtained from these communications will be used only in the recovery process and during a correct behavior of the application server. We can say that SMP is only a logging system that saves all requests and responses' information. If a crash happens during a transaction process in the database server, the transaction will rollback and the SMP will write this event only to keep track of what happened during this interaction between the application server and the database server. Finally, the Recovery manager has the responsibility to coordinate the recovery process. To define the recovery process, we have designed an architecture and a process to avoid the potential problems of the recovery process described in [13]: exactly-once execution, (where the latter means, no output to the user is duplicated to avoid confusion), the user provides input only once (to avoid user irritation) and the user attempt is carried out exactly once. If the Requests Handler detects a failure a signal is triggered to the Recovery manager to start a recovery process. First, the RM notifies this situation to the RH and SMP. When the RH receives the notification, it stops to redirect requests and redirect responses to and from the application server and it only receives requests from end-users. At the same time, the SMP avoids all communications between the application server and the data storages. After these both processes are concluded, the RM recovers (crash reboot) the application server (e.g. kill -9 pid-process) and restarts the application server waiting for a new application server instance. When the new instance is running, the RM notifies the fact to the RH and SMP. The RH redirects all requests without response (in-flight requests) to the new instance of the application server again, so the user doesn't need to provide the input again. If at any time, the RH receives a response without request associated to it, the response is discarded to avoid potential duplicates to the user in order to avoid confusion.

At the same time the SMP is monitoring the communications between the application server and avoiding potential duplicated database or session object modifications. When SMP detects a duplicated communication, the packet is not redirect to the storage if the performance of this communication was successful, otherwise the communication is redirected. On the other hand, if the communication wasn't successful, we use the SMP response saved to build a new (old) response and send it to the application server as if it'd been stored. Thanks to this control of the duplicated communications of the SMP we avoid potential problems presented in [13].

The idea of this coordination between RH and SMP using the RM is to avoid the potential crash hazards presented in [11–12]. In these papers, the authors present an architecture based on interact contracts. These contracts are thought to apply safe-recovery mechanisms after a crash, replaying all requests without response before the crash and avoid uncomfortable behaviors of the application servers. However, authors present a solution that has an important constraint for all components: even internal components have to keep the contracts to maintain the coherence of the architecture. We have used the idea presented in these papers to present the architecture to achieve crash-only software legacy application server and mask the failure to the user.

4.   How our architecture achieves the goals?

In this paper, we propose a new architecture based on two proposals to achieve a crash-safe and fast recovery. Our goals proposed at the beginning of this paper were to migrate the crash-only software concept to achieve a legacy application server with the same characteristics as a crash-only designed system. Moreover, we proposed the improvement with regards to results presented in [6] where when using the crash-only concept, the system had an unavailability time of 78 missed requests during a microreboot process based on crash-only software. We want to design an environment to avoid these missed requests, reducing to zero downtime if it is possible. We understand a legacy application server as an indivisible component to make possible the crash-only concept migration, because the crash-only software is made-up by crash-only subcomponents. Based on this premise, it is easy to understand the reasoning of how our architecture preserves the properties of the crash-only software. As we have mentioned, we have restricted our study to the "stateless" application servers: The session state is preserved in external session state storages, accomplishing the first property (a). The architecture alone cannot achieve the second property (b), though we can use virtual machines (VM) to run the legacy application server and the rest of our proposal's components: one VM for each component to guarantee the isolation between components. The third property (c) is guaranteed by the RH, the SMP components and the behavior of the application servers. All communications have a timeout configured at least at OSI 4-layer (e.g. TCP/IP protocols). The fourth property is more difficult to accomplish. Working with legacy application servers, this property has to be delegated to the Operating system, which guarantees that all resources are leased. Finally, the HTTP requests, the traditional type of message for application servers, which are completely self-described. The secondary goal is preserved thanks to the queues inside the Requests Handler. During the crash and the recovery process, the application server is unavailable for the end-users or third applications. However, our Requests Handler continues capturing requests for the application server like a proxy and when the recovery process finishes, these requests waiting on the queue will be redirected to the application server like nothing happened. This process can mask the crash for the end-users in most cases like a previous work [9] where the solution masked potential service degradation and reboot process. Our proposal also avoids error messages if it is possible, because the RH parses the requests to try to detect fine-grain application failures or the application server failures (e.g. 400 and 500 HTTP errors) avoiding that end-users may observe neither these transient failures nor temporary system unavailability. In our proposal we get crash-safe self-recovery legacy application servers and even our solution offers a "fast" recovery process. We can confirm that the Requests Handler simulates a non-stop service which is the maximum speed of the recovery, and though the end-users will suffer response delays during the recovery process, we think that that penalty delay is proportional to the advantages of the proposal.

5. Conclusions

We have presented an architecture to migrate the advantages of the crash-only software concept to the legacy application servers. Furthermore, we have to improve the crash-only designs potential by introducing the idea behind the interact contracts presented in the Phoenix project [10] in order to achieve a successful and useful self-recovery process without modifying neither the application server code nor the application code. Nevertheless, our proposal has to have all application' and all application server' information to modify the behavior of the Requests Handler and the Storage Manager Proxy to correctly capture the requests and responses and use the correct network protocol (e.g. TCP/IP, HTTP, SOAP or others).

Our solution introduces a potential time-to-service delay during the recovery process. We could reduce this time if we introduce a hot-standby application server waiting to substitute the failing server. This idea is proposed in [9] for different environments with promising results.

Acknowledgments

This research work is supported by the FP6 Network of Excellence Core-GRID funded by the European Commission (Contract IST-2002-004265) and the Ministry of Science and Technology of Spain and the European Union (FEDER funds) under contract TIN2004-07739-C02-01. We thank Ceila Hidalgo Sánchez for her contribution during the review process.

References

[1] J.Hennessy, D.Patterson. *Computer Architecture: A Quantitative Approach*, Morgan & Kaufmann Publishers, 2002.

[2] D. Patterson, et. al. *Recovery Oriented Computing (ROC): Motivation, Definition, Techniques and Case Studies.*, Technical Report UCB CSD-02-1175, U.C. Berkeley, March

2002.

[3] K. Vaidyanathan and K.S. Trivedi. *Extended Classification of Software Faults based on Aging,* In Fast Abstracts, Proc. of the IEEE IntŠl Symp. on Software Reliability Engineering, Hong Kong, November 2001.

[4] D. Scott. *Operation Zero Downtime* A Gartner Group report, Donna Scott, 2000

[5] Chet Dembeck. *Yahoo cashes in on Ebay's outage,* E-commerce Times, June 18, 1999. [web] http://www.ecommercetimes.com/perl/story/545.html

[6] G. Candea, S. Kawamoto, Y. Fujiki, G. Friedman, A. Fox. *A Microreboot - A Technique for Cheap Recovery* Proc. 6th Symp. on Operating Systems Design and Implementation (OSDI), Dec. 2004.

[7] G.Candea, A.Fox. *Crash-only Software,* Proc. 9th Workshop on Hot Topics in Operating Systems, Germany, 2001

[8] B. Ling and A. Fox. *A self-tuning, self-protecting, selfhealing session state management layer,* In Proc. 5th Int. Workshop on Active Middleware Services, Seattle, WA, 2003.

[9] Luis Silva, Javier Alonso, Paulo Silva, Jordi Torres and Artur Andrzejak. *Using Virtualization to Improve Software Rejuvenation* The 6th IEEE International Symposium on Network Computing and Applications (IEEE NCA07), 12 - 14 July 2007,Cambridge, MA USA

[10] Roger S. Barga. *Phoenix Application Recovery Project* IEEE Data Engineering Bulletin, 2002.

[11] Barga, R., Lomet, D., Paparizos, S., Yu, H., and Chandrasekaran, S. *Persistent applications via automatic recovery,* In Proceedings of the 17th International Database Engineering and Applications Symposium, Hong Kong, China, July 2003.

[12] R. Barga, D. Lomet, G. Shegalov, G. Weikum. *Recovery Guarantees for Internet Applications,* ACM Transactions on Internet Technology (TOIT), vol. 4, no. 3, pp. 289-328, 2004.

[13] R. Barga, D. Lomet, G. Shegalov, G. Weikum. *Recovery Guarantees for General Multi-tier Applications,* Proc. of the 18th Int. Conf. on Data Engineering, p. 543, Feb. 26-March, 2002.

[14] Roger S. Barga , David B. Lomet. *Measuring and Optimizing a System for Persistent Database Sessions,* Proc, of the 17th Int. Conf. on Data Engineering, p.21-30, April 02-06, 2001.

[15] M. Stonebraker. *The design of the Postgres storage system,* Proc. 13th Conf. on Very Large Databases, Brighton, England, 1987.

[16] R. Figueiredo, P. Dinda, J. Fortes. *Resource Virtualization Renaissance.* IEEE Computer, 38(5), pp. 28-69, May 2005

[17] *[website] http://roc.cs.berkeley.edu/*

BOUNDED SITE FAILURES: AN APPROACH TO UNRELIABLE GRID ENVIRONMENTS *

Joaquim Gabarro[†], Alina Garcia[‡]
Universitat Politęcnica de Catalunya
ALBCOM Research Group
Edifici Ω, Campus Nord Jordi Girona, 1-3, Barcelona 08034, Spain
gabarro@lsi.upc.edu

Maurice Clint, Peter Kilpatrick, Alan Stewart
School of Computer Science
The Queen's University of Belfast
Belfast BT7 1NN, Northern Ireland
m.clint@qub.ac.uk

Abstract   The abstract behaviour of a grid application management system can be modelled
as an Orc expression in which sites are called to perform sub-computations.
An Orc expression specifies how a set of site calls are to be orchestrated so as
to realise some overall desired computation. In this paper evaluations of Orc
expressions in untrusted environments are analysed by means of game theory. The
set of sites participating in an orchestration is partitioned into two distinct groups.
Sites belonging to the first group are called *angels*: these may fail but when they
do they try to minimize damage to the application. Sites belonging to the other
group are called *daemons*: when a daemon fails it tries to maximise damage
to the application. Neither angels nor daemons can fail excessively because
the number of failures, in both cases, is bounded. When angels and daemons
act simultaneously a competitive situation arises that can be represented by a
so-called angel–daemon game. This game is used to model realistic situations
lying between over-optimism and over-pessimism.

Keywords: fault tolerance, bounded site failures, strategic games, nash equilibria.

---

*This research is carried out under the FP6 Network of Excellence CoreGRID funded by the European
Commission (Contract IST-2002-004265).
[†]Partially supported by FET pro-active Integrated Project 15964 (AEOLUS) and by Spanish projects
TIN2005-09198-C02-02 (ASCE) and MEC-TIN2005-25859-E. This work has been done in part during a
CoreGRID Exchange Program CR38UPC-CR21QUB & CR35UNIPI.
[‡]Supported by a FPI Spanish grant BES-2003-2361.

1.   Introduction

A Grid application management system calls sites in order to perform sub-computations. Typically, it is over-optimistic to assume that all site calls made during execution of a grid application will work correctly. While, to a certain extent, such failure may be dealt with by employing time-outs and corrective action, such defensive programming may not always be easy and in some cases not possible. There may be times when the user accepts the possibility of failure, but would like to have an estimate of the likelihood of success. Such an analysis can be obtained by using Orc [4] to describe the orchestration of sites in a grid application [10] and by estimating, using probability theory, the expected number of results that will be published by an expression evaluation [9]; each site S is assumed to have a probability of failure and distinct sites are assumed to be independent. In practice, it may be difficult to provide a meaningful measure of site reliability and the assumption that distinct sites are independent may be too strong. In this paper an alternative approach based on game theory is used to analyse the behaviour of orchestrations over unreliable environments.

Grid sites are partitioned into two disjoint sets, angels A and daemons D:

- Sites in A fail in such a way as to minimize damage to an application. This kind of failure is called angelic.

- Sites in D fail in such a way as to maximise damage to the application. This kind of failure is called daemonic.

It is assumed that the number of possible failures in the sets A and D are bounded. A and D can be viewed as players in a strategic game. If only angels are present then the problem is a maximization one; if only daemons act then we have a minimization problem. The interesting case lies between the extremes, when both angels and daemons act simultaneously and a competitive situation arises that can be represented by a so-called angel-daemon game. Here, finding a Nash equilibrium gives a solution that may be used to model realistic situations for unreliable grids, where the outcome is found somewhere between over-optimism and over-pessimism.

The study of systems under failures with Nash equilibria is not new. In [3] implementation problems involving unreliable players (who fail to act optimally) are studied. In [5] the authors study distributed systems in which players may exhibit Byzantine behaviour to undermine the correctness of the system. Note that *orchestrations represent control from one party's perspective* [7]. In this sense the analysis of orchestrations is different form the analysis of distributed systems under failures. The analysis of distributed systems is based (at least in part) on the graph properties of the underlying network. In the case of orchestrations we have to abstract the network (or consider it as another web or grid service). It is this "one party perspective" that makes the following analysis new.

In §2 a brief overview of Orc is presented. In §3 a way of assessing the benefits of evaluating an expression in an unreliable environment is proposed. In §4 a means of applying game theory to analyse the outcomes of executing orchestrations on unreliable networks is proposed. In §5 we assume that only one player controls the situation. When the player is A the damage is minimized. On the other hand, when the player is D the damage is maximized. These represent the two possible extreme coordinated behaviours, one extremely good and the other extremely bad. In this case there is no competitive activity and we have an optimization problem. In §6 we consider a competitive case defining a zero sum game, the so called angel-daemon game. In this game, both A and D play simultaneously. In §7 we apply the angel-daemon game to see how a grid manager assigns macro instructions to angelic and daemonic interpreters. In §5 we conclude and identify some open points.

2.   Orc: a brief overview

A set of site calls can be orchestrated into a complex computation by means of an Orc expression [4]. A site call either returns a result or remains silent – silence corresponds to a site failure. The site which always fails (and is useless) is denoted 0. Site calls can be combined by means of three composition operations.

- Sequence: $P \gg Q$. For each output published by P an instance of Q is executed. The notation $P > x > Q(x)$ is used in situations where the computation Q depends on the output of P.

- Symmetric Parallelism: $P|Q$. The published output of $P|Q$ is *any* interleaving of the outputs of P and Q.

- Asymmetric parallelism: P where $x :\in Q$. Threads in P and Q are evaluated in parallel. Some of the threads of P may be blocked by a dependency on x. The first result published by Q is bound to x, the remainder of Q's evaluation is terminated and evaluation of the blocked threads of P is resumed.

3.   Value of an orchestration under reliability failures

Web and Grid environments are unreliable. Sites evolve and a user has little (or no) control over the execution environment. Given a complex orchestration E it is *unrealistic to assume that there will be no site failures* when this orchestration is executed.

Reliability assumption. Sites are unreliable and can fail. When a site fails it remains silent and delivers no result at all. When a site does not fail it delivers the correct result. Any kind of byzantine behaviour is excluded. Any kind of behaviour delivering an "approximate" result is also excluded.

Even though some sites fail, orchestration may still produce useful partial results. For example, robust orchestrations may contain a degree of redundant computation so that evaluations may succeed even when a number of site failures occur. Given an orchestration E let $\alpha(E)$ be the set of sites that are called in E. Let $\mathcal{F} \subseteq \alpha(E)$ denote a set of sites that fail during an evaluation of E. The behaviour of the evaluation of E in this environment is given by replacing all occurrences of s, $s \in \mathcal{F}$, by 0. Let $\varphi_{\mathcal{F}}(E)$ denote this expression.

Value assumption. The evaluation of an orchestration has value even if some sites fail. For a particular failure set $\mathcal{F}$ the usefulness of the evaluation of $\varphi_{\mathcal{F}}(E)$ is measured by $v(\varphi_{\mathcal{F}}(E))$, the *value* or *benefit* of the orchestration $\varphi_{\mathcal{F}}(E)$. The range of v should be a non-negative $\mathbb{R}$. The value function v should have the following basic properties:

- $v(\varphi_{\alpha(E)}(E))$ must equal 0 when all sites fail in an evaluation of E,

- $v(\varphi_{\mathcal{F}}(E)) \geq 0$ for all $\mathcal{F} \subseteq \alpha(E)$,

- if $\mathcal{F} \subseteq \mathcal{F}' \subseteq \alpha(E)$ then $v(\varphi_{\mathcal{F}}(E)) \geq v(\varphi_{\mathcal{F}'}(E))$.

In this paper, we measure the benefit by the number of outputs that E publishes,

$$v(E) = \text{numbers of outputs published by } E.$$

An algorithmic definition of $v(E)$, for non-recursive E, is:

$$v(0) = 0 , \quad v(s) = 1 \text{ if } s \text{ is a service site} , \quad v(if(b)) = \text{ if } b \text{ then 1 else 0}$$
$$v(E_1 | E_2) = v(E_1) + v(E_2) , \quad v(E_1 \gg E_2) = v(E_1) * v(E_2)$$
$$v(E_1 \text{ where } z :\in E_2) = \text{ if } v(E_1) \geq 1 \text{ then } v(E_1) \text{ else 0}$$

$v(E)$ has polynomial time complexity with respect to the length of the expression E.

EXAMPLE 1 *Consider the following expression*

$$E = (M_1 | M_2) > x > [(M_3 | M_4) > y > (M_5(x) > z > M_6(z) \mid (M_7 | M_8) \gg M_9(y))]$$

Then $v(E) = 12$. *If site* M_1 *fails the benefit is* $v(E') = 6$ *where*

$$E' = (0 \mid M_2) > x > [(M_3 | M_4) > y > (M_5(x) > z > M_6(z) \mid (M_7 | M_8) \gg M_9(y))]$$

4.   Assessing Orchestrations

In this section a method of partitioning a set of sites into angels and daemons based on ranking is proposed.

Reliability ranking assumption. Given an Orc expression E we assume that a ranking containing $\alpha(E)$ is available. This ranking is a measure ("objective" or "subjective") of the reliability of the sites. This ranking can be independent of any orchestration E or conversely can depend strongly of the structure of E. Let $rk(s)$ be the rank of site s.

An orchestration assessor may use such a ranking to partition a set of sites $\alpha(E)$ into angel and daemon sets as follows:

$$\mathcal{A} = \{S \mid S \in \alpha(E), rk(S) \geq \lambda_E\} , \quad \mathcal{D} = \{S \mid S \in \alpha(E), rk(S) < \lambda_E\}$$

λ_E is a *reliability degree parameter* fixed by the assessor following the suggestions of the client. We do not consider in this paper how λ_E is determined. The assessor will perform an analysis where sites in $\mathcal{A}$ perform *as well as possible* and sites in $\mathcal{D}$ perform *as badly as possible*. This is a way to perform an analysis lying between the two possible extremes "all is good" or "all is bad". We can argue this as follows. Sites with a rank higher than λ_E are "believed" by the assessor to have non-destructive behaviour. Sites with a rank lower than λ_E are unknown entities as far as the assessor is concerned and can have highly-destructive behaviour. The assessor supposes that during an evaluation of E a number of sites will fail:

- Let a small fraction β_E of angelic sites fail during the evaluation – thus, the number of failing angels is $\beta_E \times \#\mathcal{A} = \mathcal{F}(\mathcal{A})$. When an angel fails it does so in such a way as to *maximise* the value of the orchestration.

- Let a fraction γ_E of daemon sites fail. The number of failing daemons is $\gamma_E \times \#\mathcal{D} = \mathcal{F}(\mathcal{D})$. Failing daemons try to *minimize* the value of the orchestration.

For a given λ_E, β_E and γ_E the behaviour of E can be analysed:

- if λ_E is such that $\alpha(E) = \mathcal{A}$, then evaluation of the behaviour can be determined by solving a maximization problem (see §5).

- conversely, if λ_E is chosen such that $\alpha(E) = \mathcal{D}$, evaluation of the behaviour can be determined by solving a minimization problem (see §5).

If $\mathcal{A} \neq \{\}$ and $\mathcal{D} \neq \{\}$ a competitive situation arises and game theory [6] can be used to analyse system behaviour (see §6). Suppose that the set of failing sites is $a \cup d$ where $a \subseteq \mathcal{A}$, $\#a = \mathcal{F}(\mathcal{A})$ and $d \subseteq \mathcal{D}$, $\#d = \mathcal{F}(\mathcal{D})$. System behaviour is measured by $\varphi_{(a,d)}(E)$. The rewards (or utilities) of the angelic $\mathcal{A}$ and daemonic $\mathcal{D}$ players are $u_{\mathcal{A}}(a, d) = v(\varphi_{(a,d)}(E))$ and $u_{\mathcal{D}}(a, d) = -v(\varphi_{(a,d)}(E))$ (this is a zero sum game as $u_{\mathcal{A}}(a, d) = -u_{\mathcal{D}}(a, d)$). When $\varphi_{(a,d)}(E)$ is executed $\mathcal{A}$ receives $v(\varphi_{(a,d)}(E))$ from $\mathcal{D}$. The strategy a is chosen (by $\mathcal{A}$) to increase the value of $u_{\mathcal{A}}(a, d)$ as much as possible while d is chosen (by $\mathcal{D}$) to decrease this value as much as possible. Stable situations are Nash equilibria: a pure Nash equilibrium is a strategy (a, d) such that $\mathcal{A}$ cannot improve the utility by changing a and $\mathcal{D}$ cannot reduce the utility by changing d. When players choose strategies using probabilities we have mixed Nash equilibria. Let (α, β) be a mixed Nash equilibrium. As in zero sum games all the Nash equilibria have the same utilities, an assessor can measure the value of a program E by the utility of $\mathcal{A}$ on any Nash equilibrium. Given a Nash equilibrium (α, β), the expected benefit of an expression E is given by:

$$Assessment(E, rk, \lambda_E, \beta_E, \gamma_E) = v(\varphi_{(\alpha,\beta)}(E))$$

5.   Bounded failures with one player games

The two extremes of behaviour can be determined through angelic and daemonic analysis:

Angelic failures.   In an angelic analysis the viewpoint "the world is as good as possible even when failures cannot be avoided" is adopted. An angelic player $\mathcal{A}$ plays the game by choosing a list, $a = (a_1, \ldots, a_n)$, of failing sites for an expression E, when $\mathcal{F}(\mathcal{A}) = n$. Such a tuple a is called the *action* taken by the player $\mathcal{A}$. Defining $\alpha_+(E) = \alpha(E) \setminus \{0\}$ the set of eligible actions for $\mathcal{A}$ is

$$A_{\mathcal{A}} = \{(a_1, \ldots, a_n) | i \neq j \text{ implies } a_i \neq a_j \text{ and } \forall i : a_i \in \alpha_+(E)\}$$

To a strategy profile $a = (a_1, \ldots, a_n)$ we associate the set $\mathcal{F}_a = \{a_1, \ldots, a_n\}$ and the mapping $\varphi_{F_a} : \alpha_+(E) \to \alpha(E) \cup \{0\}$

$$\varphi_{F_a}(s) = \begin{cases} 0 & \text{if } s \in F_a \\ s & \text{otherwise} \end{cases}$$

is used to replace failing sites by 0 and to keep working sites unchanged. $\varphi_{F_a}(E)$ denotes the image of E under φ_{F_a}.

$$\text{ANGEL}(E, \mathcal{A}, \mathcal{F}(\mathcal{A})) = (\mathcal{A}, A_{\mathcal{A}}, u_{\mathcal{A}})$$

defines a one player ($\mathcal{A}$) strategic game ($\mathcal{A}$ is used to denote both the player and the set of sites controlled by this player): the set of actions is $A_{\mathcal{A}}$ and the utility $u_{\mathcal{A}} = v(\varphi_{F_d}(E))$. In this game, the angel $\mathcal{A}$ has to choose a strategy profile a giving a maximal utility. As there is only one player, there a maximization problem rather than a strategic conflict.

Daemonic failures.   Daemonic failures are in a sense the opposite of angelic failures. In this case there is one player, the daemon $\mathcal{D}$ trying to maximize damage. We define $\text{DAEMON}(E, \mathcal{D}, \mathcal{F}(\mathcal{D})) = (\mathcal{D}, A_{\mathcal{D}}, u_{\mathcal{D}})$ such that $F_d = \{d_1, \ldots d_n\}$, $d = (d_1, \ldots, d_n)$ and

$$A_{\mathcal{D}} = \{(d_1, \ldots, d_n) | i \neq j \text{ implies } d_i \neq d_j \text{ and } \forall i : d_i \in \alpha_+(E)\}$$

Moreover, as $\mathcal{D}$ is intent on maximising damage, a long output is a bad result and thus $u_{\mathcal{D}}(d) = -v(\varphi_{F_d}(E))$. We can imagine $u_{\mathcal{D}}(d) = -v(\varphi_{F_d}(E))$ as a quantity of money that $\mathcal{D}$ has to pay, and naturally it is interested in paying as little as possible. In this case the rational behaviour of the daemon is formalized as a minimization problem.

EXAMPLE 2 *Let us consider two well-known expressions introduced in [2] . The first is a sequential composition of parallel expressions and the second is a parallel composition of sequential expressions:*

$$SEQ\text{-}of\text{-}PAR \triangleq (P|Q) \gg (R|S) , \ PAR\text{-}of\text{-}SEQ \triangleq (P \gg Q)|(R \gg S)$$

Let us analyse both expressions with two failures. First, consider in detail a pure angelic behaviour. As we identify the player and the possible set of failures we have $\mathcal{A} = \{P, Q, R, S\}$ and the set of strategy profiles is

$$A_{\mathcal{A}} = \{(P,Q), (P,R), (P,S), (Q,R), (Q,S), (R,S)\}$$

The utilities are given in the table. In order to maximize the utility, in the case of SEQ-of-PAR, the angel has to avoid profiles (P,Q) and (R,S). In the case of PAR-of-SEQ the angel has to take precisely (P,Q) or (R,S). As expected, the daemon $\mathcal{D}$ behaves in the opposite way.

Strategy profiles	(P,Q)	(P,R)	(P,S)	(Q,R)	(Q,S)	(R,S)
Angel $\mathcal{A}$						
SEQ-of-PAR	0	1	1	1	1	0
PAR-of-SEQ	1	0	0	0	0	1
Daemon $\mathcal{D}$						
SEQ-of-PAR	0	-1	-1	-1	-1	0
PAR-of-SEQ	-1	0	0	0	0	-1

6.   Two player games: the angel-daemon case

A strategic situation will occur when E suffers the effect of two players with opposite behaviour: an angel tries to minimize damage but, at the same time, a daemon tries to increase the damage. Let us consider in more detail this case. Let E be an Orc expression and assume that $\alpha_+(E)$ is partitioned into two disjoint administrative domains, the angel domain $\mathcal{A}$ and the daemon domain $\mathcal{D}$. We assume that $\mathcal{A} \cup \mathcal{D} = \alpha_+(E)$ and $\mathcal{A} \cap \mathcal{D} = \emptyset$. The notation $\mathcal{F}(\mathcal{A}) = p$ means that p sites will fail in $\mathcal{A}$. Similarly we note $\mathcal{F}(\mathcal{D}) = q$. We define

$$\text{ANGELDAEMON}(E, \mathcal{A}, \mathcal{D}, \mathcal{F}(\mathcal{D}), \mathcal{F}(\mathcal{A})) = (\mathcal{A}, \mathcal{D}, A_{\mathcal{A}}, A_{\mathcal{D}}, u_{\mathcal{A}}, u_{\mathcal{D}})$$

as follows. The players are $\mathcal{A}$ and $\mathcal{D}$ (as usual, we use the same letter to denote the player $\mathcal{A}$ and the set of sites controlled by this player). The strategy profiles are defined as follows.

- The *angel* $\mathcal{A}$ chooses p different failing sites $F_a = \{a_1, \ldots a_p\} \subseteq \mathcal{A}$. Any call to a site in $\mathcal{A} \setminus F_a$ is successful. We associate with F_a the action $a = (a_1, \ldots, a_p)$. Formally, $\mathcal{A}$ has the following set of actions

$$A_{\mathcal{A}} = \{(a_1, \ldots, a_p)|i \neq j \text{ implies } a_i \neq a_j \text{ and } \forall i : a_i \in \mathcal{A}\}$$

- The *daemon* $\mathcal{D}$, chooses q different failing sites $F_d = \{d_1, \ldots, d_q\}$. Calls to sites in $\mathcal{A} \setminus F_d$ are successful. The daemon's action is $d = (d_1, \ldots, d_p)$ and $A_{\mathcal{D}}$ will be the set of actions.

A *strategy profile* $s = (a, d)$ with $F_s = \{a_1, \ldots, a_p, d_1, \ldots, d_q\}$ fixes a priori the set of failing sites. Given E and F_s the length of $\varphi_{F_s}(E)$ is used to define the utilities as follows:

$$u_{\mathcal{A}}(s) = v(\varphi_{F_s}(E)), \ u_{\mathcal{D}}(s) = -v(\varphi_{F_s}(E))$$

Note that ANGELDAEMON is a zero sum game because $u_{\mathcal{D}}(s) + u_{\mathcal{A}}(s) = 0$.

The players can choose the actions using probabilities. A mixed strategy for $\mathcal{D}$ is a probability distribution $\alpha : A_{\mathcal{A}} \to [0, 1]$ such that $\sum_{a \in A_{\mathcal{A}}} \alpha(a) = 1$. Similarly, a mixed strategy for the daemon player $\mathcal{D}$ is a probability distribution $\beta : A_{\mathcal{D}} \to [0, 1]$. A mixed strategy profile is a tuple (α, β) and the utilities are

$$u_{\mathcal{A}}(\alpha, \beta) = \sum_{(a,d) \in A_{\mathcal{A}} \times A_{\mathcal{D}}} \alpha(a)\beta(d)u_{\mathcal{A}}(a, b)$$

$$u_{\mathcal{D}}(\alpha, \beta) = \sum_{(a,d) \in A_{\mathcal{A}} \times A_{\mathcal{D}}} \alpha(a)\beta(d)u_{\mathcal{D}}(a, b)$$

As $\mathcal{A}$ and $\mathcal{D}$ have opposing interests there is a strategic situation and we recall the definition of Nash equilibrium as a concept solution.

DEFINITION 3 *A pure Nash equilibrium is a pair* $s = (a, d)$ *such that, for any* a' *it holds* $u_{\mathcal{A}}(a, d) \geq u_{\mathcal{A}}(a', d)$ *and for any* d' *it holds* $u_{\mathcal{D}}(a, d) \geq u_{\mathcal{D}}(a, d')$. *A mixed Nash strategy is a pair* (α, β) *with similar conditions.*

EXAMPLE 4 *Let us consider how to assess SEQ-of-PAR and PAR-of-SEQ under two different situations. In the first sites are ranked*

$$rk(P) > rk(Q) > rk(R) > rk(S).$$

Assume that the reliability parameter is such that $\mathcal{A} = \{P, Q\}$ *and* $\mathcal{D} = \{R, S\}$ *and, moreover,* $1/2$ *of angelic sites will fail and* $1/2$ *of the demonic sites will also fail (therefore* $\mathcal{F}(\mathcal{A}) = \mathcal{F}(\mathcal{D}) = 1$). *Then* $A_{\mathcal{A}} = \{P, Q\}$, $A_{\mathcal{D}} = \{R, S\}$ *and the bimatrix games are*

$$\mathcal{D}$$

	R	S
A P	1, −1	1, −1
Q	1, −1	1, −1

SEQ-of-PAR

$$\mathcal{D}$$

	R	S
A P	0, 0	0, 0
Q	0, 0	0, 0

PAR-of-SEQ

In both cases any strategy profile (pure or mixed) is a Nash equilibrium and

$$Assessment(SEQ\text{-}of\text{-}PAR, rk, 1/2, 1/2, 1/2) = 1$$
$$Assessment(PAR\text{-}of\text{-}SEQ, rk, 1/2, 1/2, 1/2) = 0$$

Thus, for example, this assessment indicates to the client that, in the present environment, there is a reasonable expectation[1] of obtaining 1 output when executing PAR-of-SEQ.

Consider a second case with $rk'(P) > rk'(R) > rk'(Q) > rk'(S)$ such that $A = \{P, R\}$ and $\mathcal{D} = \{Q, S\}$ with $\mathcal{F}(A) = \mathcal{F}(\mathcal{D}) = 1$.

$$\mathcal{D}$$

	Q	S
A P	0, 0	1, −1
R	1, −1	0, 0

SEQ-of-PAR

$$\mathcal{D}$$

	Q	S
A P	1, −1	0, 0
R	0, 0	1, −1

PAR-of-SEQ

Here no game has pure Nash equilibria. There is only one mixed Nash equilibrium with $\alpha(P) = \alpha(R) = \beta(Q) = \beta(S) = 1/2$, and in this case the angel has utility $1/2$ and the daemon has utility $-1/2$. In this case

$$Assessment(SEQ\text{-}of\text{-}PAR, rk', 1/2, 1/2, 1/2) = 1/2$$

and similarly for PAR-of-SEQ. This assessment indicates to the client that, in the present environment, an output of 1 or 0 results (with equal likelihood) is a reasonable expectation.

EXAMPLE 5 *Consider the expression $(P \mid Q \mid R) \gg (S \mid T \mid U)$ with $A = \{P, Q, S\}$ and $\mathcal{D} = \{R, T, U\}$ with $\mathcal{F}(A) = 2$ and $\mathcal{F}(\mathcal{D}) = 1$*

$$\mathcal{D}$$

	R	T	U
(P, Q)	0, 0	2, −2	2, −2
A (P, S)	2, −2	2, −2	2, −2
(Q, S)	2, −2	2, −2	2, −2

$$(P \mid Q \mid R) \gg (S \mid T \mid U)$$

---

[1] Here "reasonable expectation" is meant in the everyday sense of the phrase and is not intended to represent a probabilistic outcome.

The pure Nash equilibria are $((P, S), R)$, $((P, S), T)$, $((P, S), U)$, $((Q, S), R)$, $((Q, S), T)$ *and* $((Q, S), U)$. *In this case the assessment says that* 2 *outputs is the reasonable expectation.*

7.   Manager's placement problem

The muskel [1] skeleton-based programming system provides an example of the kind of application that can be analysed using this approach. In muskel skeletons are implemented using macro data flow instruction graphs. Macro data flow instructions are placed on (potentially unreliable) remote worker sites for execution and the results are returned to the muskel manager for consolidation. A macro data flow graph may be modelled using an Orc expression. The behaviour of the muskel system in an untrusted environment may be analysed by considering its operation under the following assumptions:

- Data flow interpreters are unreliable.

- There is no recovery mechanism.

- Some sites may fail, but all cannot fail simultaneously. This means that the number of failures is bounded.

- An application manager tries to maximize the number of outputs that are generated.

Suppose that n remote data flow interpreters $\mathcal{I} = \{I_1, \ldots I_n\}$ are available. The manager has to place the set $\alpha_+(E)$ of macro insh tructions on the different macro data flow interpreters. Assume that interpreters are partitioned into two groups: the first group tries to minimize damage and we call this group the angel; the other group of interpreters behaves like a daemon. Moreover, in both cases the number of failures is bounded. A basic question in this case is, which is the best placement? Here we do not develop a general answer, but just consider a worked example.

EXAMPLE 6 *Consider the* SEQ-of-$PAR \triangleq (P \mid Q) \gg (R \mid S)$ *with* $\mathcal{I} = \{I_1, I_2\}$ *where* I_1 *is very reliable (angelic) and* I_2 *is very unreliable (daemonic). Assume that the manager has to place two macro instructions on one interpreter and the other two on the other interpreter. We assume that in both cases the interpreters will execute half of the assigned load. What is the best placement? There are several possibilities.*

- *Consider the outputs when the manager places* P *and* R *in* I_1 *(the angel) and* Q *and* S *in* I_2 *(the daemon). If* I_1 *makes* P *fail,* I_2 *will force* Q *to fail and there is no output. This situation is not ideal for* I_1 *(the angel) because changing the failure from* P *to* R *the output improves to* 1.

> *This new situation is not too bad for I_2 (the daemon) because changing the failure from Q to S worsens the output to 0. This situation is also unstable. This never ending behaviour can be analyzed by a bimatrix game having a mixed Nash equilibrium with expected output $1/2$.*

- *If P and Q are placed in one interpreter and R and S are placed in the other, the output is 1. This is the best we can obtain.*

8. Conclusions

One of the defining characteristics of grid programming is its dynamicity. Typically, the grid user has significantly less control over resources employed than in traditional scenarios: sites used for the execution of application components may fail. Thus, an important consideration for practical grid applications is the provision of an assessment of the quality of the application based on the expected performance of its constituent execution sites. In terms of an Orc expression, E, used to model the application, an ordered list for $\alpha(E)$ is needed. How this list should be built is unclear and is perhaps a controversial question: the likely behaviour of a site may depend on subjective perceptions of its qualities. In drawing up the list two distinct classes of consideration may be identified:

- **Aspects independent of the application.** Here we consider "stand-alone" qualities of a site. For example, the availability of proxies for a site may be regarded as enhancing its reliability. We might also take into account "the reputation" of the sites [8].

- **Aspects depending of the application.** The designer has *a priori* knowledge of the available potential sites, S. >From S the designer has to choose $\alpha(E)$. Once $\alpha(E)$ has been determined the orchestration has to be developed. We suggest that in many cases the development of the application and the rank of $\alpha(E)$ are inextricably linked. For example, a site used only as a "thread" in a parallel search may fail with little consequence for the application; failure of a site which forms a constituent of a sequential backbone of an application will be catastrophic for the application.

The ordering of $\alpha(E)$ depends also on the perception of the risk. Different people have different perceptions of risk and will rank sites accordingly. For instance, consider a database D with no back-up available. Assume that D is crucial for the application so that a failure in D significantly harms the application. There are two possibilities for ranking D:

- **Moderate optimism.** As a failure of D harms the application, an optimistic view will rank D among the angels. In this way the angel will try to avoid having D fail, but if it does fail then the outcome will fall far short of expectation.

- **Safe pessimism.** Since D is crucial to the application, D is ranked among the daemons, so that the outcome (likely failure of D), although far from ideal, is at least predictable and uncertainty is removed.

To better understand these points consider the following "gedanken experiment". Imagine that in the sixties you are asked to build an orchestration for a global war involving nuclear weapons and conventional arms. In order to assess how pessimistic is the orchestration, should you place the nuclear weapons among the daemons or among the angels? If you choose the former nuclear catastrophe ensues (in the simulation); if you choose the latter there is probability of survival.

Failure of grid sites is a reality of grid computing and forms a significant part of its challenge. Assessing the likelihood of success of an application requires both an evaluation of the quality of its constituent sites and a means of combining the results to measure the quality of the assembly. We propose the use of Orc together with game theory as a way of addressing the latter point; the assessment of individual sites and the establishment of a ranking among them remain open questions, touching as they do upon issues such as degree of trust and perception of risk, issues which remain largely subjective.

References

[1] Aldinucci, M., Danelutto, M.: Algorithmic skeletons meeting grids. *Parallel Computing* 32 (7): 449–462, 2006.

[2] Bouge, L.: Le modele de programmation a parallelisme de donees: une perspective semantique. *Techniques et science informatiques*, Vol 12, 5, 541–562, 1993.

[3] Eliaz, K: Fault Tolerant Implementation. *Review of Economic Studies*, 2002, vol. 69, issue 3, pages 589-610.

[4] Misra J., Cook, W.: Computation Orchestration: A basis for wide-area computing. *Software & Systems Modeling*, 2006. DOI 10.1007/s10270-006-0012-1.

[5] Moscibroda, T., Schmid, S., Wattenhofer, R: When selfish meets evil: byzantine players in a virus inoculation game. PODC'06, 35 - 44, 2006.

[6] Osborne, M., Rubinstein, A.: *A Course on Game Theory*, MIT Press, 1994.

[7] Peltz, C: Web Services Orchestration and Choreography. IEEE Computer 36(10): 46-52 (2003)

[8] Silaghi, G.C., Arenas, A., Silva, L.: Reputation-based trust management systems and their applicability to grids. Technical Report TR-0064, Institute on Programming Models, CoreGRID-Network of Excellence, March 2007.
     http://www.coregrid.net/mambo/images/stories/TechnicalReports/tr-0064.pdf
     21 May 2007.

[9] Stewart, A., Gabarró, J., Clint, M., Harmer, T., Kilpatrick, P., Perrott, R.: Estimating the reliability of web and grid orchestrations. In Gorlatch, S., Bubak, M., Priol, T., eds.: Integrated Research in Grid Computing, Krakov. Poland, CoreGRID.

[10] Stewart, A., Gabarró, J., Clint, M., Harmer, T., Kilpatrick, P., Perrott, R.: Managing Grid Computations: An ORC-Based Approach. In ISPA 2006, LNCS Vol. 4330, pp. 278–291, 2006.

IV

WORKFLOW PROGRAMMING

WORKFLOW PROGRAM MINC

PROGRAMMING E-SCIENCE GATEWAYS

Dennis Gannon
Department of Computer Science, School of Informatics
Indiana University, Bloomington, IN
USA 40405
gannon@cs.indiana.edu

Abstract   In this paper we describe a web service oriented design for problem solving systems used by scientist to orchestrate complex computational experiments. Specifically we describe a programming model for users of a science gateway or participants in a virtual organization to express non-trivial tasks that operates equally well in a environment built from a single "many core" processor or one where the computation is completely remote.

Keywords: e-Science, Web services, multicore, cloud computing

1.   Introduction

An e-Science Gateway is an interactive framework that allows a scientific collaboration to use the resources of a Grid in a way that frees them from the complex details of Grid software and middleware. By using such a Gateway users have access to community data and applications that can be composed and programmed into new applications in a language that is very natural for scientists. The gateway itself often takes the form of specialized web portal. Significant examples include the Geophysical Network GEON [1], which provides a very large community of geo-science researchers with data and tools for that discipline; NVO [2], the national virtual observatory; the Renci BioPortal [3], a very rich set of application services for modern biology; NEESGrid, the Network of Eathquake Engineers [4]; NanoHub, a gateway for education and research in nano-technology [5]; LEAD, a gateway for advanced research and education in mesoscale meteorology (which will be discussed as a case study here); and BIRN [6], the biomedical imaging research network. These are all examples of persistent e-Science Gateways. Many more exist. However, another important set of examples include the "Virtual Organizations" (VOs) that arise out of the needs of a small set of collaborators to solve a particular problem. For example, consider the requirements of an interdisciplinary science team doing a study of the effects of genetics on political ambition. Such a study may require vast data analysis of population individual genome information, social commentary and psychological interview data from the individuals involved, and family histories of behavior. The team of experts may require a large number of specialists who will need to work together as a virtual organization for a period of a few months to a year and they will need to find ways to share access to data, scientific ontologies, and data analysis and mining tools. VOs have similar needs to the e-Science Gateways, but they have the additional challenge that they must be easy to assemble by non-grid experts in a short amount of time.

In an e-Science Gateway or VO each user has a private data and metadata space and a toolbox of components that comprise the basis data analysis tasks that are composable into the experimental scenarios that define the scientific protocols of the discipline. These composed patterns of data analysis steps that define an experiment or scientific protocal, we shall refer to as a workflow. To make science truly collaborative the Gateway must support sharing of workflows, data and data provenance. It must be possible for any member of the group to "post" discoveries to the whole no matter how trivial, and it should be possible for others to subscribe to and discover new information on a specific topic produced by anybody in the VO.

The programming challenge in these eScience Gateway and VO environments is to provide the users with a way to build new tools from old ones in a rapid and reliable manner. There are four additional principals that must be considered.

(a). Scientific experiments must be repeatable. This is fundamental to the scientific method. Consequently, the gateway or VO system must support a way to access the provenance of any data product or experiment. In the case that the data was derived from a workflow, anybody should be able to re-run the workflow with the original or new data. This has profound implications on the data and processing architecture of the system.

(b). Workflow composition models must extremely expressive, flexible and easy to use. In their simplest form workflow descriptions can be viewed as scripts, which implies they are a simple type of computer program. Hence one can ask why not use a complete programming language as the standard Gateway/VO workflow language? For example, Python and Perl are Turing complete scripting languages that have been used for many years to orchestrate scientific workflows. The problem with this solution is that it is simply too hard for the scientist to reuse, modify or adapt these scripts. The approaches described below are less complete programming languages, but have proven to be popular with the scientific community and show great promise.

(c). The programming model must works on massive multicore systems as well as Grid and the emerging distributed "cloud computing" models. Multicore computing is going to revolutionize the desktop computing environment. Systems with 100 cores per processor will dominate the computing landscape within 15 years. By computing cloud we are referring to the data centers that are being deployed by companies like Amazon, Google, Microsoft, IBM and Yahoo. These facilities provide the potential for vast amounts of data and comput capacity to be available "on-demand" and at modest cost. The rise of these data and compute clouds presents an enormous opportunity for eScience and represents the next stage of the evolution of the Grid concept.

(d). There is a strong social sharing model that is enabled by this style of organizing and orchestrating scientific computation.

2.   Programming e-Science Workflows.

The experience of many e-Science projects is that the execution of a experiment requires some form of workflow description and we have found that the most popular way to do this is with a simple graphical composition tool. There have been dozens of workflow description and enactment tools built and some are described in [7]. The most successful of these are Kepler [10], Taverna [13], Triana [7], Pegasys/Dagman [6] and BPEL based tools like XBaya [11]. Most of these allow the user to compose the workflow as a simple directed acyclic graph (DAG) where each node represents an activity such as a running an analysis program. The arrows encodes the data dependences from one activity in the workflow to another. Different systems use different approaches to encapsulating an activity. In Kepler the activities are agents. In Taverna and XBaya these are web services. As illustrated in Figure 1, an activity can have multiple inputs and produce multiple outputs and the job workflow engine is to enact an activity as soon as its inputs are all available.

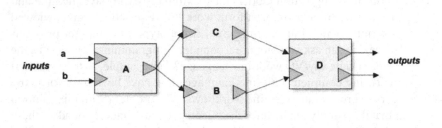

Figure 1.   A typical directed acyclic graph representation of a workflow. This is frequently called a data flow model because the edges represent a sequential data dependence of the output of one activity on the input of another.

The use of a Web service to encapsulate an activity is very attractive for several reasons. First it is relatively easy to "wrap" a standard command-line application as a web service. Second, a Web service can be a virtual entity that can be instantiated on-the-fly from a service factory [12]. This allows the service instance endpoint to be located at the most appropriate host. For example, if the service instance requires access to an application that is installed on more than one supercomputer, the machine with the lightest load can be selected.

Programming with simple DAGs is obviously not very general and there are many cases where some additional control structure can greatly extend the expressive power of the system. Figure 2 illustrates the case of control structures mixed with a data-driven graph. In this case a single source component is a listener agent which monitors external event streams. For example, it might monitor reports of severe weather events or other external activity that may trigger the workflow execution. Suppose the listener generates two type of events and each requires a different type of processing. Type A events require a single processing step, but type B events come in clusters within a fixed window of time. Each type B event can be processed independently and the results are later merged. The list of events may be a set of radar images from a cluster of storms. The merged result may be an ensemble forecast for a region. In this case we do not know if we which type of event will be generated by the listener until runtime, but suppose the listener also produces a flag is-typeA or is-typeB each time it generates an input to the rest of the system. Furthermore, we do not know how many type B events will be in a cluster. XBaya adds two simple control structures layered on top of the basic data flow graph to address this problem. A conditional node in the graph can be used to make a test to decide which downstream block of the workflow is executed.

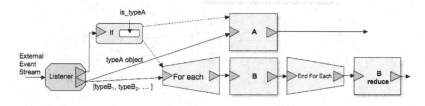

Figure 2. XBaya control structures for conditionals and map-reduce style iteration layered on top of a data-flow graph. Dotted lines in the graph indicate control paths. If the condition evaluates to true the sub-graph indicated by the upper dotted line is enabled. Otherwise the lower graph is enabled.

To create an iteration XBaya allows a "For each" control block. The input is a list, each element of which is compatible with the inputs to the sub-graph between the "For Each" and "End For Each" blocks. This control structure is a type of MapReduce operation in which an operation (in the figure, this is node B) is applied to each element of the list. The result of the "End For Each" is a list of the results. The "reduce" part of the operation can be any operation that takes a list of inputs and produces a final result. This MapReduce style computation allows a finite graphical representation of unbounded parallelism in the execution. This capability is critical for many large scale applications.

3.   A supporting Service Architecture.

A service architecture to support these capabilities is illustrated in Figure 3. The basic architecture is similar to many other gateway systems. This SOA is based on the LEAD [13] gateway (https://portal.leadproject.org) to the Teragrid Project [20]. The goal of the LEAD Gateway is to provide atmospheric scientists and students with a collection of tools that enables them to conduct research on "real time" weather forecasts of severe storms.

The gateway is composed of a portal server that is a container for "portlets" which provide the user interfaces to the cyberinfrastructure [15] services listed

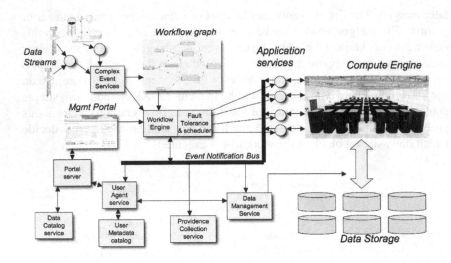

Figure 3.   The LEAD Service Oriented Architecture consists of 12 persistent services. The main services shown here include the Portal Server, the Data Catalog, the users MyLEAD metadata catalog, the workflow engine and fault tolerance services, the Data Provenance service and the Data Management Service.

above. The data search and discovery portlets in the portal server talk to the Data Catalog Service. This service is an index of data that is known to the system. The user's personal data is cataloged in the MyLEAD service [16]. MyLEAD is a metadata catalog. The large data files are stored on the back-end Grid resources under management of the Data Management Service. The myLEAD Agent manages the connection between the metadata and the data. Workflow in this architecture is described in terms of dataflow graphs, were the nodes of the graph represent computations and the edges represent data dependencies. The actual computations are programs that are pre-installed and run on the back-end Grid computing resources. However, the workflow engine, which sequences the execution of each computational task, sees these computations as just more Web services. Unlike the other services described in this section, these application services are virtual in that they are created on-demand by an application factory and each application service instance controls the execution of a specific application on a specific computing resource. The application service instances are responsible for fetching the data needed for each invocation of the application, submitting the job to the compute engine, and monitoring the execution of the application. The pattern of behavior is simple. When a user creates or selects an experiment workflow template, the required input data is identified and then bound to create a concrete instance of the workflow. Some of the input data comes from user input and others come from a search of the Data Catalog or the user's MyLEAD space. When the execution begins, the workflow engine sends work requests for specific applications to a fault tolerance/scheduler that picks the most appropriate resources and an Application Factory (not shown) instantiates the required application service.

A central component of the system is an event notification bus, which is used to convey workflow status and control messages throughout the system. The application service instances generate "event notifications" that provide details about the data being staged, the status of the execution of the application and the location of the final results. The MyLEAD agent listens to this message stream and logs the important events to the user's metadata catalog entry for the experiment. The workflow engine, provenance collection service and data management service all hear these notifications, which also contain valuable metadata about the intermediate and final data products. The Data Management service is responsible for migrating data from the Compute Engine to long-term storage. The provenance collection service [17] records all of this information and organizes it so that data provenance queries and statistics are easily satisfied.

4. The implications of the technology changes visible on the horizon.

There are three area where we can see changes in the computing landscape that will have a major impact on the way we do eScience.

4.1   The multicore future.

What does it mean for eScience when Intel and AMD and other microprocessor vendors claim that the current generation of quadcore systems will be rapidly replaced by systems with a hundred cores. Intel has already demonstrated an 80 core processor. While the implications for programming are clear: application designers of all types are going to have to learn about parallel programming. For the commercial software vendors like Microsoft, their entire software development platform will need to go through some fundamental transformations. Obviously considering the problem for software in general is beyond the scope of this paper. Fortunately there are some clear directions for e-Science gateways. We can first consider the deployment of the typical e-Science gateway. The LEAD service stack (briefly outlined in section 3 above) consists of 12 different persistent Web services. In addition, there are as many as 20 currently running application services, each of which may control several dozen parallel job invocations. Each parallel job may require from 4 to 100 concurrent processors. The LEAD SOA alone runs on a rack of 16 quad core servers.

Consequently, it is not unrealistic to suggest that the entire e-Science Gateway service set and many of the application services could run on a single manycore system. This would allow a very tightly integrated, and more reliable implementation of the core SOA that would only have to support a very small numbers of users.

Given a 100 core system, the core workflow application services and many of the applications could also be easily run on this system. Given the ability to easily express massive parallelism (such as MapReduce) using the workflow system, it is easy to utilize the full potential of multicore execution.

4.2   Cloud computing.

Companies like Google, Amazon, eBay, Yahoo!, Microsoft and IBM are building massive data and compute centers. It has been estimated that 25% of all server shipments are going to these companies to build these massive centers. There are basically two types of "clouds". The data clouds are resources that provide storage services on-demand over the Internet. For example, Amazon has the Simple Storage Service (S3) which allows a user to store and manage vast amounts of data through simple web services interfaces. S3 is easy to use and we have used it as a storage medium for workflows data products.

The more interesting cases are the "compute" clouds. These can be classified into two categories: MapReduce systems which combine a distributed file system with very large compute clusters, and virtual machine farms. Google estimates that they have approximately 1000 different use cases for MapReduce including the construction of their production web index [18] and Yahoo! has distributed the Hadoop system based on the same concept. They have made this available on a 4000 processor system available for public research. An interesting research challenge is to automatically translate MapReduce-style workflows, such as those described in section 2 into code that automatically runs on this system.

The virtual machine farms consist of clusters of processors that can be used as a parallel computing engine by remote users. These systems allow the user to configure a virtual machine with all the needed databases and applications and web services they need to create a remote service. The VM is then deployed on-demand by the user. From the perspective of the e-Science Gateway this provides an ideal way to dynamically instantiate application services from the workflow engine. An early experiment involving workflows for bioinformatics has shown this to be an effective alternative to large conventional supercomputer facilities such as the TeraGrid [19]. An interesting research challenge is to understand the trade-offs between the multiicore approach to hosting the computations locally and hosting them on a remote compute cloud. Because the the web services that represent computations are virtual, it may be possible for an instance of an application service to freely migrate between the local multicore system and the remote compute cloud. If it is more efficient to access the data when the computation is remote, the application can run there. If, on the other hand, the service needs more bandwidth in communication with other services that are running locally, the application can run locally.

4.3   Social Networking for Science

Social networking Wikis and web serves are bring communities together by providing new tools for people to interact with each other. Services like Facebook allow groups of users to create shared resource groups and networks. The LEAD gateway and others would provide a much richer experience for their users if there was more capability for dynamic creation of special interest groups with tools to support collaboration. One very interesting example of the use of social networking for e-Science is the myExperiment project [20] from the universities of Southampton and Manchester. Users of this Wiki can share workflow templates, along with notes and annotations. It should be possible to extend this idea to also include sharing of data and data provenance.

Acknowledgments

This work would not be possible without the support of NSF for the LEAD, NMI and TeraGrid projects. This paper also reflects the wisdom and hard work of many others including Satoshi Shirasuna, Suresh Marru, Dan Reed, Gopi Kandaswamy, Beth Plale, Alek Slominski, Yiming Sun, Scott Jensen and the rest of the LEAD team.

References

[1]   Geon, Welcome to the GEON Portal. http://portal.geongrid.org, visited 11/1/07.

[2]   U.S. National Virtual Observatory. http://www.us-vo.org. visited 11/1/07.

[3]   Renci Bioportal. http://www.ncbioportal.org/, visited 11/1/07.

[4]   NEES Cyberinfrastracture Center, http://it.nees.org/index.php, visited 11/1/07.

[5]   NanoHub, onlne simuation and more, http://www.nanohub.org, visited 11/1/07.

[6]   Biomedical Informatics Research Network, http://www.nanohub.org, visited 11/1/07.

[7]   I. Taylor, E. Deelman, D. Gannon, and M. Shields, Eds., Workflows in e-Science, Springer, 2006

[8]   Bertram LudŁscher, Ilkay Altintas, et. al. Scientific workflow management and the Kepler system, Concurrency and COmputation: Practice and Experience, Volume 18, Issue 10 , Pages 1039 - 1065, 2005.

[9]   T. Oinn, et. al. Taverna: a tool for the composition and enactment of bioinformatics workflows, Bioinformatics vol. 20 issue 17, Oxford University Press 2004.

[10] E. Deelman, et. al., Pegasus: A framework for mapping complex scientific workflows onto distributed systems, Scientific Programming, Volume 13, Number 3, 2005, pp. 219 - 237.

[11] S. Shirasuna, A Dynamic Scientific Workflow System for Web services Architecture, Ph.D. Thesis, Department of Computer Science, Indiana University, Sept. 2007.

[12] G. Kandaswamy, L. Fang, Y. Huang, S. Shirasuna, S. Marru, D. Gannon: Building web services for scientific grid applications. IBM Journal of Research and Development 50(2-3): 249-260 (2006).

[13] K. Droegemeier, et. al., Service-Oriented Environments for Dynamically Interacting with Mesoscale Weather, CiSE, Computing in Science & Engineering – November 2005, vol. 7, no. 6, pp. 12-29.

[14] C. Catlett, The Philosophy of TeraGrid: Building an Open, Extensible, Distributed TeraScale Facility, Proceedings of the 2nd IEEE/ACM International Symposium on Cluster Computing and the Grid, 2002.

[15] National Science Foundation Cyberinfrastructure Council, Cyberinfrastructure Vision for 21st Century Discovery. March 2007. NSF document 0728.

[16] SL Pallickara, B Plale, S Jensen, Y Sun, Structure, Sharing and Preservation of Scientific Experiment Data, IEEE 3rd International workshop on Challenges of Large Applications in Distributed Environments, Research Triangle Park, NC, 2005.

[17] Y. Simmhan, B. Plale, D. Gannon,. Querying capabilities of the karma provenance framework. Concurrency and Computation: Practice and Experience, 2007.

[18] j. Dean, S. Ghemawat, MapReduce: Simplified Data Processing on Large Clusters, OSDI'04: Sixth Symposium on Operating System Design and Implementation, San Francisco, CA, December, 2004.

[19] J. Y. Choi, Y. Yang, S. Kim, and D. Gannon, V-Lab-Protein: Virtual Collaborative Lab for Protein Sequence Analysis, Proceedings of the IEEE Workshop on High-Throughput Data Analysis for Proteomics and Genomics, Fremont, CA. Nov. 2007.

[20] myExperment. http://www.myexperiment.org. visited 11/2/07.

RE-EVALUATING THE GRID: THE SOCIAL LIFE OF PROGRAMS

David De Roure
University of Southampton,
Electronics and Computer Science
Southampton, SO17 1BJ, UK
dder@ecs.soton.ac.uk

Carole Goble
The University of Manchester,
Manchester, UK
carole.goble@manchester.ac.uk

Abstract   This paper discusses programming the Grid in the space between the Grid infrastructure and those using it to conduct scientific research. Rather than looking at any particular grid programming model, we consider the need to address 'usability' of programming solutions in this space. As a case study we consider a popular solution; i.e. scientific workflows, and we reflect on Web 2.0 approaches. We suggest that broad adoption of Grid infrastructure is dependent on ease of programming in this space.

Keywords: Scientific Wrokflow, Web 2.0

1.   Introduction

Grid computing is about bringing resources together in order to achieve something that was not possible before. In its early phase there was an emphasis on combining resources in pursuit of computational power and very large scale data processing, such as high speed wide area networking of supercomputers and clusters. This new power enabled researchers to address exciting problems that would previously have taken lifetimes, and it encouraged collaborative scientific endeavours. As it has evolved, Grid computing continues to be about providing an infrastructure which brings resources together, with an emphasis now on the notion of Virtual Organisations.

This emerging infrastructure is increasingly being considered for 'everyday science', enabling researchers in every discipline to make use of the new capabilities. However there is significant challenge in bringing the new infrastructure capabilities to broad communities of users, a problem which was perhaps masked previously by the focus on a more 'heroic' style of Grid project. Significantly, this is a programming challenge – how do we make it easy for people to assemble the services and resources they want in order to achieve the task at hand?

In this paper we look at programming in the space between the core infrastructure services and the users. This area has been the focus of attention for the Semantic Grid community for several years, initially using Semantic Web and more recently developing Web 2.0 techniques. In the next section we recap the Semantic Grid vision, then in Section 3 we take a look at scientific workflows as a case study in programming in this space, with a particular look at a system which emerged from one of the Semantic Grid projects. Section 4 reflects on everyday e-Science in the context of the principles of Web 2.0. We close by observing that success in programming the grid is not just about programming abstractions but also about ease of use and what we describe as the 'social life of programs'.

2.   The Semantic Grid

The notion of the 'Semantic Grid' was introduced in 2001 by researchers working at the intersection of the Semantic Web, Grid and software agent communities [4]. Observing the gap between aspiration and practice in grid computing, the report 'The Semantic Grid: A Future e-Science Infrastructure' stated:

> e-Science offers a promising vision of how computer and communication technology can support and enhance the scientific process. It does this by enabling scientists to generate, analyse, share and discuss their insights, experiments and results in a more effective manner. The underlying computer infrastructure that provides these facilities is commonly referred to as the Grid. At this time, there are a number of Grid applications being developed and there is a whole raft

of computer technologies that provide fragments of the necessary functionality. However there is currently a major gap between these endeavours and the vision of e-Science in which there is a high degree of easy-to-use and seamless automation and in which there are flexible collaborations and computations on a global scale.

We recognised that this emerging vision of the Grid was closely related to that of the Semantic Web – which is also, fundamentally, about joining things up. The Semantic Web is an initiative of the Worldwide Web Consortium (W3C) and at that time was defined by the W3C Activity Statement as "...an extension of the current Web in which information and services are given well-defined meaning, better enabling computers and people to work in cooperation".

To researchers aware of both worlds, the value of applying Semantic Web technologies to the information and knowledge in Grid applications was immediately apparent. At that time the service-oriented architecture of the Grid was also foreseen, and the need for machine-understandable metadata in order to facilitate automation was clear. Thus the vision of the Semantic Grid became established as the application of Semantic Web technologies both *on* and *in* the Grid [9]. Additionally, agent-based computing was proposed to achieve the necessary degree of flexibility and automation within the machinery of the Grid [8].

The dual aspects of *information* and *services* have been explored in various projects. Within the UK e-Science program, the Combechem project in particular focused on the 'Semantic Datagrid' [15], while ^{my}Grid focused on services [1]. Semantic Grid has been adopted in a range of grid projects across Europe and in 2006 the Next Generation Grids Experts Group articulated a vision for the future service-oriented Grid called the *Service Oriented Knowledge Utility*, which captured the Semantic Grid vision and identifying an agenda for future research [12].

3. Scientific Workflows

The ^{my}Grid project produced a scientific workflow system, Taverna [13], which enables scientists to assemble services in order to conduct their research – it is a programming solution in the space between the infrastructure services and the research applications. This is our case study in programming the grid. We can think of workflows as scripts, and many of the lessons from workflows extrapolate to scripts in general.

Scientific workflows are attracting considerable attention in the research community. Increasingly they support scientists in advancing research through *in silico* experimentation, while the workflow systems themselves are the subject of ongoing research and development. The National Science Foundation Workshop on the Challenges of Scientific Workflows identified the potential for scientific advance as workflow systems address more sophisticated requirements and as workflows are created through collaborative design processes involving many scientists across disciplines [5]. Rather than looking at the application or machinery of workflow systems, it is the dimension of collaboration and sharing that is of particular interest to us here.

Understanding the whole lifecycle of the workflow design, prototyping, production, management, publication and discovery is fundamental to developing systems that support the scientists' work. Reuse is a particular challenge when scientists are outside a predefined Virtual Organisation or enterprise – where there are individuals or small groups, decoupled from each other and acting independently, who are seeking workflows that cover processes outside their expertise from a common pool of components. This latter point arises when workflows are shared across discipline boundaries and when inexperienced scientists need to leverage the expertise of others.

There are many workflow systems available — we found over 75 after conducting an informal search. These systems vary in many respects: e.g. who uses them, what resources they operate over, whether the systems are open or closed, how workflows are expressed (e.g. how control flow is handled), how interactive they are, when and how tasks are allocated to resources, and how exceptions are handled. Our focus here is on scientific workflows which are near the application level rather than those further down in the infrastructure; i.e. we are interested in composing scientific applications and components using workflows, over a service oriented infrastructure (which may include Grid services). These are the workflows which are close to the scientist, or indeed the researcher whatever their domain.

3.1   The workflow as a first class citizen

One immediate attraction of workflows which encourages their uptake is the easing of the burden of repetitive manual work. However, we suggest that the key feature for scientific advancement is reuse. Workflow descriptions are not simply digital data objects like many other assets of e-Science, but rather they actually capture pieces of scientific process – they are valuable knowledge assets in their own right, capturing valuable know-how that is otherwise often tacit. Reuse is effective at multiple levels: the scientist reuses a workflow with different parameters and data, and may modify the workflow, as part of the routine of their daily scientific work; workflows can be shared with other scientists conducting similar work, so they provide a means of codifying, sharing and thus spreading the workflow designer's practice; and workflows, workflow fragments and workflow patterns can be reused to support science outside their initial application.

The latter point illustrates the tremendous potential for new scientific advance. An example of this is a workflow used to help identify genes involved in tolerance to Trypanosomiasis in east African cattle [7]. The same workflow was reused over a new dataset to identify the biological pathways implicated in the ability for mice to expel the Trichuris muris parasite (a parasite model of the human parasite Trichuris trichuria). This reuse was made easier by the explicit, high-level nature of the workflow that describes the analytical protocol.

Workflows bring challenges too. Realistic workflows require skill to produce so they can be difficult and expensive to develop. Consequently, workflow developers need development assistance, and prefer not to start from scratch. Furthermore it is easy for the reuse of a workflow to be confined to the project in which it was conceived. In the Trypanosomiasis example, the barrier to this reuse was how the knowledge about the workflow could be spread to the scientists with the potential need. In this case it was word of mouth within one institution; this barrier needs to be overcome. So, we have a situation of workflows as reusable knowledge commodities, but with potential barriers to the exchange and propagation of those scientific ideas that are captured as workflows.

Significantly, there is more to a workflow than a declaration of a process. An individual workflow description may take the form of an XML file, but these do not sit in isolation. We can identify a range of properties that are factors in guiding workflow reuse, including: descriptions of its function and purpose; documentation about the services with which it has been used, with example input and output data, and design explanations; provenance, including its version history and origins; reputation and use within the community; ownership and permissions constraints; quality, whether it is reviewed and still works; and dependencies on other workflows, components and data types. Workflows also enable us to record the provenance of the data resulting from their enactment, and logs of service invocations from workflow runs can inform later decisions about service use.

By binding workflows with this kind of information, we provide a basis for workflows to be trusted, interpreted unambiguously and reused accurately. But like the workflows themselves, the associated information is currently often confined to the system from which it originated and thus is not reusable as a useful commodity in its own right.

3.2 Workflow Systems and Communities

Scientific workflow systems with significant deployment include the Taverna workflow workbench [13], Kepler [10], Triana [2] and Pegasus [6]. Taverna, which comes from the ^{my}Grid project, is used extensively across a range of Life Science problems: gene and protein annotation; proteomics, phylogeny and phenotypical studies; microarray data analysis and medical image analysis; high throughput screening of chemical compounds and clinical statistical analysis.

Significantly, Taverna has been designed to operate in the open wild world of bioinformatics. Rather than large scale, closed collaborations which own resources, Taverna is used to enable individual scientists to access the many open resources available in the cloud, i.e. out on the Web and not necessarily within their enterprise. Many of the services are expected to be owned by parties other than those using them in a workflow. In practice they are volatile, weakly described and there is no contract in place to ensure quality of service; they have not been designed to work together, and they adhere to no common type system. Consequently, they are highly heterogeneous. By compensating for these demands, Taverna has made, at the time of writing, over 3500 bioinformatics orientated operations available to its users. This has been a major incentive to adoption. This openness also means that Taverna is not tied exclusively to the bioinformatics domain – any services can be incorporated into its workflows.

By way of comparison, the lifecycle of workflows in the Pegasus system has also been the subject of study [6]. Pegasus has more of a computational and Grid emphasis. It maps from workflow instances to executable workflows, automatically identifying physical locations for workflow components and data and finding appropriate resources to execute the components; it reuses existing data products where applicable. Pegasus is used within large scale collaborations and big projects and is perhaps more typical of traditional e-Science and grid activities, while Taverna gives an interesting insight into another part of the scientific workflow ecosystem – it is being used by many scientists on their personal projects, constituting a distributed, disconnected community of users who are also the developers of the workflows. Taverna is very much about services – and scientists – 'in the cloud'.

3.3   Sharing workflows

It is apparent then that we can view workflows as potential commodities, as valuable first class assets in their own right, to be pooled and shared, traded and reused, within communities and across communities, to propagate like memes. Workflows themselves can be the subject of peer review. Furthermore we can conceive of packs of workflows for certain topics, and of workflow pattern books – new structures above the level of the individual workflow. We call this perspective of the interacting data, services, workflow and their metadata within a scientific environment the *workflow ecosystem* and we suggest that by understanding and enabling this we can unlock the broader scientific potential of workflow systems.

Workflow management systems already provide basic sharing mechanisms, through repository stores for workflows developed as part of projects or communities. For example, the Kepler Actor Repository is an LDAP-based directory for the remote storage, query and retrieval of actors (processes) and other workflow components and the SCEC/CME workflow system has component and workflow libraries annotated with ontologies [11]. These follow the tradition of cataloguing scripting libraries and codes.

In the ^{my}Experiment project we are taking a more social approach: we believe that the key to sharing is to recognise the use of workflows by a community of scientists [3]. This acknowledges a central fact, sometimes neglected, that the lifecycle of the workflows is coupled with the process of science that the human system of workflow use is coupled to the digital system of workflows. The more workflows, the more users and the more invocations then the more evidence there is to assist in selecting a workflow. The rise of harnessing the Collective Intelligence of the Web has dramatically reminded us that it is people who generate and share knowledge and resources, and people who create network effects in communities. Blogs and wikis, shared tagging services, instant messaging, social networks and semantic descriptions of data relationships are flourishing. Within the Scientific community we have examples: OpenWetWare, Connotea, PLoS on Facebook, etc. (see corresponding .org Web Sites and facebook.com).

By mining the sharing behaviour between users within such a community we can provide recommendations for use. By using the structure and interactions between users and workflow tools we can identify what is considered to be of greater value to users. Provenance information helps track down workflows through their use in content syndication and aggregation.

4. Web 2.0

While part of e-Science has focused on infrastructure provision, everyday scientific practice has continued to evolve, especially in use of the Web. Like workflows, the mashups which characterise Web 2.0 also enable scientists to bring together resources in new ways – they provide a means of coupling robust underlying services. Significantly, creating mashups is not such a specialist activity as working with Grid or Semantic Web, and this is illustrated by the many examples of mashups being used by researchers and by ICT experts within their research domains: the Web is increasingly seen as a distributed application platform in its own right. The simple interfaces based on REST, the content behind them such as the Google Maps API, and the sharing culture that characterises their development and evolution, is leading to uptake which is having immediate impact on everyday scientific practice in many domains – and can be contrasted with the uptake of Grid.

We suggest that these two examples of programming above the service level – the scientific workflows of Taverna and mashups for everyday science – exemplify the way forward for e-Science and for Grid computing. We believe that the reason they work is that they thrive in the ecosystem between core infrastructure services and the user: an ecosystem of scientists, domain ICT experts, companies, tools, workflow systems, and indeed computer scientists.

We can demonstrate the relationship between e-Science and Web 2.0 in this space by considering e-Science in the context of the eight design patterns of Web 2.0 [14]:

The Long Tail While e-Science has often focused on specialist early-adopter scientists and large scale collaborative projects, Taverna and mashups are used by the 'long tail' of researchers doing everyday science – by which we refer to the larger number of smaller-scale specialists who are now enabled by digital science. Rather than heroic science with heroic infrastructure, new communities are coming online and bring with them the power of community intelligence. They are often using services 'in the cloud' rather than in the enterprise.

Data is the Next Intel Inside e-Science has been motivated by the need to handle the data deluge brought about by new experimental methods, and this data is large, rich, complex and increasingly real-time. Significantly there is extra value in data through new digital artefacts (such as scientific workflows) and through metadata; e.g. capturing context for interpreting data, storing provenance in order to interpret and trust data.

Users Add Value This is already a principle of the scholarly knowledge life-cycle, now revisited in the digital age. e-Science increasingly focuses on publishing as well as consuming.

Network Effects by Default Brought about by working in more and more with shared digital artefacts, the actual usage of information brings new value – through explicit reviewing but also implicitly through the recommendations and advice that can be provided automatically based on usage patterns. For example, the choice of services to run a workflow can be based on the history of service usage and performance as well as sharing of community knowledge.

Some Rights Reserved Increasingly we see mechanisms for sharing scholarly outputs – data, workflow, mashups – which by default are open. This is exemplified by preprints servers and institutional repositories, open journals, movements such as Science Commons and technologies such as the Open Archives Initiative. Open source development, and the sharing of scripts used in mashups, exemplify the openness which accelerates the creation of programming solutions.

The Perpetual Beta The technologies that scientists are choosing to use are not perfect, but they are better than what went before. The solutions being adopted in the space we are discussing are often the result of extreme programming rather than extensive software engineering, providing the essential agility in response to user needs.

Cooperate, Don't Control The success stories come from the researchers who have learned to use ICT – we are seeing an empowering of domain experts to deliver the solutions. Indeed, solutions which take away this autonomy may be resisted. This is achieved by making it as easy as possible to reuse services and code.

Software Above the Level of a Single Device e-Science is about the intersection of the digital and physical worlds. Sensor networks are responsible for the data deluge, but equally mobile handheld devices are increasingly the interface as opposed to portals in Web browsers on PCs.

5. Discussion

The Semantic Grid activities have demonstrated the value of Semantic Web technologies to meet some of the needs of e-Scientists, especially for information reuse and where automation is required. They have also demonstrated the need for ease of programming in the space above the robust services to enable agile provision of better solutions for the users.

Sometimes Web 2.0 is seen as a competitor to Grid, and criticised by the grid community for lack of robust engineering and the rigour needed to underpin scientific research. We have presented a different view: that a Web 2.0 approach is absolutely appropriate for use in the space between the robust grid infrastructure and the user. We note that the SOKU vision of robust services ('utilities') which are dependable and easy to use is entirely consistent with this.

The key point for those involved in programming the Grid is that ease of use – usability of programs – is just as important as well-designed programming models. It is necessary to think outside individual programs and think about their lifecycle, the interactions of users, developers and scientists with the programs – what we could call the 'social life of programs'. The ^{my}Experiment project adopts this approach for workflows.

One of the propositions of Grid computing has been a universal Grid achieved by a certain style of coupling of resources. The picture we have drawn is a little different: some robust services 'in the cloud', perhaps based on grid technologies, which are plumbed together towards the application level. We suggest that this latter view is more achievable and is actually what many users require. Aside from the distributed application platform, these technologies are clearly complementary within the research lifecycle; e.g. grid for capturing or generating data and Web 2.0 for working with it effectively.

e-Science is now enabling researchers to do some completely new research. As the individual pieces become easy to use, researchers can bring them together in new ways and ask new questions. Hence usability of the programming tools – workflows, mashups, whatever new techniques may emerge – is what will enable new science. This should be on the agenda for the grid programming community.

Acknowledgments

Thanks to the ^{my}Grid, Comb$e$Chem and ^{my}Experiment teams and the Taverna user community, and also to our Semantic Grid colleagues, especially Geoffrey Fox and Marlon Pierce.

References

[1] R. D. Stevens C. A. Goble, S. R. Pettifer and C. Greenhalgh. *Knowledge Integration: In silico Experiments in Bioinformatics*, pages 121–134. Morgan Kaufmann, May 2004.

[2] David Churches, Gabor Gombas, Andrew Harrison, Jason Maassen, Craig Robinson, Matthew Shields, Ian Taylor, and Ian Wang. Programming scientific and distributed workflow with triana services: Research articles. *Concurr. Comput. : Pract. Exper.*, 18(10):1021–1037, 2006.

[3] D. De Roure and C.A. Goble. myExperiment - a web 2.0 virtual research environment. In *International Workshop on Virtual Research Environments and Collaborative Work Environments*, May 2007.

[4] D. De Roure, N. R. Jennings, and N. R. Shadbolt. Research Agenda for the Semantic Grid: A future e-science infrastructure. Technical Report UK UKeS-2002-02, National e-Science Centre, Edinburgh, December 2001.

[5] E. Deelman and Y. Gil, editors. *NSF Workshop on the Challenges of Scientific Workflows*. NSF, May 2006.

[6] Ewa Deelman, Gurmeet Singh, Mei-Hui Su, James Blythe, Yolanda Gil, Carl Kesselman, Gaurang Mehta, Karan Vahi, G. Bruce Berriman, John Good, Anastasia Laity, Joseph C. Jacob, and Daniel S. Katz. Pegasus: a framework for mapping complex scientific workflows onto distributed systems. *Scientific Programming Journal*, 13(3):219–237, 2005.

[7] Paul Fisher, Cornelia Hedeler, Katherine Wolstencroft, Helen Hulme, Harry Noyes, Stephen Kemp, Robert Stevens, and Andrew Brass. A systematic strategy for the discovery of candidate genes responsible for phenotypic variation. In *Third International Society for Computational Biology (ISCB) Student Council Symposium at the Fifteenth Annual International Conference on Intelligent Systems for Molecular Biology (ISMB)*, July 2007.

[8] Ian Foster, Nicholas R. Jennings, and Carl Kesselman. Brain meets brawn: Why grid and agents need each other. In *AAMAS '04: Proceedings of the Third International Joint Conference on Autonomous Agents and Multiagent Systems*, pages 8–15, Washington, DC, USA, 2004. IEEE Computer Society.

[9] C. A. Goble, D. De Roure, N. R. Shadbolt, and A. A. A. Fernandes. *Enhancing Services and Applications with Knowledge and Semantics*, pages 431–458. Morgan-Kaufmann, 2004.

[10] Bertram Ludascher, Ilkay Altintas, Chad Berkley, Dan Higgins, Efrat Jaeger, Matthew Jones, Edward A. Lee, Jing Tao, and Yang Zhao. Scientific workflow management and the Kepler system: Research articles. *Concurr. Comput. : Pract. Exper.*, 18(10):1039–1065, 2006.

[11] Philip Maechling, Hans Chalupsky, Maureen Dougherty, Ewa Deelman, Yolanda Gil, Sridhar Gullapalli, Vipin Gupta, Carl Kesselman, Jihic Kim, Gaurang Mehta, Brian Mendenhall, Thomas Russ, Gurmeet Singh, Marc Spraragen, Garrick Staples, and Karan Vahi. Simplifying construction of complex workflows for non-expert users of the southern california earthquake center community modeling environment. *SIGMOD Rec.*, 34(3):24–30, 2005.

[12] Next Generation Grids Experts Group. Future for european grids: Grids and Service Oriented Knowledge Utilities. Technical report, EU Grid Technologies, January 2006.

[13] Tom Oinn, Mark Greenwood, Matthew Addis, M. Nedim Alpdemir, Justin Ferris, Kevin Glover, Carole Goble, Antoon Goderis, Duncan Hull, Darren Marvin, Peter Li, Phillip Lord, Matthew R. Pocock, Martin Senger, Robert Stevens, Anil Wipat, and Chris Wroe. Taverna: lessons in creating a workflow environment for the life sciences: Research articles. *Concurr. Comput. : Pract. Exper.*, 18(10):1067–1100, 2006.

[14] T. O'Reilly. What is Web 2.0 - design patterns and business models for the next generation of software, 2005. http://www.oreillynet.com/pub/a/oreilly/tim/news/2005/09/30/what-is-web-20.html.

[15] K. Taylor, R. Gledhill, J. W. Essex, J. G. Frey, S. W. Harris, and D. De Roure. A Semantic Datagrid for Combinatorial Chemistry. In *GRID '05: Proceedings of the 6th IEEE/ACM International Workshop on Grid Computing*, pages 148–155, Washington, DC, USA, 2005. IEEE Computer Society.

WORKFLOWS ON TOP OF A MACRO DATA FLOW INTERPRETER EXPLOITING ASPECTS*

Marco Danelutto
Dept. Computer Science – University of Pisa – Italy
marcod@di.unipi.it

Patrizio Dazzi
ISTI/CNR, Pisa & IMT, Lucca
patrizio.dazzi@isti.cnr.it

Abstract   We describe how aspect oriented programming techniques can be exploited to support the development of workflow-based grid applications. In particular, we use aspects to adapt simple Java workflow code to be executed on top of `muskel`, our experimental, macro data flow based skeleton programming environment. Aspects are used to extract "on-the-fly" macro data flow graphs from plain Java code where the nodes of the workflow are explicitly identified by the programmers. The macro data flow instructions in the graph are automatically submitted to the `muskel` distributed macro data flow interpreter for the execution. A proper manager, instantiated by the programmer, is used to exploit stream parallelism on the workflow. Experimental results will be presented that demonstrate scalability of the approach for suitably grained workflows.

Overall, the approach discussed here concentrates workflow exploitation responsibilities on the aspect (i.e. system) programmers leaving the application programmers only the task of properly defining logical steps in the workflow. This results in a complete separation of concerns that sensibly enhances the efficiency in workflow application development, while keeping both the system size and the additional knowledge required to application programmers reasonably small.

Keywords: workflow, data flow, aspect oriented programming.

*This research is carried out under the FP6 Network of Excellence CoreGRID funded by the European Commission (Contract IST-2002-004265).

1. Introduction

Workflow represents a popular programming model for grid applications. In a workflow, users express the data dependencies incurring among a set of blocks, possibly using a DAG. Each block processes input data to produce output data. Workflow schedulers then arrange the computations for grid execution in such a way

- all the parallelism implicitly defined through the (absence of) dependencies in the DAG is exploited, and

- the available grid resources (processing elements) are efficiently used.

Here we discuss an approach aimed at implementing workflows on top of the muskel distributed macro data flow interpreter [7]. We take into account the execution of workflows on a set of input data items. The set of input data items represents the program input stream. Each item on that stream will be submitted to a workflow process. The results of that processing will appear as a data items onto the program output stream. Usually the workflows considered in grids are such that nodes in the DAGs are complex, possibly parallel applications that process data contained in one or more input files to produce data in one or more output files [11]. Here we consider a much simpler class of workflows: those whose DAG nodes are (possibly complex) Java "functions" processing generic (possibly complex)Object input parameters to produce (possibly complex) Object output results.

The muskel distributed macro data flow interpreter [1] has been developed to support structured parallel programming on clusters, networks of workstations and grids. Using muskel, programmers write parallel applications according to the algorithmic skeletons programming model [4–5]. Parallel code is therefore expressed as a composition of skeletons: parallel design patterns modelling well known parallelism exploitation patterns, specialized through proper sequential code parameters.

In muskel, each skeleton program is translated in a macro data flow graph whose instructions (nodes) model large chunks of side effect free (i.e. functional) sequential Java code. "Functional" code is provided as classes implementing the Compute interface. This interface only includes a Object compute (Object in) method, which is the one use to wrap the sequential computation implementing the function. Each time a new data item is submitted to the program input stream, an instance of the data flow graph with the input data placed in the proper data flow tokens is submitted to the muskel distributed interpreter for the evaluation. The distributed interpreter schedules fireable[1] macro data

---

[1]a data flow instruction is *fireable* iff all the input tokens it needs are present

flow instructions for execution on the available processing resources and then it stores back result data tokens either in the proper positions of the graph (target macro data flow instructions) or on the program output stream (final result tokens only).

2.   Aspects to implement workflows

In a sense, the way muskel implements skeleton programs on top of the macro data flow interpreter is definetly close to the way workflows are usually implemented on distributed architectures and grids. As muskel distributed macro data flow interpreter efficiency has already been demonstrated [1], we tried to exploit muskel to implement workflow computations. As already stated, we considered workflows processing stream of input data to produce stream of output data. This allows to express both parallelism implicit in the workflow definition (and therefore exploited within the computation of a single instance of the workflow) and stream parallelism (parallelism among dinstinct instances of workflow computation, relative to independent input data items). In order to obtain a macro data flow graph from the workflow abstract code, we exploit Aspect Oriented Programming (AOP) techniques [10], as follows[2]:

- Users express workflows as plain Java code, with the constraint the nodes of the workflow must be expressed using Compute object calls.

- Users declare a Manager object passing it an Iterator providing the input tasks. The Manager object completely and transparently takes care of implementing stream parallelism using the muskel distributed macro data flow interpreter.

- AOP pointcuts and advices are used to intercept the calls to the compute methods and to transform such calls into proper fireable macro data flow instructions submitted to the muskel distributed macro data flow interpreter.

Sample code used to model workflows is shown in Figure 1. The right part of the Figure lists the Java code modelling the workflow graphically depicted in the left part of the Figure. Multiple results are modelled returning Vector objects and multiple input parameters are modelled with a "vararg" compute method[3].

More in detail, the calls to compute methods are transformed into the submission of a proper (already fireable) macro data flow instruction to the muskel

---

[2]we used AspectJ AOP framework through the AspectJ [13, 2] Eclispe plugin, actually
[3]varargs have been introduced in Java 1.5 and allow to pass a variable number of arguments (of the same type) to a method; the arguments are referred to in the method body as array elements

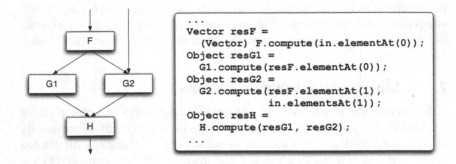

```
...
Vector resF =
  (Vector) F.compute(in.elementAt(0));
Object resG1 =
  G1.compute(resF.elementAt(0));
Object resG2 =
  G2.compute(resF.elementAt(1),
            in.elementsAt(1));
Object resH =
  H.compute(resG1, resG2);
...
```

Figure 1.   Sample workflow (left) and relative Java code (right)

distributed macro data flow interpreter modified in such a way a Future for the result is immediately returned. If one of the input arguments of the compute call is a Future, the advice intercepting the compute method call takes care of waiting for its actual value to be computed before submitting the macro data flow instruction to the interpreter.

As input Future actual values are only required by the advice right before the workflow node is started, parallelism implicit in the workflow is correctly delegated to the underlying muskel interpreter. As an example, consider the workflow of Figure 1. The functions G1 and G2 are evaluated (their evaluation is requested by the advice to muskel interpreter) sequentially. However, as the first one immediately returns a Future, the second one (also returning a Future) will eventually run in parallel on a distinct remote processing element as outlined in Figure 2. When the evaluation of the H node is requested, the advice intercepting the request will realize two futures are passed as input parameters and therefore it will wait before submitting the node evaluation request to the muskel interpreter up to the moment the two actual values of the "input" Futures are available. Overall, advices transforming calls to compute methods into fireable macro data flow instructions act as the data flow *matching unit*, according to classical data flow jargon.

The approach suggested here to implement workflows on top of the muskel macro data flow interpreter presents at least two significant advantages:

- the whole, already existing, efficient and assessed muskel macro data flow interpreter structure is fully exploited. The muskel interpreter takes completely care of ensuring load balancing, fault tolerance (w.r.t. remote resource faults) and security;

- users are only asked to express workflows with elementary Java code, possibly spending some time wrapping workflow node code in Compute objects and declaring a Manager object which is used to supply input data, retrieve output data, control non functional features (e.g. parallelism degree in the execution of the workflow) and to ask the evaluation of the workflow code.

3. Implementation details

We shortly recall `muskel` features (§ 3.1), then we point out the most notable aspects related to workflow implementation on top of `muskel` (§ 3.2). The interested reader may find more details concerning `muskel` features in [14, 7, 8].

3.1 `muskel`

`muskel` executes macro data flow code derived from user defined skeletons by exploiting a distributed macro data flow interpreter. Load balancing is guaranteed as the fireable macro data flow instructions are delivered to remote data flow interpreter instances according to an auto scheduling policy: idle

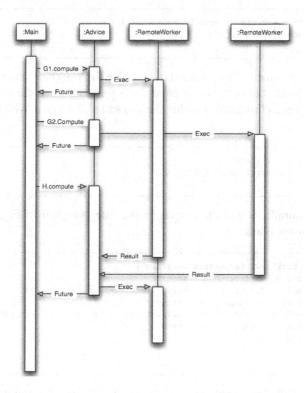

Figure 2.   Transition diagram relative to the execution of part of the workflow of Figure 1.

remote interpreter instances ask the instruction repository for new fireable instructions to be executed. Efficiency in the execution of `muskel` programs is close to 1 provided the average grain of the macro data flow instructions is sufficiently high (see Fig. 3). The more innovative feature of `muskel`, however, has been the introduction of the *computation manager* concept: an entity taking care of all the non functional aspect of distributed/parallel program execution. The `muskel` manager, in particular, completely deals with fault tolerance aspects. In case of a failure of a remote interpreter instance, it arranges to reschedule the computations (fireable instructions) scheduled to the failing node to other nodes, possibly recruited *on-the-fly* exploiting a simple peer-to-peer algorithm.

3.2   Workflows on top of `muskel`

In order to be able to express workflows, the user must write one class per workflow node. The class has to implement the `Compute` interface, that is a very simple interface such as:

```
public interface Compute extends Serializable {
   public Object compute(Object ... params);
}
```

The `compute` method is assumed to compute the workflow node results (the returned `Object`) out of the input parameters `params`. Then the workflow can be described in a class implementing the `Workflow` interface, which is defined as follows:

```
public interface Workflow {
   public Object doWorkflow(Object param);
}
```

As an example, a workflow such as the one sketched in Fig. 1 can be described by the class:

```
public class WorkFlow1 implements Workflow {
   public Object doWorkflow(Object task) {
      Vector resF = (Vector) F.compute(((Vector)task).elementAt(0));
      Object resG1 = G1.compute(resF.elementAt(0));
      Object resG2 = G2.compute(resF.elementAt(1),((Vector)task).elementAt(1));
      Object resH = H.compute(resG1, resG2);
      return resH;
   }
}
```

The code style here is quite close to the style used when programming plain Java applications, actually.

We capture the execution of the Compute calls in the workflow exploiting aspects. The pointcut is defined on the call of the compute method of any object implementing Compute:

```
pointcut computeRemotely(Object param[], itfs.Compute code) :
  call(Object itfs.Compute.compute(Object ... )) &&
  !within(execEngine.Engine) &&
  args(param) && target(code) ;
```

The advice invoked on the pointcut is an around advice such as:

```
execEngine.Engine eng = new execEngine.Engine();

Future around(Object param[], itfs.Compute code) : computeRemotely(param, code) {
  for(int i=0; i<param.length; i++) {
    if(param[i] instanceof Future) {  // reifing each parameter right before call
      param[i] = ((Future) param[i]).getValue();
    }
  }
  Object future = eng.exec(codice, param); // deliver fireable instruction
  return future; // and return the corresponding Future object
}
```

It arranges to collect the Compute class name and the input parameters and creates a macro data flow instruction which is submitted to the distributed muskel macro data flow interpreter via the (muskel predefined) exec.Engine object instance declared in the aspect class. Input tokens to the macro data flow instruction that are Future instances rather than plain reified objects, are eventually reified *on the fly* within the advice. Eventually, a Future object is returned. Each Future object represents an handle that can be eventually used to retrieve the actual data computed by the distributed interpreter during the compute call. In particular, Future interface provides two methods: a Object getValue() method to get the actual value of the Future, possibly waiting for the completion of the corresponding computation, and a boolean isReady() method to test whether the computation producing the actual value of the Future is already terminated (this is used to support asynchronous calls).

It is worth pointing out that the task of properly designing AOP code is not in charge to the application programmer. All AOP related code is developed by system programmers. Application programers just exploit it by properly defining the proper Compute and Workflow code incorporating the "business logic" of the application or, rephrasing, fully detailing the functional aspects of the application.

As a whole, the procedure just described models an asynchronous execution of the macro data flow instructions implementing the workflow nodes. It allows to fully exploit the parallelism intrinsic to the workflow, by properly using Futures. It derives from the approach we first suggested in [9] where we used annotations to denote side effect free method calls in plain Java codeto be executed in parallel. However, the approach discussed in this work presents several peculiarities.:

- First of all, here there is a sharp-cut distinction between the "control" and "business" code, actually contained in separate files, whereas with PAL programmers write business code and annotations (that behaves as control code) inside the same file.

- PAL was conceived for exploiting method-level parallelism: through a simple program enrichment process, programmers choose which Java methods-call should be transformed in asynchronous ones i.e. PAL allows to add parallelism to legacy java code with a minimum intervention. Instead, here we ask the programmers to structure their application as a workflow.

- PAL provides a fixed number of annotations (hence a very limited number of action can be performed) that an adapter-based architecture exploits to transform bytecode at runtime. The transformation process depends, in a way, on the adapter used. The approach described in this work is strongly coupled with *muskel* but the code transformation policies implementation is based on AspectJ, the most widely diffused tool for aspect oriented programming, which offers a rich set of mechanisms for customizing the "aspectization" process. As a consequence, the programmers can customize/optimize/change the transformation process by simply modifying the aspects (without a direct code update).

As already stated, we are interested not only in the exploitation of parallelism within the evaluation of a single workflow instance, but also in exploiting the parallelism between different instances of workflows run on distinct input data sets. In order to support stream parallelisms, we provide the user with a `StreamIterator` manager. This manager takes as parameters an `Iterator` (providing the input data sets to be processed by the `Workflow`) and a `Workflow`. It provides a method to compute the whole bunch of inputs, as well as a method to get an `Iterator` that can be used to retrieve workflow results. Using the `StreamIterator` manager, the main code relative to our example can therefore be expressed as follows:

```
public static void main(String[] args) {
  Workflow wf = new WorkFlow1();            // workflow to be used (userdef)
  InTaskIterator intIt =                    // provide the input tasks ...
      new InTaskIterator();                 // ... via an iterator (userdef)
  Manager mgr = new StreamIterator(wf,intIt);// declare the manager
  mgr.go();                                 // start parallel computation
  Iterator resIt = mgr.getResultIterator(); // get access to result iterator
  while(resIt.hasNext()) {                  // while there are more results ...
```

```
        Object result = resIt.next();        // get one and
        ...                                   // process it (userdef)
    }                                         // that's all
}
```

The main task of the `StreamIterator` manager is to invoke execution of the parameter `Workflow` instances on all the input data sets provided by the `Iterator`. This is achieved exploiting a proper `Thread` pool and activating one thread in the pool for each independent workflow computation. Then, the AOP procedure illustrated above intercepts the calls to `compute` methods and arrange to run them in parallel through the `muskel` distributed macro data flow interpreter.

4.   Experiments

In order to prove the effectiveness of the approach, we performed some experiments on a newtwork of workstations with Java 1.5 accessible via plain `ssh/scp` rather than with other more sophisticated grid middleware. The scalability of plain `muskel` has actually already been demonstrated. Figure 3 shows how with suitable grain of the workflow nodes (i.e. of the `Compute` functions) efficiency close to the ideal one is achieved. In this context, the grain $G = T_{compute}/T_{communication}$ is the time spent to compute a workflow node (i.e. a fireable macro data flow instruction) on a machine divided by the time spent to sent the parameters and to receive the results to and from the machine. The main (and only) difference between plain `muskel` and the system proposed here to execute workflows on top of `muskel` lies in the way fireable instructions are provided to the distributed data flow interpreter of `muskel`. In plain `muskel`, fireable instructions are taken from a compiled representation of a macro data flow graph. In particular, each time a new token arrives to a macro data flow instruction in the graph (either from the input stream or as the result of the distributed computation of another macro data flow instruction) the target macro data flow instruction is checked for "fireability" and, possibly, delivered to the distributed macro data flow interpreter. The time spent is in the sub-micro second range (net time, not taking into account time spent to copy parameters in memory during the interpreter call). When executing workflows according to the approach discussed in this work, instead, fireable instructions come from the advice invoked on the pointcut intercepting the `compute` calls. We measured the overhead in this case and the results are shown in the following table (times are in milliseconds):

Average	23.09	Minimum	19
Standard deviation	3.01	Maximum	27

These values are relative to a 2 GHz Core 2 Duo machine, running Mac OS/X 10.4.9, Java 1.5.0-07, AspectJ 1.5.4 with AspectJ tools 1.4.2 and Eclipse 3.2.2.

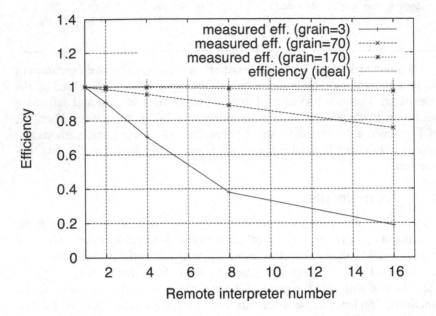

Figure 3.   Efficiency of the muskel/aspect workflow prototype

On the same machine, delivering a fireable instruction to the macro data flow interpreter with plain `muskel` requires an average of 0.004 milliseconds. The difference in the times is not surprising: in the former case, we go through pure meta programming tools and we "interpret" each call, while in the latter we use plain (compiled) Java to handle each one of the calls. Therefore, we can conclude the average 23 milliseconds represent the pure overhead spent each time a new fireable instruction has to be computed (i.e. each time one of the workflow `Compute` nodes is computed). The time spent in reifiyng a `Future`, instead, is negligible (this not taking into account the time spent to wait for actual production of `Future` values, of course). This allows us to conclude that the parallel execution of workflows on top of `muskel` slightly increases the grain required to achieve almost perfect scalability

5.   Related work & Conclusions

Sobral et al. discussed the usage of AOP to support modular computing [16, 15, 6]. They use AOP techniques to separately solve partition, concurrency and distribution problems and eventually show how the related aspects can be used to provide a (kernel for a) general purpose, modular parallel computing framework. The proper usage of the aspects proposed, however, requires in general more specific programmer knowledge than the one required to exploit the approach we present here. Other authors [3] demonstrated that AOP can be efficiently exploited in conjunction with components and patterns to derive parallel applications for distributed memory systems. Although their work targets the same kind of systems we target here, again the approach followed in [3] highly relies on the ability of the programmer to find out the right places to exploit aspects. In [12] another approach exploiting aspects to parallelize Java applications from the Java Grande forum using AspectJ is presented. Good results are shown in the paper, but the procedure used to exploit aspects requires entering the program details to find out possibilities for parallelization.

We have shown how AOP techniques can be seamlessly used to transform a very basic kind of workflows in such a way they can be executed on distributed target architectures through the muskel macro data flow interpreter. Exploitation of AOP techniques allow to completely separate the concerns relative to parallelism exploitation and application functional core. In particular, the same application code used to perform functional debugging on a single, sequential machine may be turned into parallel code by adding aspects, compiling it through AspectJ and then running it on the muskel runtime.

The way used to write workflow code is quite basic Java programming. Workflow components must implement a simple interface, and programmers are explicitly required to provide them as side effect free sequential components. We are currently completing a simple GUI that can be used to derive automatically Java code from a graphic representation of the workflow.

Preliminary experiments show that the approach is perfectly feasible and that actual speedups can be achieved provided that the workflow nodes are medium to coarse grain.

References

[1] M. Aldinucci, M. Danelutto, and P. Dazzi. Muskel: an expandable skeleton environment. *Scalable Computing: Practice and Experience*, 2007. To appear.

[2] AspectJ Home page, 2007. http://www.eclipse.org/aspectj/.

[3] P. V. Bangalore. Generating Parallel Applications for Distributed Memory Systems Using Aspects, Components, and Patterns. In *The 6th AOSD Workshop on Aspects, Components and Patterns for Infrastructure Software (ACP4IS)*, Vancouver, BC, Canada, March 2006. ACM 978-1-59593-657-8/07/03.

[4] M. Cole. A skeletal approach to exploitation of parallelism. In *Proc. of CONPAR 88*, British Computer Society Workshop Series, pages 667–675. Cambridge University Press, 1989.

[5] M. Cole. Bringing skeletons out of the closet: A pragmatic manifesto for skeletal parallel programming. *Parallel Computing*, 30(3):389–406, 2004.

[6] C. A. Cunha and J. L. Sobral. An annotation-based framework for parallel computing. In *Proc. of Intl. Euromicro PDP: Parallel Distributed and network-based Processing*, pages 113–120, Los Alamitos, CA, USA, 2007. IEEE Computer Society.

[7] M. Danelutto. QoS in parallel programming through application managers. In *Proc. of Intl. Euromicro PDP: Parallel Distributed and network-based Processing*, pages 282–289, Lugano, Switzerland, Feb. 2005. IEEE.

[8] M. Danelutto and P. Dazzi. Joint structured/non structured parallelism exploitation through data flow. In V. Alexandrov, D. van Albada, P. Sloot, and J. Dongarra, editors, *Proc. of ICCS: Intl. Conference on Computational Science, Workshop on Practical Aspects of High-level Parallel Programming*, LNCS, Reading, UK, May 2006. Springer.

[9] M. Danelutto, M. Pasin, M. Vanneschi, P. Dazzi, L. Presti, and D. Laforenza. Pal: towards a new approach to high level parallel programming. In M. Bubak, S. Golatch, and T. Priol, editors, *Proc. of the Integrated Research in Grid Computing Workshop*, CoreGRID, Krakøw, Poland, oct 2006. Academic Computing Centre CYFRONET AGH. submitted.

[10] R. E. Filman, T. Elrad, S. Clarke, and M. Aksit. *Aspect-Oriented Software Development*. Addison-Wesley, 2005. ISBN 0-321-21976-7.

[11] Survey on Grid Workflows, http://wiki.cogkit.org/index.php/Survey-on-Grid-Workflows, 2007.

[12] B. Harbulot and J. R. Gurd. Using AspectJ to Separate Concerns in Parallel Scientific Java Code. In *Proceedings of the 3rd International Conference on Aspect-Oriented Software Development (AOSD)*, Lancaster, UK, March 2004.

[13] R. Laddad. *AspectJ in Action: Practical Aspect-Oriented Programming*. 2003. ISBN 1-930110-93-6.

[14] muskel Home Page, 2006. http://www.di.unipi.it/~marcod/Muskel.

[15] J. Sobral. Incrementally developing parallel applications with aspectj. In *20th IEEE International Parallel & Distributed Processing Symposium*. IEEE Press, 4 2006.

[16] J. L. Sobral, M. P. Monteiro, and C. A. Cunha. Aspect-oriented support for modular parallel computing. In *Proceedings of the Fifth AOSD Workshop on Aspects, Components, and Patterns for Infrastructure Software*, pages 37–41, Bonn, Germany, 2006. Published as University of Virginia Computer Science Technical Report CS–2006–01.

UTILIZING HETEROGENEOUS DATA SOURCES IN COMPUTATIONAL GRID WORKFLOWS

Tamas Kiss, Alexandru Tudose, Gabor Terstyanszky
Centre for Parallel Computing, School of Informatics, University of Westminster 115 New Cavendish Street, London, W1W 6UW
kisst@wmin.ac.uk A.Tudose@student.westminster.ac.uk terstyg@wmin.ac.uk

Peter Kacsuk, Gergely Sipos
MTA SZTAKI Lab. of Parallel and Distributed Systems, H-1518 Budapest, P.O. Box 63, Hungary
kacsuk@sztaki.hu sipos@sztaki.hu

Abstract

Besides computation intensive tasks, the Grid also facilitates sharing and processing very large databases and file systems that are distributed over multiple resources and administrative domains. Although accessing data in the Grid is supported by various lower level tools, end-users find it difficult to utilise these solutions directly. High level environments, such as Grid portal and workflow solutions provide little or no support for data access and manipulation. Workflow systems are widely utilised in Grid computing to automate computational tasks. Unfortunately, the ways of feeding data into these workflows is limited and in most cases requires additional tools and manual intervention. This paper describes how data can be fed into computational workflows from heterogeneous data sources. The P-GRADE Grid portal and workflow engine have been integrated with the SDSC Storage Resource Broker (SRB) in order to access SRB data resources as inputs and outputs of workflow components. The solution automates data interaction in computational workflows allowing users to seamlessly access and process data stored in SRB resources. The implemented solution also enables the seamless interoperation of SRB, SRM (Storage Resource Manager) and GridFTP file catalogues.

Keywords: grid workflow,SRB,P-GRADE portal,interoperation,data management

1.   Introduction

Current production Grid systems all aim to support data intensive applications and offer solutions such as OGSA-DAI [1] (Open Grid Services Architecture Data Access and Integration) or SRB [2] (SDSC Storage Resource Broker) to access large data collections. These tools provide the required abstraction of data that may span over several resources and administrative domains. However, most end-users find it difficult to access these relatively low-level tools directly. End-users require a graphical user interface, typically a Grid portal, where they can create, execute and monitor their applications in an integrated environment. Besides simple job execution Grid portals may also offer additional functionalities, for example workflow composition, or selection and execution of applications from code repositories with custom input parameter values. These applications may require access to large data collections.

Unfortunately, current Grid portals and application hosting environments provide very little or no support at all to access advanced data manipulation tools. Solutions are limited to browser portlets that enable accessing data collections and doing the necessary data movements and transformations prior or after job execution manually. Examples include the BIRN (Biomedical Informatics Research Network) [17] and the NCMIR (National Center for Microscopy and Imaging Research) [18] portals that both provide SRB browsing and manipulation capabilities for end-users. The NGS Application Repository [15] supports data browsing and staging, currently only from GridFTP [8] servers, but it will also be extended with SRB support in the near future.

In case of more complex application scenarios, that require the execution of several jobs with complex dependencies between them, manual data manipulation provided by the above solutions is not feasible. Workflow solutions, such as Triana [3] or Taverna [4] provide automatic orchestration of these complex scenarios, staging and automatically transferring data along the workflow. However, these solutions are currently limited concerning their data manipulation capabilities and the data sources they can utilise. Taverna, for example, is a very effective workflow management environment but not easily adaptable for current production Grids. Its main aim is not job submission rather the connection and orchestration of pre-deployed services. As a consequence, data input is defined by the implementation of the actual service. Using Triana, our other example, programs can be assembled from a set of building-blocks by dragging them into a workspace window and connecting them. However, Triana is not integrated with Grid data solutions such as SRB or OGSA-DAI.

The aim of this paper is to describe how computational workflows can be extended with more sophisticated data management capabilities. In order to demonstrate this concept the workflow engine of the P-GRADE grid portal has been extended to seamlessly access data stored in SRB repositories. Section 2 of this paper describes how data is currently handled by the P-GRADE portal, followed by the description of the SRB/P-GRADE integration in section 3. Finally, future work and conclusions are given in section 4.

2. Data Driven Workflows in P-GRADE

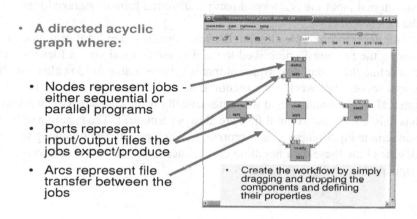

- **A directed acyclic graph where:**
  - **Nodes represent jobs - either sequential or parallel programs**
  - **Ports represent input/output files the jobs expect/produce**
  - **Arcs represent file transfer between the jobs**

- Create the workflow by simply dragging and dropping the components and defining their properties

Figure 1. A P-GRADE portal workflow

The P-GRADE portal is a general purpose, workflow oriented computational Grid portal that supports the development and execution of workflow-based Grid applications. Detailed description of the portal can be found in several publications such as [5], or on the P-GRADE portal Website [10]. Here we only concentrate on describing the current data manipulation and transfer capabilities of the portal.

The basic unit of execution in the P-GRADE portal is the workflow. A P-GRADE portal workflow is a directed acyclic graph where the nodes of the graph represent sequential or parallel jobs, as illustrated on Figure 1. The nodes are communicating with each other via the means of file transfer. Each job requires zero or more input files and produces zero or more output files. The files are currently transferred between the nodes via GridFTP [8] file transfer, represented by the arcs of the graph on Figure 1. The arcs are connecting the output ports of one job to the input ports of another.

When creating a computational workflow the user either uploads the executables to the portal server from a local machine, or selects the codes from a legacy code repository [11]. In both cases the input files to workflow components can either be local or remote. Local input files are uploaded from the user's local file system to the portal server during workflow creation, and from here at execution time they are transferred to the Grid compute resource. Local input files are typically small in size. However, a Grid application may require huge amount of input data that is stored in external servers. In this case the user can define the input as "remote" and provide its GridFTP address (in case of Globus based Grids) [8] or LFC logical file name (in case of EGEE type of Grids) [7]. An external input file is always directly transferred form its storage location to the executor site.

Similarly to input files, output files can also be either local or remote, following the previously described logic. In case of local output files the user can define the output as permanent that will be available for download on the portal server after workflow execution, or volatile that will only be used for internal communication and will automatically be deleted when the workflow has finished. Remote output files are always permanent. The handling of local and remote input/output files is represented on figure 2. The following section descries how these data handling capabilities have been extended with SRB support.

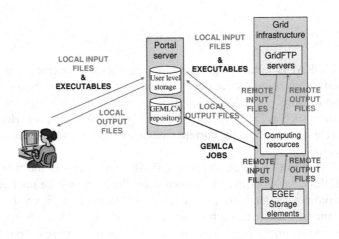

Figure 2.   Local and remote files in P-GRADE workflows

3. SRB Data Resources in P-GRADE Portal Workflows

3.1 SRB Integration Options

The SDSC Storage Resource Broker [13] is a software product developed by the San Diego Supercomputing Centre that provides access to files and database objects seamlessly across a distributed environment. SRB abstracts the physical location of the data and the way it is stored by presenting the user with a single file hierarchy for data that is actually distributed across multiple storage systems. SRB provides a way to access data sets and resources based on their logical names or attributes rather than their physical locations. The solution is widely deployed in production Grid systems including the UK National Grid Service (NGS) [6].

SRB functionalities can be offered in the P-GRADE portal in different ways. The most obvious solution is to extend the portal with an SRB browser portlet. Adding an SRB browser portlet to P-GRADE definitely enhances its capabilities and it is a rather useful tool for many end-users. They can perform a wide range of operations on SRB resources using the portal's graphical user interface. However, it takes us only a little bit closer to workflow level integration as the data still has to be manually copied from and to the SRB resource and fed into the workflow. Figure 3 illustrates the SRB browser portlet implemented for P-GRADE. Although there are some other similar portlets available (e.g. in the BIRN portal [17]), the reason for implementing our own solution was justified by its flexible architecture.

The portlet was designed in a plug-in structure which allows easily extending its functionality towards other file storage systems such as GridFTP or EGEE file catalogues. The portlet, besides the usual file and directory operations, also supports metadata creation and handling. Figure 3 shows the SRB portlet with data and metadata management.

Besides an SRB browser portlet, the major interest of our work is integrating SRB at workflow level. This integration can be done at two different levels: at port level or at job level.

The port level integration means that input or output ports of a P-GRADE portal job could refer to files stored on SRB storage facilities and consequently, utilise SRB data stores for file storage and file retrieval. The current types of ports, "local" and "remote", are extended with a third port type that refers to SRB resources. The solution allows users to process input data in workflow jobs stored in SRB data stores, and also to write the output of the jobs back to an SRB resource.

The second option is the job level integration. Portal users can currently define and execute "standard" or "GEMLCA" jobs. A standard job represents a GT2 or g-Lite job submission, while a GEMLCA job [11] is a service invocation that refers to code stored in the GEMLCA legacy code repository. This

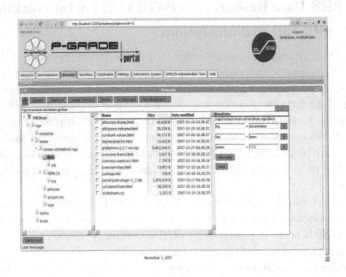

Figure 3.   SRB browser portlet in the P-GRADE portal

framework can be extended with a third job type, called "SRB" job. The "SRB" job is a set of SRB commands, potentially created with the help of a built in GUI within the portal, which manipulates an SRB data collection. This job can still be connected to other "standard", "GEMLCA" or "SRB" jobs with the help of "local", "remote" or "SRB" ports.

The second half of this section describes the port level integration, while the job level solution will be introduced in a forthcoming paper.

3.2   SRB resources as input/output ports

The port level integration of SRB into the P-GRADE portal raises three different challenges:

- the SRB client environment has to be properly set up and configured,

- SRB port definition and input file selection have to be enabled in the workflow editor of the portal,

- and finally, data has to be retrieved from SRB resources before job execution, and transferred back afterwards.

3.2.1   Setting up the SRB client environment.   When dealing with SRB environment descriptions, the aim was to enable access to multiple SRB

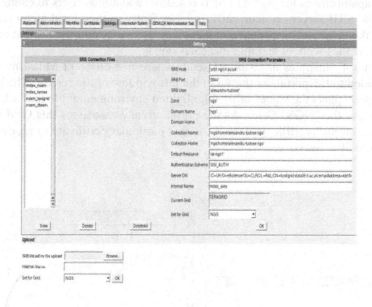

Figure 4. SRB settings portlet in the P-GRADE portal

servers at the same time. These SRB servers can be located in different Grids and may require different certificates to access. The P-GRADE portal is a multi-Grid portal [14] that allows users to map jobs to and access data located in different production Grids (which may use different Grid middleware and require different certificates) within the same workflow. The portal allows storing multiple certificate proxies on the portal server at the same time mapping them to different Grids. Our aim was to extend this multi-Grid capability to SRB resources.

Before running any SRB client, the client environmental variables need to be set up. Usually, this is accomplished via a configuration file named MdasEnv. This is a simple text file that contains lines of parameter/value pairs where each value is given in quotes. In order to set up the client environmental variables, an SRB Settings portlet has been developed and added to the P-GRADE portal. Users can load MdasEnv files from their own file-system, can view and modify existing SRB environmental files, and most importantly, can create new ones on the fly. This portlet has been designed and implemented in such way that enables the portal to handle multiple MdasEnv files for a particular user. These environmental files are mapped to Grids and this way linked to potentially different Grid user certificates. The solution extends the multi-

Grid capabilities of the portal to SRB resources and allows users to connect to multiple SRB servers concurrently, independently of their Grid membership. Using the graphical user interface, users can also easily edit the content of the MdasEnv files without learning its actual syntax.

Figure 4 illustrates an example setup where five different MdasEnv files are loaded to the portal, as shown in the left window of the screen. The right window displays the values of the highlighted environmental file that is being mapped to the "NGS" Grid. As the portal already associates this Grid with a particular user certificate, it will use that particular certificate to access the specified SRB resource.

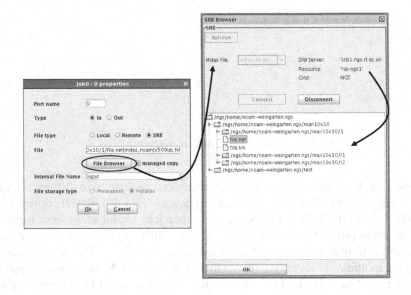

Figure 5.   Port properties window and SRB File Browser

3.2.2   Workflow creation and execution using SRB ports.   The next challenge after setting up the SRB environment was to modify the workflow editor of the portal and enable the creation of SRB input and output ports. This required the introduction of a new port type called "SRB" besides the currently existing "Local" and "Remote" types.

The left hand side of figure 5 depicts the port properties window, modified to handle SRB file types. The user sets "File type" to SRB and clicks on the "File Brower". The next task is to select the Mdas file to be used from a drop-down list. As this file is mapped to a particular Grid, the portal knows which certificate to use when accessing the selected collection, as it was explained in the previous section. After connecting to the selected collection, the built in SRB file browser can be used to find the required input file, as shown on the right hand side of figure 5.

The final challenge is to access the SRB data collection and retrieve the selected files before job execution, and also to copy SRB output files back to the SRB resource. In its current implementation, the P-GRADE portal employs a script-based solution for file staging. These scripts suffered necessary modifications to extend this file staging to SRB resources. SRB is accessible from various client solutions like Scommands (UNIX-like command-line interface), Jargon (JAVA API), C client (C API), inQ (Windows based browser/query tool) and mySRB (web-based browser/query tool). After a critical analysis of SRB client solutions, the SRB command-line client (s-commands) was selected and installed on the portal server. The grounds of this decision were completeness of the command line client giving access to all the SRB functionality, and also its suitability to be integrated with the P-GRADE portal scripts.

If all SRB file transfers occur and terminate on the portal server then this machine can easily become a bottleneck. In order to overcome this shortcoming the implemented solution utilises direct file transfer between the SRB resource and the executor site whenever it is possible (see figure 6). The portal checks whether the executor site has an SRB client installed (Executor site 1 on figure 6). If it finds a client on the site then the portal utilises this client to directly transfer input/output files. If the executor site does not support SRB (Executor site 2) or the direct transfer fails, then the file is first transferred to the portal server utilising the portal's SRB client, and then to the executor site by the means of GridFTP (in this case the maximum size of the transferred file has to be limited to protect the portal server).

3.3 Results of the integration

The integration of SRB data resources into P-GRADE workflows allows utilizing data coming from and going to SRB file catalogues. Moreover, the different port types, including local, remote and SRB ports, can be freely mixed as input or output of workflow components. This solution allows the seamless interoperation of SRB catalogues, GridFTP file systems and EGEE storage elements (based on SRM [16]) at the level of P-GRADE workflows. In order to demonstrate these capabilities a workflow simulating urban car traffic [12] was created. As it is shown on figure 7, jobs of the workflow are running in different grids (US OSG [9], UK NGS [6], EGEE [7]) and utilise data resources based on different technologies (SRB, SRM [16], GridFTP [8], local) from these different grids.

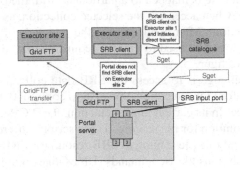

Figure 6.   Direct and indirect transfer of SRB data in P-GRADE

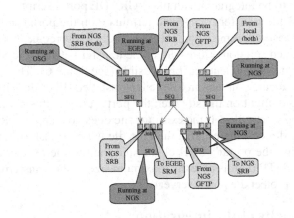

Figure 7.   P-GRADE workflow using SRB, GridFTP, SRM and local data resources

4.   Conclusions and Further Work

The P-GRADE Grid portal is a high-level integrated application hosting environment that assists the user-friendly creation and execution of workflow based Grid applications spanning multiple Grids. The current portal supports access to local files, SRM-based EGEE logical file systems and GridFTP file collections as inputs and outputs of workflow components. The aim of our research is to extend these capabilities to other widely used distributed Grid data management solutions. As a first reference implementation the P-GRADE portal workflow engine has been extended with SRB support capabilities. SRB is one of the most widely used distributed data management systems by the Grid community, and this way the integration is potentially a huge interest to both SRB and P-GRADE portal user groups.

The described solution will be put into production level operation at the beginning of 2008 on the NGS P-GRADE portal [19]. On the other hand, further Grid data management solutions are also analysed and considered for integration. An OGSA-DAI browser portlet has already been implemented and added to the P-GRADE portal, and the workflow level OGSA-DAI integration is also work in progress. These new additions to P-GRADE will provide interoperation of all widely used Grid data and file storage systems at the level of workflows.

References

[1] Mario Antonioletti et. al.: The design and implementation of Grid database services in OGSA-DAI, Concurrency and Computation: Practice and Experience, Volume 17, Issue 2-4, Pages 357 - 376, Special Issue: Grids and Web Services for e-Science, 2005 John Wiley & Sons, Ltd.

[2] Arcot Rajasekar et. al. Storage Resource Broker - Managing Distributed Data in a Grid, Computer Society of India Journal, Special Issue on SAN, Vol. 33, No. 4, pp. 42-54, Oct 2003.

[3] D. Churches et.al: Programming Scientific and Distributed Workflow with Triana Services. Grid Workflow 2004, Concurrency and Computation: Practice and Experience, Vol 18, Issue 10, August 2006, pp 1021-1037, ISSN 1532-0626

[4] T. Oinn, M. Addis, J. Ferris, D. Marvin, M. Greenwood, T. Carver, M. R. Pocock, A. Wipat and P. Li. Taverna: a tool for the composition and enactment of bioinformatics workflows, Bioinformatics, Vol. 20 no. 17, 2004, pages 3045-3054.

[5] P. Kacsuk and G. Sipos: Multi-Grid, Multi-User Workflows in the P-GRADE Grid Portal, Journal of Grid Computing Vol. 3. No. 3-4., 2005, Springer, 1570-7873, pp 221-238

[6] The UK National Grid Service Website, http://www.ngs.ac.uk/

[7] The EGEE web page, http://public.eu-egee.org/

[8] W. Allcock, J. Bester, J. Bresnahan, A. Chervenak, L. Liming, S. Tuecke: GridFTP: Protocol Extension to FTP for the Grid, March 2001, http://wwwfp.mcs.anl.gov/dsl/GridFTP-ProtocolRFCDraft.pdf

[9] The Open Science Grid Website, http://www.opensciencegrid.org/

[10] The P-GRADE portal Website, http://www.lpds.sztaki.hu/pgportal/

[11] T. Delaittre, T. Kiss, A. Goyeneche, G. Terstyanszky, S.Winter, P. Kacsuk: GEMLCA: Running Legacy Code Applications as Grid Services, Journal of Grid Computing Vol. 3. No. 1-2. June 2005, Springer Science + Business Media B.V.

[12] T. Delaitre, A.Goyeneche, T.Kiss, G.Z. Terstyanszky, N. Weingarten, P. Maselino, A. Gourgoulis, S.C. Winter: Traffic Simulation in P-Grade as a Grid Service, Conf. Proc. of the DAPSYS 2004 Conference, pp 129-136, ISBN 0-387-23094-7, September 19-22, 2004, Budapest, Hungary

[13] SRB project homepage http:www.sdsc.edusrbindex.phpMain-Page

[14] P. Kacsuk, T. Kiss, G. Sipos, Solving the Grid Interoperability Problem by P-GRADE Portal at Workflow Level, Conf. Proc. of the Grid-Enabling Legacy Applications and Supporting End Users Workshop, within the framework of the 15th IEEE International Symposium on High Performance Distributed Computing , HPDC¥5, Paris, France, pp 3-7, June 19-23, 2006

[15] D. Meredith, M. Maniopoulou, A. Richards, M. Mineter: A JSDL Application Repository and Artefact Sharing Portal for Heterogeneous Grids and the NGS, Proceedings of the UK e-Science All Hands Meeting 2007, Nottingham, UK, 10th-13th September 2007, pp 110-118, ISBN 978-0-9553988-3-4

[16] A. Sim, A. Soshani editors, Storage Resource Manager Interface Specification version 2.2, 09.05.2007, http:www.ogf.orgPublic-Comment-DocsDocuments2007-10OGFGSM-SRMv2.2.pdf

[17] Jason   Novotny,   Ramil   Manansala,   Thien   Nguyen: BIRN   Portal Overview,   Portals   &   Portlets   2006,   17-18   July   2006,   Edinburgh,   UK http://www.nesc.ac.uk/action/esi/download.cfm?index=3246

[18] The National Center for Microscopy and Imaging Research (NCMIR) - SRB portlet http://ncmir.ucsd.edu/Software/srbportlet.htm

[19] NGS P-GRADE portal: https://grid-portal.cpc.wmin.ac.uk:8080/gridsphere/gridsphere

V

CHECKPOINTING AND MONITORING

RESULT ERROR DETECTION ON HETEROGENEOUS AND VOLATILE RESOURCES VIA INTERMEDIATE CHECKPOINTING *

Derrick Kondo
Laboratoire d'Informatique de Grenoble/INRIA Rhone-Alpes, France
dkondo@imag.fr

Filipe Araujo and Luis Silva
CISUC, Department of Informatics Engineering, University of Coimbra, Portugal
filipius,luis@dei.uc.pt

Patricio Domingues
School of Technology and Management, Polytechnic Institute of Leiria, Portugal
patricio@estg.ipleiria.pt

Abstract
Desktop grids use the free resources in Intranet and Internet environments for large-scale computation and storage. While desktop grids offer tremendous computational power and a high return on investment, one critical issue is the validation of results returned by participating hosts that are volatile, anonymous, and potentially malicious. We conduct a benefit analysis of a mechanism for result validation that we proposed recently for the detection of errors in long-running applications. This mechanism is based on using the digest of intermediate checkpoints, and we show in theory and simulation that the relative benefit of this method compared to the state-of-the-art is as high as 45%.

Keywords: desktop grids, error detection, result validation, checkpointing, digest

---

*This work was supported by the CoreGRID Network of Excellence, funded by the European Commission under the Sixth Framework Programme. Project no. FP6-004265.

1.   Introduction

For over a decade, one of the largest distributed computing platforms in the world have been desktop grids, which use the idle computing power and free storage of a large set of networked (and often shared) hosts to support large-scale applications [14, 13–1]. Desktop grids are an extremely attractive platform because they offer huge computational power at relatively low cost. Currently, many desktop grid projects, such as SETI@home [14], FOLDING@home [13], and EINSTEIN@home [1], use TeraFLOPS of computing power of hundreds of thousands of desktop PC's to execute large, high-throughput applications from a variety of scientific domains, including computational biology, astronomy, and physics.

Despite the huge return-on-investment that desktop grids offer, one critical issue is the correctness of results returned from volatile, anonymous, and potentially malicious hosts. A number of different factors can influence the correctness of the results returned from the desktop grid worker to the server. These factors can be due to computational errors (for example, overclocking of the CPU or incorrectly modified application binaries [15]) or input/output errors (for example, a machine crash during an out-of-order flush of in-memory blocks [11]).

Given the risk of erroneous results, effective error detection mechanisms are essential. In this paper, we conduct a benefit analysis of a mechanism that we proposed recently for the detection of errors in long-running applications. This mechanisms uses the digest of intermediate checkpoints to accelerate the detection of result errors, especially for long running applications. A number of projects such as `climateprediction.net`, `climatechange`, and `seasonalattribution` have workunits whose execution span months [6], and we believe early error detection for these projects would be useful. We present theoretical upper and lower bounds on the benefits of our mechanism *for heterogeneous and volatile resources*, using error rates derived from a real desktop grid system. Finally, we present simulation results that loosen the assumptions of our theoretical analysis, but nevertheless confirm our theoretical results.

The paper is structured as follows. In Section 2, we describe how our work in this paper relates to previous research. Then, in Section 3, we detail our mechanism for error detection, give theoretical upper and lower bounds on its benefits, and confirm our analysis with simulation results. Finally, in Section 4, we summarize our conclusions and describe future research directions.

2.   Related Work

In [4], we presented the theoretical analysis and simulation results of the same error detection mechanism presented here, but there were two main limitations. First, the previous analysis was conducted using hypothetical error rates instead of error rates obtained empirically from a real project. In fact, our previous work assumed error rates that were orders of magnitude higher than the rates we determined in this study. *Nevertheless, we show here that substantial benefits can still be achieved using this novel technique with real but relatively lower error rates.* Second, the theoretical analysis previously conducted made the assumption that checkpoints occur simultaneously across hosts at constant intervals. For reasons that we detail in the next section, this is an unrealistic assumption in volatile and heterogeneous desktop grids. *We loosen the assumption to consider variable checkpointing intervals, and give new theoretical upper and lower bounds on the benefits of this technique using a mathematical approach based on order statistics.*

3. Comparing Intermediate Checkpoints for Long-Running Workunits

In this section, we present novel benefit analysis of a mechanism for error detection that we proposed recently in [4]. This mechanism is based on check-pointing and replication, and is well-suited for long-running workunits. The technique involves comparing intermediate checkpoint digests (provided for example by the MD5 [12] family of algorithms) of redundant instances of the same task. (Note that often computations occupy a large space in memory often near the 100MB range [6] and/or sending a small, intermediate result for comparison may not be possible nor efficient.) If differences are found, the conclusion is that at least one task's execution is wrong. In contrast to the simple redundancy mechanism, where diverging computations can only be detected after a majority of tasks have completed, intermediate checkpoint comparison allows for earlier and more precise detection of errors, since execution divergence can be spotted at the next checkpoint following any error. This allows one to take proactive and corrective measures without having to wait for the completion of the tasks, and it allows for faster task completion, since faulty tasks can immediately be rescheduled.

We assume the following. First, if the digests differ from the correct digest, then the divergent digest differs from all other digests (including other divergent ones). Second, the errors occur independently of one another. Finally, each task is checkpointed locally and periodically (as is done in several existing desktop grid systems [3, 15]). (Note that later we relax these assumptions in our simulations.) With respect to CPU time, the application could conduct local checkpointing periodically (for example, every 10 minutes). However, with respect to wall-clock time, the time between checkpoints is random because of non-deterministic events that could delay checkpointing such as a host being powered off, or the worker being suspended or killed because of user activity [8].

Parameter	Definition
W	Benefit in time of intermediate checkpointing relative to the state-of-the-art method
$T_{k,j}$	Time from start of workunit to the time of checkpointing segment j on worker k
R	Number of workers on which a checkpointed task is replicated
c	Number of segments or equivalently checkpoints per task
$S_{k,g}$	Time from start of segment g to the time of checkpointing segment g on worker k
p, v	p is the probability of getting an error within a segment on any host. $v = 1 - p$
X	Random variable distributed geometrically with parameters p and v representing the number of task segments before an error occurs

Table 1.   Parameter Definitions.

Thus, we model the time between checkpoints as a random variable. In particular, each checkpoint delineates the end of a task segment to create a total of c segments. Let R be the number of workers on which a checkpointed task is replicated (see Table 1). Let $S_{k,g}$ be a random variable that represents the time to checkpoint the current segment g, beginning from the last checkpoint (or start of the task, in the case of the first checkpoint), on worker k where $1 \leq g \leq c$, and $1 \leq k \leq R$.

Let $T_{k,j}$ be a random variable that represents the amount of time elapsed since the start of the task up to the checkpoint time of segment j, on worker k. Specifically, $T_{k,j} = \sum_{g=1}^{j} S_{k,g}$ (see Figure 1 for an example).

We assume that $S_{k,g}$ is distributed exponentially with parameter λ across all workers. While a number of previous studies have characterized the distribution of availability intervals on *enterprise* desktop resources (for example, [8]), it is unclear how these periods of availability relate to the time of checkpointing a segment on *Internet* environments. Thus, for future work, we will verify our assumption using resource traces, for example, those currently being collected on Internet desktop environments [10].

Given that $S_{k,g}$ is distributed exponentially, $T_{k,j}$ has a gamma distribution with parameters $\alpha = j$ and $\beta = 1/\lambda$.

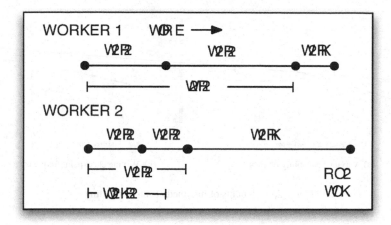

Figure 1. Example of Intermediate Checkpointing

The time to validate the ith segment is given by $T_{(R),i}$, which is the Rth order statistic of the set $T_{1,i}, ..., T_{R,i}$. That is, $T_{(R),i}$ represents the maximum time to complete segment i among all R workers.

The expected gain $E[W]$ for using intermediate checkpoints compared to state-of-the-art methods where the comparison is done at the end of the workunit is then given by:

$$E[W] = E[T_{(R),c} - T_{(R),i}] \qquad (1)$$

where $1 \leq i \leq c$.

Let X be the number of trials, i.e., the segment in which an error occurs on any of the hosts, and let X have a geometric distribution with parameters p and v, where p is the probability of getting an error within a segment in any of the hosts, and $v = 1 - p$.

From [5], a lower bound on the expectation of the maximum of a set of random variables is the maximum of the expected value of each random variable in the set. Moreover, Hartley and David [7] report that an upper bound for the expectation of the maximum is $\mu + \sigma \times (n - 1)/\sqrt{2n - 1}$, given a set of n independent random variables with identical means and variances (μ, σ^2).

In Figure 2, we show the upper and lower bounds on the benefit $E[W]$ relative to the upper and lower bounds of the expected maximum time $E[T_{(R),c}]$ for checkpointing at the end of the task. In particular, in Figure 2(a), the number of checkpoints c is fixed to 1000, and p varies between [0.0005, 0.0015]. In

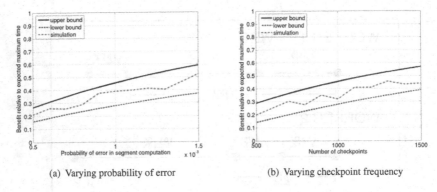

(a) Varying probability of error   (b) Varying checkpoint frequency

Figure 2.   Benefits of intermediate checkpointing

Figure 2(b), the probability of error within each segment p is fixed at 0.001, and c varies between [500, 1000]. (The range of error rates are based upon those observed in a real desktop grid system [16]. In that study, the authors checked syntactically and semantically the results returned from about 600 hosts in an Internet-wide desktop grids to determine error rates of hosts.)

We observe potentially significant gains even for small error rates. For example, in Figure 2(a), we find that if the probability of error p is 0.001 and the number of checkpoints per task c is 1000, then the potential benefit of intermediate checkpointing is between $\sim 30 - 45\%$. While 1000 checkpoints may seem abnormally large, if we assume a task checkpoints every 10 minutes a thousand times, this equates to a 7-day workunit. (This is a reasonable checkpoint frequency and workunit length as the frequency in real projects EINSTEIN@home, PREDICTOR@Home, and SIMAP is on the order of minutes [2] and execution is on the order of days or months [6].) In Figure 2(b), we find that if the number of checkpoints is 1050 (and the probability of error is 0.001), then the potential benefit of intermediate checkpointing is between $\sim 30 - 45\%$.

We then confirmed and extended the theoretical results through simulation. We assign a number of tasks to a set of workers. Whenever a worker computes a checkpoint, it randomly determines whether that computation is wrong or correct. Once a checkpoint is wrong, all the remaining checkpoints from that worker are also considered as wrong. In our experiments, the time that a worker needed to compute a checkpoint was given by an exponential distribution. We chose an arbitrary average checkpoint time (as it does not impact the *relative* benefit of our technique). We varied the number of checkpoints of each task and the probability of error in each checkpoint. (We used a constant value for the probability of error. We also tried random variables (truncated Gaussian, exponential and others), with little if any impact on the outcome of the trials.)

In Figures 2(a) and 2(b), we show the results of our experiments for the same range of parameters as used for the theoretical analysis. The curve of the observed benefit is the average of 300 trials.

Our results show that the there is a considerable benefit in comparing intermediate checkpoints, especially for long-running workunits. Even for very small probabilities of error, which correspond to real values observed in real systems, the time savings can amount to 20%-45% of the time corresponding to state-of-the-art solutions. (One potential limitation of this method is scalability of receiving the high-frequency digest messages if digests are sent centrally to a "supervisor" for comparison. We are currently working on secure load-balancing techniques via distributed hash tables (DHT) to remove this limitation, and we will report on this in future work.)

4. Conclusion

We showed the benefits of a recently proposed method for accelerating error detection on large-scale and volatile resources. In particular, we gave novel theoretical analysis for our proposed method based on the digest of intermediate checkpoints, *where each task segment can take a variable amount of time* due to host volatility or heterogeneity, for example. For error rates often found in real systems, we found that the time savings bounded by theoretical analysis can often range from 20% to 45%. We then verified our theoretical bounds on the potential benefit through simulation experiments, while loosening assumptions of the analysis. We find that our simulation experiments validate our theoretical analysis, even for various distributions of the probability of error. For future work, we will develop scalable ways to collect and compare checkpoint digests, for example using mechanisms based on DHT's.

References

[1] EINSTEN@home. http://einstein.phys.uwm.edu.

[2] B. Allen, C. An, and T. Rattel. Personal communications, April 2006.

[3] D. Anderson. Boinc: A system for public-resource computing and storage. In *Proceedings of the 5th IEEE/ACM International Workshop on Grid Computing*, Pittsburgh, USA, 2004.

[4] F. Araujo, P. Domingues, D. Kondo, and L. M. Silva. Validating Desktop Grid Results By Comparing Intermediate Checkpoints. *Submitted to 2nd Coregrid Integration Workshop*, 2006.

[5] T. Aven. Upper (lower) bounds on the mean of the maximum (minimum) of a number of random variables. *Journal of Applied Probability*, 22:723–728, 1985.

[6] Catalog of boinc projects. http://boinc-wiki.ath.cx/index.php?title=Catalog_of_BOINC_Powered_Projects.

[7] H. Hartely and H. David. Universal bounds for mean range and extreme observations. *The Annals of Mathematical Statistics*, 25:85–89, 1954.

[8] D. Kondo, M. Taufer, C. Brooks, H. Casanova, and A. Chien. Characterizing and Evaluating Desktop Grids: An Empirical Study. In *Proceedings of the IPDPS'04*, April 2004.

[9] M. Litzkow, M. Livny, and M. Mutka. Condor - A Hunter of Idle Workstations. In *Proceedings of the 8th International Conference of Distributed Computing Systems (ICDCS)*, 1988.

[10] P. Malecot, D. Kondo, and G. Fedak. Xtremlab: A system for characterizing internet desktop grids (abstract). In *in Proceedings of the 6th IEEE Symposium on High-Performance Distributed Computing*, 2006.

[11] A. Oltean. How to do atomic writes in a file. http://blogs.msdn.com/adioltean/archive/2005/12/28/507866.aspx, December 2005.

[12] R. Rivest. RFC-1321 The MD5 Message-Digest Algorithm. *Network Working Group, IETF*, April 1992.

[13] M. Shirts and V. Pande. Screen Savers of the World, Unite! *Science*, 290:1903–1904, 2000.

[14] W. T. Sullivan, D. Werthimer, S. Bowyer, J. Cobb, G. Gedye, and D. Anderson. A new major SETI project based on Project Serendip data and 100,000 personal computers. In *Proc. of the Fifth Intl. Conf. on Bioastronomy*, 1997.

[15] M. Taufer, D. Anderson, P. Cicotti, and C. L. B. III. Homogeneous redundancy: a technique to ensure integrity of molecular simulation results using public computing. In *Proceedings of the International Heterogeneity in Computing Workshop*, 2005.

[16] D. Kondo, F. Araujo, P. Domingues, P. Malecot, G. Fedak, F. Cappello Characterization Error Rates on Internet Desktop Grids. To appear in *Proceedings of Euro-Par*, 2007.

FAILRANK: TOWARDS A UNIFIED GRID FAILURE MONITORING AND RANKING SYSTEM

D. Zeinalipour-Yazti*, K. Neocleous‡, C. Georgiou‡, M.D. Dikaiakos‡

* School of Pure and Applied Sciences, Open University of Cyprus, CY-1304, Nicosia, Cyprus
‡ Department of Computer Science, University of Cyprus, CY-1678, Nicosia, Cyprus
zeinalipour@ouc.ac.cy and {kyriacos, chryssis, mdd}@cs.ucy.ac.cy

Abstract   The objective of Grid computing is to make processing power as accessible and easy to use as electricity and water. The last decade has seen an unprecedented growth in Grid infrastructures which nowadays enables large-scale deployment of applications in the scientific computation domain. One of the main challenges in realizing the full potential of Grids is making these systems *dependable*.

In this paper we present *FailRank*, a novel framework for integrating and ranking information sources that characterize failures in a grid system. After the failing sites have been ranked, these can be eliminated from the job scheduling resource pool yielding in that way a more predictable and dependable infrastructure. We also present the tools we developed towards evaluating the FailRank framework. In particular, we present the *FailBase Repository* which is a 38GB corpus of state information that characterizes the EGEE Grid for one month in 2007. Such a corpus paves the way for the community to systematically uncover new, previously unknown patterns and rules between the multitudes of parameters that can contribute to failures in a Grid environment. Additionally, we present an experimental evaluation study of the FailRank system over 30 days which shows that our framework identifies failures in 91% of the cases.

Keywords: failure monitoring, FailRank, FailBase repository.

1.   Introduction

Grids have emerged as wide-scale, distributed infrastructures that comprise heterogeneous computing and storage resources, operating over open standards and distributed administration control [10–11]. Grids are quickly gaining popularity, especially in the scientific sector, where projects like *EGEE (Enabling Grids for E-sciencE)* [6], *TeraGrid* [20] and *Open Science Grid* [18] , provide the infrastructure that accommodates large experiments with thousands of scientists, tens of thousands of computers, trillions of commands per second and petabytes of storage [6, 20, 18]. At the time of writing, EGEE assembles over 250 sites around the world with more than 30,000 CPUs and 5PB of storage, supporting over 100 Virtual Organizations.

While the aforementioned discussion shows that Grid Computing will play a vital role in many different scientific domains, realizing its full potential will require to make these infrastructures *dependable*. As a measure of dependability of grids we use the ratio of successfully fulfilled job requests over the total number of jobs submitted to the resource brokers of a grid infrastructure. The FlexX and Autodock data challenges of the WISDOM [25] project, conducted in August 2005, have shown that only 32% and 57% of the jobs completed successfully (with an "OK" status). Additionally, our group conducted a nine-month characterization of the South-Eastern-Europe resource broker (rb101.grid.ucy.ac.cy) in [4] and showed that only 48% of the submitted jobs completed successfully. Consequently, the dependability of large-scale grids needs to be improved substantially.

Detecting and managing failures is an important step toward the goal of a dependable grid. Currently, this is an extremely complex task that relies on over-provisioning of resources, ad-hoc monitoring and user intervention. Adapting ideas from other contexts such as cluster computing [16], Internet services [14–15] and software systems [17] seems also difficult due to the intrinsic characteristics of grid environments. Firstly, a grid system is not administered centrally; thus it is hard to access the remote sites in order to monitor failures. Moreover we cannot easily encapsulate failure feedback mechanisms in the application logic of each individual grid software, as the grid is an amalgam of pre-existing software libraries, services and components with no centralized control. Secondly, these systems are extremely large; thus, it is difficult to acquire and analyze failure feedback at a fine granularity. Lastly, identifying the overall state of the system and excluding the sites with the highest potential for causing failures from the job scheduling process, can be much more efficient than identifying many individual failures. Of course the latter information will be essential to identify the root cause of a failure [15], but this operation can be performed in a offline phase, and thus it is complementary to our framework.

In the FailRank architecture, feedback sources (i.e., websites, representative low-level measurements, data from the Information Index, etc.) are continuously coalesced into a representative array of numeric vectors, the *FailShot Matrix (FSM)*. FSM is then continuously ranked in order to identify the K sites with the highest potential to feature some failure. This allows the system to automatically exclude the respective sites from the job scheduling process.

The advantages of our approach are summarized as follows: (i) FailRank is a simple yet powerful framework to integrate and quantify the multi-dimensional parameters that affect failures in a grid system; (ii) our system is tunable, allowing system administrators to drive the ranking process through user-defined ranking functions; (iii) we eliminate the need for human intervention, thus our approach gives space for automated exploitation of the extracted failure semantics; (iv) we expect that the FailRank logic will be implemented as a filter outside the Grid job scheduler (i.e., Resource Broker or Workload Management System), thus imposing minimum changes to the Grid infrastructure.

2. Monitoring Failures in a Grid Environment

In this subsection we overview typical failure feedback sources provided in a grid environment. These sources contain information that is utilized by our system in order to deduct, in an a priori manner, the failing sites. Our discussion is in the context of the EGEE infrastructure, but similar tools and sources exist in other grids [20, 18].

Meta-information sources: Several methods for detecting failures have been deployed so far. Examples include (for a detailed description see [22]): (i) *Information Index Queries:* these are performed on the Information Service and enable the extraction of fine-grained information regarding the complete status of a grid site; (ii) *Service Availability Monitoring (SAM)* [26]: a reporting web site that is maintained for publishing periodic test-job results for all sites of the infrastructure; (iii) *Grid statistics:* provided by services such as *GStat* [12]; (iv) *Network Tomography Data:* these can be obtained by actively *pinging* and *tracerouting* other hosts in order to obtain delay, loss and topological structure information. Network tomography enables the extraction of network-related failures; (v) *Global Grid User Support (GGUS)* ticketing system [7]: system administrators use this system to report component failures as well as needed updates for sites. Such tickets are typically opened due to errors appearing in the SAM reports; (vi) *Core Infrastructure Center (CIC)* broadcasts [3]: allow site managers to report site downtime events to all affected parties through a web-based interface; and (vii) *Machine log-files*: administrators can use these files to extract error information that is automatically maintained by each grid node.

Active benchmarking: Deploying a number of lower level probes to the remote sites is another direction towards the extraction of meaningful failure semantics. In particular, one can utilize tools such as GridBench [21, 23], the Grid Assessment Probes [2] and DiPerF [5], in order to determine in real time the value of certain low level and application-level failure semantics that can not be furnished by the meta-information sources. For example, GridBench provides a corpus of over 20 benchmarks that can be used to evaluate and rank the performance of Grid sites and individual Grid nodes.

Both the Meta-Information Sources and the Active Benchmarking approaches have a major drawback: *their operation relies heavily on human intervention*. As Grid infrastructures become larger, human intervention becomes less feasible and efficient. As we would like Grid Dependability to be scalable, our proposed architecture does not rely on human intervention but instead provides the means for acquiring and analyzing the data from the above resources in an *automated* manner.

3.   The FailRank System

In this section we describe the underlying structure that supports the FailRank system. We start out with an architecture overview and then proceed with basic definitions in order to formalize our description. We follow with the description of the failure ranking mechanism deployed in FailRank.

3.1   Architecture Overview

The FailRank architecture (see Figure 1), consists of four major components: (i) a *FailShot Matrix (FSM)*, which is a compact representation of the parameters that contribute to failures, as these are furnished by the feedback sources; (ii) a temporal sequence of FSMs defines an *FSM timeseries* which is stored on local disk; (iii) a *Top-K Ranking Module* which continuously ranks the FSM matrix and identifies the K sites with the highest potential to run into a failure using a user defined scoring function; and (iv) a set of data exploration tools which allow the extraction of failure trends, similarities, enable learning and prediction. FailRank is tunable because it allows system administrators and domain experts to drive the ranking process through the provisioning of custom scoring functions.

3.2   Definitions and System Model

Definition (*FailShot Matrix (FSM)*): Let S denote a set of n grid *sites* (i.e. $S = \{s_1, s_2, ..., s_n\}$). Also assume that each element in S is characterized by a set of m attributes (i.e. $A = \{a_1, a_2, ..., a_m\}$). These attributes are obtained

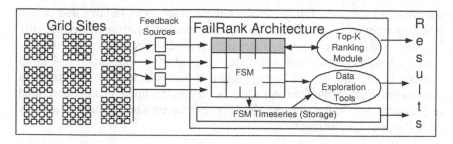

Figure 1. The FailRank System Architecture: Feedback sources are continuously coalesced into a representative array of numeric vectors, the *FailShot Matrix (FSM)*. FSM is then continuously ranked in order to identify the K sites with the highest potential to feature some failure.

Site	CPU	DISK	QUEUE	NET	FAIL
s_1="USC-LCG2"	0.63	0.61	0.01	0.28	0.35
s_2="TAU-LCG2"	0.66	0.91	0.92	0.56	0.58
s_3="ELTE"	0.48	0.01	0.16	0.56	0.54
s_4="UCL-CCC"	0.99	0.90	0.75	0.74	0.67
s_5="CY01-KIMON"	0.44	0.07	0.70	0.19	0.67

Table 1. The *FailShot Matrix (FSM)* coalesces the failure information, available in a variety of formats and sources, into a representative array of numeric vectors.

by the feedback sources described in Section 2. The rows in Table 1 represent the sites while the columns represent the respective attributes. The jth attribute of the ith site is denoted as s_{ij}. The j-th attribute specifies a *rating* (or *score*) which characterizes some grid site s_i ($i \leq n$) at a given time moment. These ratings are extracted by custom-implemented parsers, which map the respective information to real numerics in the range [0..1] (1 denotes a higher possibility towards failure). The $m \times n$ table of scores defines the *FailShot Matrix (FSM)*, while a *Site Vector* is any of the n rows of FSM.

A graphical illustration for some synthetic example is given in Table 1. The figure shows five sites $\{s_1, ..., s_5\}$ where each site is characterized by five attributes: CPU (% of cpu units utilized), DISK (% of storage occupied), QUEUE (% of job queue occupied), NET (% of dropped network packets) and FAIL (% of jobs that don't complete with an "OK" status).

Definition (*FSM Timeseries*): A temporal sequence of l FailShot Matrices defines an *FSM Timeseries of order l*.

Keeping a history of the failure state for various prior time instances is important as it enables the automatic post-analysis of the dimensions that contributed to a given failure, enables the prediction of failures and others. It is important to notice that the FSM timeseries can be stored incrementally in order to reduce the amount of storage required to keep the matrix on disk. Nevertheless, even the most naive storage plan of storing each FSM in its entirety, is still much more storage efficient than keeping the raw html/text sources provided by the feedback sources. In constructing FailBase, described in Section 4, we found that the FSM representation saves us approximately 350GB of storage per month.

3.3   The Ranking Module

Although the snapshot of site vectors in FSM greatly simplifies the representation of information coming from different sources, observing individually hundreds of parameters in real time in order to identify the sites that are running into trouble is still a difficult task. For example a typical LDAP query to the Grid Information Service returns around 200 attributes. Monitoring these parameters in separation is a cumbersome process that is very expensive in terms of human resources, can rarely lead to any sort of a priori decision-making and is extremely prone to mistakes and human omissions. Instead, automatically deducting the sites with the highest potential to suffer from failures is much more practical and useful. Since this information will be manipulated with high frequencies, we focus on computing the K sites with the highest potential to suffer from failures rather than finding all of them (K is a user-defined parameter). Therefore we don't have to manipulate the whole universe of answers but only the K most important answers, quickly and efficiently. The answer will allow the Resource Broker to automatically and dynamically divert job submissions away from sites running into problems as well as notify administrators in advance (compared to SAM & tickets) to take preventive measures for the sites more prone to failures.

Scoring Function: In order to rank sites we utilize some aggregate scoring function which is provided by the user (or system administrator). For ease of exposition we use, similarly to [1], the function:

$$Score(s_i) = \sum_{j=1}^{m} w_j * s_{ij} \tag{1}$$

where s_{ij} denotes the score for the jth attribute of the ith site and w_j ($w_j > 0$) a weight factor which calibrates the significance of each attribute according to the user preferences. For example if the CPU load is more significant than the DISK load, then the former parameter is given a higher weight. Should we need to capture more complex interactions between different dimensions of FSM we could construct, with the help of a domain expert, a custom scoring function or

CPU	DISK	QUEUE	NET	FAIL	RANK
$s_4, .99$	$s_2, .91$	$s_2, .92$	$s_4, .74$	$s_4, .67$	$s_4, 4.05$
$s_2, .66$	$s_4, .90$	$s_4, .75$	$s_2, .56$	$s_5, .67$	$s_2, 3.63$
$s_1, .63$	$s_1, .61$	$s_5, .70$	$s_3, .56$	$s_2, .58$	$s_5, 2.07$
$s_3, .48$	$s_5, .07$	$s_3, .16$	$s_1, .28$	$s_3, .54$	$s_1, 1.88$
$s_5, .44$	$s_3, .01$	$s_1, .01$	$s_5, .19$	$s_1, .35$	$s_3, 1.75$

Table 2. The Sorted (by column score) FSM (Sorted-FSM) is utilized by the top-K engine to continuously identify K highest ranked answers, where K is a user parameter.

we could train such a function automatically using historic information. It is expected that the scoring function will be much more complex in a real setting (e.g. a linear combination of averages over n' correlated attributes, where $n' << n$) and we are currently working towards evaluating these alternatives.

Example: In order to stimulate our description, consider the example of Table 1. In order to infer the overall rank for two site vectors, such as $s_2 = \{0.66, 0.91, 0.92, 0.56, 0.58\}$ and $s_4 = \{0.99, 0.90, 0.75, 0.74, 0.67\}$, we apply the scoring function with $w_j = 1$ (i.e. all dimensions are of equal importance), and find that $s_2 = 3.63$ and $s_4 = 4.05$.

In order to minimize the computation of the scoring function, which potentially has to join hundreds of columns in each run, we will utilize the *Threshold Algorithm (TA)* [9]. *TA* is one of the most widely recognized algorithms for finding the K highest rank answers in database and middleware scenarios. Suppose that we are interested in finding the $K = 1$ objects with the highest score. *TA* starts out by performing a parallel access to the n lists of the Sorted-FSM (see Table 2). While an object s_i is seen, *TA* performs a random access to the other lists to find the exact score for s_i using the given scoring function. In our working example the exact score would be computed for the two objects in the first row (i.e. $s_4 = 4.05$ and $s_2 = 3.63$) since sorted access is executed on a row-at-a-time basis. It then computes a *threshold* value τ as the sum of all scores in the first row (i.e. $\tau = .99 + .91 + .92 + .74 + .67 = 4.23$). Since τ is larger than both scores of s_4 and s_2, the *TA* algorithm performs another iteration in which the threshold τ is refined as the sum of scores across the second row (i.e. $\tau = 3.54$). It also computes the exact score for $s_5 = 2.07$ (the only unresolved object in the second row). Now the algorithm finds at least $K=1$ objects above the threshold (i.e. $s_4 \geq \tau$ and $s_2 \geq \tau$) and therefore terminates. It is easy to prove that no other object can have a score above s_4 thus the score function calculation can be omitted for these objects.

4. The EGEE FailBase Repository

In the previous section we outlined the main components of the FailRank architecture. In this section we present the tools we developed in order to evaluate the proposed architecture. In particular, we present the *FailBase*

Repository which is a 38GB corpus of state information that characterizes the EGEE Grid for one month in 2007. Such a corpus paves the way for the community to systematically uncover new, previously unknown patterns and rules between the multitudes of parameters that can contribute to failures in a grid environment.

4.1   Overview

FailBase currently contains 32 days of monitoring data obtained from tests executed on the EGEE Grid Infrastructure between 16/3/2007 and 17/4/2007. The trace was collected at the High Performance Computing systems Lab (HPCL) at the University of Cyprus. We utilized a dual Xeon 2.4GHz CPU machine with 1GB of RAM connected to the European Academic Network (GEANT) at 155Mbps.

The trace maintains information for 2,565 Computing Element (CE) queues. It is important to note that resource brokers perform the *matchmaking* between the requests and the available and appropriate queues at the CE-queue granularity rather than on individual nodes. Thus, we focus on characterizing failures at the same granularity as well. Each CE-queue is stored in an individual folder that currently contains 72 attributes (i.e., files) and each file characterizes the CE-queue it is stored in. For example, `ce101.grid.ucy.ac.cy-jobmanager-lcgpbs-atlas` is the directory that contains measurements specific to the ATLAS experiment job queue that is maintained on the Computing Element `ce101.grid.ucy.ac.cy`.

Each of the files in the CE-queue folders can be thought of as a timeseries (i.e., a sequence of [timestamp,value] pairs) for the given attribute using a time step of approximately 1 to 10 minutes (varies according to the type of source). We currently share the Failbase repository with the researchers of our group using the UNIX filesystem interface which maintains openness and portability. In the future we have plans to store the information in a relational database on the EGEE grid in order to allow researchers from other institutes to access and manipulate the stored information using the expressive power of the Structured Query Language (SQL).

4.2   Meta-information Sources

We shall next describe the adopted methodology for acquiring the 72 failure-related attributes from the respective meta-information sources:

(i) *Service Availability Monitoring (SAM)*: We obtained approximately 260MB of data in raw html form (one html file for each CE) using the UNIX system utility *curl*. We then processed these pages using a set of perl scripts and generated 18 attributes. These attributes contain information such as the version number of the middleware running on the CE, results of various replica manager tests and results from test job submissions.

(ii) *Information Index Queries (BDII)*: We used the *ldapsearch* system utility tool to perform approximately 2 million LDAP queries on the Information Index hosted on *bdii101.grid.ucy.ac.cy*. We then performed a projection in order to extract another 15 failure-related attributes. This yielded attributes such as the number of free CPUs and the maximum number of running and waiting jobs for each respective CE-queue.

(iii) *Grid Statistics (GStat)*: We downloaded, again using curl, and parsed data files from the monitoring website of Academia Sinica. From these files we generated 19 attributes for each given center and then replicated these attributes to all the respective queues. The 19 attributes contain information such as the geographical region of a Resource Center, the available storage space on the Storage Element used by a particular CE, and results from various tests concerning BDII hosts.

(iv) *Host sensor data (GridICE)*: We performed over 500,000 LDAP queries on every EGEE Computing Element host that published GridICE [8] sensor data (i.e., on ≈184 computing element hosts). The interval between consecutive probes was 10 minutes. We were able to extract 18 attributes of interest that includes information such as the total and available sizes of RAM, virtual memory and filesystem-specific information.

(v) *Network Tomography Data (SmokePing)*: We obtained a 313MB snapshot of the *gPing* database from ICS-FORTH (Greece) for the studied period. The database contains network monitoring data for all the EGEE sites. From this collection we measured the average round-trip-time (RTT) and the packet loss rate relevant to each South East Europe CE (see Figure 2) which therefore yielded 2 additional attributes. In order to make the information consistent with the FailBase repository schema, we replicated files from the CE-level to CE-queue-level using a one-to-one mapping function.

5. Experimental Evaluation

In this section we describe an experimental study of the FailRank framework as well as our methodology.

5.1 Methodology

We have implemented a trace-driven tool in GNU C++ which processes the Failbase repository and then simulates the execution of the FailRank framework. In particular, we replay the trace in our simulator and at each timestamp we identify the K sites that might fail to respond. We will denote these $(timestamp, siteID)$ tuples as the *Identified Set* (I_{set}). The I_{set} is constructed by select-

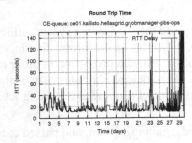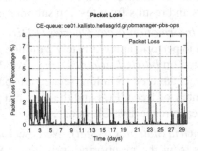

Figure 2.   Round-Trip-Time (left) and Packet Loss (right) for the CE-queue
ce01.kallisto.hellasgrid.gr-jobmanager-pbs-ops. These attributes are two of the
72 attributes maintained for the 2,565 CE-queues in the Failbase Repository.

ing the K highest-ranked answers from the execution of the scoring function
described in Section 3.3 with equal weights on the FSM table.

Note the resource broker can compute the I_{set} directly from the FSM matrix,
before the timestamp at which the actual error happens, thus such an approach
provides an a priori failure detection mechanism. In order to assess this claim
and validate that the I_{set} corresponds to the actual sites that have failed to
respond, we need a set of $(timestamp, siteID)$ tuples at which real site failures
happened. We shall denote such a set as the *Real Set (R_{set})* and we construct it
by combining the 18 attributes provided by the SAM service (described in 4.2)
using the scoring function described in Section 3.3. That yields an average
score per site for every timestamp. For each timestamp, we then again choose
the K sites which have the highest score. We define the *penalty*, for not finding
the correct sites at timestamp i, using a set-theoretic notation as follows:

$$Penalty_i = |R_{set} - I_{set}| \qquad (2)$$

where $|R_{set}| = |I_{set}| = K$ and the penalty at each timestamp i is defined as
the cardinality of the set difference $R_{set} - I_{set}$. In our experimentation, we
shall also use the *Aggregate Penalty* (i.e., $\mathcal{A} = \sum_{i=1}^{timestamps} Penalty_i$), which
provides a measure of overall efficiency for the I_{set} in all timestamps.

Having identified the correct I_{set} sites, our objective is to blacklist these sites
and exclude them from the job scheduling process, decreasing in that way the
number of failures.

5.2   Evaluating FailRank

In this subsection we evaluate the efficiency of the FailRank framework in
identifying the sites that will fail. In particular, we obtain the I_{set} using two
alternative strategies: i) *FailRank Selection*, which utilizes the FSM matrix and
selects the $K = 20$ sites ($\approx 10\%$ of all sites) that maximize the scoring function

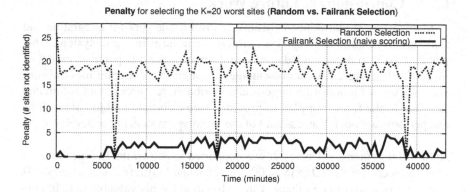

Figure 3. **FailRank selection vs. Random selection:** FailRank identifies the site that have failed as opposed to Random which always identifies very few of the K=20 sites.

of Section 3.3 with equal weights; and ii) *Random Selection*, which does not utilize the FSM matrix and simply selects the $K = 20$ sites at random.

We then measure the respective penalty using our provided definition. Note that for this experiment we utilize a subset of the Failbase repository (i.e., 197 OPS queues monitored for 32 days) for which we had the largest number of available attributes. We also apply a spline interpolation smoothing between consecutive time points in our graph in order to facilitate presentation.

Figure 3 illustrates that FailRank selection always has an extremely low penalty (i.e. on average 2.14 ± 1.41 with $\mathcal{A} = 92,596$) while Random selection is always very close to 20 (i.e. on average 18.19 ± 3.5 with $\mathcal{A} = 786,148$). We can conclude that FailRank misses the correct sites in only 9% of the cases while Random misses the correct results in 91% of the cases. Another observation is at time instances 6000, 16000 and 39000, both selection curves drop to zero. This is attributed to the fact that our meta-information trace contained missing values at the given points (i.e., $I_{set} = R_{set} = \emptyset$). One final observation is that the Random selection curve is in some cases above 20. This is attributed to the fact that the cardinality of the R_{set} might be bigger than K, instead of equal to K, in certain cases. This is explained as follows: to construct the R_{set} we identified the K highest ranked tuples for each timestamp. In some cases the Kth tuple has an equal score to the $K^{th} + 1$ tuple (or maybe even the $K^{th} + 2$ tuples, etc.). As a result, $|R_{set}|$ might be bigger than $|I_{set}|$ which consequently might yield a penalty larger than K (e.g. consider the case where $R_{set} \cap I_{set} = \emptyset$).

6.   Conclusions & Future Work

In this paper we introduce FailRank, a novel framework for integrating and ranking information sources that characterize failures in a grid system. This perspective is to our knowledge new and fits well the computation model of grid infrastructures. Another advantage is that FailRank streamlines the very complex task of monitoring large-scale distributed resources in an automated manner. In the future we plan to provide more elaborate ranking algorithms and perform an in-depth assessment of our prototype system under development.

Acknowledgements: This work was supported in part by the European Union under projects CoreGRID (# IST-2002-004265) and EGEE (#IST-2003-508833). The authors would like to thank Yannis Ioannou for his valuable help in constructing the Failbase repository and Charalampos Gkikas for providing access to the Hellas-FORTH gPing data.

References

[1] Bruno N., Gravano L. and Marian A., "Evaluating Top-K Queries Over Web Accessible Databases", In ICDE 2002.

[2] Chun G., Dail H., Casanova H., and Snavely A., "Benchmark probes for grid assessment", In IEEE IPDPS 2004.

[3] "CIC", http://cic.gridops.org/

[4] Da Costa G., Orlando S., Dikaiakos M.D., "Nine months in the life of EGEE: a look from the South", In *IEEE MASCOTS* 2007.

[5] Dumitrescu C., Raicu I., Ripeanu M., Foster I., "DiPerF: An automated DIstributed PERformance testing Framework", In *IEEE/ACM Grid 2004*.

[6] "EGEE", http://www.eu-egee.org/.

[7] "Global Grid User Support (GGUS) ticketing", https://gus.fzk.de/pages/home.php

[8] "GridICE", http://grid.infn.it/gridice/

[9] Fagin R., Lotem A. and Naor M., "Optimal Aggregation Algorithms For Middleware", In *PODS* 2001.

[10] Foster I. and Kesselman C., "The Grid: Blueprint for a New Computing Infrastructure", Elsevier, 2004.

[11] Foster I., Kesselman C., and Tuecke S., "The Anatomy of the Grid: Enabling Scalable Virtual Organizations", In *Intl. J. Supercomputer Applications*, 15(3):200–222, 2001.

[12] Grid Statistics (GStat) http://goc.grid.sinica.edu.tw/gstat/

[13] Junqueira, F. P., and Marzullo, K., "The virtue of dependent failures in multi-site systems", In *HotDep* 2005.

[14] Kiciman E. and Fox A., "Detecting Application-Level Failures in Component-based Internet Services", In *IEEE Transactions on Neural Networks*, 2004.

[15] Kiciman E. and Subramanian L., "Root Cause Localization in Large Scale Systems", In *HotDep* 2005.

[16] Krishnamurthy S., Sanders W.H., Cukier M.: "A Dynamic Replica Selection Algorithm for Tolerating Timing Faults", In *DSN* 2001.

[17] Locasto M.E., Sidiroglou S., and Keromytis A.D., "Application Communities: Using Monoculture for Dependability", In *HotDep* 2005.

[18] "OSG", http://www.opensciencegrid.org.

[19] Raman R., Livny M., Solomon M.H., "Matchmaking: An extensible framework for distributed resource management", In *Cluster Computing*, Vol 2, pp 129-138, 1999.

[20] "TeraGrid", http://www.teragrid.org/

[21] Tsouloupas G., Dikaiakos M.D., "GridBench: A Tool for the Interactive Performance Exploration of Grid Infrastructures", In *Journal of Parallel and Distributed Computing*, Vol 67, pp 1029-1045, 2007.

[22] Neokleous K., Dikaiakos M.D., Fragopoulou P., Markatos E.P., "Failure Management in Grids: The Case of the EGEE Infrastructure", In *Parallel Processing Letters* (in press, Dec. 2007).

[23] Tsouloupas G. and Dikaiakos M.D., "Grid Resource Ranking using Low-level Performance Measurements.", In *Euro-Par* 2007.

[24] Vlachos M., Hadjieleftheriou M., Gunopulos D. , Keogh E., "Indexing multi-dimensional time-series with support for multiple distance measures" In *KDD* 2003.

[25] "WISDOM", http://wisdom.eu-egee.fr/

[26] "Service Availability Monitoring (SAM)", http://goc.grid.sinica.edu.tw/gocwiki/SAM

A FAULT-INJECTOR TOOL TO EVALUATE FAILURE DETECTORS IN GRID-SERVICES

Nuno Rodrigues, Décio Sousa, Luis Silva
Dep. Engenharia Informática, University of Coimbra,
Polo II, 3030-Coimbra
Portugal
luis@dei.uc.pt

Abstract   In this paper we present a fault-injector tool, named JAFL (Java Fault Loader), that was developed with the target of testing the fault-tolerance mechanisms of Grid and Web applications. Along with the JAFL internals description, we will present some results collected from synthetic experiments where we used both our injector and fault detection mechanisms. With these results we expect to prove that our fault injection tool can be actively used to evaluate fault detection mechanisms.

Keywords: fault injection, fault detection, performance evaluation

1. Introduction

Before the deployment of Grid applications or any Grid middleware it is necessary to be sure that the software is robust and reliable. The software modules that are most difficult to be tested are the ones related with failure-detection and recovery. To exercise these modules we propose the use of synthetic fault-injection. By using fault injection techniques we will be able to reproduce the occurrence of failures in a system and measure the latency and coverage of the built-in fault-detection mechanisms.

To reproduce valid failures, the fault injector tools must be developed based on todays most common failures. In surveys such as [6] or [7] we can see that the main causes of failure are divided in four big groups: software failures, operator errors, hardware failures and security violations. Since hardware failures and security violation are out of the scope of this paper, we will only discuss software failures and operator error issues, which, in their turn, account for 80% of system failures (software (40%), operator error (40%)).

After deeply analyzing these two groups (software and operator errors) we realized that operator errors occur mainly during system maintenance, software upgrades and system integration while the software failures normally occur due to system overload, resource exhaustion and complex fault-recovery routines. Since these are the most common causes of system failures, our work will be completely focused on them.

In this paper we present a fault-injector tool, named JAFL (Java Fault Loader) that was developed based on the previous issues and with the target of testing the fault-tolerance mechanisms of Grid and Web applications. Furthermore, we can say that this fault-injector was developed as an aditional package of the QUAKE benchmarking tool [28]. In the next sections we will describe JAFL internals, we will expose some of the most common fault detection mechanisms and we will present some results that were collected from experiments where we used both our injector and some fault detection mechanisms. In the end of this paper we expect to prove that our fault injector can be helpful in the evaluation of the fault-detection mechanisms used in Web and Grid systems.

2. Fault Injector

There are three categories of fault injectors: hardware implemented, simulator based and software implemented [1]. Our fault injector is included in the later category.

The most known software fault injection tools targeted for Grid systems are: Cecium [8], Doctor [9], Orchestra [10], NFTAPE [11], LOKI [12], Mendosus [13], FAIL-FCI [14] and OGSA [15]. Some of them are able to inject real failures in the system, applications or network while the others are simple simulator-based injectors.

While most of the software injection tools only consider the injection at low level (with the objective of emulating hardware failures such as processor or memory faults [2, 3]) or at software-level (with the objective of corrupting code or data [4, 5]), our fault-injector was based on a slightly different approach.

Our goal is more targeted to the synthetic consumption of JVM and operating system resources and to the injection of human-operator errors. As we have said previously, these types of failures represent a considerable amount of failures that occur in real systems. Since our objective is to reproduce the most common failures, we developed our fault injector with the ability to inject the following faults: Memory consumption; CPU consumption; Thread consumption, Disk Storage consumption, I/O consumption, Database connections consumption, File handler consumption, Exception Throwing, Database Table Deletion and Database Table Lock. Later in this section we will explain each one of them.

2.1   Architecture

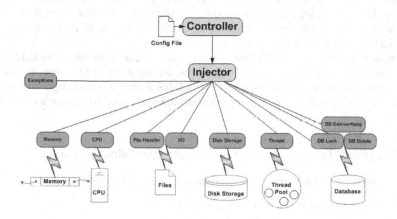

Figure 1.   JAFL Architecture

Our fault injector, as shown in Figure 1, is composed by 2 main modules: the Controller and the Injector.

The Controller is responsible for reading a configuration file where all the configurations for the next fault injection are stored. In this configuration file the user can define the fault load, the specific parameters for that fault load, the start time, the interval between injections and the end time (it can be infinite) of the next fault injection.

The Injector module has two main functions: receive the fault load parameters from the Controller module and deliver them to the respective fault load sub-module. There are ten sub-modules in the Injector module, each one representing one specific fault:

Memory Consumption: With this sub-module we are able to consume, along the time, a given amount of memory in the JVM. If we don't define an end point it will consume all the memory and throw an Out Of Memory Error.

CPU Consumption: By using various threads to do some hard calculations, this sub-module can increase substantially the CPU Load .

Thread Consumption: With this fault we are able to create various threads along the time and wait to see how the system responds.

Disk Storage Consumption: We can use this kind of fault to see how the system handle the lack of disk space. If we don't define an end point it will consume all the disk space.

I/O Consumption: This sub-module is responsible for doing read/write operations on our system. If we want to burst our system we can check our maximum read/write speed and configure the fault for those values.

Database Connections Consumption: With this fault we can consume various database connections and check whether our applications behave with the connection pool being filled up.

File Handler Consumption: By using this fault we can consume the file descriptors which are available for the user running the Java application.

Exception Throwing: This sub-module is able to throw some exceptions. We implemented this sub-module because after the occurrence of an exception the application can change its behavior.

Database Table Lock: With this sub-module we can emulate some database lock problems that occur, most of the times, during maintenance operations.

Database Table Deletion: This fault simulates a very common operator error which normally occurs when an erroneous backup is used to restore a database.

2.2   Usage

As JAFL is written in Java, it can be used in the following ways:

- Deployed in a Web/Grid container using the Java Technology

- Integrated with standalone applications

- Run as a standalone application

In figure 2 we can see a sample scenario where JAFL can be used in the 3 ways. In the frontend server, JAFL is used to actively consume the Web/Grid container resources; in "node b" it is used to perturb a simple application running on that node and in "node e" it is running as a standalone application with the goal of consuming operating system resources. This sample scenario shows that JAFL can be very helpful to test the reliability of a Web/Grid application.

3.   Detectors

In the previous section we presented our fault injector tool. In this section we will present the failure detection mechanisms that we have chosen to detect the faults produced by the JAFL tool.

Fault-detection mechanisms are the responsible for measuring the health of an application. If they are accurate enough they can help the system operators to keep the system up and running. Otherwise, if they are not able to detect a failure and trigger an alarm, the system can become unavailable and the system administrators would not notice that.

To guarantee a good detection coverage we have chosen four types of failure detectors:

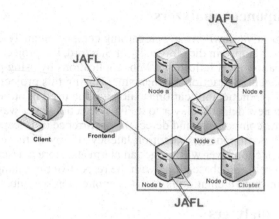

Figure 2. JAFL Usage Scenario

- System and Application Monitoring and Failure Detection Tools

- Component analyzers

- Log analyzers

- External Monitoring

Since each of these mechanisms has its own advantages and drawbacks, we will now describe them in detail.

3.1 System and Application Failure Detectors

This is the most common type of failure detectors. They are able to monitor the operating system resources (memory, cpu, etc), network interfaces, system services and others. With an accurate configuration they are also able to monitor applications and check the resources that they are consuming, their availability etc.

In the field of commercial solutions we have names such as HP Openview [18] or IBM Tivoli [19] to accomplish this task. Otherwise, if we prefer public domain solutions we can choose Zabbix [20], Nagios [21], Big Sister [22] and others.

In our study we adopted Zabbix, which is one of the powerful and easiest platforms to work with. It is very easy to deploy and to configure, provides a wide variety of features and stores all the data in a database, allowing external programs to collect data from there. It is composed by a Zabbix Server and Zabbix Agent. The Agent is deployed in the monitored host and sends all the information to the Server. The Server is then responsible for all the data analysis and alarm triggering.

3.2   Component analyzers

One of the mostly known projects regarding component analysis is Pinpoint [16]. Pinpoint, developed in the University of Stanford, is a project which aim is to detect application-level failures in Web Applications by using path-analysis [17] and component interaction mechanisms. Having this project in mind, we instrumented a synthetic application (which will be used in our experiments) and we added a new detection layer to it. This detection layer was responsible for analyzing the components and detect the occurrence of Exceptions or high variations on the components execution latency. If any of these problems is detected, this detection layer will trigger an alarm and store a description of the problem on a specific database along with the respective timestamp. The major drawback of our implementation is that it is application specific.

3.3   Log analyzers

Log analyzers are applications that parse log files and extract information from them. Two of the mostly known standalone rule-based log analyzers are Swatch [23] and Logsurfer [24]. These log analyzers are commonly used to do real-time analysis of the log files and check if certain regular expressions are found there. If a certain regular expression, (e.g. an error message) is found, the tools will throw ouput events that can be converted in alarms. In our experiments we decided to use a tool developed by ourselves but with the same design as the ones presented before. We developed a tool that simply sweeps the log files and tries to locate keywords that can indicate any kind of error. If the tool detects keywords such as "Exception", "Error" or "OutOfMemory" an alarm is triggered and the description of the problem is stored in an external database with the respective timestamp.

3.4   External Monitoring

The external monitors are agents that run outside of the Grid platform and that are able to behave like real users. They can visit webpages, do shopping and use services. These external agents are able to detect DNS problems, TCP problems, HTTP errors, content matching errors and high response times. If any of these problems is detected, the agent will store the timestamp and all the available information about the problem in a database. Once again, this was an implementation from ourselves which was based on external monitoring tools such as [29] and [30].

4.   Experimental Results

In this section, we will present two of the many results collected from experiments run in the CISUC cluster in Coimbra. We used eight nodes of the Cluster and they were divided by: Main Server, Zabbix Server, External Agent and normal clients.

Our main server was configured to expose TPC-W in Java [25]. TPC-W is a synthetic application written in Java which is composed by a set of servlets that simulate an e-business like Amazon.com. We deployed TPC-W over Apache Tomcat (with 1024 MB JVM) [26] and we used MySQL [27] for data storage. As we have said before, we added a failure detection layer to the TPC-W application with the goal of detecting component failures. In the same machine we configured our log analyzer tool, which was constantly analyzing the Apache Tomcat logs and we configured the Zabbix Agent which was responsible for analyzing the operating system resources and monitor the Tomcat container activity.

In another node we deployed the Zabbix Server and a MySQL database. This database was very useful to synchronize all the failure detection times since all the detection mechanism store the information about the failures in this database.

The other single node was configured as an external monitoring agent. This agent executes transactions in the TPC-W Web application and checks if errors appear during those transactions.

The remaining nodes were used to inject workload in the application. This workload consists in various transactions according to the TPC distribution.

All the internal detectors (Zabbix, Component, Log) were configured with a 15 seconds polling interval while the external agent was configured with 1 minute between each transaction.

After configuring our experimental framework we started our experiments. We configured our fault injector to inject failures in the Tomcat container and we obtained very interesting results.

4.1 Memory Consumption

In this experiment we used our fault injector to simulate memory leaks in the Tomcat container. To achieve this, we configured our fault injector to consume 1 MB of memory per second, we define 120 seconds as our ramp-up time and we did not defined any stoppage time. In Figure 3 we can see the detectors reaction to the fault.

By looking carefully at the Figure 3 we can see that the red line represents the injection period, the dark blue dots represent the mechanism that detected the failure and the light blue dots represent the activated trigger.

If we check the detection points along the time we can see that the Zabbix Agent spotted the problem at 540 seconds. Since Zabbix was configured to trigger an alarm when the JVM reaches 90% of its maximum heap space, this was as expeced result. At this point, the JVM Memory is almost full and the application starts getting unstable. This instability is immediately noticed by the components when they understand that the request latencies are getting very high. After the components, also the external monitors detected the problem when they caught some HTTP timeout errors. By last, the Log analyzer tool detected an error in the log file. Therefore, we can say that the errors detected in the log files were OutOfMemory errors. Since here, the service gets completely unavailable and only the external agents are able to detect the HTTP timeouts.

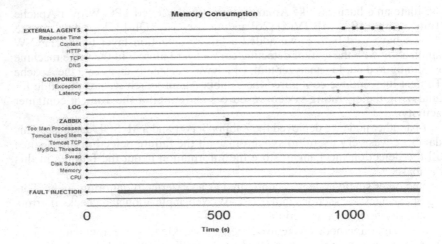

Figure 3.   Memory Consumption

With this experiment we were able to test the capabilities of both our fault injector and our four detection mechanisms. Figure 3 can prove that both of them produced the expected results.

4.2   Table Deletion

With this experiment we have seen how the system handles a table deletion operator error and what detectors are able to detect this kind of problem. Since TPC-W uses various database tables, we configured our fault injector to delete each one of those tables with a rate of 1 table per 10 seconds. The objective of this table deletion fault is to simulate an erroneous database backup.

If we look at Figure 4 we can see that the component detector was the quickest to spot the failure. This time, instead of detecting high latency in the components execution, it has detected an exception at component level. Since Tomcat logs exceptions to log files, the Log Analyzer tool was also able to catch these exceptions; but lately. Besides the component and log analyzers, also the external agents were able to catch this failure. They understood that the content of the page that they were requesting was different from the expected one. By analysing the content, they have seen that the exception

Once again our injector was able to accomplish its objective: triggering the detection systems.

5.   Conclusions and Future Work

Using fault injectors to test the robustness of an application is one of the most common practices in the process of development.

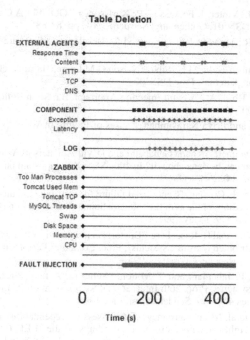

Figure 4.   Table Deletion

In this paper we presented a new fault injection tool, named JAFL, which is slightly different from the common injectors. JAFL was developed to consume operating system resources and simulate operator errors.

After choosing different detection mechanisms, we conducted several experiments where we used JAFL to inject faults in a synthetic application and we observed that almost all of them were detected by our detection mechanisms. While resource consumption and low-level issues were mainly detected by Zabbix and by the component analyzer tool, application-level failures were mainly detected by the component analyzer tool, by the external monitoring agent and, in some situations, by the log analyzer tool. This is a very positive result since our objective was to develop a tool capable of triggering the various fault detection mechanisms used in Web/Grid services.

In the future we want to add more features to the JAFL tool and make it available to the community. Our objective is to allow the community to use JAFL in their own applications.

References

[1] H. Ammar, B. Cukic, C. Fuhrman, and A. Mili. A Comparative Analysis of Hardware and Software Fault Tolerance. Annals of Software Engineering, 10:103 - 150, 2000.

[2] Aidemark, J.; Vinter, J; Folkesson, P.; Karlsson, J. "GOOFI - A Generic Fault Injection
     Tool". Proc DSN'01, Gothenburg, Sewden, 2001, pp. 83-88

[3] Avresky, D.R.; Tapadiya P.K; "A method for Developing a Software-Based Fault Injection
     Tool"

[4] Eliane Martins, Cecilia M.F. Rubira, Nelson G.M Leme, "Jaca: A reflective fault injection
     tool based on patterns". Proc DSN'02

[5] Martins, E.; Rosa, A. "A Fault Injection Approach Based on Reflective Programming".
     Proc DSN'00

[6] Soila Pertet and Priya Narasimhan. Causes of Failure in Web Applications. December
     2005

[7] David Openheimer, Archana Ganapathi and David A. Paterson. Why do Internet services
     fail, and what can be done about it? In 4th USENIX Symposium on Internet Technologies
     and Systems, 2003

[8] G. Avarez and F. Cristian, "Centralized failure for distributed, fault-tolerant protocol test-
     ing," in Proceedings of the 17th IEEE Internationnal Conference on Distributed Computing
     Systems (ICDCS'97) May 1997.

[9] S. Han, K. Shin, and H. Rosenberg. "Doctor: An integrated software fault injection environ-
     ment for distributed real-time systems", Proc. Computer Performance and Dependability
     Symposium, Erlangen, Germany, 1995.

[10] S. Dawson, F. Jahanian, and T. Mitton. Orchestra: A fault injection environment for
     distributed systems. Proc. 26th International Symposium on Fault-Tolerant Computing
     (FTCS), pages 404-414, Sendai, Japan, June 1996.

[11] D.T. Stott and al. Nftape: a framework for assessing dependability in distributed systems
     with lightweight fault injectors. In Proceedings of the IEEE International Computer
     Performance and Dependability Symposium, pages 91-100, March 2000.

[12] R. Chandra, R. M. Lefever, M. Cukier, and W. H. Sanders. Loki: A state-driven fault
     injector for distributed systems. In In Proc. of the Int.Conf. on Dependable Systems and
     Networks, June 2000.

[13] X. Li, R. Martin, K. Nagaraja, T. Nguyen, B.Zhang. "Mendosus: A SAN-based Fault-
     Injection Test-Bed for the Construction of Highly Network Services", Proc. 1st Workshop
     on Novel Use of System Area Networks (SAN-1), 2002

[14] William Hoarau, and Sbastien Tixeuil. "A language-driven tool for fault injection in
     distributed applications". In Proceedings of the IEEE/ACMWorkshop GRID 2005, page
     to appear, Seattle, USA, November 2005.

[15] N. Looker, J.Xu. "Assessing the Dependability of OGSA Middleware by Fault-Injection",
     Proc. 22nd Int. Symposium on Reliable Distributed Systems, SRDS, 2003

[16] E. Kiciman and A. Fox. Detecting Application-Level Failures in Component-based Internet
     Services. IEEE Transactions on Neural Networks, Vol. 16, Issue 5, 2005

[17] M.Y. Chen, A. Accardi, E. Kiciman, D. Patterson, A. Fox and E. Brewer. Path-based
     failure and evolution management. In The 1st USENIX/ACM Symposium on Networked
     Systems Design and Implementation (NSDI '04), San Francisco, CA, March 2004

[18] HP Openview - www.managementsoftware.hp.com/,

[19] Tivoli - http://www-306.ibm.com/software/tivoli/products/monitor/

[20] Zabbix - http://www.zabbix.org/

[21] Nagios - http://nagios.org/

[22] Big Sister - http:// bigsister.graeff.com

[23] Swatch - http://swatch.sourceforge.net

[24] Logsurfer - http://www.dfn-cert.de/eng/logsurf/index.html

[25] TPC-W in Java - http://www.ece.wisc.edu/ pharm/tpcw.shtml

[26] Apache Tomcat - http://tomcat.apache.org/

[27] MySQL - http://www.mysql.com/

[28] Quake Benchmarking tool - Presented in the CoreGRID Industrial Conference, CICŠ2006

[29] Site24x7 - http://site24x7.com

[30] Gomez - http://www.gomez.com

PERFORMANCE MONITORING OF GRID SUPERSCALAR WITH OCM-G/G-PM: TUNING AND IMPROVEMENTS*

Rosa M. Badia and Raul Sirvent
Univ. Politècnica de Catalunya, C/ Jordi Girona, 1-3, E-08034 Barcelona, Spain
rosab@ac.upc.edu
rsirvent@ac.upc.edu

Marian Bubak
Inst. Computer Science, AGH, al. Mickiewicza 30, 30-059 Kraków, Poland
Academic Computer Centre – CYFRONET, Nawojki 11, 30-950 Kraków, Poland
bubak@agh.edu.pl

Wlodzimierz Funika and Piotr Machner
Inst. Computer Science, AGH, al. Mickiewicza 30, 30-059 Kraków, Poland
funika@agh.edu.pl
machner@student.agh.edu.pl

Abstract

This paper addresses further research work on the use of a Grid-enabled system for performance monitoring of GRID superscalar-compliant applications. Performance facilities are based on the extended functionality of the OCM-G monitoring system and a graphical tool G-PM used to interpret information received from the monitoring system. Previous papers focused mainly on the integration issues related to performance analysis of GRID superscalar applications and presented ideas for required changes to the G-PM architecture. Here we show with two case studies how the implemented changes enhance GS application monitoring. Summary follows a discussion of problems and presents plans for the future with a focus on tuning the whole infrastructure.

Keywords: grid programming models, monitoring tools, performance analysis

*This research is partly funded by the EU IST FP6-0004265 CoreGRID project and by the Ministry of Science and Technology of Spain (TIN-2004-07739-C02-01).

1.   Introduction

Developing parallel and distributed applications is often a difficult task. One has to take into account many issues that are not present when writing sequential applications, such as inter-process communication, synchronization or data transfer. Grid environments provide many facilities that should ease the developer but sometimes we come across problems that we simply did not anticipate. Our program can work in an apparently strange and unexpected way or its performance may prove to be far lower than we expected. This is why performance monitoring is so important, especially when writing applications for the Grid. We need ways of analyzing the behaviour of our code in order to detect potential bottlenecks, instabilities or other defects.

The Grid superscalar (GS) [1] is an environment which helps the application developer by bridging the gap between writing sequential and parallel applications. One of its aims is to make the latter as easy as the first. It's based on the master-worker model. The user has to write the master code and so called grid-enabled functions which in the end will be run as separate worker processes. In the master these functions are called, thus delegating the work load to the workers. The developer is also provided by GS with special methods for initializing the environment, reading and writing files (which can be used for inter-process communication), making barriers etc.

Our aim is to have the means of monitoring this highly dynamic environment but the existing monitoring systems are mainly off-line ones. A GS application programmer might have the need for a more reactive tool. This is what motivated us to start efforts to monitor GS with the Grid-enabled OMIS Compliant Monitoring system (OCM-G), developed in the EU IST CrossGrid project [5] and allowing on-line monitoring of Grid applications. This should give much better insight into program runtime. The requirements imposed by OCM-G on the application to be monitored are registration of each process in the system and library instrumentation (so that OCM-G gets notifications of the main events, especially function execution). The system acquires monitoring data, but it does not interpret or visualize it in any way. This is to be done by other tools that should get this information by issuing requests and interpreting it according to the user's needs.

One of such tools is the G-PM (Grid-enabled Performance Measurement tool) which provides many ways of performance analysis of application runtime. It is supplied with various visualization methods allowing to see for example function execution time and count. It connects to OCM-G and listens to events specified by the user defining the performance measurement.

The purpose of our efforts is to allow GS application monitoring by integrating OCM-G and G-PM with Grid superscalar, which is not an entirely straightforward task, because these environments were created separately and some incompatibilities exist, making changes necessary. Some of them have already been described in [8] and [9], additional ones will be shown in this paper. This time, our main focus will be on the presentation of first real-life monitoring cases and further improvements of the whole infrastructure.

This paper is organized as follows: Section 2 summarizes the integration issues concerning GS application monitoring, described in [9]. It also depicts the current progress of work, especially how we've solved some of our earlier problems (focusing on the modifications in the G-PM tool). Section 3 shows two case studies, which allow to see the benefits and possibilities provided by the environment. Section 4 shows an analysis of application execution delay due to monitoring. Section 5 presents the problems we've encountered along with their possible solutions and ideas for the future that could allow us to improve the whole infrastructure. Section 6 sums up the results and shows plans for further research.

2. Current progress of work

As mentioned above, the Grid superscalar programming paradigm is based on the master-worker model. The user writes a master application in a fashion very similar to writing a sequential application. The environment takes care of producing a "glue" between the master and workers. To be monitored, both the master and the worker processes need to register in OCM-G prior to doing any real work.

In [9] we described how GS library instrumentation is realised in order to keep OCM-G informed of GS functions being invoked. We showed how me made use of the OCM-G facilities allowing this, especially the cg-ocmg-libinstr tool in order to instrument the relevant libGS-master and libGS-worker libraries. Thanks to the work done then, the user don't need to insert any code to the their applications to make monitoring possible. We also showed our own instrumentation facility - a GS library instrumentation script. Another important part of our infrastructure was the monGS script through which all monitored Grid superscalar applications should be executed. It supplies them with the necessary data (such as the main monitor address and application name) needed to register in OCM-G. It passes this information both to the master and worker processes, since every monitored process needs to be registered. We also showed the new G-PM metrics representing the time spent executing GS functions and the number of their invocations. We are going to use these metrics now in both of our case studies.

One of the main problems we encountered was the fact that G-PM was created with MPI applications in mind and that it works on a fixed number of processes. It waits for a given number of processes to register, then attaches to all of them and never updates their list afterwards. This approach (shown in Fig. 1) is completely inadequate in the Grid superscalar environment, because workers can be created and destroyed all the time. There can be thousands of them and any of them can take an arbitrary amount of time to complete. It is just much more dynamic. Because of this it was not possible to monitor workers - G-PM had no way of attaching to them. The idea for solving this problem was to allow G-PM to dynamically respond on the events of worker registration in OCM-G by automatically attaching to the newly created processes. It is shown in Fig. 2. We have implemented this approach - at its start G-PM issues a service request to OCM-G, which specifies the app-proc-registered event as an interesting one. Thanks to it, each time a new worker process registers, its ID is notified to G-PM that attaches to it. This allows the tool to get notifications for all the subscribed events occurring during worker lifetime. These events include the beginning and end of instrumented function calls. Workers can now be fully monitored. Also, when a new worker registers in OCM-G, its execution is automatically stopped. It can be awoken by G-PM after the tool had attached to it. This provides additional synchronization between G-PM and the monitored processes. We make sure that they do not continue their tasks before the tool is ready to handle them. In practice, they are resumed almost at once, so this procedure does not slow them down significantly which is showed later on in this paper, in Section 5.

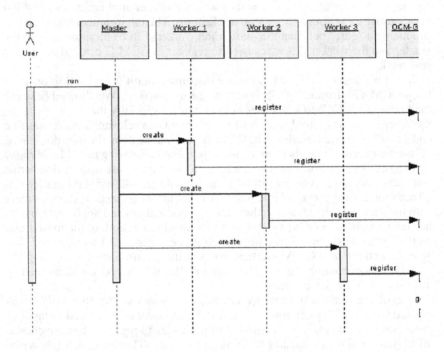

Figure 1.   The original way G-PM attaches to processes

Another new feature is the GS-Worker-delay metric that represents the amount of time spent in the execution of a single worker process. This metric measures the time between the execution of the IniWorker() and EndWorker() functions which begin and end the worker lifetime, respectively. This allows us to see how much time the worker process actually spent doing its tasks.

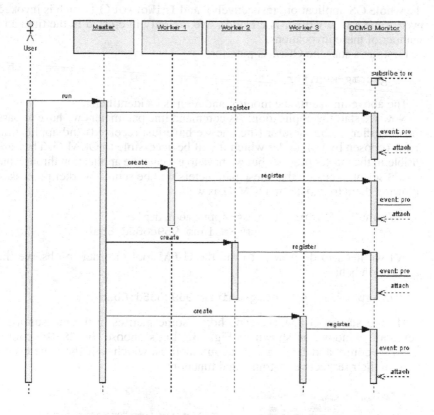

Figure 2. The mode of attaching G-PM to processes modified for GS needs

Thanks to these modifications G-PM was made aware of the invocations of all the Grid superscalar instrumented functions (almost all of the main ones) both in the worker and master processes. The user only need to choose which functions should be monitored to be able to see when each execution took place, how much time it took or how many times it was invoked. This information is provided in a user-friendly graphical manner. G-PM allows for different visualization methods (i.e. histograms, multicurves, bargraphs etc.). This will be shown in the next section.

3. Case study

Let's take a look at two monitoring scenarios. We have an application that executes a user-defined grid-enabled function an arbitrary number of times to perform some calculations. Each time this function is executed, a new worker process is created. In the first scenario we would like to track the execution of the main Grid superscalar functions - GS-On(), GS-Off() (which start and end the whole GS application, respectively), and `IniWorker()` (which is invoked every time a new worker is created). We are only interested in the time and number of these invocations.

First, let's start the OCM-G monitor:

```
cg-ocmg-monitor
```

The above line starts the monitor and returns its identifier.

Now we start the application. As command line parameters we have to pass the identifier of the monitor (the one we have just received) and application name (chosen by us), under which it will be accessible to OCM-G. They are visible in the master process, but we have to execute the application through the monGS script to ensure that these parameters will be sent to worker processes, allowing them to register in OCM-G as well.

```
./monGS ./simple --ocmg-appname simple
                 --ocmg-mainsm 959c635d:8bab
```

All we need to do now is to run the G-PM tool in order to observe the application behaviour.

```
cg-gpm simple --ocmg-mainsm 959c635d:8bab
```

Having started G-PM, we can choose some metrics in the measurement definition window, as shown in Fig. 3. Let's choose the `GS-On-count`, `GS-Off-count` and `IniWorker-count` metrics, which will show the executions of their respective instrumented functions.

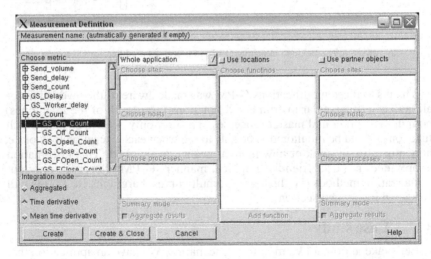

Figure 3.   G-PM: Defining a measurement for the instrumented functions (invocation count)

Next we can choose a way to visualize our measurements. For the purpose of this use case we shall choose a multicurve. Now we need to resume the program execution (applications by default pause their execution after having registered in OCM-G) and have a look at the measurement display. We can observe (in Fig. 4) that the execution of the mentioned functions was spotted by GP-M - the visualization presents two invocations of the `IniWorker()` function (which means that two worker processes have been created and registered in OCM-G) and invocations of `GS-On()` and `GS-Off()` at the beginning and end of application execution.

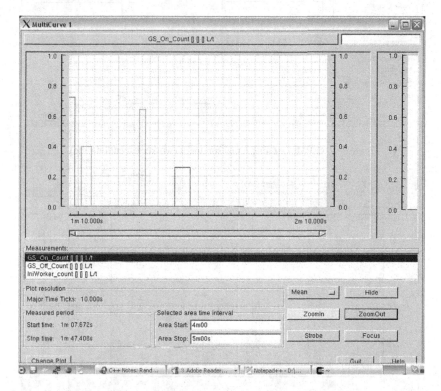

Figure 4. G-PM: Application flow of the monitored application (count metrics observed)

In the second monitoring scenario, we are interested in the amount of time taken by each of the workers. To observe it we go through all of the steps mentioned above, but we choose a different metric (`GS-Worker-delay` - see Fig. 5)

Our multicurve display (Fig. 6) shows that 5 worker processes have been created, at what time each one was created and how much time each of them took.

This way we can monitor any of the main Grid superscalar functions - for example we can see how much time was spent in opening or closing a file (the `GS-Open()` and `GS-Close()` functions) or synchronizing processes (the `GS-Barrier()` function).

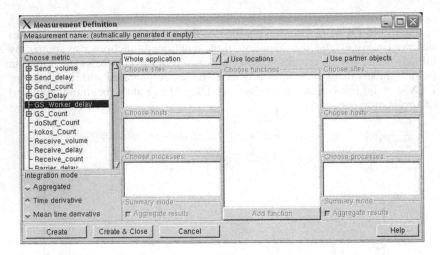

Figure 5.   G-PM: Defining a measurement (worker execution time)

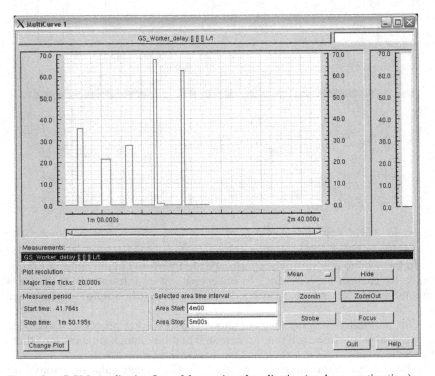

Figure 6.   G-PM: Application flow of the monitored application (worker execution time)

4.   Application delay analysis

Monitoring practically always provides some overhead and slows the monitored application. In our case the program needs to communicate with OCM-G and this procedure does entail delay. To measure it, we ran the application shown above in a couple of different scenarios. The first one included no monitoring (no delay), the second one was the application communicating only with OCM-G (lag caused by OCM-G registration and notifications) and in the third one we also had G-PM running, so all the processes stopped after registration and were instantly awoken by the tool (no measurements were defined). The results are depicted in Fig. 7. They show how much more time it took to execute the application in the second and third scenario with regard to the first one.

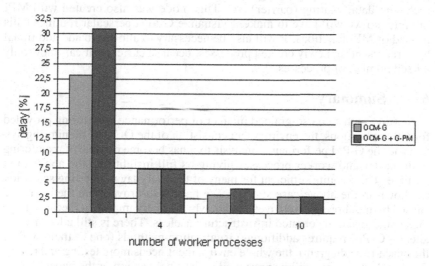

Figure 7.   Delay caused by performance monitoring

As we can see, the delay is really small and in our case was at most a couple percent compared to the application execution time. We consider this kind of lag entirely acceptable. One should realize that these measurements where performed on the same hardware configuration - the bigger was the number of processes the more work was to be done. This is why we can't see the parallelization speedup - there weren't any additional free processors to delegate the workers to.

5.   Problems and ideas for the future

Currently, the most important problem is the issue of tuning the whole environment which doesn't appear entirely stable yet. It certainly requires further testing and additional research and implementation effort in order to find and fix any errors that might show up. Moving between different hardware configurations is a good way to identify more imperfections. Our current implementation should be considered as the alpha version of the whole platform - additional maintenance will be needed to clean up and document the existing code.

Another case is the instrumentation of some additional GS routines, that haven't been instrumented yet and have been pointed out as important in the program execution and worth monitoring.

There is also a need to enhance some of the G-PM display modes to make them more suitable for the Grid superscalar environment requirements. One of the new G-PM visualization modes is the a space-time diagram. We are planning to integrate it into the GS-dedicated G-PM version. This diagram shows the work done by each of the processes as a bar divided into coloured pieces, each piece representing some part of functionality such as sending or receiving data, waiting (barrier) etc. This mode was also created with MPI in mind, so we will have to make it visualize Grid superscalar routines calls instead of MPI functions. It will also be necessary to allow it to add additional bars, representing newly created processes, because currently it can show only a fixed number of processes.

6.   Summary

Starting with a coarse-grained manner of performance monitoring provided for GS applications, the environment consisting of the OCM-G monitoring system and the G-PM performance analysis tool has become capable of monitoring both master and worker processes giving us full insight into the application runtime. This is quite sufficient for many of the everyday monitoring scenarios, as shown in the above case studies. We have also proved that the overhead caused by monitoring is relatively small, which is very important, because large lags could make the created infrastructure useless. There is still a lot of work ahead - G-PM requires additional visualization methods (one of them will be the space-time diagram), the whole environment needs more testing and tuning. These enhancements will be presented in the final version of the paper.

Acknowledgements. Our thanks go to colleagues Bartosz Balis, Marcin Smætek, and Tomasz Szepieniec for valuable discussions.

References

[1] Rosa M. Badia, Jesus Labarta, Raul Sirvent, Josep M. Perez, Jose M. Cela and Rogeli Grima. *Programming Grid Applications with GRID superscalar*. Journal of Grid Computing, vol. 1, 2003, pp. 151-170.

[2] T. Ludwig, R. Wismuller, V. Sunderam and A. Bode. *OMIS – On-line Monitoring Interface Specification (Version 2.0)*. Shaker Verlag, Aachen, vol. 9, LRR-TUM Research Report Series, (1997)
http://wwwbode.in.tum.de/~omis/OMIS/Version-2.0/version-2.0.ps.gz

[3] Globus Project homepage http://www.globus.org/

[4] Y. Tanaka, H. Nakada, S. Sekiguchi, T. Suzumura, S. Matsuoka. *Ninf-G: A Reference Implementation of RPC-based Programming Middleware for Grid Computing.* Journal of Grid Computing, 1(1):41-51, 2003.

[5] EU IST CrossGrid project page http://www.eu-crossgrid.org/

[6] Balis, B., Bubak, M., Funika, W., Wismueller, R., Radecki, M., Szepieniec, T., Arodz, T., Kurdziel, M. *Grid Environment for On-line Application Monitoring and Performance Analysis.* Scientific Pogramming, vol. 12, no. 4, 2004, pp. 239-251.

[7] R. Wismuller, M. Bubak, W. Funika, and B. Balis. *A Performance Analysis Tool for Interactive Applications on the Grid.* Intl. Journal of High Performance Computing Applications, 18(3):305-316, Fall 2004.

[8] Badia R.M., Bubak, M., Funika, W., and Smetek, M. *Performance Monitoring of GRID superscalar applications with OCM-G.* In: Sergei Gorlatch, Marco Danelutto (Eds.), Proceedings of the CoreGRID Workshop "Integrated Research in Grid Computing", Pisa, Italy, November 28-30, 2005, pp. 229-236, TR-05-22, University of Pisa, 2005

[9] Badia R.M., Sirvent R., Bubak M., Funika W., Klus C., Machner P. and Smetek M. *Performance monitoring of GRID superscalar with OCM-G/G-PM: integration issues,* Proceedings of the CoreGRID Workshop "Integrated Research in Grid Computing", Krakow, Poland, October 19-20, 2006, pp. 321-331

[10] Funika W., Duell J., Jojczyk P., Strack R. *Enhancing the G-PM performance measurement tool by Spacetime diagram,* Proc. Cracow Integration Workshop 2006, Krakow, 11-18 October 2006, ACC CYFRONET AGH, Krakow, 2007(to be published).

A SCALABLE MULTI-AGENT INFRASTRUCTURE FOR REMOTE FAILURE DETECTION IN WEB APPLICATIONS

Decio Sousa, Nuno Rodrigues, Luis Silva
Dep. Engenharia Informática, University of Coimbra,
Coimbra, Portugal
Portugal
luis@dei.uc.pt

Abstract   In this paper we present GOA-Net, a multi-agent architecture for remote detection of application-level failures in web-sites. It has been stated in the literature that despite the effort on system-level monitoring tools the internet applications and web-sites still face some application-level faults that end up to be seen by the end-user. This tool tries to overcome this problem and makes use of multi-agent technology and possibly later internet-grid computing. The monitoring of web-site failures can be done through different views: inside the network of the application, from the internet backbone and from the perspective of the end-user. The tool includes some data-correlation policies to reduce the occurrence of false-alarms and provide more accurate results.

Keywords: failure detection, multi-agents, internet applications.

1.   Introduction

In the two past decades the industry have been developing a wide variety of monitoring tools to detect failures and anomalies in IT systems. The most compelling examples include HP OpenView [1], IBM Tivoli [2], Altaworks Panorama [3], the open source Zabbix [4] and Nagios [5]. These tools are excellent to detect failures that occur or show up at the level of the operating system and the middleware. Despite this evidence there are unfortunately some subtle application-level failures that escape these system-level monitoring and end up to be seen by the end-user [10, 11]. Typically these failures occur because of operator errors or software bugs (typically non-deterministic) that escaped offline testing. These failures (Software and Human Operator) still account for 80% of total failures present in Internet Applications [13].

To detect these user-level failures there have been several proposals for external detectors [6, 7, 8, 9]. Some of these solutions are simple academic proposals [7], others are already commercial products [6, 8, 9]. We have analyzed the state-of-the-art of external monitoring tools and we have identified some opportunities of enhancement. In this paper we present the design of GOA-NET, (Global Observation Multi-Agent Network) a scalable multi-agent network for remote detection of user-visible failures in web-applications. Its architecture is composed by a coordinator and a standalone, lightweight agent that can be easily massively distributed around the globe through the integration with other large-scale distributed applications.

Our agent-detectors are able to simulate entire web-site transactions collecting performance data at the various network-levels and also checking and validating web-site content. Furthermore, they will be able to forecast performance degradation and web-site malfunction. This list of features is directly competitive with the existing solutions. Apart from these features of the agent-detectors we have designed a highly-scalable architecture that can be deployed in the Internet by being potentially integrated with some middleware for large-scale volunteer computing like BOINC [14] or similar. Although there are some challenges to overcome we feel this is a potential idea and we now starting an experimental study with our first prototype of our architecture.

2.   Related Work

Fortunately, we are not alone developing this network as several remote monitoring systems already exist. We could state hundreds of different platforms, networks or frameworks that exist throughout the Internet, but as this would be an extremely exhaustive list, we present 4 that we consider to be representative.

Site24x7 [7] from AdventNet [12] is a monitoring service that comprehends a simple architecture based on a single monitoring station providing monitoring only from 1 location. This is a free service that has support for single web-page monitoring and transactions. Although it provides content checking for single-pages it does not allow such for entire transactions. Users are alerted via e-mail and/or SMS and it generates user-friendly reports with charts on availability and response time of the monitored web-site.

Watchmouse [8] is a commercial online service that can monitor different Internet services for correct functioning and availability. Based on 20 monitoring stations 3 continents dispersed, is capable of monitoring most Internet protocols (PING, HTTP, HTTPS, SMTP, POP3, IMAP, FTP, TELNET, DNSa, DNSns). Is a complete solution that also provides web-site content checking and validation, although its most prominent drawback is the unsupported web-site transactions making it only capable of monitoring one specific web-page of a configured web-site. Alerts are also generated via e-mail or sms and charted reports are also available on response time and availability.

Another commercial remote monitoring solution is provided by AlertSite Monitoring Suite [9]. This suite is focused on monitoring web-sites and e-mail transactions. It is composed by a set of products that can be acquired concerning the needs of each individual customer. Its main advantages are its capability of collecting very detailed performance metrics for each web-page monitored (DNS resolution time, TCP Connect time, Time to first byte, time for whole page download, content download time, simulation of cached and non-cached users, etc) and also capable of generating SLA proof reports on web-sites service level. Although very complete on performance metrics, this platform does not make any content validation making this the most revealing drawback.

Finally, the platform we consider to be the most advanced. Gomez Performance Network (GPN) [6] is a network of agents placed all over the world that perform performance tracking and remote web-site monitoring. The GPN agents are present in ISP federated servers, client intranets and 10 000+ real-users that provide First-, Middle- and Last-mile perspectives of monitored web-sites. This is, to the best of our knowledge, the only platform of its kind that covers all three perspectives. Recently, Gomez has joined a partnership with HP Labs, having integrated GPN with the popular HP OpenView platform, being now the first platform that is capable of external and internal monitoring of web-sites.

As we can see from these platforms, not all of them, except maybe for Gomez, incorporate all the desired features. Some have better detectors but lack in the architecture; others have a good base of architecture but fail in other aspects. GOA-Net wants to implement all these features allying a scalable architecture with good detectors and forecasting techniques that will act according to the data collected. Our network wants not only to equal the features present in others of its kind, but also to bring new aspects and techniques to help reducing the time to detect failures in web-sites.

3.   GOA-Net

In this section we will describe GOA-Net, Global Observation Agent Network. Figure 1 represents the network architecture. It is composed by two base components: A Master Agent (MA) or coordinator and several Global Observation Agents (GOA). GOAs are all connected to the Master Agent, and each GOA is assigned N web-sites to monitor that can be updated serving the needs of the network. The communication between GOAs and the MA is made

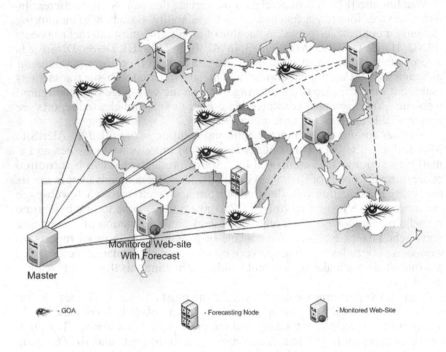

Figure 1.   GOA-Net Architecture

though encrypted messages and an important aspect is that any communication is always initiated by the GOAs to the Master and never otherwise. This is most helpful in solving connectivity problems like GOAs residing inside firewalls. Another important aspect to take into account is the fact that the Master Agent requires some processing power and therefore when the network scales up we believe we will need a powerful and probably replicated server.

Besides these two base components, a third exists. Forecasting Aggregation Nodes (FAN) are federated nodes that aggregate and process data gathered by GOAs in order to produced performance degradation forecasting. These nodes are hosted in federated data-centers in order to have processing and storage resources at their disposal. As it is not likely to expect that every monitored web-site also needs or desires to have this type of prediction service the number of these nodes in the architecture grows on-demand. In figure 1 is represented a web-site that requires performance forecasting. Both agents monitoring it are sending all gathered data to a FAN which is found through an indexing DHT.

The next two sub-sections explain in deep the mechanisms behind the two base components of the architecture: GOA and GOA-Master

3.1   GOA

GOAs are the basic unit of the infrastructure. A GOA is an automaton that acts similarly to a web-crawler, but instead of permanently sweeping the Internet for content indexation (as web-crawlers do), these agents execute, at a given polling frequency, predefined transactions in monitored web-sites, as a user would typically do. Each transaction is operator-defined and can be more or less complex, being able to include an unlimited number of web-pages to be accessed and checked for correct functionality. GOAs are able to perform every kind of user interaction in order to simulate real user behaviour. Forms can be filled, products browsed, searches conducted, products added to a shopping cart and business transactions complete. These agents possess error detection mechanisms that range from pure performance metric collections to higher-level content validation. With these mechanisms they are able to understand the correct functioning of a web-site, not only based in pure QoS and performance metrics but also understanding if the content presented by the site is the one it should really be presented.

3.1.1   Detection Mechanisms.   In order to detect that a certain web-site is in trouble or is facing difficulties, GOAs collect several metrics when accessing each page of a certain transaction. We can distinguish these metrics in two distinct groups: (1) Performance and (2) Content Checking. For the first group, agents collect several response times, such as DNS resolution time, TCP connect time, whole page download time and content download time. Collecting these performance metrics and comparing them with operator-defined thresholds makes the CA able to infer an incorrect behaviour from the web-site. Naturally, if the agent fails to resolve the DNS name, fails to open a TCP socket to the server or receives a HTTP error (4xx or 5xx HTTP codes), he will immediately report the incident to the MA. These performance metrics make it possible not only to detect failures but also to perceive their origin (DNS, TCP or HTTP).

Although these performance metrics are often good indicators about the web-sites behaviour and correct functioning, there are some types of failures (namely application level failures and operator errors) that may not produce any visible performance disturbance. These are those types of failures that sometimes escape from system-level monitors and tend to become user-visible failures. For example, if a database connection is broken between an application server and a DB server, the web-site may still respond properly (in terms of HTTP) and the server system probably will not show any sign of disturbance, but the content presented will appear corrupted. In order to detect these kinds of failures, GOAs have content checking and validation mechanisms. They are able to verify both static and dynamic content in a web-page. Operators can define regular expressions that each page must contain in order to be considered valid. Also, they can define expressions that the page must not contain. This is most useful in web-sites that usually throw error messages when an exception occurs or display some apology message when for example the database is not available. Furthermore, operators can define a percentage of dynamic content present in a certain page. This way, the GOA knows that the page size is not expected to vary more or less than the specified percentage. Naturally, if such variation is exceeded or if a regular expression is/is not matched the MA will be warned.

3.1.2   Agent Distribution - First-, Middle- and Last-Mile.   Each GOA
is assigned a number of web-sites to monitor by the MA. The importance in having several GOAs monitoring the same web-site with the same transactions is that different GOAs can provide different perspectives of the Web-Sites' correct functioning.

Although GOAs are agents that simulate user behaviour when accessing web-sites, they are not constraint to be run only on client machines. Because this agent is written in Java, it can be run on every machine with internet connection. Also, as Global Observation Agents are generic automatons they can be spread all over the Internet, making this multi-agent grid capable of providing and analyzing, in real time, different perspectives of the web-site as perceived in the First, Middle and Last miles of the network path. Figure 2 represents these perspectives.

First mile coverage, or inside the firewall coverage, provides the perspective of the web-site behaviour without any network interference (present in middle- and last-mile). This perspective represents the pure performance of the web-application without the impact of the network. Simply by placing an agent running on a machine inside the servers' firewall, or running the agent on the server itself can accomplish the collection of these metrics.

The Middle-Mile perspective is collected from the Internet Backbones geographically disperse on multiple networks. The information collected here can be used to diagnose and identify problems that are not visible in the first-mile such as DNS resolution problems, network congestion issues and internal ISP connectivity problems.

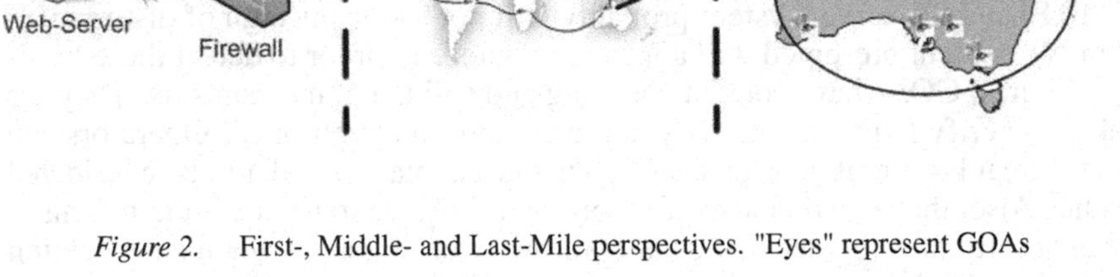

| FIRST-MILE | MIDDLE-MILE | LAST-MILE |
| Inside-Firewall Monitoring | Internet Backbone Monitoring | The End-User Perspective |

Figure 2.   First-, Middle- and Last-Mile perspectives. "Eyes" represent GOAs

The collection of this perspective however, requires the collaboration of ISPs that must agree in running our agent somewhere inside their own backbones.

Last-Mile information represents the entire transaction as whole, exactly as perceived by end-users themselves. This gives us the perception of how web-site users are experiencing their interactions with the web-site. Also, this perspective is useful in diagnosing problems present only in end-users, such as performance or reliability problems associated with over weighted web-pages (typically present in users with smaller bandwidth).

3.1.3   Error Location.   Although we have seen that GOAs by themselves incorporate some mechanisms that help identify the source of an identified error (DNS, TCP and HTTP error detection enables the inferring of the error location, DNS server, network or server respectively), more accuracy can be achieved by correlating the information of different GOAs.

Table 1 summarizes the different errors that can be seen in each of the three different perspectives. Correlation between these perspectives leads to better pinpoint the source of the problem originating the anomaly detected.

Table 1.   Visible Failures in each of the three perspectives

	Routing Problems	Network Cong. Problems	Server Conect. Problems	DNS Res. Problems	Internal Server Problems
First-Mile	-	-	-	-	x
Middle-Mile	-	x	x	x	x
Last-Mile	x	x	x	x	x

Failures originated by routing problems are expected to trigger only the agents present in last-mile since middle and first are not prone to be affected by these failures.

In order for GOA-Net to consider network congestion, server connectivity or DNS resolution problems as the origin of a failure, only agents placed in middle and last mile should report the incident since the first mile is not affected by any of these problems. In this case, differentiation between the three possible origins is made by the type of error perceived by each GOA. Remember from the previous section, that GOAs are able to distinguish between DNS, TCP and HTTP errors. If they report DNS problems, then the cause must reside within the DNS server. If TCP connection reports host unreachable then it is most probably due to the server lacking Internet connectivity. Although, if GOAs timeout connecting to the server, it indicates that there is probably a network congestion between them and the server.

Finally, we can infer the cause of the problem to reside inside the server itself if all the agents in the three perspectives report the incident, as this is the only cause of failure that will result in visibility in all three perspectives.

3.2   Master Agent

The Master Agent is a central point of coordination of all the GOAs. The MA holds every configuration for every monitored Web-Site. These configurations include the detailed specification of the transactions to be reproduced by the GOAs when accessing the web-site together with some parameters that define the frequency in which each GOA should reproduce the defined transaction. As a central coordinator, the MA has the mission of assigning each GOA with WSs to monitor. Furthermore, the MA is responsible for all the data correlation between GOAs and for confirming the alerts received by them.

When an alert is received from any GOA, the MA will issue an error report to the system administrator. In order to provide accurate reports the MA needs to correlate information between every GOA monitoring the same web-site. To do this the following algorithm is applied.

Error Reporting Algorithm

MA generates error reports upon reception of a notification from a GOA indicating an erroneous condition with a monitored web-site. The generation of such reports is made by the MA which correlates information about all the GOAs monitoring that web-site. To do this, MA keeps an internal table for each monitored web-site that keeps the notifications received from GOAs. Upon reception of such notification the corresponding table is updated reflecting the information received from the GOA. In order to correctly timestamp the reports, MA keeps the mean RTT value for each GOA. The notification timestamp is then computed as the MA timestamp at the moment notification is received minus the mean RTT (Round Trip Time) of the GOA that sent the notification.

Because GOAs are not expected to issue notifications all at the same time (because they only run their transactions from time to time) it is possible that upon the reception of a notification, other GOAs monitoring the same web-site may still have not notice the anomaly reported. Therefore, the MA has to wait before he can have the perspective of all the GOAs monitoring the web-site. The waiting interval is computed as the defined polling interval for the web-site plus the maximum mean RTT of the agents monitoring that web-site. GOAs that do not issue a notification within this interval are considered not to be eatchingthe anomaly.

In order not to delay failure reports to system administrators, issued reports can have different accuracies depending on the number of GOAs on the different perspectives that noticed the anomaly in the moment the report is generated. Three levels of accuracy exist: Low, Medium and High. Upon the reception of a notification from a GOA, the MA always issues a report. The notification of a problem P implicates that N GOAs notify that same problem (Remember table 1 where we can see which GOAs should report a determined problem). If at least 1 GOA of each level that is supposed to notice the problem has already issued a notification, then the error report is considered accurate (High accuracy level). If only some of the GOAs have issue the notification, but timestamps indicate that others still have time to notify, the report is considered Medium accurate. In case that none of the expected GOAs notified the MA about the problem but again the waiting period is not yet over, the report is considered to be of Low accuracy.

When the MAs' waiting period is over and no High accuracy report has been issued, the first notification is considered a false one and a new report is issued disconfirming any previous reports that had been generated.

With this mechanisms GOA-Net is capable of quickly issuing error reports although not compromising the filtering of any possible false positive alerts.

4.   Objectives

Having summarized the architecture and design specifications of GOA-Net, we now present the list of features and objectives for this platform. The network must be capable of (1) Support for web-transactions, (2) checking and validating static and dynamic content, (3) monitor from First-, Middle- and Last-Mile, (4) Large-Scale coverage with integration with volunteer computer initiatives or any other mean of large-scale deployment, (5) collecting and analyzing performance metrics in real time.

Most of these features (except 4) are already present in most of the platforms we analyzed in section 2 of this paper but the main differentiation objective we have, is to incorporate some intelligence in our agent. To the best of our knowledge, all the agents/monitoring stations of the platforms we analyzed are pure reactive. They simply monitor and react when some variable scopes out of a threshold. It is our goal to make our GOA not only reactive but also proactive in the sense that it should be (6) capable of proactively forecast performance degradations and web-site malfunctions.

Briefly, objectives 1-5 are those which make GOA-Net competitive in relation to other solutions available. 6 differentiates our network.

5.   Future Work

In this paper we presented a scalable multi-agent architecture for failure detection and performance degradation forecasting in web-sites. This is an idea we feel can contribute to better detect failures and reduce unavailability. We have now finished a first prototypal implementation and are running experiments that help us validate and better understand the potential behind this tool. We expect in near future to present these results and also to extend our implementation to a more professional one that we hope can be used by both industry and academic community.

References

[1] Hewlett Packard Corporation, HP OpenView Software. http://www.openview.hp.com

[2] IBM Corporation, IBM Tivoli Software. http://www.ibm.com/software/tivoli

[3] Altaworks Panorama. http://www.altaworks.com/solutionsPanorama.htm

[4] Zabbix. http://www.zabbix.org/

[5] Nagios. http://nagios.org/

[6] Gomez Performance Network. http://www.gomez.com/products/index.html

[7] Site24x7. http://www.site24x7.com

[8] Watchmouse. http://www.watchmouse.com

[9] AlertSite. http://www.alertsite.com

[10] E. Kiciman and A. Fox, "Detecting Application-Level Failures in Component-based Internet Services", IEEE Transactions on Neural Networks, Vol. 16, Issue 5, 2005

[11] A study about online transactions, prepared for TeaLeaf Technology Inc, by Harris Inter-active, October 2005

[12] Adventnet, Inc - http://www.adventnet.com

[13] Soila Pertet and Priya Narasimhan, "Causes of Failure in Web Applications", Parallel Data Laboratory, Carnegie Mellon University, CMU-PDL-05-109

[14] Berkeley Open Infrastructure for Network Computing - http://boinc.berkeley.edu/

A DISTRIBUTED AND REPLICATED SERVICE FOR CHECKPOINT STORAGE

Fatiha Bouabache
Laboratoire de Recherche en Informatique
Universite Paris Sud-XI, 91405 ORSAY, FRANCE.
fatiha.bouabache@lri.fr

Thomas Herault
INRIA Futurs/Laboratoire de Recherche en Informatique
Universite Paris Sud-XI, 91405 ORSAY, FRANCE.
thomas.herault@lri.fr

Gilles Fedak
INRIA Futurs/Laboratoire de Recherche en Informatique
Universite Paris Sud-XI, 91405 ORSAY, FRANCE.
fedak@lri.fr

Franck Cappello
INRIA Futurs/Laboratoire de Recherche en Informatique
Universite Paris Sud-XI, 91405 ORSAY, FRANCE.
fci@lri.fr

Abstract   As High Performance platforms (Clusters, Grids, etc.) continue to grow in size, the average time between failures decreases to a critical level. An efficient and reliable fault tolerance protocol plays a key role in High Performance Computing. Rollback recovery is the most common fault tolerance technique used in High Performance Computing and especially in MPI applications. This technique relies on the reliability of the checkpoint storage, most of the rollback recovery protocols assume that the checkpoint servers machines are reliable. However, in a grid environment any unit can fail at any moment, including components used to connect different administrative domains. Such a failure leads to the loss of a whole set of machines, including the more reliable machines used to store the checkpoints in this administrative domain. It is thus not safe to rely on the high MTBF of specific machines to store the checkpoint images.

This paper introduces a new protocol that ensure the checkpoint storage reliability even if one or more Checkpoint Servers fail. To provide this reliability the protocol is based on a replication process. We evaluate our solution through simulations against several criteria: scalability, topology, and reliability of the nodes. We also compare between two replication strategies to decide which one should be used in the implementation.

Keywords: high performance computing,fault tolerance,replication,rollback recovery

1.   Introduction

High Performance Computing has an important role in scientific and engineering researches. As the size of High Performance Systems increases
continuously, the average time between failures becomes increasingly small. So
Fault Tolerance becomes a critical property for Parallel applications running
on these systems. MPI (Message Passing Interface) paradigm is actually the
most used to write parallel applications. However, in traditional implementations, when a failure occurs, the whole distributed application is shutdown and
restarted [1]. To avoid this, many solutions have been proposed, but the most
used is Rollback Recovery [2]. Rollback recovery is based upon the concept
of a checkpoint. A checkpoint describes the state of one or more components
of the system at a given time of its execution. These checkpoints are built
from images of processes and the state of communication channels. During
its execution, the system takes checkpoints according to a scheduling policy.
When a failure occurs, some processes rollback to their last images. The fault
tolerance protocol must ensure that the system is in a coherent state which allows it to continue its execution. With coordinated checkpoint protocols, all the
processes are synchronized and take their images at the same time, by building
a coherent state and a global image of the system called a snapshot. A snapshot
is a collection of checkpoint images (one per process) with the state of the
different communication channels [3]. When a failure occurs, all the processes
must rollback together to the last coherent state, so the checkpoint images of
all the processes must be available simultaneously. Usually, checkpoint images
are kept for the two last checkpoint waves in order to spare storage resources.
If the checkpoint images are not available, the rollback technique fails. These
protocols often assume that Checkpoint storage is made by special dedicated
and reliable machines named Checkpoint servers.

A grid is an infrastructure consisting of the aggregation of several distributed
resources, usually from different administrative domains. There are many
kind of grids, and we focus in this study on the cluster of clusters: companies
and universities build large supercomputers by aggregating the resources of
different clusters. Using such a grid, users expect to obtain larger systems more
suitable to address the complexity of their problems. One of the features of
a grid is its size, orders of magnitude larger than a single cluster. Moreover,
a grid spans multiple domains and is characterized by a topology including
few interconnection points linking many components. In a single cluster, if
the failure hits the switch or the interconnection mechanism, each component
is disconnected from the others and the failure may be considered as fatal. If
one of the interconnection point fails, a whole cluster is lost for the rest of
the system, including its most reliable components. So, no machine can be
considered as reliable anymore. In a grid, however, the amount of resources lost
by the failure of a router may be tolerable.

In this paper, we introduce a distributed checkpoint storage service of coordinated Rollback Recovery Protocols suited for clusters of clusters. It addresses
the issues related to the Grid Model: to ensure the checkpoint storage reliability,
even though one or more checkpoint servers fail, we use a replication process.

We compare two different strategies of replication named simple and hierarchical. The paper is organized as follows. Section 2 presents the Grid and failure models we consider. Section 3 presents the related works. Section 4 introduces our protocol for distributed checkpoint storage. We evaluate performances of our approach and we compare two different replication techniques in section 5. Last, we draw our conclusions in Section6.

2. System Model

We consider a High Performance Grid made up of powerful computer servers. We also consider the grid environment as an aggregation of C clusters, each cluster i includes N_i machines. To store the checkpoint images, we define in each cluster a set of checkpoint servers. Thus, in a cluster, we have two kinds of processes. Clients processes that carry out calculations and regularly transfer their checkpoint images to the storage service; and checkpoint servers (CS), which maintain the checkpoint storage. All checkpoint servers within the same cluster are pooled in a group. The different clusters are linked over front-end machines. Figure 1 illustrates the architecture of our system.

We assume that any component of the system can fail at any time, and we consider that there exists a coordinated checkpoint protocol which handles the clients failures. Therefore, we propose a solution to handle the checkpoint server failures to ensure the storage service reliability even when a checkpoint server fails. We consider two types of behaviors:

- a failure may hit a checkpoint server in a cluster.

- a failure may hit the cluster's front-end machine, or a set of failures disconnects a whole cluster from the rest of the grid. For the clusters which remain connected, all the components of the cluster fail simultaneously.

To increase the protocol flexibility, we make the following assumptions :

- We consider a group failure if we lose a connection with the checkpoint servers of this group (e.g.: a front-end failure). We suppose that it cannot be more than K group failures, with $0 \leq K \leq C - 1$.

- In the case of a group failure, the computation which was executed in this cluster get restarted on new one.

- We suppose that for a number of checkpoint servers n_i in group i, $0 \leq i \leq C - 1$, at a given moment, there cannot be more than k_i checkpoint servers failures, $0 \leq k_i < n_i$.

These numbers are fixed according to the mean time between failures in the system. Our solution relies on a distributed checkpoint service. To ensure the reliability of this service, we use a replication protocol. We replicate Checkpoint images over checkpoint servers, so that a valid replica is available even though one or more checkpoint servers fail. To tolerate k_i failures in a group i, $0 \leq i \leq C - 1$, we must have at least $k_i + 1$ replicas in this group. To tolerate a group failure, we also replicate the checkpoint images outside the cluster which hold them. So, to tolerate K group failures, with $0 \leq K \leq C - 1$, we replicate the checkpoint images over $K + 1$ different groups.

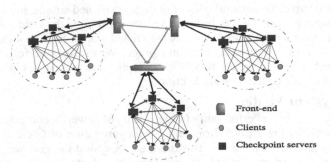

Figure 1.   System Architecture

3.   Related Works

In checkpoint-based protocols, during the execution the computation state is periodically saved. Then when a failure occurs, the computation is restarted from the last saved state. Checkpoint based protocols can be classified into three categories: coordinated checkpointing, uncoordinated checkpointing, and message logging [4]. The first coordinated checkpointing protocol for distributed applications was proposed by Chandy and Lamport in [3]. This solution assumes that all the channels are FIFO and any process can decide to initiate a checkpoint wave. This algorithm is implemented in many fault tolerant message passing libraries, such as LAMMPI [5], MPICH-V [4]. Other techniques like Checkpoint Induced Communication [6] try to limit the size of the coordinated set to build the global coherent snapshot. This technique has also been implemented in other fault-tolerant libraries, like the proactive communication library [5]. All these techniques assume the ability to store the checkpoint images in a reliable media which is not subject to failures.

Other checkpoint based solutions exists without relying on stable storage, [8] introduces a disk-less checkpointing solution. This solution defines a way to perform fast, incremental checkpointing by using $N+1$ parity, which reduces high memory overhead required by disk-less checkpointing methods. However, after a failure, all processors communicate with the parity, which can cause a communication bottleneck. Also, the solution is based on the parity machine which should never fail. Others distribute the checkpoint images directly in the memory of the computing peers, like for the FT-MPI project [9], or the Charm++ project [10]. However, storing the checkpoint image in the memory of the other processes implies either to use twice the memory necessary for the application or remove the transparency assumption and to use user-driven serialization of the checkpoint image. [11] describes disk-based and memory-based checkpointing fault tolerance schemes. The goal of this solution is to automate the checkpointing and the restarting of the tasks, and thus to avoid writing additional code. These schemes are based on the works presented in [12] and [13]. In [14] a new solution based on the assumption that some failures are predictable is introduced. It pro-actively migrates execution from processors suspected to fail. This solution is based on processor virtualization and dynamic task migration ideas provided on [15] and [12]. [16] introduces a fault tolerance protocol that provide fast restarts. This protocol uses the concepts of message logging and processor virtualization. It does not assume the existence of reliable component that never fails.

The goal of the replication services is to keep the states of the different replicas coherent, by implementing the adequate primitives. The two major classes of replication techniques ensuring this consistency are: active replication [17] and passive replication [18]. Simple replication is not adequate for high performance computing. Indeed, to tolerate n failures every component must be replicated n times. Thus, the computation resources are divided by n. Replication is however a mechanism used to ensure the accessibility of data in fault tolerance protocols. [19] considered distributing generic data on the grid using distributed hash tables, and evaluated the efficiency of this approach for storing checkpoint images for fault tolerance. However, this technique is not focused on the coordinated checkpoint protocols, which induce a peak overload on the EDG network, and we believe that hierarchical techniques are more suited than DHTs for this kind of topology. [20] and [21] introduce solutions to ensure availability of some failures points (e.g. the head node of a cluster architecture) using redundancy. These solutions are based on the asymmetric and symmetric Active/Active High availability. Active/Active High availability means that several replicas are active in the same time. Whereas in the asymmetric one there is not any coordination between the active replicas, in the symmetric one the active replicas maintain a common global component state.

4. Checkpoint Storage Protocol

Our checkpoint storage protocol, based on a distributed checkpointing service and a replication process, proceeds in two phases. The recording phase, responsible for images storage, and the recovery phase executed when a failure occurs on some calculation nodes.

4.1 The Recording Phase

The recording phase proceeds in two steps. First, clients send their images to the CSs within the same cluster. Second, those images are replicated amongst the CS group within the local cluster, and in remote clusters. In order to improve the performances, image sending is made on a distributed way. A checkpoint image is split in several parts of fixed size named *chunks*. We call f_c^j the jth chunk of the cth client checkpoint image. During the building of the checkpoint image, the client builds his chunks and sends them to the CSs of its cluster. The client memorizes a list of CSs that received its chunks. At the end, the client keeps a local copy of its checkpoint image, then it sends to all the CSs on its cluster the finalize message which contains the chunks number. The image is considered safely stored, when the client receives acknowledgments (ACKs) for all its chunks. If the client detects a CS failure before the reception of the corresponding ACK, it selects another CS and resends the corresponding chunks. If the client fails during the transfer, the checkpoint wave get cancelled, a new resource equivalent is allocated, and the application is restarted from its last checkpoint.

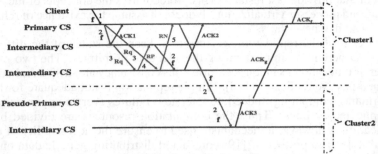

Figure 2.   Example of execution

In the second step, chunks are replicated on the CSs, we consider that a chunk f is *correctly replicated* in the group i if and only if f is replicated on $k_i + 1$ servers in this group. According to the assumption on the number of tolerated failures, a chunk is considered *recorded*, if it is *correctly replicated* in $K + 1$ groups.

4.1.1   Replication Strategies.   .

1. Simple Replication Strategy: We have adapted the passive replication technique : each checkpoint server receiving a chunk ck_c^j from the client c becomes primary of this chunk, and must ensure its replication. When a checkpoint server s primary of a certain number of chunks fails, a new server is selected to become primary of all the chunks of s.

During the replication step, a CS s can play several roles according to the origins of the received chunks. First, receiving a chunk from the client, s is considered *primary* of this chunk. It is responsible of the correct replication of this chunk in its group and on K different groups before sending the acknowledgement to the client (ACK_f in figure 2). Second, if it receives a chunk from a CS $s' \neq s$ from another group $i' \neq i$, it is considered as a *pseudo-primary* of this chunk in its group. It is then responsible to replicate the chunk in its group and to send the acknowledgement to the primary s' (ACK_g in figure 2). The last role, *intermediary* is played by a CS when it receives a chunk from another CS within its group. In this case, the CS sends directly the acknowledgement to the primary or to the pseudo-primary ($ACK1$, $ACK2$, and $ACK3$ in figure 2). During the replication step, the chunks received from clients have the greatest priority, than those received from the other CSs, and finally those received from the other clusters.

With the Simple Replication Strategy (SRS), the primary CS does the replication over all the other CSs of its group, then over the other groups. Then each *pseudo-primary* does the replication over all the other CSs of its group. So a CS s receiving a chunk ck from a client or from another group sends it to $(s + i)mod[2^m], 1 \leq i < 2^m$. With this technique, an *intermediary* CS has no active role in the replication process.

2. Hierarchical Replication Strategy: To accelerate the replication process, we introduce another strategy. Its goal is that each CS in the system has an active role, including the *intermediary* ones. For that we define for each CS s a

set of CSs with identifiers $\{s, s + 2^0, s + 2^1, \cdots, s + 2^{m-1}\}$ called *children*. Fig.2 presents a diagram of an execution of the replication step with this strategy. The primary server of a chunk ck_c^j replicates it on the *children* servers which constitute the first level of replication, then, each CS receiving this chunk must replicate it over its own *children* servers, carrying on that way until all the CS have received the chunk. To avoid replicating a chunk twice on the same CS, a request is sent before each replication (the third step in Fig.2).

During the execution of a checkpoint wave, two cases may happen : 1) the execution finishes without any CS failure, and 2) some checkpoint servers fail before the end of the wave. If a primary CS s fails during the replication, a new primary s' is selected to handle the primary chunks of s. A client detecting the failure of s before the reception of its acknowledgement, resends the chunk to s'. The CSs are organized on a circular list, so when a primary CS fails the new primary is simply the next in the list. s' will check the replication status before the breakdown. In case the replication was started before the failure, it sends a request to collect the acknowledgements from the other CSs to know if they have received the chunk by the last primary. When a CS in the same group receives this request, it acknowledges the previous reception of the chunk, or asks for it if it has not received it before. When a CS from another group receives this request, it checks the previous reception of the chunk, then it verifies if a correct replication was made in its group before sending an acknowledgment to the primary, otherwise, it asks for it.

At the end of the recording phase the CS has to check if all the clients of the same distributed application have correctly recorded their images, then validate locally the checkpoint wave.

4.2 The Recovery Phase

In the beginning of this phase, a consensus is executed between the different CSs to define the last valid wave: each CS proposes the number of its last valid wave, and the goal is to arrive at an agreement. As several checkpoint wave can be done before failure, the client starts by asking for the last valid wave, and checks whether the image is available locally. Otherwise, it requests its image from the CSs within its cluster. As for the recording, recovery is done in a distributed way: the client sends its request of recovery to all the CS of its group, then a CS receiving the request provides chunks of which is primary. Finally, once all the chunks are recovered, the image is reconstituted, and the client is restarted.

5. Performance Evaluation

We study our solution using the SimGrid [22] simulator. SimGrid provides the main functionalities for the simulation of distributed applications in heterogeneous distributed environments. We particularly use MSG, the first distributed programming environment provided within SimGrid. It allows us to study the different heuristics of the issues before the implementation. It makes it possible, in the first stage, to validate our solution and especially to carry out a good comparison between the two replication strategies.

Running a simulation with Simgrid requires as input two files in XML formats. These files do not only describe the simulation parameters and dynamics (e.g. links and machines failures) but also the network topology. We suppose that the Checkpoint Servers of a group are connected between them through a complete graph. The number of CS is small, so we will have a realistic number of connections to manage. However, for the inter clusters connections, we choose a graph much less connected, where each CS will only have one outgoing connection. For all the experimentation, the links within a cluster are homogenous, as are the CSs and the clients.

5.1   Impact of the Topology

We first investigated the impact of the clients number, and thus the size of the data to be stored. For that, we fixed the cluster and the CSs numbers in the system ($c = 1$ cluster and $s = 6$ CSs), and we varied the clients number. The first curve in Fig.3, the checkpoint wave, presents the wave execution time according to the number of clients. We notice that the execution time is proportional to the number of clients. This is not surprising since more clients means a larger quantity of data to store and to replicate, and thus the wave of checkpoint takes more time. To identify which one of the two checkpoint phases influences the execution time, we isolated the recording phase. The corresponding measurement in Fig.3 shows that the execution time of the recording step increases slowly. This is expected, because in theory this step is executed in a parallel way and it takes xl/N time unit (where x is the number of chunks per client, l the size of a chunk, and N the link capacity) whatever the clients number is . In practice, the observed increasement is due to the saturation of the communication bottleneck. So the growing of the checkpoint wave execution time when a clients number increases is caused by the replication phase execution time. In theory the execution time t of the replication phase is:

$$t = kxl(\frac{1}{N} - \frac{1}{sN})$$

Thus when the clients number k increases the execution time of the replication phase increases proportionally.

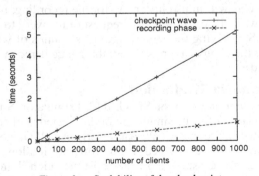

Figure 3.   Scalability of the checkpoint

The goal of the second experimentation is to evaluate the impact of the network topology. In order to do this, we consider a fixed number of clients

$k = 100$, a fixed number of CSs $s = 30$, and we make vary the number of clusters c. Thus, there is k/c clients and s/c servers in each cluster; every client has x chunks of size l. The links have a capacity of N MB/s within a cluster and N' MB/s between clusters. Theoretically, the checkpoint wave over c clusters takes the time t defined so:

$$t = \frac{xl}{N} + \frac{2xkl}{N} + \frac{xkl}{sN} + \frac{xkl}{N'} - \frac{1}{c}\left(\frac{xkl}{N} + \frac{xkl}{N'}\right) - \frac{cxkl}{sN}$$

The curve resulting from this equation is presented in Fig.4.

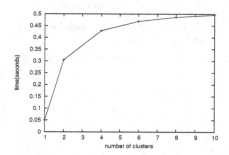

Figure 4.   Impact of the topology and comparison with the thoeretical result

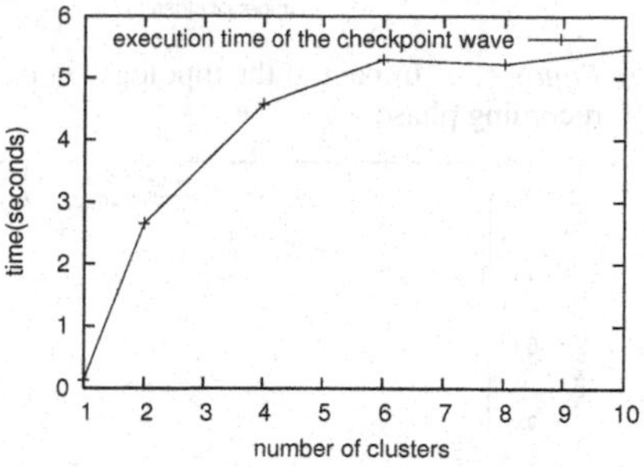

Figure 5.   Impact of the topology

The first curve, Fig.5, presents the result of this second experimentation. To better understand the result we isolated the recording phase (the second curve, Fig.6), and the local replication (the last one, Fig.7). When the cluster number increases, the clients number per cluster decreases, and thus the recording phase execution time decreases. However, although the number of checkpoint servers per cluster decreases, the execution time of the local replication increases, because there is overlapping between this phase and the rest of the execution, which reduces the global execution time of the checkpoint wave.

5.2   Impact of the Replication

To evaluate the two replication strategies, we first investigated the effect of the CSs in the system and thus the effect of the replication. For doing this, we fixed the clients number $k = 200$ and we varied the CSs number s. Figure 8 shows that the execution time of the checkpoint wave, particularly the replication phase increases considerably and proportionally with the CSs number. Theoretically, the execution time t of the replication phase is:

$$t = \frac{kxl}{N} - \frac{kxl}{sN}$$

So when s increases the execution time of the replication phase increases too.

To compare the effect of the hierarchical replication versus the simple one, we fixed the clients and the chunks numbers per client, and we varied the CSs number. Then we launch two series of executions with the two strategies. These experiments are carried out to decide which replication strategy will be used in the implementation. As we can see in Fig.9, the best replication strategy depends on the number of CSs. The hierarchical one does additional checks

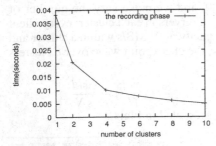

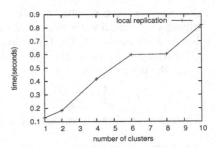

Figure 6. Impact of the topology on the recording phase

Figure 7. Impact of the topology on the replication phase

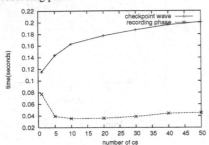

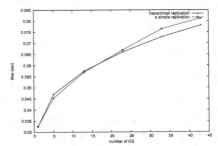

Figure 8. Impact of the Replication.

Figure 9. Comparison between hierarchical and simple replication.

for the presence of chunks onto the secondary CSs before each sending. As we give the first priority to the chunks received from clients, and every CS received data from clients when Css number is low, the additional checks increases needlessly the execution time, which makes the simple replication better than the hierarchacal. However, when the CSs number increases, the hierarchical replication allows overlapping of communications to secondary CSs, and so the acceleration of the replication phase. We observe that when the simple replication is better, the difference is small because the checks message size is smaller than the chunk size. Although the execution time of the recording phase should be fixed, increasing the number of clients or decreasing the number of CSs makes the recording phase more aggressive, in the sense that the size of data to be stored increases or the storage devices number decreases which causes communication bottleneck.

6.   Conclusion

An efficient and reliable fault tolerance protocol plays a key role in High Performance Computing and especially in MPI applications. Rollback recovery is the most used technique in such environments. To ensure a high level of fault tolerance, the rollback recovery techniques rely on the availability of checkpoint images at rollback time. Usually, rollback/recovery protocols often assume that Checkpoint storage is made by special dedicated and reliable machines named Checkpoint servers. In a grid, however, no machine can be considered as reliable anymore, since even machines with a high MTBF are located inside a cluster which may be entirely disconnected from the rest of the grid.

In this work, we introduced a distributed checkpoint storage service of coordinated Rollback Recovery Protocols suited for clusters of clusters. It addresses the issues related to the Grid Model: to ensure the checkpoint storage reliability, even though one or more checkpoint servers fail, we use a replication process.

We compared two replication strategies, a simple direct strategy, where a CS receiving image from a client uploads this image to each and every one of the CSs; and a hierarchical one, where CSs synchronize with each others to ensure the replication. This comparison shows that the strategy choice depends on the system topology, particularly the CSs and the clients numbers.

The different experimentations show that the execution time of the replication phase takes much more time than the recording one. A long time of the checkpoint wave execution decreases the checkpoint wave frequency. To avoid this we propose to consider the checkpoint wave as done when the recording phase is finished. So, a CS sends the acknowledgments when it received the data, then it does the replication. Thus we increase the checkpoint wave frequency. If a CS fails before the end of the replication, and some data is lost, we cancel this step, and we consider the last wave for which the replication is successfully finished.

For the future, first we will evaluate our approach via an experimenation in a real experimental grid. Then, we would like propose a new scheduling scheme and a new replication strategy that improve the performances of our protocol.

References

[1] W. Groop and E. Lusk, Fault Tolerance in MP Programs. *OAI-PMH server at cs1.ist.psu.edu*, 2002

[2] E. N. Elnozahy et al.A survey of Rollback-Recovery Protocols in Message-Passing Systems, Journal "CSURV: Computer Surveys", volume 34, 2002.

[3] K.M. Chandy and L. Lamport, Distributed snapshots: Determining global states of distributed systems.
ACM Transactions on Computer Systems (TOCS), 3(1):63? 75, 1985.

[4] A. Bouteiller et al.Mpich-v: a multiprotocol fault tolerant mpi. *International Journal of High Performance Computing and Applications, 20(8):319?333, fall*, 2006.

[5] G. Burns, R. Daoud, and J. Vaigl. *LAM: An open cluster environment forMPI*, 1994.

[6] L. Alvisi et al.*An analysis of communication induced checkpointing. In Proceedings of the symposium on fault-tolerant computing, pages 242?249*, 1999.

[7] F. Baude et al.A hybrid message logging-cic protocol for constrained checkpointability. In Proceedings of EuroPar2005, LNCS, 2005.

[8] James S. Plank and Kai Li, Faster Checkpointing with N+1 Parity, 24th International Symposium on Fault-Tolerant Computing, Austin, TX, June, 1994, pp 288–297.

[9] Z. Chen et al.Building fault survivable MPI programs with FT-MPI using diskless-checkpointing. In Proceedings of the tenth ACM SIGPLAN Symposium on (PPoPP), June 2005.

[10] G. Zheng, L. Shi, and L. V. Kale. Ftc-charm++: an inmemory checkpoint-based fault tolerant runtime for charm++ and mpi. In Proceedings of the IEEE International Conference on Cluster Computing, USA, 2004. IEEE Computer Society.

[11] C. Huang et al.Performance evaluation of adaptive MPI. PPOPP 2006: 12-21

[12] L. V. Kale and S. Krishnan. Charm++: Parallel programming with message-driven objects. In Wilson, G.V., Lu, P., eds.: Parallel programming using C++. MIT Press (1996) 175-213.

[13] L. V. Kale. The Virtualization approach to Parallel Programming: Runtime Optimization
      and the State of Art. In LACSI 2002, Albuquerque, October 2002.
[14] S. Chakravorty, C. L. Mendes, and L. V. Kalé, Proactive Fault Tolerance in MPI Applica-
      tions Via Task Migration. HiPC 2006; 485-496
[15] L. V. Kale and S. Krishnan. Charm++: Parallel programming with message-driven objects.
      In Wilson, G.V., Lu, P., eds.: Parallel programming using C++. MIT Press (1996) 175-213.
[16] S. Chakravorty and L. V. Kalé, A fault tolerance Protocol with Fast Fault Recovery,
      Accepted for publication at IPDPS 2007.
[17] R. Guerraoui and A. Schiper. Software based replication for fault tolerance. IEEE Com-
      puter, 30(4):68?74, Apr. 1997.
[18] N. Budhiraja et al.The primary-backup approach, Dec. 01 1993.
[19] L. Rilling and C. Morin. A practical transparent data sharing service for the grid. In Proc.
      Fifth InternationalWorkshop on Distributed SharedMemory (DSM 2005), Cardiff, UK,
      May 2005. Held in conjunction with CCGrid 2005.
[20] C. Leangsuksun et al.Asymmetric active-active high availability for high-end computing.
      In Proceedings of (COSET-2), in conjunction with the 19th ACM International Conference
      on Supercomputing (ICS), Cambridge, MA, USA, 2005.
[21] C. Engelmann et al.Symmetric active/active high availability for high-performance com-
      puting system services. Journal of Computers (JCP), 1(8), 2006.
[22] INRIA. Simgrid project. http://simgrid.gforge.inria.fr.

VI

APPLICATIONS AND USE CASES

APPLICATIONS AND USES

HIGH-LEVEL SCRIPTING APPROACH FOR BUILDING COMPONENT-BASED APPLICATIONS ON THE GRID *

Maciej Malawski[†], Tomasz Guba_la, Marek Kasztelnik, Tomasz Bartynski, Marian Bubak
Institute of Computer Science and ACC CYFRONET
AGH University of Science and Technology
Krakow, Poland
malawski@agh.edu.pl

Francoise Baude and Ludovic Henrio
INRIA Sophia Antipolis – CNRS – Univ. of Nice Sophia Antipolis
Sophia Antipolis, France
francoise.baude@inria.fr

Abstract   In this paper, we describe a top-down approach to solution of the problem of component composition on the Grid. The proposed method is based on the use of a dynamic scripting language. It enables designing a simple API to define component composition in an elegant and concise way. GScript [17] provides constructs to create component instances (deployment), connect their ports (composition) and invoke the component methods with the minimum amount of code. As GScript is based on Ruby [26], it also provides the full flexibility of a programming language, with a rich set of control constructs of component applications (workflows). GScript hides all the details of the underlying Grid infrastructure, so the programmer may focus on the application logic, while the process of resource selection and component deployment is performed automatically. We describe the architecture of the runtime library needed to support the high-level features, and propose a set of development tools, based on the Eclipse platform. We report on a prototype which demonstrates the applicability of the approach to construct applications from both MOCCA (CCA) and ProActive (GCM) components.

Keywords: component composition, dynamic scripting, GScript.

*This work is supported by EU IST CoreGRID project and Polish grant SPUB-M.
[†]Maciej Malawski kindly acknowledges the support from the Foundation for Polish Science.

1.   Introduction

Component-based programming is considered an important paradigm for constructing Grid applications [15]. It offers a well-structured abstraction of processing elements represented by components, their interfaces and protocols realized as component ports and connections between ports that constitute the information flow. Although the conceptual model is simple, the task of delivering such a programming platform remains a challenge due to the complexity of the Grid.

There are two ways of composing components: composition in space and composition in time. Both are relevant to Grid applications [25, 16]. *Composition in space* involves direct connections between component ports, while control and a data flow passes directly between connected components. Composition in space can be either *static* – the connections are established prior to the actual application execution or *dynamic* – the connections may change during application execution which may involve reconfiguration or creation of connections on demand. *Composition in time* assumes that components do not have to be directly connected, but their server interfaces can be invoked by a client, which coordinates the whole application. In this case both control and data flow pass through the client, which can be a specific application or a more generic workflow engine [18].

There is a need for a high-level programming approach which would enable combining both types of component composition in a way which is flexible and convenient for a programmer. The approach should not be limited to a single component model, since many models are available for programming Grid applications [15]. Moreover, being focused on the Grid environment, it should conceal the complexity of the underlying infrastructure, automating the process of component deployment and resource selection where possible. It would be also valuable if the solution could facilitate such aspects as component configuration and passing parameters to the application. Such a solution would eventually form a powerful application development, deployment and execution tool for the Grid.

In this paper we describe a top-down approach to solving the problem of component composition on the Grid. The proposed solution is based on a dynamic scripting language [29]. This solution is especially well suited for rapid application development (RAD), prototyping and experimenting scenarios. A scripting approach also provides the full flexibility of using a programming language, enabling a rich set of control constructs of component applications (workflows). The high-level notation allows hiding all the details of the underlying Grid infrastructure, so the programmer may focus on the application logic and automating the process of resource selection and component deployment. The following section describes current work related to component composition. Next, we present the concept of our language and show how it can be applied to the Common Component Architecture (CCA) [3] with MOCCA framework [24] and Grid Component Model (GCM) [14] with the ProActive [5] implementation. After introducing the basic features of the notation, we briefly describe the architecture of a runtime system which is needed to support the high-level functionality. Finally, we report on the progress of a prototype implementation and conclude with presenting prospects for future work.

2. Related work

There are several ways of component composition: low-level API, scripting languages, descriptor based programming (ADL), skeletons and high order components, and graphical tools.

Each component standard, such as CCA or Fractal, provides an API (possibly in many programming languages) to perform basic operations on components. This API is then used by other high-level interfaces, facilitating the composition process.

A common approach to component composition is to use a scripting language. Some frameworks define their specific notation, as in the case of the CCAFFEINE framework [1], while others offer direct interfaces from a script to the framework API. The latter case is implemented in XCAT [21] and MOCCA, where applications can be assembled using a script written in Jython [20] or JRuby [19]. These languages have been selected partially because they use Java-based interpreters and allow seamless integration with Java client-side libraries or component frameworks. When using such scripts, it is possible to combine composition in time with composition in space, since both Python and Ruby are powerful programming languages which allow expressing the control flow and the sophisticated logic of any application, as is the case in the XCAT framework [16].

Composition in space may be performed using an Architecture Description Language (ADL). Such a notation, which is present in the component standards such as Fractal [2] or CORBA Component Model (CCM) [10], allows specifying the application structure in the form of a graph showing the connections between components. By introducing a concept of virtual nodes in ProActive and in GCM [5], it is possible to separate the architecture description from the deployment information, which is then provided in auxiliary deployment descriptor files. The ADL approach can be supported by graphical tools, however, it is limited in describing dynamic application behavior and does not allow composition in time.

For composition in time, there are specific notations available, called workflow languages, which specify application flow (control or data) in the form of a graph. Some workflow systems, such as Kepler [2], Triana [30], Pegasus [13] and K-WfGrid [18] may be used on the Grid. They enable editing the workflow using graphical tools and support conditions, parallel execution and specific constructs such as loops, etc. They are intended to assist non-programmer users in developing applications; however for workflows with many components and complex interactions, they may become difficult to use. Workflows may be expressed in an imperative language, e.g. in Grid Superscalar [27]. Some authors suggest using graphical languages to combine both temporal and spatial composition. As the examples of ICENI [25] and GriCoL [6] suggest, this requires creation of specialized component model extensions.

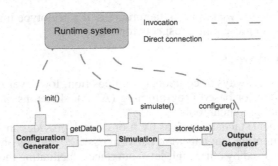

```
generator = GS.create("org.example.ConfigurationGenerator")
simulation = GS.create("org.example.Simulation")
output = GS.create("org.example.OutputGenerator")

simulation.inputPort.connect(generator.dataPort)
simulation.outputPort.connect(output.outputPort)

generator.init(steps, size)

simulator.simulate()
```

Figure 1.   Example of application using composition in space

3.   Composition with a High-level Scripting Language

The proposed approach to composition of component-based grid applications bases on a dynamic scripting language. This basis allows designing a high-level API for application composition and deployment, which enables specifying the application structure in a concise way. Modern scripting languages allow the programmer to specify the same functionality with considerably less lines of code than e.g. Java, making the code more readable and thus less error-prone. Additionally, they provide full expressiveness needed to specify application behavior in more flexible way than any workflow notation. Following careful analysis of possible candidates, we have selected Ruby [26] which is an object-oriented, dynamic scripting language with a clear and powerful syntax. As the interpreter we chose JRuby [19] which is implemented in pure Java and allows seamless integration with all available Java libraries.

To illustrate the concept of a script, let us consider a simplified application, built of three components (see Fig.1 or Fig.2):

- *Generator* for preparing initial data,

- *Simulation* part performing some computations and

- *Output* element responsible for storing the results.

Such an application can be modeled either using direct connections between components, or as a workflow which is coordinated by an external entity, labeled as the *RuntimeSystem*.

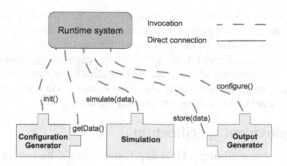

```
generator = GS.create("org.example.ConfigurationGenerator")
simulation = GS.create("org.example.Simulation")
output = GS.create("org.example.OutputGenerator")

generator.init(steps, size)

for i in (1..steps)
    data = generator.getData()
    result = simulator.simulate(data)
    output.store(result)
end
```

Figure 2.   Example application using composition in time

As Ruby is an object-oriented language, component instances in the script are represented by objects. With dynamic method definition and invocation it is possible to refer to their ports and port operations using a single method. Simple loops enable us to create collections of components and then iterate over them or connect them in required topologies, such as graphs or meshes. It is also possible to mix the various types of composition and control the dynamic behaviour of the application.

3.1   Composition support

A script allows us to easily express both types of composition (see Fig. 1 and 2) while preserving a clear and concise notation. In Fig. 1 the script is used to create direct connections between component ports, but also to configure the components and launch the simulation. Subsequently, control is passed to the components and the data flows directly between them using established bindings (e.g. *simulate()* execution invokes *getData()* and *storeData()* methods on bound components whenever needed). In Fig. 2, the components are implemented in such a way that they do not need connections, as data is passed through the runtime system under the supervision of the runtime system. Such composition may be useful for more loosely-coupled scenarios, since it does not require direct dependencies between components.

In both scenarios the *Generator* and *Output* components may be implemented in the same way, so their usage is invariant in both composition types. This is, however, not the case for the *Simulation* component, since it needs to get *data* either via a connected *uses* port or as a parameter of the *simulate(data)* method. Nevertheless, it is possible to design and implement a *Simulation* component, which can be compatible with both types of interactions. It should have both *uses* ports and two versions of the *simulate()* method: the *simulate()* which tries to fetch the *data* from the uses port and then stores it via the output port, and *result simulate(data)* which does not rely on the uses ports.

3.2   Deployment specification

A programmer assembling a Grid application should be free to specify how much information about deployment is to be provided manually and which decisions could be left for automatic tools. We consider three levels of detail:

- Fully automatic: the programmer specifies only the class of a component to create. The location for component deployment is determined automatically by the system:
  `GS.create(componentClassName)`

- Using a virtual node: the programmer specifies a virtual node which the component should be deployed on:
  `GS.createOnVN(componentClassName, vn)`

- Manual, by specifying a concrete location, e.g.
  `GS.createConcrete(techInfo)` where `techInfo` is the descriptor specifying all concrete information needed to create the component (e.g. H2O kernel in the case of MOCCA) and to invoke methods on it (e.g. names of the ports).

All these levels should be supported by the runtime system and might be combined by the programmer, e.g. to specify a concrete location for a master component and let the system automatically select resources for worker components from the available pool.

3.3   Framework interoperability

The scripting API for composition and deployment of components is neutral with respect to the used component model. Script invocations are translated to underlying Fractal, CCA or CCM APIs. If more than one component model is supported, it is possible to combine components from different models into a single application. In the case of a component workflow, the runtime system is the central point of inter-component communication, so it acts as an intermediary passing results from one component invocation to another. It is also possible to integrate modules developed in other technologies, e.g. Web services or WSRF in such a workflow. In the case of composition in space, when direct links between components are involved, it may be necessary to introduce *glue* ports between the heterogeneous components, to enable translation of invocations between them. As our research on interoperability between GCM and CCA [22] suggests, it is possible to introduce such a generic glue which can bridge components from different models and frameworks.

3.4 Optimizing communications

As can be seen in Fig. 2, composition in time requires that all the data has to flow through the central workflow engine (runtime system), which may lead to bottlenecks and poor scalability in larger systems. One of the solutions to this problem is to use a *pass-by-reference*-like model, where a *data* object does not contain actual data payload, but only a reference to that data, e.g. in the form of a URL. This requires both producer and consumer components to support storing and retrieving data from URL-specified locations, but then the actual data transfer can proceed directly between them.

There is however an alternative solution, which involves *futures*. The statement:

```
data = generator.getData()
```
may not block until the invocation is realized, instead creating a promise (a *future*) for the actual data. Subsequently, invoking:

```
result=simulator.simulate(data)
```
will copy the future reference to the simulator which will automatically retrieve the value of the data when the generator computes it (and it will be automatically blocked whenever the data is needed but not yet computed and received). In a framework that supports first-class futures, this mechanism is automatic and transparent, but it could also be implemented specifically for the script interpreter. Finally, as the value of data is not needed in the script interpreter, communicating the value to the interpreter could be avoided (this would correspond to garbage collection of future references).

The mechanism consisting of transmitting a future reference and automatically updating the value has been formalized for ProActive, and the ASP calculus in [9]. In practice, the ProActive framework partially provides what is needed in our particular case: futures are automatically created and transmitted by copy between objects or components, while future update is automatic. If by relying on ProActive the script interpreter were not to be blocked waiting for the result of the first invocation, it could proceed to the following phases. However, the future update strategy currently implemented in the ProActive framework implies that all copies of the future are updated with the result; consequently, a copy of the data would also be sent to the script interpreter itself, even if it did not need this data.

3.5 Prospects for decentralized script evaluation

Another drawback of the script interpreter is that it provides a single central point for managing all reconfigurations of connections and data communications, which may become a bottleneck. This issue could be addressed in a hierarchical component model, such as the GCM, by encapsulating a script interpreter inside each composite component. An additional construct (*subscript*) would be added to the script language that would delegate part of a script to the script interpreter associated with another component, and would consequently distribute the induced data communications more evenly.

Scalability would thus be ensured, but synchronization between those sub-script interpreters in a real distributed environment may be complex and is out of the scope of this study.

3.6   Alternative notation for composition in space

Currently, the proposed and implemented API for composition in space requires explicit invocation of *connect* methods on components. Although the notation proposed is as concise as possible, we suggest that it would be feasible to use an alternative notation, similar to the *imperative* programming as in the case of composition in time. It would require adoption of a combination of decentralized script evaluation and imposing a specific convention on component code.

As a result of the following statement:
```
data = generator.getData()
```
the interpreter should not invoke the method, but only return a proxy to a *data* object with the dependency information. Then, the call:
```
result=simulator.simulate(data)
```
should be interpreted as a request to create a connection to the port through which the data could be retrieved:
```
simulator.inputPort.connect(generator.outputPort)
```
and then a *simulate()* call which would actually invoke *getData()* using the created binding.

4.   Runtime and Development Support

As the goal of our Ruby-based GScript language is to provide constructs for component deployment, composition and invocation of component methods, there is a need to provide a runtime library. The library provides information on components in use and hides the complexity of the underlying Grid infrastructure. The architecture of the Runtime system is shown in Fig. 3. *Registry* is used for storing all technical information about available components, containers and the state of the Grid resources, updated by the *Monitoring* system. The *Optimizer* module is responsible for supporting decisions on (automatic) component deployment. The role of the optimizer is similar to that of the *deployment framework*, as proposed in [11]. The *Invoker* module

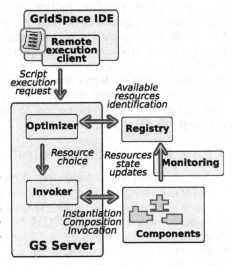

Figure 3.   Runtime system of GridSpace

transparently performs remote calls on component ports of different frameworks.

The invoker has an extensible architecture which allows plugging in adapters responsible for interacting with different technologies. So far, we have developed adapters for communicating with MOCCA and ProActive components, as well as with Web Services. Support for WSRF services is under development. We have also implemented an adapter for the MOCCA-ProActive Glue components; those glue components allow composition in space (direct connections) between the two frameworks [22]. This adapter is used in the experiment presented in the next section. More details on the invoker and the architecture of the system can be found in [4].

Although programming in a scripting language such as Ruby is convenient, there is always a need to support the development process with user friendly tools which assist programmers and help reduce the number of mistakes. For GScript we offer an integrated development environment based on the Eclipse platform with the Ruby Development Tools enriched by additional plugins. One of them is the Registry Browser which lists all available component classes, their ports and methods. It is connected with a script editor and allows us to insert automatically-generated code snippets. Another plugin may be used to browse the component classes categorized using an ontology-based taxonomy. It can be especially useful when searching for a component based on its functionality and finding similar components which are available.

The registry is available as a Web service, and stores technical information about registered components and services. It is also possible to use a local registry, which stores the same information in the Ruby script format, which is useful for quick development and debugging.

The current prototype of the optimizer allows us to specify an optimization policy (goal) in a pluggable way, however no advanced algorithms have been implemented so far.

5.   Experiments

The prototype functionality has been verified on a number of testing components using sample scripts demonstrating the functionality of the whole runtime system. One of the scenarios includes a scientific application used for simulation of clustered gold atoms. The application was initially developed using the MOCCA framework [23] alone and in the scenario depicted in Fig. 4 it was possible to plug an alternative output generator component, developed using ProActive, into the running application. A sample script which creates a ProActive output component oComp and connects it to the running MOCCA component subsystem (wrapped in wComp) is shown in Fig. 5 (techInfo details are omitted).

The runtime system of GridSpace serves as the engine of the Virtual Laboratory, developed for the ViroLab project [12]. The scripting notation is used to develop experiments in bioinformatics and virology, including data access, genetic sequence analysis, drug resistance prediction and data mining [28, 8].

6.   Conclusions and Future Work

In this paper we presented the concept of a high-level scripting language for programming component applications on the Grid. By using a dynamic interpreted language approach, it is possible to design a flexible and powerful notation, which covers the aspects of deployment, space and time composition, parametrization and configuration of components. The scripting approach can be applied to the process of rapid application development, prototyping and conducting scientific experiments on the Grid. A prototype which was developed demonstrates the feasibility of the proposed solution.

As our discussion in Section 3 suggests, it is possible to enrich the scripting model with decentralized and lazy script evaluation. In the case of composition in time, this may lead to an optimized communication pattern in workflow execution, while for composition in space it suggests an interesting alternative notation for dependency specification. This approach is worth further investigation, especially in the context of decentralized and hierarchical component environments for the Grid.

Future work also includes enriching the programming language with a set of constructs for parallel execution, development of deployment automation (optimization algorithms) and expanding support for other technologies. Another interesting open prospect is the possibility to deploy developed scripts *as new components* which may be subject to further composition. Such compo-

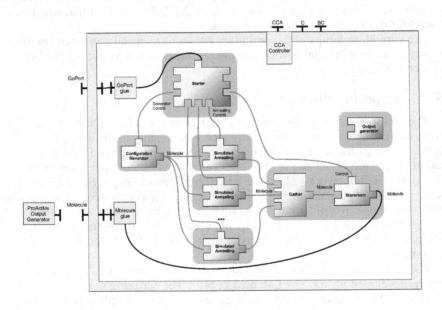

Figure 4.   CCA simulation running in MOCCA connected to a ProActive component

```
#  create component from tech info

wComp = GS.createConcrete(wrapperTechInfo)
oComp = GS.createConcrete(outputTechInfo)

# bind output to the wrapper
oComp.UsesMoleculePort.connect(wComponent.MyMoleculePort)

# start wrapper component
wComp.startFc()

# start output generator component
oComp.startFc()

# Invoke Go port
wComp.go();
```

Figure 5. Script for connecting the ProActive OutputGenerator component (*oComp*) to the running components of the application running in MOCCA and wrapped as a composite ProActive/MOCCA component (*wComp*).

nents could then be reused in more complex applications, as suggested by the GridSpace [17] concept.

Acknowledgments

The authors would like to express their gratitude to the team working on GridSpace: Bartosz Baliś, W_lodek Funika, Eryk Ciepiela, Joanna Kocot, Daniel Harezlak, Piotr Nowakowski, Darek Król and Kuba Wach.

References

[1] B. A. Allan et al. The CCA core specification in a distributed memory SPMD framework. *Concurrency Computat.*, 14:1–23, 2002.

[2] I. Altintas, E. Jaeger, K. Lin, B. Ludaescher, and A. Memon. A web service composition and deployment framework for scientific workflows. *ICWS*, 0:814, 2004.

[3] R. Armstrong, G. Kumfert, L. C. McInnes, S. Parker, B. Allan, M. Sottile, T. Epperly, and T. Dahlgren. The CCA component model for high-performance scientific computing. *Concurr. Comput. : Pract. Exper.*, 18(2):215–229, 2006.

[4] T. Bartynski, M. Malawski, T. Gubala, and M. Bubak. Universal grid client: Grid operation invoker. In R. Wyrzykowski, editor, *Parallel Processing and Applied Mathematics, 7th International Conference, PPAM 2007, Gdansk, Poland, September 2007, Revised Selected Papers*, Lecture Notes in Computer Science. Springer, 2007. to appear.

[5] F. Baude et al. From distributed objects to hierarchical grid components. In *Int. Symp. on Distributed Objects and Applications (DOA), Catania, Italy*, volume 2888 of *LNCS*, pages 1226 – 1242. Springer, 2003.

[6] H. L. Bouziane, C. Perez, N. Currle-Linde, and M. Resch. Analysis of Component Model Extensions to Support the GriCoL Language. Technical report, CoreGRID Workshop on Grid Programming Model, Grid and P2P Systems Architecture, Grid Systems, Tools and Environments, Heraklion - Crete, Greece, 12-13 June 2007.

[7] E. Bruneton, T. Coupaye, and J.-B. Stefani. Recursive and dynamic software composition with sharing. In *Proceedings of Seventh International Workshop on Component-Oriented Programming*, June 2002.

[8] M. Bubak, T. Gubala, M. Kasztelnik, M. Malawski, P. Nowakowski, and P. Sloot. Collaborative virtual laboratory for e-health. In P. Cunningham and M. Cunningham, editors, *Expanding the Knowledge Economy: Issues, Applications, Case Studies, eChallenges e-2007 Conference Proceedings*, page 8, Amsterdam, 2007. IOS Press.

[9] D. Caromel and L. Henrio. *A Theory of Distributed Object*. Springer-Verlag, 2005.

[10] CORBA Component Model, v3.0, 2002. http://www.omg.org/technology/documents/formal/components.htm.

[11] M. Coppola, M. Danelutto, S. Lacour, C. Perez, T. Priol, N. Tonellotto, and C. Zoccolo. Towards a common deployment model for grid systems. In S. Gorlatch and M. Danelutto, editors, *Proc. of the Integrated Research in Grid Computing Workshop*, volume TR-05-22, pages 31–40, Pisa, Italy, Nov. 2005. Universita di Pisa, Dipartimento di Informatica.

[12] Cyfronet. ViroLab Virtual Laboratory, 2007. http://virolab.cyfronet.pl.

[13] E. Deelman, J. Blythe, Y. Gil, C. Kesselman, G. Mehta, S. Patil, M.-H. Su, K. Vahi, and M. Livny. Pegasus: Mapping scientific workflows onto the grid. In *Grid Computing: Second European AcrossGrids Conference, AxGrids*, volume 3165 of *Lecture Notes in Computer Science*, pages 11–20. Springer, 2004.

[14] Deliverable D.PM.02 - proposals for a Grid component model, 2006. http://www.coregrid.net.

[15] V. Getov and T. Kielmann, editors. *Component Models and Systems for Grid Applications*. Springer, 2005.

[16] M. Govindaraju, S. Krishnan, K. Chiu, A. Slominski, D. Gannon, and R. Bramley. Merging the CCA component model with the OGSI framework. In *CCGRID '03: Proceedings of the 3st International Symposium on Cluster Computing and the Grid*, page 182, Washington, DC, USA, 2003. IEEE Computer Society.

[17] T. Gubala and M. Bubak. Gridspace - semantic programming environment for the grid. In R. Wyrzykowski, J. Dongarra, N. Meyer, and J. Wasniewski, editors, *PPAM*, volume 3911 of *Lecture Notes in Computer Science*, pages 172–179. Springer, 2005.

[18] T. Gubala and A. Hoheisel. Highly dynamic workflow orchestration for scientific applications. In *CoreGRID Intergation Workshop 2006 (CIW06)*, pages 309–320. ACC CYFRONET AGH, 2006.

[19] Java powered Ruby implementation, 2007. http://jruby.codehaus.org/.

[20] The Jython Website, 2004. http://www.jython.org.

[21] S. Krishnan and D. Gannon. XCAT3: A Framework for CCA Components as OGSA Services. In *Proc. Int. Workshop on High-Level Parallel Progr. Models and Supportive Environments (HIPS)*, pages 90–97, Santa Fe, New Mexico, USA, Apr. 2004.

[22] M. Malawski, M. Bubak, F. Baude, D. Caromel, L. Henrio, and M. Morel. Interoperability of grid component models: GCM and CCA case study. In T. Priol and M. Vanneschi, editors, *Towards Next Generation Grids: Proceedings of the CoreGRID Symposium*, pages 95–105, Rennes, France, August 2007. Springer.

[23] M. Malawski, M. Bubak, M. Placek, D. Kurzyniec, and V. Sunderam. Experiments with distributed component computing across grid boundaries. In *Proceedings of the HPC-GECO/CompFrame workshop in conjunction with HPDC 2006*, Paris, France, 2006.

[24] M. Malawski, D. Kurzyniec, and V. Sunderam. MOCCA – towards a distributed CCA framework for metacomputing. In *Proceedings of the 10th International Workshop on High-Level Parallel Programming Models and Supportive Environments (HIPS2005) in conjunction with International Parallel and Distributed Processing Symposium (IPDPS 2005)*. IEEE Computer Society, 2005.

[25] A. Mayer, S. McGough, N. Furmento, W. Lee, S. Newhouse, and J. Darlington. ICENI Dataflow and Workflow: Composition and Scheduling in Space and Time. In *UK e-Science All Hands Meeting*, pages 627–634, Nottingham, UK, Sept. 2003. ISBN 1-904425-11-9.

[26] The Ruby programming language, 2007. http://www.ruby-lang.org.

[27] R. Sirvent, J. M. Perez, R. Badia, and J. Labarta. Automatic grid workflow based on imperative programming languages. *Concurrency and Computation: Practice and Experience*, 18:1169–1186, 2005.

[28] P. M. Sloot, A. Tirado-Ramos, I. Altintas, M. Bubak, and C. Boucher. From molecule to man: Decision support in individualized e-health. *Computer*, 39(11):40–46, 2006.

[29] B. A. Tate. *Beyond Java*. O'Reilly, 2005.

[30] I. Taylor, M. Shields, I. Wang, and A. Harrison. Visual grid workflow in Triana. *Journal of Grid Computing*, 3(3-4):153–169, Sept. 2005.

DKS: DISTRIBUTED *K*-ARY SYSTEM
A MIDDLEWARE FOR BUILDING LARGE
SCALE DYNAMIC DISTRIBUTED
APPLICATIONS

Roberto Roverso, Cosmin Arad, Ali Ghodsi, Seif Haridi
School for Information and Communication Technology (ICT),
Royal Institute of Technology (KTH), Stockholm, Sweden.
{roverso, icarad, aligh, seif}@kth.se

Abstract   This report presents the design and implementation of a middleware for building large-scale, dynamic, and self-organizing distributed applications for the Internet. First, we identify the challenges that are faced when building this type of applications and the constraints imposed on the middleware that is to support them. We derive a set of essential services that are to be provided by our middleware in order to facilitate the development of distributed applications. These services include *scalable communication, failure detection, name-based overlay routing, group communication* and a *distributed hash table* abstraction. We present the *event-based component-oriented* architecture of the system, discussing the design choices that we made in order to meet the aforementioned challenges and constraints while providing the essential services for distributed applications. We describe in detail the event scheduling mechanism, the communication and failure detection, as well as the interface to applications and other miscellaneous services.

Keywords: overlay networks, distributed hash tables, group communication, failure detection, middleware, peer-to-peer

1.   Introduction

Internet-scale distributed applications and services such as wide-area storage systems [12, 6, 15], content distribution networks [5, 9], media streaming systems [17, 14, 3] or peer-to-peer and GRID computing and resource sharing systems [1] have motivated considerable advancements in the research on large-scale distributed systems in the last few years. Quite often, cooperating computer nodes that form these distributed systems are organized in an overlay network operating over the Internet.

Building real implementations of this type of systems poses a common set of challenges. First, given the nature of the provided services, these applications should accommodate a large number of users and participating machines. Thus, their implementation should be *scalable* in terms of the size of the network and the communication, storage, and computational load they are subjected to.

Second, these applications should operate in an environment of dynamic membership, where nodes are constantly joining, leaving the network or failing. Hence, the applications need to be *fault-tolerant*. Nodes should accurately detect the failure of neighboring nodes and act accordingly. Moreover, these applications should accommodate dynamic peer connectivity, and be able to continuously maintain certain connections and *garbage collect* others.

In order to facilitate the development and quick prototyping of new large-scale, dynamic, and self-organizing distributed applications, we decided to build a middleware library that provides basic reusable services for this type of applications and encapsulates solutions to the aforementioned set of challenges.

DKS, the middleware that we have implemented provides the following services: a *distributed hash table* (DHT) indexing service, that allows for storing and retrieving <key, value> pairs, an overlay network allowing for reliable name-based routing of messages, and group communication services. In addition, we provide lower level essential services like failure detection, timers, and web-based testing support.

Implementing a middleware library brings certain constraints. Large-scale systems imply a certain degree of heterogeneity in the performance and capacity of participating machines. In order to accommodate this heterogeneity the library should be as lightweight as possible, thus it should have a low memory footprint and should use a number of threads that accommodates the number of processing cores available on the machine where the middleware is executed. Moreover, it should be extensible and easily integrated with applications.

In the following sections we discuss the services provided by DKS and then we describe the DKS system architecture.

2.   Middleware services

We have derived a set of middleware services that we believe are essential to any large-scale distributed application, and which, if available, facilitate the quick implementation and deployment of new distributed algorithms.

First of all, application nodes need a reliable and efficient communication infrastructure for point-to-point communication and name-based routing. Second, they need to detect the failure of peer nodes in a timely manner and take fail-over measures. Extending these basic abstractions, we believe many applications would benefit from the use of a distributed index provided by a DHT service or from a group communication abstraction. Also, DKS provides timers handling and built-in support for application testing. We now look at each of these services in turn.

2.1   Reliable name-based communication and routing

The application nodes running the DKS middleware form a *structured overlay network* (SON). Each node can be addresed by a name that is actually a numeric identifier.

DKS provides both point-to-point message passing and message routing through the overlay network while hiding the connection management from the application. Messages can be sent to node names, the sender not having to know the Internet address of the receiver. For point-to-point communication, new temporary connections are established automatically if needed. Endpoints of each connection negotiate whether any of them needs the connection to be permanent or temporary. Temporary connections are automatically garbage collected and closed if not used for a certain period of time. Permanent connections are established between overlay network neighbors, for instance, but the application can chose to make a connection permanent should it be used for a longer time, to avoid connection establishment trashing.

The overlay network topology is induced by the Distributed k-ary System [10] DHT. The topology is maintained automatically and it is used for name-based routing of messages.

2.2   Failure detection

In order to be able to tolerate failures, applications need to detect them first. A node failure detection service is thus crucial for a distributed application. Due to the possibility of network congestion and message loss in the Internet, no bound on transmission delay can be guaranteed thus it is impossible to implement a strongly accurate [4, 11] failure detector using predefined message acknowledgment timeouts. Therefore, DKS provides an *eventually perfect* failure detector, which adapts its timeouts, hence its accuracy, to the variation of network latency, for each connection, thus for each neighboring node in part. At times it can falsely suspect alive nodes to have failed, due to temporary increased network latency, but eventually it adapts and resumes accurate failure detection.

2.3   Distributed hashtables

Distributed hashtables (DHTs) are an essential component of robust large-scale distributed systems. They provide a directory/index service in the form of a hash table abstraction, which distributed applications can use to reliably store various kind of meta-data. Data items in the DHT are replicated to keep them available as nodes join and leave the system.

The basic DHT operations are storing <key, value> pairs and retrieving the values associated to a key. DKS also provides bulk operations [10], whereby the storage or retrieval of a set of items is optimized in terms of message complexity.

DKS provides multiple DHT tables, with different characteristics such as replication degree or worst-case routing complexity. We are currently working on providing a transactional database abstraction on top of the DHT.

2.4   Group communication

Exploiting the structure of the overlay network, DKS provides an efficient overlay broadcast service as well as pseudo-reliable version of it [10]. Broadcast messages reach all nodes in the overlay network in a number of communication steps that is logarithmic in the size of the network, with no redundancy. A broadcast with feedback operation is also provided. This allows any node to aggregate global information from every other node in the system.

2.5   Other services

DKS provides testing support for overlying applications by means of a built-in web-server instance in each application node. Applications can expose internal state though dynamic web pages published on the server. From a central testing node, a script can automatically web-browse application nodes and assert the validity of their published internal state.

Another service provided by the DKS middleware is the management of timers. DKS allows overlying applications to register and cancel timers and triggers notifications on timers' expiration.

3.   System architecture

For reasons of modularity, readability and easy maintainability the DKS middleware is structured into *components*. Each component implements one service that it provides to other components through an *event-based* interface. In general, components are event-driven but there are some exceptions. For instance, components that deal with I/O operations or timers are control oriented and have their own thread of control.

Event-driven components are implemented as Java objects. They are comprised of some local state variables and a set of event handlers, which are ordinary Java methods. Each event handler handles events of one type. Events are ordinary Java objects and event types are Java types (classes). An event handler is executed whenever an event of the corresponding type is triggered. Event handlers are executed by the worker threads of a *thread pool* of adjustable size. While being executed, event handlers might trigger other events.

Triggering and execution of events relies on a *publish-subscribe* mechanism. Components *subscribe* for all the event types that they can handle. Whenever a new event is triggered, it is *published* for scheduling and when scheduled, the corresponding event handlers or all components that had subscribed for that event type are executed.

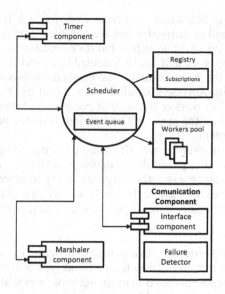

Figure 1. General Architecture of the middleware

An event subscription contains a reference to the subscriber component instance, a reference to the event handler method, and the event type for which the subscription is made. All event subscriptions are stored in a hashtable indexed by event type. In fact, a set of subscriptions is associated to an event type as there can be more than one component subscribing for the same event type.

Figure 1 shows a graphical representation of the middleware's architecture. The services mentioned in the previous section, such as overlay routing and group communication, are provided by single components, which interacts with each others using events of specific types.

3.1 Event scheduling

When an event is triggered a new event instance is created and placed on an event queue. The event queue is a priority queue and is used for prioritization of events. Events can have one of three priorities: low, medium, or high. By convention timer expiration events are given high priority, middleware events are given medium priority, and application events are given low priority. In general, high priority events are scheduled before medium and low priority ones and medium priority events are scheduled before low priority ones. However, to avoid starvation of low priority events we implement the following fairness mechanism: not more than f events are consecutively scheduled from a higher priority queue if there exist events in lower priority queues. f is a fairness parameter.

When an event is dequeued for scheduling, its type is looked up in the subscription table and all subscriptions are retrieved. For each subscription in part a *work* item is created and submitted for execution to the thread pool. A work item is a unit of work that can be executed by a worker thread in the thread pool. It consists of the event instance that needs to be handled and references to the component instance and handler method that need to be executed for handling the event. A worker thread that processes a work item will invoke the handler method on the specified component instance passing it the event instance as an argument.

While invoking an event handler method on some component instance, a worker thread locks that particular component instance. This enforces that one component instance executes only one event handler at a time so the component writer does not have to deal with concurrency. We can say that event handlers execute atomically with respect to each other, or that components are concurrency-safe.

3.1.1   Event consumers.   Components subscribe to events by type. As a result, a component that subscribes to one event type will handle all events of that type. Some components need to exchange messages with their peer components in other application nodes. Message sending and receiving is handled by a communication component. Whenever the communication component receives a message, it triggers a message received event. If all components that handle messages subscribed to this event, many of them would only handle it to find out that it contains a message they are not interested in. Therefore, to avoid this event trashing, we introduce the notion of event consumers.

Certain events, like the ones encapsulating received messages, may have associated with then, a *consumer*. A consumer is a pair containing the component designated to handle the event, together with its event handler method. If an event has an associated list of consumers, these will be scheduled to handle the event, together with other subscribers for the event type.

Currently, this mechanism is only used for events encapsulating messages. Components handling messages register as consumers by specifying a message type and a message handler method. Consumer registrations are kept in a hashtable indexed by message type. Whenever a message is received, based on its type, the list of consumers is retrieved from the consumer registry and all of them are scheduled to handle the message.

The consumers mechanism is a mechanism for message scheduling. Like events, messages have types, and different components handle different types of messages. Registering as a message consumer is the analogue of subscribing for an event type. The alternative approach to message scheduling would be for every message to be an event and use the event scheduling mechanism.

3.1.2   Component mutual exclusion.   There exist situations where multiple components need to access some shared state. Typically, the shared state resides in one component and needs to be accessed by other components. As we execute components concurrently in the thread pool, we may introduce race conditions on the shared state. To avoid such race conditions, we want to prevent executing a component event handler that is accessing state of a running component and delay its execution until the conflicting running component has finished executing its handler.

When subscribing for an event type, a component A registers an event handler. At the same time it has to state what other component's (say B) state that handler accesses. We assume that all handlers of component B access the state that the handler of component A accesses. Thus, the handler of component A cannot run concurrently with any handler of component B. We say that the handler of component A depends on the handlers of component B and vice-versa. All such dependencies are stored in a dependency table. For each event handler we have a dependency set consisting of all the handlers the respective event depends on. These dependency sets are created both ways at handler subscription time.

The scheduler maintains a set of running handlers. Whenever a new event handler is to be executed, its dependency set is intersected with the set of running handlers and the new event handler is executed only if this intersection is empty. Otherwise, the coresponding work item is placed in a waiting set. Whenever one of the running handlers finishes executing, the waiting set is inspected for handlers that are now ready to execute.

3.2 Communication

A communication component handles the sending and receiving of messages between middleware nodes over TCP connections. Middleware nodes are addressed by a reference comprising of their Internet address and overlay address. The communication component provides the service of sending a message to a specified node reference by handling the corresponding event and triggers a message received event when a new message is received from a remote node. In providing these basic services the communication component hides the connection management from the other components of the middleware and from the application.

Hidden connection management includes initiating or accepting a new connection that is needed to send a message, periodically garbage collecting not recently used connections, and tie-breaking when two nodes have open two different connections to each other simultaneously, by closing one of them. Every middleware node listens for incoming connections on a TCP port that is part of its node reference.

The communication component also offers explicit control to connection management to other components. Connections are tagged as *permanent* or *temporary*. Permanent connections are never closed while temporary connections are subject to garbage collection. Other components can change the status of a specific connection through specific events. The status of a connection is negotiated with the other peer and a connection can be made temporary only if both end-points agree that they don't need it as a permanent connection. Automatically created connections are initially temporary, but other components can also explicitly create permanent or temporary connections. For instance, a node should have permanent connections to its neighbors in the overlay routing table.

3.2.1   Message transmission and reception.   Message transmission and reception is done with a selector model rather than with a thread per connection model. This is mainly because as the middleware node is part of an overlay network it may have a considerable number of neighbors and therefore many open connections. Having one thread per connection would lead to a too large number of threads in the system and to considerable context-switching overhead as the Java threads are heavyweight threads. Hence, the communication component contains its own thread that blocks on all pending I/O operation and immediately unblocks and handles I/O operations that become ready. This mechanism enables scalable communication.

Message transmission and reception is done by copying message bytes from memory buffers to socket buffers and vice-versa. The selector thread blocks on a receive operation until some bytes are available in the receive socket buffer. It can also block on a transmit operation if the transmit socket buffer is full.

We use *direct* memory buffers for efficient communication as the Java Virtual Machine make a best effort to perform native I/O operations on direct buffers, avoiding extra byte copying. However, direct buffers have a higher allocation cost than normal buffers. For this reason we pre-allocate a pool of direct buffers at component initialization time. Buffers are acquired from the buffer pool as they are needed and released back thereafter.

Each connection may have an active I/O operation and some state associated with it. When the respective I/O operation becomes ready, the selector continues the operation (by sending or receiving some bytes) and updates its state. Hence, the selector transmit and receive operations are state machines. Whenever all bytes of a message have been received, and are available in a list of buffers, they are passed to a marshaler component for unmarshaling. Each connection has an associated queue of messages to be sent. These are already marshaled messages and are represented as lists of buffers. Whenever all bytes of a message have been sent, the next message is dequeued, a message header is composed and sent and then the bytes of the message are sent. The communication component guarantees FIFO message transmission which is relied upon by the failure detector and some of the DKS [10] protocols.

Message headers are 9 bytes long and include the message type, the message sequence number and the payload length. All messages are acknowledged. This enables the continuous estimation of the round-trip time (RTT) of each connection which is used for failure detection (see Section 3.3).

When triggering the sending of a message, other components can subscribe to notifications. They can be notified, through a specified event, either when all the bytes of the message have been sent or when the message receipt has been acknowledged.

3.3   Failure detection

As our middleware nodes are to be deployed over the Internet which behaves as a partially synchronous network [11], we provide an *eventually perfect* [4, 11] failure detector. This failure detector triggers *suspicion* events when it suspects that a peer node has crashed, and *rectification* events when it finds that the suspicion was in fact a false positive. False positives can happen in the Internet where most of the time the message transmission delay is bounded but sometimes, due to congestion, messages or acknowledgements may take longer than expected to arrive, thus resulting into a timeout and triggering a false suspicion.

The failure detector relies on a prediction of round-trip time for each connection in part. As all messages exchanged by the middleware are acknowledged, the RTT can be measured for each sent message. For each connection the average RTT is kept together with the RTT variance. These values are used to compute an expected round-trip timeout (RTTO). $RTTO = E(RTT) + 4 \times VAR(RTT)$. This timeout value is used to set a timer every time a message is sent. If the timer expires before an acknowledgement is received, the peer is suspected to have crashed. If an acknowledgement is eventually received, the RTTO is recomputed to adapt to the new RTT. If an acknowledgement is received before the timer expires the timer is just canceled.

In the case when the local peer doesn't actively send messages to the remote peer, the failure detector periodically sends *ping* probes awaiting for *pong* acknowledgements within a timeout of RTTO milliseconds. From the failure detection point of view, pings are equivalent to ordinary messages and pongs are equivalent to message acknowledgements. The local peer waits for γ milliseconds from the time it receives a pong until is sends the next ping. No ping is sent if the remote peer is suspected, but the local peer awaits for the pong to the last sent ping.

As the failure detection mechanism closely relies on the RTTO estimation, computed per each link in part, and on message acknowledgements, it is implemented inside the communication component. Because each connection may have a different expected RTTO we have a failure detector instance for each connection in part.

If the local peer sends a sequence of messages, only the first message is used for failure detection. From the failure detection point of view, all messages sent before the acknowledgement to the first sent message is received are ignored. This behavior relies on the fact that connections are FIFO.

3.4 Application interface

Applications making use of the middleware may interact with it in two different ways. One way, suitable for new applications, is to fit the application to the middleware architecture, that is, to have a component-oriented event-driven application.

For applications written in a control-oriented manner we provide an interfacing component whose role is to provide blocking calls to the application. Typically, middleware services are used by triggering a request event. When the service operation has been completed a response event is triggered by the middleware. The interfacing component wraps this event-based interface into a blocking call interface, thus every service is made into a call which starts by triggering the corresponding request event and then blocks awaiting for the response event. Handling the response event results in the middleware call returning to the application.

A middle ground between a fully synchronous interface and having a complete event-based application is an asynchronous interface for control-oriented applications. That is, request events are triggered by the application but the application does not have to block waiting for the response event. It can continue to run and can later check whether the response event has been triggered or not. The check can be blocking or non-blocking, that is if the response event has not been triggered yet, the application can either block awaiting it or continue to run and check again at a later time. This way, the application can trigger a number of middleware services, whereby the response events are stored in a mailbox that the application checks.

3.4.1   Web-based testing support.   The middleware includes a web-server which serves pages with statistics and state of the middleware components.By default, the web-server replies with a human readable web-page containing statistics about the open connections, failure detection and status of some of the middleware components. However, every component including application components can publish their own dynamic pages on the web-server. These pages should have an easily parsable format and should contain <variable,value> pairs. Thus the value of certain variables can be automatically asserted from a unit testing framework which can browse the middleware nodes' web-servers and retrieve interesting state information.

4.   Performance evaluation

We have evaluated the performance of some of the services provided by our middleware by running it on a cluster of machines with Intel Xeon CPUs running at 3GHz and equipped with 4GB of RAM. We conducted experiments to measure the performance of the communication component, the group communication component, the overlay routing and the event scheduling capacity of the system.

4.1   Point-to-point communication performance

We evaluated the communication component by measuring the message forwarding performance of a node. For this purpose, we set up a network of three nodes: the first node A sends messages to a second B, which then forwards them to C. Node C collects the messages and measures the number of messages received per second, i.e. how fast messages are forwarded by B. For providing a deeper understanding of the communication component's performance, we conducted a number of experiments with different message sizes. The test's result is shown in Figure 2.

4.2   Overlay routing performance

We tested the performance of our overlay routing system by issuing a fixed number of lookups to random identifiers in an identifier's space of size 1024.

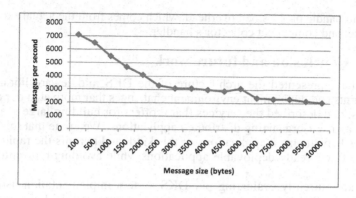

Figure 2.   Message forwarding capacity

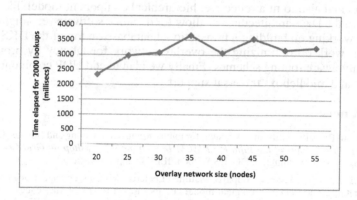

Figure 3.   Lookup performance's test result

We then measured how long it takes, on average, to receive a reply from all the responsible nodes. Figure 3 shows the results of the aforementioned test with 2000 lookups for random identifiers for different numbers of participating nodes in the network.

4.3   Event scheduling performance

To measure the performance of the middleware's scheduler, we created a simple system with two components: one that triggers a number of events and another one which handles them and measures how fast they are delivered. Given this test configuration, we injected 500 thousand events from the first component and found out that they were delivered to the second component in 2,015 seconds, on average. This gives a mean of 248.139 events delivered per second, which represents approximately the average load which the scheduler is able to handle plus a small overhead, which comes from the actual execution of the second component collector's handler.

5.   Conclusion and future work

We have presented the architecture of the DKS middleware library, the constraints and deployment environment challenges that motivated our design choices, and described the services that it offers for building large-scale, dynamic, and self-organizing distributed applications. We argue that this set of services benefits most applications of this kind, and permits the rapid prototyping of new ready-deployable applications while avoiding reinventing the wheel.

We are currently evaluating our DKS system implementation using the ModelNet [18, 13] network emulator with a network model built from real Internet measurements [16, 7, 8].

As future work, we plan to enrich the set of services provided by the DKS platform and also to fit a reflective, hierarchical component model, like Fractal [2], to the DKS architecture, to allow for dynamic software reconfiguration. We are working on building a transactional database on top of the DKS DHT. We also work on optimizing the overlay network for latency by providing proximity-aware routing schemes. Finally we plan to add UDP communication support and middlebox[1] traversal support.

References

[1] David P. Anderson. Boinc: A system for public-resource computing and storage. In *GRID '04: Proceedings of the Fifth IEEE/ACM International Workshop on Grid Computing*, pages 4–10, Washington, DC, USA, 2004. IEEE Computer Society.

[2] Eric Bruneton, Thierry Coupaye, Matthieu Leclercq, Vivien Quema, and Jean-Bernard Stefani. The fractal component model and its support in java: Experiences with auto-adaptive and reconfigurable systems. *Softw. Pract. Exper.*, 36(11-12):1257–1284, 2006.

[3] Miguel Castro, Peter Druschel, Anne-Marie Kermarrec, Animesh Nandi, Antony Rowstron, and Atul Singh. Splitstream: high-bandwidth multicast in cooperative environments. In *SOSP '03: Proceedings of the nineteenth ACM symposium on Operating systems principles*, pages 298–313, New York, NY, USA, 2003. ACM Press.

[4] Tushar Deepak Chandra and Sam Toueg. Unreliable failure detectors for reliable distributed systems. *J. ACM*, 43(2):225–267, 1996.

[5] Bram Cohen. Incentives build robustness in bittorrent. Technical report, bittorrent.org, 2003.

[6] F. Dabek, M. F. Kaashoek, D. R. Karger, R. Morris, and I. Stoica. Wide-area cooperative storage with CFS. In *Proceedings of the 18th ACM Symposium on Operating Systems Principles (SOSP'01)*, pages 202–215, Chateau Lake Louise, Banff, Canada, October 2001. ACM Press.

[7] DIMES. http://www.netdimes.org, 2004-2007.

[8] ETOMIC. http://www.etomic.org, 2004-2007.

---

[1] NAT or firewall devices.

[9] Michael J. Freedman, Eric Freudenthal, and David Mazières. Democratizing content publication with coral. In *NSDI'04: Proceedings of the 1st conference on Symposium on Networked Systems Design and Implementation*, pages 18–18, Berkeley, CA, USA, 2004. USENIX Association.

[10] Ali Ghodsi. *Distributed k-ary System: Algorithms for Distributed Hash Tables*. PhD dissertation, KTH—Royal Institute of Technology, Stockholm, Sweden, December 2006.

[11] R. Guerraoui and L. Rondrigues. *Introduction to Reliable Distributed Programming*. Springer-Verlag, Heidelberg, Germany, 2006.

[12] John Kubiatowicz, David Bindel, Yan Chen, Steven Czerwinski, Patrick Eaton, Dennis Geels, Ramakrishan Gummadi, Sean Rhea, Hakim Weatherspoon, Westley Weimer, Chris Wells, and Ben Zhao. Oceanstore: an architecture for global-scale persistent storage. *SIGPLAN Not.*, 35(11):190–201, 2000.

[13] ModelNet. http://modelnet.ucsd.edu, 2002-2007.

[14] J. J. D. Mol, D. H. J. Epema, and H. J. Sips. The orchard algorithm: P2p multicasting without free-riding. In *P2P '06: Proceedings of the Sixth IEEE International Conference on Peer-to-Peer Computing*, pages 275–282, Washington, DC, USA, 2006. IEEE Computer Society.

[15] A. Rowstron and P. Druschel. Storage management and caching in past, a large-scale, persistent peer-to-peer storage utility. In *Proceedings of the 18th ACM Symposium on Operating Systems Principles (SOSP'01)*, Chateau Lake Louise, Banff, Canada, October 2001. ACM Press.

[16] Yuval Shavitt and Eran Shir. Dimes: let the internet measure itself. *SIGCOMM Comput. Commun. Rev.*, 35(5):71–74, 2005.

[17] Kunwadee Sripanidkulchai, Aditya Ganjam, Bruce Maggs, and Hui Zhang. The feasibility of supporting large-scale live streaming applications with dynamic application end-points. In *SIGCOMM '04: Proceedings of the 2004 conference on Applications, technologies, architectures, and protocols for computer communications*, pages 107–120, New York, NY, USA, 2004. ACM Press.

[18] Amin Vahdat, Ken Yocum, Kevin Walsh, Priya Mahadevan, Dejan Kostic, Jeff Chase, and David Becker. Scalability and accuracy in a large-scale network emulator. In *OSDI '02: Proceedings of the 5th symposium on Operating systems design and implementation*, pages 271–284, New York, NY, USA, 2002. ACM Press.

TRANSACTIONS AND CONCURRENCY CONTROL FOR PEER-TO-PEER WIKIS: AN EVALUATION*

Stefan Plantikow, Alexander Reinefeld, Florian Schintke
Zuse Institute Berlin
<surname>@zib.de

Abstract   Supporting atomic transactions and concurrency control in peer-to-peer networks is difficult because nodes may leave, crash or join at any time. We propose a transaction processing scheme for peer-to-peer networks that ensures consistency and durability by constructing the overlay from replicated state machines. Our scheme supports a mixture of pessimistic, hybrid optimistic and multiversioning concurrency control techniques to minimize the impact of replication on latency and to maximize the speed of read operations.

We apply the transaction scheme to a distributed Wiki application and present pseudocode of the relevant functions. Our Wiki supports rich metadata and indices for navigation purposes. We compare the presented concurrency control techniques in various scenarios and evaluate their performance in terms of communication cost and message latency.

Keywords: wikis, distributed transactions, concurrency control, consistency, overlay networks.

*This work was supported by the EU Network of Excellence Core-GRID and the EU SELFMAN project

1.   Introduction

Peer-to-peer databases allow storing and retrieving data efficiently in distributed environments without central control. To achieve high scalability, such databases are built using structured overlay networks. Unfortunately, in their most basic implementation, structured overlays do not guarantee any predictable ordering of concurrently executed operations and thus are unsuited for the data consistency requirements of complex applications.

Extending our previous work in [15] we propose and evaluate a transactional system for a distributed content management system built on a structured overlay. Our emphasis is here on the comparative evaluation of the various concurrency control methods that support long-running transactions in dynamic decentralized systems where nodes may fail with a relatively high rate.

In the following Section we describe the requirements for a scalable distributed Wiki. In Section 3 we present our transaction processing scheme with a focus on concurrency control. This schema is extended to the relational model and exemplified using the distributed Wiki in Section 4. In Section 5 we evaluate the proposed concurrency control schemes and compare their required number of messages and latency.

2.   Requirements for Distributed Wikis

A *Wiki* is a content management system that embraces the principle of minimizing access barriers for non-expert users. Wikis like www.wikipedia.org comprise millions of pages that are written in a simplified, human-readable markup syntax. Users may concurrently view (read) or change (write) pages over the Internet. To be able to revert malicious page changes, the edit history is also stored.

Since the content of Wikis is provided and maintained by a large user community, page edits are quite frequent. If two users start editing the same version of a page, the user who first finishes gets her version stored while the other is informed about the update conflict. This requires to serialize all requests. Common Wiki software implements this using the transactional ACID semantics of relational database systems.

However, central databases may become a bottleneck for popular Internet Wikis like Wikipedia. We therefore propose to implement the Wiki as a distributed peer-to-peer system extended by transaction mechanisms that guarantee the ACID properties. We chose the *page model* as our basis, which, according to Gray [4], treats a database as a set of uniquely addressable, single objects that can be read and written. This model fits the structured overlay paradigm in which objects are stored by their identifier using the overlay's policy for data placement. In Section 4.1, we show how database schemas can be mapped onto the page model.

2.1   Distributed Transactions

As the database becomes distributed over several nodes in our overlay, we need a *distributed transaction processing scheme* to guarantee the ACID properties. All accesses to local objects are controlled by *resource manager (RM)* processes. In the overlay, each peer performs the resource management for all its local objects. Additionally, for each active transaction, a *transaction manager (TM)* coordinates the transaction execution with the involved RMs. The transaction management includes the execution of the distributed atomic commit protocol (see Section 3.2) and is performed by the peer that initiated the transaction.

2.2   Churn and Asynchronism

Large-scale overlays are subject to a considerable amount of churn [9] and the system must therefore be able to ensure the ACID properties in the presence of node joins, leaves, and failures. Implementing transactions on overlays requires *lookup consistency*, which is needed, for example, to acquire locks from the responsible RMs and to inhibit the delivery of outdated data. Protocols for consistent lookups based on atomic commit [3, 7] must be executed by all joining and leaving nodes. This, however, is difficult to implement because nodes may crash at any time: In contrast to DBMSs structured overlays are based on the *crash-stop model* rather than the *crash-recovery* model.

We therefore propose *replicated state machines* (RSMs) [19] to ensure lookup consistency, availability, and durability. Instead of constructing the overlay network from single nodes, it is made up by cells.

Cell Model.   A *cell* is a dynamically sized group of physical nodes [18] that constitute an RSM. Performing replication below the overlay's topology reduces the communication cost and masks crashes of single nodes. When too many nodes of a cell crash, the remaining nodes initiate the removal of the complete cell from the overlay by invoking the overlay's leave-protocol. The freed nodes may then join other cells.

Executing a state machine replication protocol within a cell incurs a high overhead because RSM protocols are based on consensus algorithms. Even modern consensus algorithms like Fast Paxos [8] require three communication rounds with a total of at least $N(\lfloor 2N/3 \rfloor + 1)$ messages. When using the cell model, however, the routing process can be improved by using dirty reads (see Fig. 1). This may cause routing errors when the state of a node does

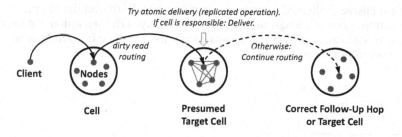

Figure 1.   Cell routing using dirty reads.

not properly reflect the cell's state, but consistency is not affected because messages are only delivered by a replicated operation if the presumed target cell is actually responsible. If the cell is not responsible for the message, the routing is continued. Figure 1 illustrates the routing process.

Note that the cell model provides a cheap method for data replication because all nodes holding replicas are known within a cell. Other schemes [3] require additional routing costs for locating the replica holders.

3.   Building Blocks for Transactions on Overlays

We use hybrid optimistic concurrency control (HOCC) [22] and two phase commit on top of replicated state machines. Additionally we support optimized fast-read transactions using read-only multiversioning (Section 3.3).

3.1   Hybrid Optimistic Concurrency Control (HOCC)

HOCC is an optimistic concurrency control scheme. First, HOCC executes the transaction optimistically under the assumption that there are no conflicts (work phase) and then, at commit time, validates that this assumption is actually true (validation phase). HOCC executes *strong two phase locking (2PL)* for the transaction's read and write sets at the beginning of the validation phase. In case of a validation failure due to conflicts, the locks are kept and the transaction logic is re-executed. Because access invariance is assumed (i.e. repeated executions of the same transaction have identical read and write sets), this second execution cannot fail as all necessary locks are already held by the transaction.

Using strong 2PL allows to avoid distributed deadlock detection if a global validation order between transactions with non-disjoint sets of accessed objects can be established. For this, as proposed by Agrawal et. al [1], every cell v maintains a strictly monotonic increasing timestamp t_v for the largest, validated transaction. Before a validation starts, the transaction manager suggests a validation time stamp $t > t_v$ to all involved cells v. After every cell v has acknowledged that $t > t_v$ and updated t_v to t, the validation phase is started. Otherwise the algorithm is repeated.[1]

Alternatively to HOCC, transaction processing could be implemented by cells using pessimistic, strong 2PL and an additional distributed atomic commit protocol. This has worse performance because, compared to HOCC, more of the expensive replicated operations are necessary. With traditional optimistic concurrency control, long-running transactions may suffer starvation due to consecutive validation failures if they work on objects that are frequently accessed by short-running transactions

---

[1]Gruber [5] optimized this approach by including the largest validation timestamp in every message, thereby decreasing the necessary latency.

3.2   Distributed Atomic Commit

Distributed atomic commit requires consensus between all transaction participants on the transaction's termination state (committed or aborted). If commit
atomicity is not guaranteed, all four ACID properties are violated.

We propose a blocking protocol for distributed atomic commit that uses cells
to treat TM failures by replicating the termination state of transactions.[2] A
commit record that holds this termination state is stored under the transaction's
unique identifier (TXID) in the overlay network (for example, in the same cell
as the transaction manager's node). If no failures occur, regular two-phase
atomic commit (2PC) is executed. Additionally, after the prepared-messages
have been received from the RMs and before the final commit messages are
sent, the TM writes the commit record. If the record is already set to abort,
the TM aborts the transaction. If the RMs suspect a TM failure, they read the
commit record to either determine the termination state or initiate transaction
abort.

3.3   Fast-Read Transactions

In many practical applications, like Wikis, read transactions are more frequent
than update transactions. Therefore, we optimize and extend our transaction
processing scheme for fast, read-only transactions by applying techniques
similar to read-only multiversioning (ROMV) [12].

All data items are versioned using unique timestamps generated from each
node's loosely synchronized clock and globally unique node identifier. For
each data item, we maintain a *current version*. This version is accessed and
locked exclusively by HOCC transactions as described above and implicitly
associated with the cell's maximum validation timestamp t_v. This current
version decouples read-only multiversioning and HOCC.

Our approach moves newly created versions to the future such that they never
interfere with read operations from ongoing read-only transactions. This avoids
the cost associated with distributed atomic commit for read-only transactions but
necessitates to execute reads as replicated operations. Read-only transactions
are associated with their start time. Every read operation is executed as a
replicated operation using the multiversioning rule [16]: The result is the oldest
version that is younger than the transaction start time. If this version is the
current version, the maximum validation timestamp t_v is updated. This may
block the read operation until a currently running validation is finished. Update
transactions create new versions of all written objects using $t > t_v$ during
atomic commit.

---

[2]For an alternative, non-blocking approach, see, e.g., [13].

4.   Algorithms for a Distributed Wiki

Next, we describe the basic algorithms of a distributed lightweight content management system that is built on a structured overlay with transaction support.

4.1   Supporting Relational Schemas on Overlays

So far, we only considered uniquely addressable, uniform objects. In practice, many applications use more complex, relational data structures. This rises the question of how multiple relations with possibly multiple attributes can be stored in a single structured overlay.

Since current overlays only support few index dimensions efficiently, it is necessary to partition additional attributes into disjoint groups and map these groups instead. The partition must be chosen in such a way that fast primary-key based access is still possible. Depending on their group membership, attributes are either primary, index, or data attributes. Multiple relations can be modeled by introducing an additional primary attribute that contains a unique relation identifier.

4.2   Relational Schema for Wikis

Each Wiki page is addressed by a unique identifier which is also used for hyperlinking from other Wiki pages. All pages can be read and edited by any user. This may result in many concurrent modifications of hotspot pages, making Wikis a perfect test-case for our distributed transaction algorithm.

Modern Wikis provide a host of additional features beyond mere reading and writing of pages, particularly to simplify navigation. In this paper we exemplarily consider backlinks (list of other pages linking to a page) and recent changes (list of recent modifications of a page). We model our Wiki using the two relations CONTENT and BACKLINKS:

Relation	Primary attributes	Index attributes	Data attributes
CONTENT	*pageName*	*ctime* (change time)	*content*
BACKLINKS	*referencing* (page), *referenced* (page)	-	-

4.3   Core Wiki Functions

All Wiki operations use transactions to maintain the consistency invariants:

- CONTENT always contains the page's current content,
- BACKLINKS contains proper backlinks for all pages given by CONTENT,
- users cannot modify pages whose content has never been seen by them (explained below).

We describe the Wiki algorithms using the pseudocode notation in Table 1. The function WikiRead (Fig. 2) delivers the content of a page and all backlinks pointing to it. In the cell model, this first requires a lookup operation for the

Table 1. Pseudocode notation [15] used in this article. Relations are represented as sets of tuples and written in CAPITALS. Relation tuples are addressed using values for the primary attributes in the fixed order given by the relation. Tuple components are identified by unique labels. Range queries are expressed using labels and marked with a "?".

Procedure Proc $(arg_1, arg_2, \ldots, arg_n)$	Procedure declaration
begin transaction ... commit (abort) transaction	Transaction boundaries
ADDRESS"$_{ZIB}$"	Read tuple from relation
ADDRESS"$_{ZIB}$" $\leftarrow$ $("Takustr.\ 7", "Berlin")$	Write tuple to relation
$\Pi_{attr_1, \ldots, attr_n}(M) = \{\pi_{attr_1, \ldots, attr_n}(t) \mid t \in M\}$	Projection, M is a tuple set
$\forall t \in$ tuple set : RELATION $\overset{+}{\leftarrow} t$ bzw. $\overset{-}{\leftarrow} t$	Bulk insert and delete
$\mathrm{DHT}^?_{key_1 = "a",\ key_2}$ or $\mathrm{DHT}^?_{key_1 = "a",\ key_2 = *}$	Range query ($*$ asks for any value)
ADDRESS$^?_{"ZI" < \overline{orga} < "ZZ"}$ $\overline{street}$ $_{\#<50}$	Sorted range query with result limit

page's cell and a range query[3] for all cells that contain backlinking information. After these lookups, depending on the chosen concurrency control scheme, data access is performed in parallel and a properly formatted result is returned to the user.

The function RecentChanges (Fig. 2) issues a range query to find all cells that store a sorted list of the *limit* newest pages that have been changed *beforeTime*.

The function WikiWrite (Fig. 2) is more complex because conflicting writes by multiple users must be resolved. This can be done by serializing the write requests using locks or request queues. In case of conflicts, the WikiWrite is aborted. Users may then manually merge their changes and retry. This approach is similar to the compare-and-swap instruction available in some microprocessors and to the concurrency control in version control systems.[4] For our distributed Wiki, we implement the compare-and-swap by using transactions. First, we precompute which backlinks should be inserted or deleted. Then, we compare the current and old page content and abort if they differ. Otherwise all updates are performed by writing the new page content and modifying BACKLINKS. Update operations can be performed in parallel.

4.4   Supporting Metadata

Often additional metadata needs to be stored with each page (e.g. page author, category). To support this, we add a third relation METADATA with primary key attributes *pageName* and *attrName* and data attribute *attrValue*. Alternatively,

---

[3]We assume that the overlay supports range queries over a finite number of index dimensions [20, 2].
[4]Most version control systems provide heuristics (e.g. content merging) for automatic conflict resolution that could be used for our distributed Wiki as well.

Figure 2.   Algorithms for a distributed Wiki: WikiRead reads the page content, RecentChanges lists the recently modified pages, and WikiWrite writes new page content and updates the backlinks.

1: **function** WikiRead $(pageName)$
2:     **begin transaction** *read-only*
3:         $content \leftarrow \pi_{content}(\text{CONTENT}_{pageName})$
4:         $backlinks \leftarrow \Pi_{referenced}(\text{BACKLINKS}^{?}_{referencing=pageName, \ referenced})$
5:     **commit transaction**
6:     **return** $content, backlinks$
7: **end function**

1: **function** RecentChanges $(beforeTime, \ limit)$
2:     **begin transaction** *read-only*
3:         $result \leftarrow \{\text{CONTENT}^{?}_{pageName, \ ctime > beforeTime}\}^{\overleftarrow{ctime}}_{\# < limit}$
4:     **commit transaction**
5:     **return** $result$
6: **end function**

1: **procedure** WikiWrite $(pageName, \ content_{old}, \ content_{new})$
2:     $refs_{old} \leftarrow$ Refs $(content_{old})$
3:     $refs_{new} \leftarrow$ Refs $(content_{new})$
4:     $refs_{del} \leftarrow refs_{old} \setminus refs_{new}$ — pre-calculation
5:     $refs_{add} \leftarrow refs_{new} \setminus refs_{old}$
6:     $txStartTime \leftarrow$ CurrentTimeUTC $()$
7:     **begin transaction**
8:         **if** $\pi_{content}(\text{CONTENT}_{pageName}) = content_{old}$ **then**
9:             $\text{CONTENT}_{pageName} = (txStartTime, \ content_{new})$
10:            $\forall t \in \{(ref, \ pageName) \mid ref \in refs_{add}\} : \text{BACKLINKS} \xleftarrow{+} t$
11:            $\forall t \in \{(ref, \ pageName) \mid ref \in refs_{del}\} : \text{BACKLINKS} \xleftarrow{-} t$
12:        **else**
13:            **abort transaction**
14:        **end if**
15:    **commit transaction**
16: **end procedure**

---

we could also add metadata attributes to CONTENT but this would hardly scale because current overlays only provide a limited number of index dimensions.

Note that changes to metadata must also be executed in transactions because they could be based on previously read, outdated page contents—similar to backlinks. For reading page metadata, a simple range query suffices [15].

5.   Evaluation

Table 2 presents the communication overhead of the concurrency control schemes using transactions of k serial steps. Each such step comprises the parallel execution of operations on n different data items. We consider three cases:

(1) $k = 1, n = 1$

(2a) $k > 1$, $n > 1$ and the set of different items is fixed for all steps. A typical read–write–cycle as used by WikiWrite would be $k = 2$.

(2b) $k > 1$, $n > 1$ and the set of different items is *not* fixed for all steps. In Table 2 we show the worst case where all sets are pairwise disjoint.

The last operation on an item is assumed to be known in advance and therefore can be bundled with the corresponding prepare-and-validate message of the distributed atomic commit.

For each concurrency control scheme and for each sample transaction, the table gives the required number of lookup operations in the overlay (L), replicated operations on cells (R), and simple operations directly sent to single nodes (S). Additionally it contains upper bounds on latency that are expressed using the operations' worst-case execution times t_L, t_R, and t_S. The evaluated concurrency control schemes are:

Atomic Write	simple, replicated operation on a single cell
Pess. 2PL	pessimistic 2PL transaction
HOCC	HOCC transaction without validation failure (Sec. 3.1)
HOCC w. conflicts	HOCC transaction with validation failure and re-execution of transaction logic
Fast-Read	read-only multiversioning transaction (Sec. 3.3)

Table 2. Comparison of the presented concurrency control schemes with regard to the required number of messages and latency of the described sample transactions. All bounds are expressed using cost variables for one-time overlay lookup overhead (L, t_L), replicated cell operations (R, t_R), and simple remote calls (S, t_S).

Concurrency control scheme	(1) Single operation	(2a) k operations with same n items per step	(2b) k operations with n new items per step
#Network Operations			
Atomic Write	$L + R$	-	-
Pess. 2PL	$2L + 3R$	$(n+1)L + (1+(k+1)n)R$	$(1+kn)L + 1+(3k-1)n)R$
HOCC	$2L + 3R$	$(n+1)L + \frac{(k-1)nS}{+(1+2n)R}$	$(1+kn)L + 1+(3k-1)n)R$
HOCC w. conflicts	$2L + 4R$	$(n+1)L + \frac{2(k-1)nS}{+(1+3n)R}$	$(1+kn)L + 1+(5k-2)n)R$
Fast-Read	$L + R$	$nL + \quad +knR$	$knL + knR$
Latency			
Atomic Write	$t_L + t_R$	-	-
Pess.2PL	$t_L + 3t_R$	$t_L + (k+2)t_R$	$kt_L + (k+2)t_R$
HOCC	$t_L + 3t_R$	$t_L + \frac{(k-1)t_S}{+3t_R}$	$kt_L + (k+2)t_R$
HOCC w. conflicts	$t_L + 4t_R$	$t_L + \frac{2(k-1)t_S}{+4t_R}$	$kt_L + (2k+2)t_R$
Fast-Read	$t_L + t_R$	$t_L + kt_R$	$kt_L + kt_R$

The data operations on the different cells are combined with validate-and-prepare messages and executed as single replicated operations. The HOCC variants and pessimistic 2PL are committed using the distributed atomic commit protocol from Section 3.2.

The results are summarized in Table 2. We made the simplifying assumption, that cell nodes that have been selected for optimistic execution using HOCC do not leave their cell. Further we assume that no network failures occur and that all data items and the commit record are stored on different cells and that this assignment does not change, i.e. the overlay's topology is static during transaction execution.

As can be seen in Table 2, HOCC reduces the number of necessary replicated operations for consecutive operations on the same item, hence it is well suited for typical read-and-update transactions like WikiWrite. For $k = 1$, $n = 1$, ACID is already provided by using a replicated state machine and no distributed atomic commit is necessary. For $k > 1$ and operations over pairwise disjoint item sets (case 2b), HOCC needs the same amount of replicated operations as pessimistic 2PL.

Fast-Read transactions use more replicated operations but save the distributed atomic commit costs of HOCC. Therefore, they are well-suited for quick, parallel read functions like WikiRead. However, multi-step read-only transactions are better off by choosing HOCC if the performance gained by optimism outweighs the overhead of distributed atomic commit.

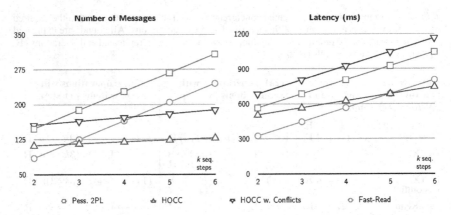

Figure 3. Effect of the different concurrency control schemes on the required number of messages and latency of k-step transactions over $n = 2$ initially fixed items. We assume that **S** needs 2, **L** 3, and **R** 20 messages and use $t_S = 60\,ms$, $t_L = 90\,ms$, $t_R = 120\,ms$ as latency bounds. With 5 nodes per cell, the transaction involves $N = 15$ physical nodes (one extra cell for the commit record, client is part of that cell).

Figure 3 illustrates k-step transactions over a set of $n = 2$ initially fixed data items (case 2a) using parameters chosen from practical experience. It can be seen that HOCC outperforms pessimistic 2PL in general and has only a slightly higher latency in the presence of conflicts/revalidation. At the same time, HOCC provides support for long-running transactions where pessimistic 2PL has to abort transactions upon deadlock detection. As discussed earlier, fast-read transactions outperform the other schemes for $k < 5$ in both cases 2a and 2b because they do not need to execute distributed atomic commit.

6.   Related Work

There has been extensive research on distributed hash tables and structured overlay networks. However, there is comparatively little work on extending such systems with support for transaction processing. New approaches to transaction handling for other kinds of distributed systems, like Grid computing [23] and mobile agents [6], try to eliminate the need for the centralized coordination of transaction participants.

For structured overlays, a transaction processing scheme based on 2PL is described by Mesaros et al. [11] that resolves lock conflicts by giving older transactions higher priority and forcing the loosing transaction into the 2PL shrinking phase. Transactions are committed by forming a dynamic multicast group that consists of all participating nodes.

OceanStore [17] implements multiversioning-based replication using a two-tier architecture. On the first layer, a primary ring stores a small set of replicas. On the second layer, additional replicas of object versions are cached. All replicas are located using the Tapestry overlay network. Atomic updates on the primary ring are serialized and performed by executing a Byzantine agreement protocol.

Muthitacharoen et al. [14] describe Etna, a system for executing atomic read and write operations in a Chord-like overlay network. Operations are serialized using a primary copy and replicated over k successors using a consensus algorithm.

Both articles do not describe how full transaction processing can be built on top of atomic operations. For OceanStore, multiversioning [16] is proposed [17]. The caching tier is used to keep the inherent cost of atomic updates small–at the price of reduced consistency.

Another approach for implementing Wikis is BubbleStorm [21] which supports rich queries over all documents stored in the overlay. However, BubbleStorm lacks means for implementing consistent reverse navigational indices.

Distributed atomic commit has also been solved for overlays using a non-blocking approach based on Paxos [13]. Contrary to our solution, the algorithm works over the complete set of all replicas of all accessed items and fixes this set at commit time. Availability is achieved by using symmetric replication [3].

Instead of using state machine replication inside cells, Reed-Solomon codes or similar encoding schemes could be used (as proposed Litwin et al. [10]) to ensure proper availability.

7.   Summary

We presented and evaluated a distributed transaction processing scheme that supports relational schemas on top of structured overlay networks. We identified lookup inconsistency caused by node unreliability and message asynchronism as the core obstacle for implementing the ACID properties. As a remedy, we introduced cells made of multiple (unreliable) nodes that together constitute a replicated state machine. We used this cell model as the basis for overlay transaction processing.

For best performance, the application can choose from different concurrency control schemes: Hybrid optimistic concurrency control, for example, for long running transactions, atomic cell-write for simple updates, or fast-read transactions for read-only access. Moreover, all of these control schemes may be concurrently used in the same overlay network.

We applied our approach to a distributed Wiki and presented algorithms for writing and reading replicated Wiki pages.

References

[1] D. Agrawal, A.J. Bernstein, P. Gupta, and S. Soumitra. Distributed optimistic concurrency control with reduced rollback. In: *Distributed Computing* (2), pages 45–59, 1987.

[2] A. Andrzejak and Z. Xu, Scalable, Efficient Range Queries for Grid Information Systems. In: *2nd IEEE International Conference on Peer-to-Peer Computing (P2P2002)*, pages 5–7, Sweden, Sep. 2002

[3] A. Ghodsi. Distributed k-Ary System: Algorithms for Distributed Hash Tables. PhD thesis, KTH Stockholm, Stockholm, 2006.

[4] J. Gray. The Transaction Concept: Virtues and Limitations. In: *Proceedings of the 7th International Conference on Very Large Databases*, pages 144–154, 1981.

[5] R.E. Gruber. Optimistic Concurrency Control for Nested Distributed Transactions. *Technical Report MIT-LCS/TR-453*, Laboratory of Computer Science, Massachusetts Institute of Technology, Jun. 1989.

[6] K. Haller, H. Schuldt, and H.J. Scheck. Transactional Peer-to-Peer Information Processing: The AMOR Approach. In: *Mobile Data Management: 4th Intl. Conf. (LNCS 2574)*, pages 356–362, Springer, 2003.

[7] S.E. Johnson. Consistent lookup during Churn in Distributed Hash Tables. Master thesis, Norwegian University of Science and Technology, Trondheim, Sep. 2005.

[8] L. Lamport. Fast Paxos. *Technical Report MSR-TR-2005-112*, Microsoft Research, 2nd edition, Jan. 2006.

[9] J. Li, J. Stribling, T. M. Gil, R. Morris, and M.F. Kaashoek. Comparing the performance of distributed hash tables under churn. In: *IPTPS 2004*, Feb. 2004.

[10] W. Litwin and T.W. Schwarz. LH*RS: a high-availability scalable distributed data structure using Reed Solomon Codes. In: *SIGMOD '00: Proceedings of the 2000 ACM SIGMOD Intl. Conf. on Management of data, ACM Press*, pages 237–248, 2000.

[11] V. Mesaros, R. Collet, K. Glynn, and P. van Roy. A Transactional System for Structured Overlay Networks. *Technical Report RR2005-01*, Department of Computing Science and Engineering, Universite catholique de Louvain, Mar. 2005.

[12] C. Mohan, H. Pirahesh, and R. Lorie. Efficient and flexible methods for transient versioning of record to avoid locking by read-only transactions. In: *SIGMOD '92: Proceedings of the 1992 ACM SIGMOD International Conference on Management of Data.*, pages 124–133, 1992.

[13] M. Moser and S. Haridi. Atomic Commitment in Transactional DHTs. In: *First CoreGRID European Network of Excellence Symposium*, Aug. 2007.

[14] A. Muthitacharoen, S. Gilbert, and R. Morris. Etna: A Fault-tolerant Algorithm for Atomic Mutable DHT Data. *Technical Report MIT-CSAIL-TR-2005-044*, Computer Science and Artificial Intelligence Laboratory, Massachusetts Institute of Technology, 2005.

[15] S. Plantikow, A. Reinefeld, and F. Schintke. Transactions for Distributed Wikis on Structured Overlays. In: *8th IFIP/IEEE Distributed Systems: Operations and Management (DSOM 2007)*, Oct. 2007.

[16] D. Reed. Naming and Synchronization in a Decentralized Computer System. PhD thesis, Published as: *Technical Report MIT-LCS/TR-205.*, Laboratory of Computer Science, Massachusetts Institute of Technology, Sep. 1978.

[17] S. Rhea, P. Eaton, P. Geels, D. Weatherspoon, H. Zhao, and J.B. Kubiatowicz. Pond: The OceanStore Prototype. In: *Proceedings of the 2nd USENIX Conf. on File and Storage Technologies*, pages 1–14, 2003.

[18] A. Schiper. Dynamic group communication. In: *Distributed Computing* 18 (5), pages 359–374, 2006.

[19] F.B. Schneider. The State Machine Approach: A Tutorial. *Technical Report TR-86-800*, Department of Computer Science, Cornell University, 1986.

[20] T. Schütt, F. Schintke, and A. Reinefeld. A Structured Overlay for Multi-dimensional Range Queries. *Euro-Par 2007 Parallel Processing*, pages 503–513, Aug. 2007.

[21] W.W. Terpstra, J. Kangasharju, C. Leng, and A.P. Buchmann. BubbleStorm: Resilient, Probabilistic, and Exhaustive Peer-to-Peer Search. *SIGCOMM'07*, pages 49–60, Aug. 2007.

[22] A. Thomasian. Distributed Optimistic Concurrency Control Methods for High-Performance Transaction Processing. In: *IEEE Transactions on Knowledge and Data Engineering* 10 (1), pages 173–189, Feb. 1998.

[23] C. Türker, K. Haller, C. Schuler, and H.J. Scheck. How can we support Grid Transactions? Towards Peer-to-Peer Transaction Processing. In: *Proceedings of the 2005 CIDR Conference*, pages 174–185, 2005.

[24] G. Urdaneta, G. Pierre, and M. van Steen. A Decentralized Wiki Engine for Collaborative Wikipedia Hosting. In: *Proceedings of the 3rd International Conference on Web Information Systems and Technologies*, Mar. 2007.

A HIGHER-ORDER COMPONENT FOR EFFICIENT GENOME PROCESSING IN THE GRID

Philipp Ludeking, Jan Dunnweber and Sergei Gorlatch
University of Munster, Department of Mathematics and Computer Science
Munster, Germany
{duennweb|luedeking|gorlatch}@uni-muenster.de

Abstract   Computational grids combine computers in the Internet for distributed data processing and are an attractive platform for the data-intensive applications of bioinformatics. We present an extensible genome processing software for the grid and evaluate its performance. Our software was able to discover previously unknown circular permutations (CP) in the ProDom database containing more than 70 MB of protein data. A specific feature of our software is its design as a component: the Alignment HOC, a Higher-Order Component that makes use of the latest Globus toolkit as grid middleware. Besides genome data, the Alignment HOC accepts plugin code for processing this data as its input, and contains all the required configuration to run the component on top of Globus, thus, freeing the non-grid-expert user from dealing with grid middleware. Instead of writing data distribution procedures and configuring the middleware appropriately for every new algorithm, Alignment HOC users reuse the existing component and only write application-specific plugins. To maintain plugins persistently in a reusable manner, we built a web-accessible plugin database with a comfortable administration GUI. The flexible component-based implementation makes it easy to study CPs in other databases (e.g. UniProt/Swiss-Prot) or to use an alignment algorithm different than the standard Needleman-Wunsch. For the efficient distribution of workload, we developed a library of group communication operations for HOCs.

Keywords: higher-order components, genome processing, sequence alignment, middleware

1.   Introduction

Genome processing algorithms which are used for sequence alignment or protein structure prediction typically compute one or more result matrices and have the time complexity of $O(n^2)$ or higher for sequence length n [12, 16]. The recently developed hashing-based alignment algorithms, e. g., SSAHA [13], offer better performance but these algorithms raster the sequences and applications that require full sensitivity still need to run one of the traditional algorithms despite of its complexity. Depending on algorithm and database, a genome analysis can take several months or even years of calculation time on a standard computer. A promising alternative platform are computational grids [7]. However, the proper use of grid technology requires a lot of technical knowledge, especially with respect to network communication, since a portable encoding is necessary for all data that is exchanged over the network. Porting genome processing software to a grid requires additional time and redundant re-implementations of the same software, distracting the programmer from developing new algorithms which are interesting for biologists.

In this work we present a component-based software for the efficient pairwise processing of huge genome sequences. The specific type of software component we developed is a Higher-Order Component (HOC) [8], called Alignment HOC, which is configured to run on the grid and accepts, besides genome data, executable code as parameters from the user over a remote connection. The purpose of these code parameters or plugins is to adapt the Alignment HOC to the user's application, i. e., different kinds of similarity detections can be performed by sending to the component different application-specific code parameters. The Alignment HOC encapsulates all the technical details of the processing in the grid (e.g. data transfer, data distribution) and allows its users to specify the application-specific operations by implementing a simple Java interface.

2.   Detection of circular permutations

Circular permuted protein sequences (CPs) occur in a number of protein families [17] and can be found in all large databases of protein data. Their linear order may be quite different but the 3-dimensional structure of their resulting protein and its biological functionality are often the same.

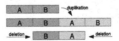

Figure 1.   Possible development of a circular permutation

In Fig. 1, A and B are arbitrary subsequences of a protein sequence. The figure shows an example of one possible development of circular permutations, by doubling the original sequence and inserting afterwards new start and end codons (tri-nucleotide codes that define begin and end of a gene expression [10]).

Such a circular permuted sequence consists of two parts from the original sequence, but in a different order [4].

The problem with circular permuted sequences is caused by the non-linear rearrangement of the amino acid order. Different from other mutations like insertions or deletions of single amino acids, a CP shifts the beginning of the sequence to the end. Standard alignment algorithms will not detect a significant similarity between the original and the circular permuted sequence (shown in Figure 2), although the tertiary structures (the 3-dimensional folding of the amino acid chain) of the resulting proteins may be nearly the same.

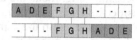

Figure 2.   Standard alignment of a circular permuted sequence

In order to find these similarities, the whole database must be processed by a sensitive algorithm, adjusted for the non-linear sequence rearrangement of CPs.

2.1   Implementation of the Genome Analysis Algorithm

CP detection is the locating of protein sequences, which are highly similar to each other after the circular permutation (see Sect. 2) has been made undone. We implemented two CP detection algorithms, one working on sequences of protein domains (domains are functional units in a protein consisting of up to several hundred amino acids), the other processing the underlying amino acid sequences. The domain variant of our implementation is similar to a hashing-based method, such as SSAHA [13], as both use highly shortened representations of the processed sequences (domain IDs instead of hash values, in our HOC).

Both CP detection algorithms have their advantages and disadvantages in different applications. Thus, we implemented both of them as code parameters for the Alignment HOC, i. e., our Alignment HOC can be used for processing either domain data or amino acid strings. The code parameters (which we provide in a Web-accessible database) contain the code for the input format-relevant operations. In different applications, users can interchange the code parameters by selecting via a Web service the one which is appropriate for processing their application input.

Our code parameters for the Alignment HOC perform the following three main steps:

(a). An optional preprocessing of the input sequences, e. g., for on the fly translation from DNA to amino acids or vice versa.

(b). Calculation of a scoring matrix wherein each element holds the result of a user-defined scoring function that rates differences between pairs of protein residues (i. e., elements of the genome code) and is applied to the two subsequences, delimited by the matrix elements' indices.

(c). The detection of traceback paths, i. e. paths following high values in the scoring matrix which start at the bottom and the right side of the matrix.

A standard global alignment of two similar sequences results in a scoring matrix with one main traceback path that always starts in the most bottom right element and runs almost diagonal through the whole scoring matrix. Typically, there are variations in the diagonal path, since the compared sequences have point mutations. Fig. 3, left shows a traceback running straight along the middle diagonal. Optionally, users can easily adapt the Alignment HOC to perform more specific kinds of preprocessing, alignment and traceback: each of the three steps above is performed inside the code parameters of the Alignment HOC, i. e., users can modify the alignment steps in the same way as they can choose between processing protein domains or amino acid strings via the selection of the code parameters required for the application.

Figure 3.   Standard alignment (left) and CP detection algorithm (right)

The right part of Fig. 3 shows what the Alignment HOC does in the traceback step when users select our non-default traceback code parameter which we implemented for CP detection. In case of a circular permutation between two compared sequences, the first part of each analyzed sequence is strongly similar to the last part of the other sequence. Instead of one main traceback path, an alignment between two circular permuted sequences has two traceback paths starting from two local maximum scores, one in the bottom row and the other one in the rightmost column of the scoring matrix. If such two maxima cannot be located, since there is almost no variation in the matrix, the sequences are not circular permutated.

Our traceback code parameter for detecting CPs tests the matrix with respect to the criterion *traceback paths run almost along shifted diagonals* as follows: we start from the two maxima, follow the high scores and count the number of quandrants passed on these paths. The test is positive, if there is no intersection (i. e., a common element) and both paths pass three quadrants.

To avoid false-positive detections of CPs, both compared sequences are doubled before the scoring matrix is calculated. Figure 4 shows how we use this extension to increase the sensitivity of the CP detection: we compare the lengths of the four line segments which the traceback paths mark by their intersections with the inner borders of the matrix quadrants. Only if the corresponding lengths (i. e., the segments of a single line, such as α and β on the inner vertical border in the figure) have nearly the same ratio, the CP test is considered to be positive. Doubling the sequence lengths obviously results in a matrix that is four times larger, but experiments justify the higher computation costs: tests [17] have

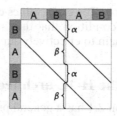

Figure 4. Detection with increased sensitivity

shown that without doubling the input more than half of the detected CPs are false-positive results.

We started the implementation of our traceback procedure for detecting CPs by porting the C program Raspodom [17] (which only works on protein domains) to Java. Our version of this CP detection algorithm is portable, as required for the grid, and we were able to decrease the requirements for main memory, as compared to Raspodom, by 60%. This optimization is realized by storing only the part of the alignment data that is necessary for CP detection in the main memory. Instead of working on both doubled sequences at the same time, our algorithm processes half the sequences separately and, thus, when a matrix quadrant is computed, only the relevant half of the input is loaded. Moreover, not all matrix elements are relevant in our application but rather only the matrix elements which are crucial for choosing the traceback directions; for each row of the matrix, we, therefore, only store the position of the maximum element.

Since there are only 20 different amino acids used in the protein biosynthesis, there are many equal scores, when aligning amino acid sequences (instead of domains). A high number of matches in a scoring matrix produces noise in the scoring matrix, i.e., variations in the distribution of high scores, which complicates the detection similarities.

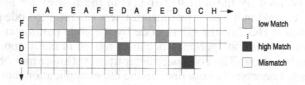

Figure 5. Reducing noise by using dynamic match values in the scoring matrix

Fig. 5 shows the method that we have developed to work around the described similarity noise problem by rating the matches. Whenever input elements match, a different value than the scoring function output is assigned to the corresponding matrix element, e.g., score 1 for a simple match, score 10 for a double match (i.e. matching elements plus a match in the upper left neighbor cell), score 20 for a triple match and score 50 for four successive matches on the main diagonal. Thus, our rating counts neighboring matches for rating the degree of a match. The exact values chosen for the rating schema are arbitrary, except for the condition that they range approximately within the scoring function's codomain to effectively suppress low similarities in the aligned sequences.

2.2   Advantages of the HOC architecture

The algorithm from Section 2.1 has a general processing structure but three application-dependent steps. Thus Higher-Order Components (HOCs) are the ideal technology for porting this algorithm to the grid.

The schema of the Alignment HOC is depicted in Fig. 6: The client runs an application that uses the Alignment HOC which computes the alignment on the remote High-Performance Computers (HPC) with code parameters (e. g., the CP-detection traceback) sent by the client.

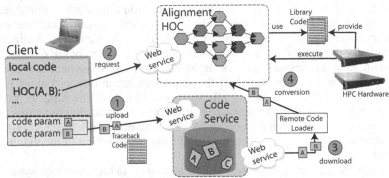

Figure 6.   Communication between Client, Code Service and Alignment HOC

In the upload step (1), the application code is intermediately stored in the Code Service, a Web service connected to a database (via OGSA-DAI [14]). Identifiers specified by the user ([A] and [B] in the figure) are linked to the uploaded code, making it a code parameter. Users can refer to code parameters of the Alignment HOC in the client code by the code parameter identifiers. Both HOCs and their code parameters can be reused in many applications in different combinations. The code parameter transfer (lower part of the client-side code) is not necessarily contained in the client application, but it is rather an administrative action. We developed a Web-based portal allowing to browse the Code Service and check if a code parameter with the functionality required for their application is available: if not, then a new code parameter can be developed and made publicly available using our portal. The transfer can of course also be handled with hand-written code, if a self-contained client should be developed that is independent from our portal.

The HOC(A,B)-call in step (2) is an ordinary Web service request that is served by the Alignment HOC (i. e., only the primitive identifiers are sent as parameters, not the code itself, as there is no standard representation of executable code as a Web service parameter). HOCs execute recurring communication patterns. The pattern in the Alignment HOC in Fig. 6 is called wavefront [6]: a varying number of parallel processes compute matrix elements during the alignment procedure. For transparently inserting code parameters into appropriate positions in the pattern implementation, the Alignment HOC performs two steps invisible to the application programmer: in the download step (3), the code that the identifiers refer to is transferred to the HPC hardware (which are multiple servers communicating via RMI for the Alignment HOC). The conversion step (4) is performed by the Remote Code Loader which is locally placed on each execution host and makes the downloaded code parameters executable there. This conversion is done by cast operations which assign the code parameters their proper types, i. e. the interface definitions for the user-defined initialization, the alignment and the traceback step.

2.3   Optimised group communication

To share the calculation data in the grid, we implemented efficient group communication procedures for distributed networked computers: a broadcast and a scatter operation. Our group communication procedures for the data distribution are based on *orthogonal communication patterns* [15], which have been proven to be a very efficient variant of implementing MPI-based collective operations on local clusters. We implemented the orthogonal patterns using Java and RMI, allowing to communicate efficiently on a grid platform.

Figure 7.   Different group communication structures

Figure 7 shows two examples of group communication for eight grid nodes (i. e., networked computers). On the left, it shows a linear group communication starting from node 'S0' to the nodes 'S1-S7', which leads to a bottleneck on the S0-link. The HOC communication operations avoid the bottleneck effect by continuously dividing the available nodes into a hierarchy of groups and subgroups until the deepest subgroups contain only two or less nodes. These groups can be graphically arranged in rows and columns, therefore, the name orthogonal communication. The right part of Figure 7 shows the communication paths used in the HOC-Broadcast in an example with eight nodes. The horizontal line represents the division in a top and a bottom group, each containing four nodes. Both groups contain two subgroups represented by dashed boxes.

During a group communication starting from the node S0, the message is first passed from the top group to one node in the bottom group (in the example in Fig.7 from S0 to S4). Inside each of these groups, the message is then sent to the subgroups (from S0 to S2 and from S4 to S6). These two send operations are executed simultaneously. In the third and final step, the message is shared inside each of the four subgroups. When the group-based communication structure of the HOC-Broadcast and HOC-Scatter is used, the number of sequentially communicating processes grows logarithmically instead of linearly with an increasing number of grid nodes.

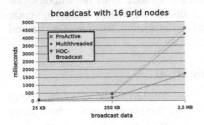
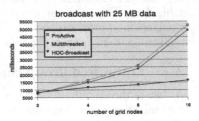

Figure 8.   Results of the HOC broadcast experiments

Commonly used grid programming libraries, e. g. , ProActive [2] offer group communication operations, similar to our HOC-Broadcast and HOC-Scatter operations. Contrary to our implementation, these libraries implement group communication following a linear structure which leads to decreasing performance with a growing number of communicated data and participating grid nodes. In the ProActive implementation, a broadcast or scatter operation does not only distribute data, but the data can be immediately processed: any method in a Java class can be declared a ProActive group operation, and Java reflection is used to execute the method on multiple hosts while supplying input either in broadcast or scatter mode [2]. This mechanism provides a convenient abstraction over network communication, helping the ProActive user to concentrate on the application-level operations instead of data distribution, but it leads to a certain overhead. To estimate the overhead of using reflection for running arbitrary user-defined methods on group-wise communicated data, we experimentally implemented another set of communication that follow a linear structure (like ProActive) but do not use reflection. To avoid I/O-delays, we use a thread pool and start multiple linear sending processes at once. Therefore, our experimental linear operations are called 'Multithreaded' in the diagrams in Fig. 8.

The left part of Figure 8 shows a test involving 16 grid nodes and a growing amount of data. The right part of the figure shows the same group communication, but with a fixed amount of data (25 MB) and a growing number of involved grid nodes. In both cases the advantage of our new HOC broadcast can be directly recognised from the diagram. Instead of exponentially growing communication times we achieved linear growth when increasing the number of involved grid nodes.

2.4   Detected CPs

Running our CP detection application (see Section 2) using the Alignment HOC (see Section 2.2) we scanned the protein database ProDom and found similarities that were not known previously [3].

ProDom Version	Raspodom	Alignment HOC
2003.1	36	129(40)
2004.1	93	850(192)

Table 1.   Number of detected CPs with different databases and algorithms

Table 1 shows the number of detected circular permutations by using our Alignment HOC and, in turn, Raspodom for two versions of the ProDom database.

The numbers in parentheses are those CPs where two ore more protein domains are involved in the sequence rearrangement. These results are particularly reliable true-positive detections, because larger parts of the sequence (at least two functional parts of the protein) are involved in the rearrangement, allowing to assure the presence of a CP.

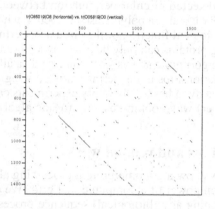

Figure 9.   CPs in microbacteria

Two of the newly detected CPs are shown as dot plots in Figure 9. In each dot plot, the two characteristic shifted diagonals (see Sect. 2.1) are observable (compare Figure 3). The new CP, shown in the dot plot on the left, compares the sequences *'Peptide synthetase MBTF'* (O05819) and *'FxbB'* (O85019). Both are parts of mycobacteria genomes, but only the function of *'FxbB'* is known in the Swiss-Prot database as part of an AMP binding enzyme family. The relationship between *'Peptide synthetase MBTF'* and *'FxbB'* of being circular permutations of each other leads to the hypothesis that *'Peptide synthetase MBTF'* is also part of the same AMP binding enzyme family with a similar function.

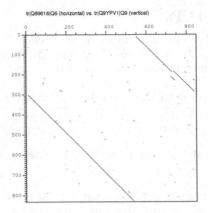

Figure 10.   Dot plot from Swiss-Prot

The dot plot in figure 10 compares the two nameless sequences Q69616 and Q9YPV1. Both are listed in the Swiss-Prot database as polymerases but only about Q9YPV1 there is the additional information that it is a DNA-polymerase. The detected circular permutation between the two sequences indicates that Q9YPV1 is also a polymerase interacting with DNA. The ultimate proof about the biological function of the circularly permuted sequences and their corresponding proteins can only be given by a laboratory experiment.

Our theoretical algorithmic analysis of sequence data allows the detection of such interesting relationships in the permanently growing databases. Based on the relationships and hypotheses, laboratory experiments can be done in a more precise (and cheaper) way, looking exactly for the algorithmically predicted functions.

3.   Conclusions and related work

This paper shows how a genome/protein processing algorithm can benefit from the calculation power of a computational grid. We developed a generic component for running any (biological) sequence processing application on multiple distributed high-performance computers.

The domain version of our implementation is similar to a hashing-based method, such as SSAHA [13], as both use highly shortened representations of the processed sequences (domain IDs instead of hash values, in our HOC). Some other projects are aim at using modern Grid technology (including Globus) for research in bioinformatics, e. g., the North Carolina BioGRID [1]and the GrADS-based implementation of sequence alignment [18]. The main difference of the HOC-based approach is that each part of the algorithm (the preprocessing, the traceback and the computation of the matrix itself, see Section 2.1) can be exchanged without affecting the complex infrastructure for running the distributed computations. The Alignment HOC can, thus, e. g., be used for protein structure prediction. The introduction of this new component to the

HOC-SA [5] is the main contribution in the field of component-based programming, while the new communication routines explained in Section 2.3 and the newly detected relationships between sequences in the ProDom and Swiss-Prot databases can be viewed as a useful coproduct. A quantitative comparison (in terms of detected CPs) with an earlier project (Raspodom [3]) was conducted in Section 2.4.

Our Alignment HOC is able to handle the pairwise processing of hundreds of megabytes of data (as present in total genome databases) by distributing the computations. The calculation power offered by the Alignment HOC makes it possible to keep up with the exponentially growing size of biological sequence databases when performing CP detection and other kinds of biological data analysis applications. The Alignment HOC is available as open-source software from the Globus Web site [5] (including a GUI and the new group communication library). It offers biologists new opportunities to easily develop and adapt the sequence processing in their applications to run on grids.

References

[1] M. Altunay, D. Colonnese, and C. Warade. High Throughput Web Services for Life Sciences. In *IT Coding and Computing*, pages 329–334, Washington, DC, USA, 2005. IEEE.

[2] Laurent Baduel, Françoise Baude, and Denis Caromel. Efficient, Flexible, and Typed Group Communications in Java. In *Java Grande Conference*, pages 28–36, Seattle, 2002. ACM Press.

[3] Bornberg-Bauer et al. Raspodom Results.
http://www.uni-muenster.de/Biologie.Botanik/ebb/projects/raspodom

[4] Janusz M. Bujnicki. Sequence Permutations in the Molecular Evolution of DNA methyltransferases. *BMC Evolutionary Biology*, 2:3, 2002.

[5] Jan Dünnweber and Catalin L. Dumitrescu et al. . The HOC-SA Globus Incubator Project. Web page: http://dev.globus.org/incubator/hoc-sa/, 2006.

[6] Jan Dünnweber, Sergei Gorlatch, Marco Aldinucci, Marco Danelutto, and Sonia Campa. Adaptable Parallel Components for Grid Programming. In *Integrated Research in GRID Computing*, pages 43–59. Springer Verlag, December 2006.

[7] Ian T. Foster. Globus Toolkit Version 4: Software for Service-Oriented Systems. In *NPC*, pages 2–13, 2005.

[8] Sergei Gorlatch and Jan Dünnweber. From Grid Middleware to Grid Applications: Bridging the Gap with HOCs. In *Future Generation Grids*, pages 299–306. Springer Verlag, 2005.

[9] O. Gotoh. An Improved Algorithm for Matching Biological Sequences. *J. Mol. Biol.*, 162:705–708, 1982.

[10] A. Jeltsch. Circular Permutations in the Molecular Evolution of DNA Methyltransferases. *J. Mol. Evol.*, 49:161âĂŞ164, 1999.

[11] Ahmed Moustafa. The JAligner Library for Biological Sequence Alignment, 2007. http://jaligner.sourceforge.net.

[12] S. B. Needleman and C. D. Wunsch. A General Method Applicable to Search for Similarities in the Amino Acid Sequences of two Proteins. *Journal of Molecular Biology*, 48:443–453, 1970.

[13] Zemin Ning, Anthony Cox, and James Mullikin. SSAHA: A Fast Search Method for Large DNA Databases. In *Genome Research 11*, pages 1725–1729, 2001.

[14] OGSA-DAI project team. The Open Grid Service Architecture - Data Access and Integration OGSA-DAI, 2007. http://www.ogsadai.org.uk.

[15] T. Rauber, R. Reilein-Ruı, and G. Runger. ORT - A Communication Library for Orthogonal Processor Groups. In *Proc. of the ACM/IEEE Supercomputing Conf. 2001 (SC'01)*, Denver, Colorado, USA, 2001. ACM.

[16] T. F. Smith and M. S. Waterman. Identification of Common Molecular Subsequences. *Journal of Molecular Biology*, 147:195–197, 1981.

[17] J. 3rd Weiner, G. Thomas, and E. Bornberg-Bauer. Rapid motif-based Prediction of Circular Permutations in multi-domain Proteins. *Bioinformatics*, 21:932 – 937, 2005.

[18] Asim YarKhan and Jack J. Dongarra. Biological Sequence Alignment on Computational Grids using the GrADS Framework. *Future Gener. Comput. Syst.*, 21(6):980–986, 2005.

VII

DESIGN METHODOLOGIES FOR GRID SYSTEMS

SZTAKI DESKTOP GRID:
BUILDING A SCALABLE, SECURE PLATFORM
FOR DESKTOP GRID COMPUTING

Attila Marosi, Gabor Gombas, Zoltan Balaton, Peter Kacsuk
{atisu, gombasg, balaton, kacsuk}@sztaki.hu
MTA SZTAKI
Computer and Automation Research Institute of the Hungarian Academy of Sciences
Budapest, Hungary

Tamas Kiss
kisst@wmin.ac.uk
Centre for Parallel Computing, University of Westminster,
London, UK

Abstract   In this paper we present a concept how separate desktop grids can be used as building blocks for larger scale grids by organizing them in a hierarchical tree. We describe an enhanced security model which satisfies the requirements of the hierarchical setup and is aimed for real-world deployment.

Keywords: desktop grid, heirarchical tree, security model

1.   Introduction

Contrary to traditional grid systems where the maintainers of the grid infrastructure provide resources where users of the infrastructure can run their applications, desktop grids provide the applications and the users of the desktop grid provide the resources.

The common architecture of desktop grids typically consists of one or more central servers and a large number of clients. The central server provides the applications and their input data. Clients join the desktop grid voluntarily, offering to download and run tasks of an application with a set of input data. When the task has finished, the client uploads the results to the server where the application assembles the final output from the results returned by clients.

A major advantage of desktop grids over traditional grid systems is that they are able to utilize non-dedicated machines. Besides, the requirements for providing resources to a desktop grid are very low compared to traditional grid systems using a complex middleware. Thus, a huge amount of resources can be gathered that were not available for traditional grid computing previously. Based on the environment where the desktop grid is deployed we can distinguish between two different desktop grid flavors.

Global Desktop Grids   Global Desktop Grids (also known as Public Desktop Grids or Public Resource Computing) consist of a server which is publicly accessible over the Internet, and the attached clients are offered by their owners to help out projects they sympathize with. There are several unique aspects of this computing model compared to traditional grid systems. First, clients may come and go at any time, and there is no guarantee that a client which started a computation will indeed finish it. Furthermore, the clients cannot be trusted to be free of either hardware or software defects or malicious intent, meaning the server can never be sure that an uploaded result is in fact correct. Therefore, redundancy is often used by giving the same piece of work to multiple clients and comparing the results to filter out corrupt ones.

Local Desktop Grids   Local Desktop Grids are to fill the gap between traditional grids and desktop grids. They are intended for institutional or industrial use, especially for businesses it is often not acceptable to send out application code and data to untrusted third parties (sometimes, such as for medical applications, this is even forbidden by law). Thus, in a Local Desktop Grid the project and clients are usually shielded from the world by firewalls or other means and only known and trusted clients are allowed to offer their resources. This environment gives more flexibility by allowing the clients to access local resources securely and since the resources are not voluntarily offered the performance may be limited but more predictable. However, new security requirements arise in Local Desktop Grids that require authentication of clients and servers and establishing trust between parties.

The rest of the paper is organized as follows. The next section discusses related work, section 3 introduces SZTAKI Desktop Grid and we describe our extension of BOINC to be able to support hierarchy. In section 4 we describe an enhanced BOINC security model. We present the future work in section 5. Then the conclusion section closes the paper.

2. Related work

Condor   Condor[1] is a complex cycle-scavenger platform which is originating from the Condor research project at the University of Wisconsin-Madison. Its approach is radically different from the DG model, while aiming for the same goal. First it uses the push model to submit jobs to the workers, while the DG model implies using the pull model, where always the clients request work for themselves. It does not use one of the wellknown ports (defined by RFC739) for communication, rather has it's own. Condor provides a complex matchmaking feature to pair jobs and resources. It trust it's own resources and the tasks are mapped to local user on the execute node. Scalability is limited by the centralized management implied by the push model. Largest experiments are at the level of 10000 jobs in EGEE[11] but it requires a very complicated Grid middleware infrastructure that is difficult to install and maintain at the desktop level.

Berkeley Open Infrastructure for Network Computing   BOINC[2] is originating form the SETI@home project, it aims to provide an open infrastructure for deploying large-scale scientific projects which are attractive to the public interest. BOINC is a general framework which can run many distributed applications and yet anyone can join easily by installing a client software. BOINC is the most popular DG system with more than 250000 participants and 475 TeraFLOPS.

XtremWeb   XtremWeb[4] is a research project, which, similarly to BOINC aims to serve as a substrate for Global Computing experiments. It supports the cenralized setup of servers and PCs as workers. In addition it can be used to build a peer-to-peer system with centralized control, where any worker node can become a client that submits jobs.

There are several commercial solutions available, the most wellknown being provided by United Devices and Entropia Inc.[3] . What they have in common is that they run in isolation, there is no adherence to grid standards or interoperability amongst them or with any grid middleware.

3. SZDG: A hierarchical BOINC-based DG system

As we can see there is a huge difference between traditional grids and desktop grids. We also have to make a distinction between the publicly used Global Desktop Grids and the Local Desktop Grid concept. The SZTAKI Local Desktop Grid[5] implements the latter. It is based on BOINC and is aimed to satisfy the needs of both academical institutions and enterprises (there is also a Global Desktop Grid version[9] running currently with more than

20000 registered users). What if there are several departments using their own resources independently and there is a project at a higher organizational level (e.g. at a campus or enterprise level)? Ideally, this project would be able to use free resources from all departments. However, using BOINC this would require individuals providing resources to manually register to the higher level project which is a high administrative overhead and it is against the centrally managed nature of IT infrastructure within an enterprise.

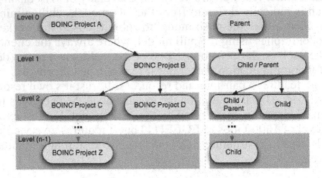

Figure 1.   Roles in the hierarchy

One of the enhancements of the SZTAKI Local Desktop Grid is hierarchy. It allows the use of desktop grid projects as building blocks for larger grids, for example divisions of a company or departments of a university can form a company or faculty wide desktop grid. The hierarchical desktop grid allows a set of projects to be connected to form a directed acyclic graph. Work is distributed among the edges of the directed graph. The projects are ordered into levels based on the distance between them and the top level.

Every project has a classical parent-child relationship with the others. A project may request work from a project above (*child*) or may provide work for a project below (*parent*). The hierarchical interaction is always between a parent and a child regardless of how many levels of hierarchy are above or below them. For a child every workunit regarded originating from it's parent regardless where it is originally from or from where was the input data for the workunit fetched (the data is not always from the parent). It is allowed for a project to have more children and parents. Figure 2 shows a three-level example.

The Hierarchy Client, which is based on the BOINC Core Client, is always running beside the child project. Thus at the top level there is no need for any modifications, it is just an ordinary BOINC project. Generally, a project acting as a parent does not have to be aware of the hierarchy, it only sees the child as one powerful client. The client reports to the parent a pre-configured number of processors, thus allowing to download the desired number of workunits. There can be limitations set on the server side to maximize the allowed number of workunits downloaded per client, so the only requirement for the parent side is to set these limits sufficiently high. It has two components (see Figure 2):

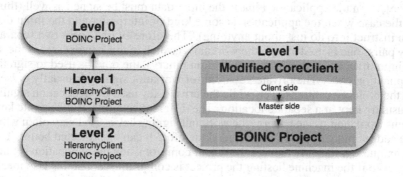

Figure 2.   The split architecture of the Hierarchy Client.

a master side which puts retrieved workunits in the database of the LDG and retrieves the completed results, and a client side which downloads workunits from the parent and uploads results.

Using a prototype with this functionality we were able to provide basic hierarchical functionality without any other modifications, but it had several drawbacks:

- the application binaries had to be deployed manually on each level.

- since workunits refer to an application by its name and version for execution, there is no guarantee that there won't be name collisions between new and already deployed applications when there are a large number of applications deployed in the hierarchy.

- work distribution is based on the local scheduling[7] method implemented in the BOINC Core Client which is not ideal in a hierarchical setup as it was not designed for this task.

4.   Extending BOINC for Use in Hierarchy

Although the hierarchy prototype presented in the previous section is very simple and was easy to implement, it had a major drawback: applications must be installed manually at every child level in order to be able to process workunits originating from the parent. Overcoming this limitation also requires replacing of the security model of BOINC.

The most important factor in desktop grid computing is the trust between the clients and the project providing the application. Allowing foreign code to run on a computer always has a risk of either accidental or intended misbehavior. BOINC mitigates this risk by only allowing to run code that has been digitally signed by the project the client is connected to. Clients trust the operators of the BOINC project not to offer malicious code, and digitally signing the application provides technical means to ensure this trust relation. Of course it is not enough to only sign the application binary, the input data must be signed as well (think of the case when the application is some kind of interpreter and the input data can instruct it to do just about anything).?Therefore BOINC uses two separate key pairs: one is used to sign the workunits (which in this context means the set of input files and a link to the application binary), the other is used to sign the application code. The private key used for workunit signing is usually present on the project's central server, while the private key used for application signing is usually kept at a separate location. The different handling of the private keys stems from their usage pattern: the workunit signing key is used very often while the code signing key is seldom needed therefore it can be protected better. This technique significantly reduces the risk of compromising the application signing key even if the machine hosting the project is compromised, but this also means that installing new applications is a manual process – which is unfortunate for a hierarchical setup. Therefore, solving the automatic application deployment issue presents two challenges:

- a lower-level project in a hierarchical desktop grid system must be able to automatically obtain an application's binary from its parent and be able to offer the application to its clients without manual intervention, and

- this process must not increase the risk of injecting untrusted applications into the system.

These requirements mean that a lower-level project can not simply re-sign the application it has obtained from the parent, since that would require the private key to be accessible on the machine hosting the lower-level project which in turn would significantly increase the risk of a key compromise if the machine hosting the project is compromised.

4.1   Extending the Security Model to Support Hierarchy

As discussed above the security model used by BOINC is not adequate in a hierarchical setup and a new model is needed. The model must provide enough information for the operator of the client machine (*User* from now on) to decide if a downloaded workunit should be trusted to run on the client machine or not, independent from where in the hierarchy the workunit is originated from. The model must provide enough information for the following decision scenarios:

(a). The *User* wants to trust any workunits of applications installed locally on the BOINC project she is directly connected to (i.e., the *User* trusts the project itself). This is the original trust model of BOINC.

(b). The *User* wants to trust any workunits from a given project, regardless of how many levels of hierarchy did the workunit travel through. This is in fact a generalization of the previous requirement.

(c). The *User* wants to trust a specific application regardless of where in the hierarchy it is hosted and regardless of what other applications does the hosting project offer.

The $t(\langle subject \rangle, \langle object \rangle)$ trust relation for a workunit can be broken down to three parts:

- trusting the application code: $t(User, App)$,

- trusting the set of input files: $t(User, Input)$, and

- trusting the link between the application, its inputs and the desired location of its outputs to prevent the application from processing data that was meant for an other application: $t(User, \langle App, Input, Output \rangle)$. We will use the shorthand $WUDesc$ for the $\langle App, Input, Output \rangle$ triplet.

A workunit WU is trusted if all components are trusted: $t(User, App) \wedge t(User, Input) \wedge t(User, WUDesc) \rightarrow t(User, WU)$.

The trust relation is realized by digital signature verification. Therefore, each of the three classes of objects App, $Input$ and $WUDesc$ are accompanied by one or more digital signatures $Sig_X : X \in \{App, Input, WUDesc\}$, and it is assumed that $User$ has a set of trusted identities marked $TrustedID_{User}$. Thus the trust relation becomes $t(User, X) \Leftrightarrow \exists s \in Sig_X :$ $verify\text{-}sig(X, s) \wedge subject\text{-}of(s) \in TrustedID_{User}$, where the $subject\text{-}of(s)$ function provides the identity that created the signature s. We also allow special $Any_X : X \in \{App, Input, WUDesc\}$ elements which satisfy the $\forall s : verify\text{-}sig(Any_X, s) = TRUE$. $Any_X \in TrustedID_X$ means that the user does not require a valid signature for that particular component.

We decided to use the X.509 Public Key Infrastructure, since it is a widely accepted and used infrastructure that provides all the technical elements we need. Therefore, the $TrustedID_{User}$ set becomes a list of X.509 certificates.

We define 3 entities responsible for signing various components of the system. The Application Developer ($AppDev$ from now on) can sign application code. This kind of signature testifies that the application binary comes from a known source and does not contain malicious code. The Project is the administrative body of the BOINC project and it may also sign application code testifying that said application is in fact part of the project. The $Server$ is the machine where the project is hosted, and it signs input files and workunit descriptors. Using the original BOINC terms the $AppDev$ provides the code-signing key, while the $Server$ provides the workunit-signing key.

The $TrustedID_{User}$ list of trusted certificates must be determined by the user, since the trust is ultimately a human relation. This may be simplified by the $Project$ by providing a list of $Server$ and optionally $AppDev$ certificates it trusts – this means the user can delegate the trust to the $Project$. This realizes the first scenario described in 4.1. The second scenario is realized if the $Project$ also provides the aggregated list of certificates from all levels above it in the hierarchy. The third scenario is realized if the user lists only the certificate of the appropriate $AppDev$ and specifies that she does not care about the signature of $Input$ or $WUDesc$.

4.2   Extending the Security Model for Industrial Needs

The previous section described a model how a user can trust work received from a hierarchical desktop grid system. In an industrial environment however more is needed: it is not enough for the user to trust the workunit, but the project must also trust the user before it gives out possibly confidential information. Also it is not enough just to trust the receiving user, but the data also has to be protected from being disclosed to untrusted parties. This is a new requirement that is not present in public projects.

Protecting the confidentiality of the data can be easily achieved. BOINC by default uses plain HTTP protocol for communication, but it also supports the HTTPS protocol where the communication is encrypted. The *Server* certificate can be used with the HTTPS protocol to ensure that the *User* in fact talks to the server she thinks is talking to. Although BOINC uses a simple shared-secret based authentication scheme to identify users, this authentication applies only to interactions with the scheduler. Together with the use of HTTPS this may be adequate to prevent unauthorized users from uploading results, but it does not prevent unauthorized users to download application code and input data if they are able to guess the file name used on the server.

The protection of input data from unauthorized download can be achieved by giving every user a certificate. The *Project* can act as a Certificate Authority and can sign the certificates of all authorized users. Then, the web server that is used for downloading the input files can be configured to only allow downloading if the client authenticated itself with a properly signed certificate. The workunits are always signed by the server running a specific project, so the projects need a way to make their known and accepted signing certificates available for their clients and other projects. This is solved by an extension to the web based interface of the BOINC project allowing to query for the certificates via the HTTP(S) protocol and depending on the trust model described in 4.1. Although it is a simple extension on the server side the BOINC Core Client needs modifications.

4.3   Automatic Application Deployment

BOINC allows the creation of a workunit that refers to external servers for the input files. This means that lower-level projects in a hierarchy do not need to install the input files locally, they may just refer to the original location of the files in the workunit description. However due to security considerations BOINC does not allow to refer to outside of the project for application binaries, they must always reside on the project's server. Thus, lower-level (child) projects must deploy all applications whose workunits they offer locally.

The automatic deployment of applications presents two problems. The first problem arises from the need to properly sign the binary and is solved by the introduction of the *AppDev* role as described in the previous section. If the users have configured their *TrustedID* $_{User}$ sets to contain the appropriate certificate of the *AppDev*, then the project does not need to sign the application binary, thus its secret key is not needed for application deployment.

The second problem arises from the fact that BOINC uses the $\langle AppName,\ Version \rangle$ tuple to identify applications and in a complex hierarchy it is possible that at different levels different applications are installed under the same name. This problem can be solved by automatically renaming the application when a workunit is transferred from a parent to lower level child project. Using an Universally Unique Identifier (UUID) as the new application name ensures that there will be no name collisions.

For the following we assume that the application consists of just a single binary. Compound applications or applications with accompanying shared libraries are not considered in this paper. The Hierarchy Client keeps track of the name mapping of the application between parent projects and child project. Such a renaming is possible because on the sever side only the workunit-generating master application cares about the name of the application, and in this case this master application is the link between the members of the hierarchy and therefore has full control. Additionally, the following requirements have to be met for the application registration in a Hierarchical Desktop Grid:

- The registration method should be consistent with the original registration method, allowing already deployed projects to be added to a hierarchy without any modification and any project to leave the hierarchy anytime.

- Different versions of the same application should be allowed to run in parallel, since each parent may run different version of the same application.

- Since each application instance is tied to a platform, the application name should be the same for all platforms, allowing any child to query for the different platform instances of the application.

- Instances of the same application originating from different parents should be treated as different ones, to ensure that results are reported to the appropriate parent.

The details of the flow of the application deployment and work distribution are described in [6] .

It is ensured that applications can still be installed manually as in a regular BOINC project and that will not cause inconsistency between the configuration files of the project, the database of the project and the Hierarchy Client. There is one significant difference though: an automatically deployed application is not signed using the code-signing key of BOINC, instead the signature retrieved by the Hierarchy Client is used. This requires that the Core Client requesting work is able to retrieve the certificates (depending on the trust scenario described in 4.1) from the given project, and is able to validate signatures using the certificates.

5.   Future Work

Our enhancements improve BOINC in many ways, but there are several limitations we are aware of. In this section we discuss what we think are the most crucial challenges.

Sandboxing   Another aspect of security that we did not mention yet is isolating the application from the rest of the computer it is running on. The BOINC Core Client simply *fork*s a new process for each application it is executing, meaning that the application process has access to the same resources as the Core Client itself. In an industrial environment sometimes the data on the computer (confidential information) is needed to be shielded off from the application code run by the client. To achieve this the Core Client may be run as a restricted user which also restrict the processes created by it, but in industrial environments the platform used is often Windows and it is sometimes not enough to only rely on the operating system facilities to ensure isolation from the rest of the system. In a UNIX environment the sandboxing can be easily achieved, since there are several tools like XEN [8] or *chroot* available. According to our present knowledge there are no similar mechanisms for widely used versions of Windows (2000, 2003 or XP) available. A possible solution would be using virtualization technologies available for all platforms like VMware, VirtualBox or QEMU [10].

We propose that instead the simple *fork* mechanism a lightweight virtual machine with a minimalist Linux image should be started with a virtual machine monitor like QEMU. This would properly isolate the application from the rest of the computer of the User. Also because the virtual machine runs Linux independent of the operating system on the Users computer this way only a version of the application for the Linux platform would be required that simplifies application development and deployment.

Scheduling   The Hierarchy Client currently uses the scheduling method in the BOINC Core Client, which is intended for clients requesting work for themselves, not for hierarchical work distribution. Currently we are adjusting the number of processors reported by the client to adjust the number of requested workunits. Another problem comes from the fact that BOINC assigns a deadline to each downloaded workunit to prohibit workunit-hijacking by users. The deadline is set when the workunit is downloaded and after it passes, the workunit is considered invalid and resent to another client. The deadline is the sum of the time of download and a delay bound value. Since each level of hierarchy is recreating workunits from those it got from its parent for distribution, the deadline of the original workunit at the top level is not propagated. Thus the lower level projects have no information if their workunits will be invalidated on a higher level because the deadline has already passed. A solution would be to make the workunits carry the original deadline with them via their descriptors as they traverse the hierarchy. This would allow to give the lower level projects some idea how to set the delay bound value of their workunits upon registration.In a hierarchy there is the problem of requesting the exact amount of work.

If requesting too much, the clients (that may be Core or Hierarchy Clients) won't be able to upload them before the deadline passes, if too little, some of the clients are left without work. We are working on developing scheduling strategies specific for the Hierarchical Desktop Grid.

6. Conclusion

In this paper we demonstrated how can stand-alone desktop grid installations be combined to form a large-scale grid system. We described our extensions for the security model that allows SZTAKI Desktop Grid to fulfill the additional security requirements that follow from the hierarchical setup and those required by industrial use cases.

7. Acknowledgments

The research and development published in this paper is partly supported by the Hungarian Government under grant NKFP2-00007/2005 and by the European Commission under contract number IST-2002-004265 (CoreGRID).

References

[1] Douglas Thain and Todd Tannenbaum and Miron Livny: *Distributed computing in practice: the Condor experience.*, In Journal of Concurrency - Practice and Experience, Volume 17, number 2-4, Pages 323-356, 2005

[2] David P. Anderson: *BOINC: A System for Public-Resource Computing and Storage.* In proceedings of the Fifth IEEE/ACM International Workshop on Grid Computing, Pages 4-10., 2004.

[3] Andrew A. Chien: *Architecture of a commercial enterprise desktop Grid: the Entropia system*, In Grid Computing: Making the Global Infrastructure a Reality, Chapter 12, Pages 337-350, 2003

[4] Franck Cappello, Samir Djilali, Gilles Fedak, Thomas Herault, Frederic Magniette, Vincent Neri, Oleg Lodygensky: *Computing on large-scale distributed systems: XtremWeb architecture, programming models, security, tests and convergence with grid*, Future Generation Computer Systems, Volume 21/3, Pages 417-437, 2005

[5] Zoltan Balaton, Gabor Gombas, Peter Kacsuk, Adam Kornafeld, Attila Csaba Marosi, Gabor Vida, Norbert Podhorszki, Tamas Kiss: *SZTAKI Desktop Grid: a Modular and Scalable Way of Building Large Computing Grids*, Parallel and Distributed Processing Symposium, 2007. IPDPS 2007. IEEE International 26-30 March 2007

[6] Attila Csaba Marosi, Gabor Gombas, Zoltan Balaton, Peter Kacsuk, Tamas Kiss: *SZTAKI Desktop Grid: Building a scalable, secure platform for Deskop Grid Computing*, CoreGRID technical report TR-100, Institute on Architectural Issues: Scalability, Dependability, Adaptability (WP4)

[7] David P. Anderson, John McLeod VII.:*Local Scheduling for Volunteer Computing*, Workshop on Large-Scale, Volatile Desktop Grids (PCGrid 2007), 2007

[8] P. Barham, B. Dragovic, K. Fraser, S. Hand, T. Harris, A. Ho, R. Neugebauer, I. Pratt, A. Warfield: *Xen and the Art of Virtualization.* In Proceedings of the 19th ACM SOSP, pages 164-177, October 2003.

[9] SZTAKI Desktop Grid Public Project. http://szdg.lpds.sztaki.hu/szdg/.

[10] Fabrice Bellard: *QEMU, a fast and portable dynamic translator*, ATEC'05: Proceedings of the USENIX Annual Technical Conference 2005 on USENIX Annual Technical Conference, 2005

[11] EGEE Enabling Grids for E-SciencE. http://www.eu-egee.org.

PEER-TO-PEER TECHNIQUES FOR DATA DISTRIBUTION IN DESKTOP GRID COMPUTING PLATFORMS

Fernando Costa, Luis Silva
CISUC, Dep Eng Informatica,
University of Coimbra,
Portugal
flcosta@student.dei.uc.pt
luis@dei.uc.pt

Ian Kelley, Ian Taylor
School of Computer Science,
Cardiff University,
United Kingdom
and
Center for Computation & Technology
Louisiana State University,
United States
I.R.Kelley@cs.cardiff.ac.uk
Ian.J.Taylor@cs.cardiff.ac.uk

Abstract   In this paper, we discuss how Peer-to-Peer data distribution techniques can be adapted to Desktop Grid computing environments, particularly to the BOINC platform. To date, Desktop Grid systems have focused primarily on utilizing spare CPU cycles, yet have neglected to take advantage of client network capabilities. Leveraging client bandwidth will not only benefit current projects by lowering their overheads but also will facilitate Desktop Grid adoption by data-heavy applications. We propose two approaches to Peer-to-Peer data sharing that could be adapted for volunteer computing platforms: the highly successful BitTorrent protocol and a secure and customizable Peer-to-Peer data center approach.

Keywords: peer-to-peer, P2P, BitTorrent, P2P-ADICS, P2PS, BOINC

1.   Introduction

Desktop Grids have been extremely successful in bringing large numbers of donated computing systems together to form computing communities with vast resource pools. These types of systems are well suited to perform highly parallel computations that do not require any interaction between network participants. Currently, the most successful Desktop Grid systems are volunteer computing platforms such as the Berkeley Open Infrastructure for Network Computing (BOINC), which rely on donated computer cycles from ordinary citizen communities. BOINC is currently being successfully used by many projects to analyze data, and with a supportive user community, can provide compute power to rival that of the world's supercomputers. In the current implementation of these systems, network topology is restricted to a strict master/worker scheme, generally with a fixed set of centrally managed project computers distributing and retrieving results from network participants. The potentially large user communities that become involved in volunteer computing initiatives can easily result in large network requirements for host projects, forcing them to upgrade their computer hardware and network availability as their projects rise in popularity.

These centralized data architectures currently employed by BOINC and other Desktop Grid systems can be a potential bottleneck when tasks share large input files or the central server has limited bandwidth. With new data management technologies, Desktop Grid users will be able to explore new types of data-intensive application scenarios, i.e., ones that are currently overly prohibitive given their large data transfer needs. This lack of a robust data solution often discourages application developers from embracing a Desktop Grid environment, or forces users to scale back their applications to problems that do not rely upon large data sets. There are many applications that, given more robust data capabilities, could either expand their current problem scope or migrate to a Desktop Grid environment.

Peer-to-Peer (P2P) data sharing techniques can be used to introduce a new kind of data distribution system for volunteer and Desktop Grid projects – one that takes advantage of client-side network capabilities. This functionality could be implemented in a variety of forms, ranging from BitTorrent-style networks where all participants share equally, to more constrained and customizable unstructured P2P networks where certain groups are in charge of data distribution and discovery. These approaches, although similar in nature, each have their own distinct advantages and disadvantages, especially when considered in relation to a scientific research community utilizing volunteer resources. In this paper, we make the argument for P2P data distribution, discuss the relative advantages and disadvantages of these two approaches, and explore how they could be applied to the Desktop Grid community, with particular emphasis on BOINC.

The paper is organized as follows: section 2 gives background on the technologies involved; section 4 introduces related work; section 4 discusses how P2P technologies could be applied to Desktop Grid systems such as BOINC; section 5 introduces how the BitTorrent protocol could be used in this facility; section 6 presents a more complex data center approach; and, section 5 concludes.

2.   Background

To begin the discussion on how P2P technologies can be integrated into Desktop Grids, specifically BOINC, it is advantageous to first give a brief overview of the software technologies involved. Naturally, there are many [3] [14][21] Peer-to-Peer technologies available and several different systems that can be classified as Desktop Grids [1][6][11][15]. However, for the purposes of this paper, we limit our scope to exploring how the very popular BitTorrent protocol as well as another in-development secure data center approach can both be applied to the most widespread "volunteer computing" Desktop Grid platform, the Berkeley Open Infrastructure for Network Computing (BOINC).

The Berkeley Open Infrastructure for Network Computing (BOINC) [1][4] is a software platform for distributed computation using otherwise idle cycles from volunteered computing resources. BOINC's use is widespread, with many different and varying projects employing the core infrastructure to distribute their data processing jobs. The diverse scientific domains utilizing BOINC range from gravitational wave analysis, to protein folding, to the search for extraterrestrial life [22]. Although these projects are diverse in their scientific nature, each one has something in common with the others: they have work units that can easily be distributed to run autonomously in a highly distributed and volatile environment. To achieve this task, each project must not only prepare its data and executable code to work with the BOINC libraries and client/server infrastructure, but they must also setup and maintain their own individual servers and databases to manage the project's data distribution and result aggregation. BOINC has been highly successful, and to date, over 5 million participants have joined various BOINC projects, giving an overall computing power equivalent to 450 TeraFlops [2].

BitTorrent [7] is a popular file distribution protocol based on a P2P paradigm. However, unlike other well-known P2P applications such as Gnutella or KaZaA, which incorporate peer and file discovery algorithms, BitTorrent's focus is more on optimising the distribution of files by enabling multiple download sources through the use of file partitioning, tracking and file swarming techniques. The main idea of BitTorrent is the collaboration between users accessing the same file by sharing chunks of the file with each other. To obtain information about the file to download, a peer must download a corresponding .torrent file. This file contains the file's length, name and hashing information, and the url of a tracker, which keeps a global registry of all the peers sharing the file. Trackers help peers establish connections between themselves by responding to a user's file request with a partial list of the peers having parts, or chunks of the file. A tracker does not participate in the actual file distribution; each peer decides locally which data to download based on data collected from its neighbors. Therefore, each peer is responsible for maximizing its own download rate. Peers do this by downloading from whomever they can and deciding which peers to upload to via a variant of tit-for-tat policy to prevent parasitic behavior.

The Peer-to-Peer Architecture for Data-Intensive Cycle Sharing (P2P-ADICS) [16] is a research and development project at Cardiff University, working to build a multi-purpose and adaptable super-peer architecture for data caching that can be used by scientific applications to distribute large data files and large data sets in Desktop Grid environments. P2P-ADICS's is being designed with the scientific user in mind, taking into account such issues as customizable network membership and data security policies, as well as the more traditional scalability challenges. For its low-level network building layer, P2P-ADICS is currently relying on a software package entitled "Peer-to-Peer Simplified," or P2PS [19], which is also being developed by the same group. Although P2PS is a light-weight system for building decentralized Peer-to-Peer networks, and is similar in nature to JXTA, it is more focused on the fundamental network building tools and provides much simpler mechanisms for advertisement queries and service discovery. P2PS can be used by a variety of applications to construct P2P overlay networks, for a variety of purposes, including data exchange and caching.

3. Related Work

The creation of Condor [15] as one of the first Grid Computing middleware projects paved the way for numerous Desktop Grid projects, that, instead of harnessing computational power from clusters on organizations, sought to take advantage of the internet and distributed desktop users. Many of these projects follow a centralized architecture [1][6][18], using a data distribution system that has one (or few when using mirrors) point of failure. To distribute data sharing, numerous alternatives are available today, in the form P2P file-sharing systems or data storage systems. In this section we discuss some of the more significant ones as they relate to the work proposed here.

OceanStore [12] is a global, distributed, Internet-based storage infrastructure. It consists of cooperating servers that work as both server and client. The data is split up into fragments which are stored redundantly on the servers. For search, OceanStore provides the Tapestry [21] subsystem and updates are performed by using Byzantine consensus protocol. This adds an unnecessary overhead since file search is not a requisite for BOINC and supporting replication implies the use of a distributed locking service, which incurs further performance penalties. Farsite also uses the Byzantine agreement protocol to establish trust within an untrusted environment. Farsite aims to provide the user with persistent non-volatile storage with a filesystem like interface, by utilizing unused storage from user workstations, while operating within the boundaries of an institution.

Freeloader [17] aggregates unused desktop storage space and I/O bandwidth into a shared cache/scratch space for hosting large, immutable datasets and exploiting data access locality. It is designed for large scientific results (outputs of simulations). The overall architecture of Freeloader shares many similarities to Google File System (GFS). GFS is a distributed storage solution which scales in performance and capacity while being resilient to hardware failures. GFS was designed to operate in a trusted environment where the application is the main influence of usage patterns. The GFS typical file size was expected to be in the order of gigabytes and the application workload would consist of large continuous reads and writes, which does not apply to the BOINC environment.

Gnutella [9] is a decentralized file-sharing system whose participants form a virtual network, communicating via the Gnutella protocol, which is a simple protocol for distributed file search. To participate in Gnutella, a peer first must connect to a known Gnutella host, lists of which are available on specialized sites.

KaZaA [14] is similar to Gnutella, although it extends upon this by exploiting peer heterogeneity and organizing the peers into two classes, Super Nodes (SNs) and Ordinary Nodes (ONs). SNs are generally more powerful in terms of connectivity, bandwidth, processing processing power, and are not behind NAT systems. In order to bypass firewall and NAT systems, KaZaA uses dynamic port numbers along with a hierarchical design where a node can act as a relay between two other nodes. Like Gnutella, KaZaA's file discovery mechanism creates unnecessary traffic and its Super Node architecture applied to data distribution on BOINC could generate an unacceptable level of network traffic while relaying requests.

4. Applying a Peer-to-Peer Data Architecture to BOINC

The BOINC architecture is based on a strict master/worker model, with a central server responsible for dividing applications in thousands of small independent tasks and then distributing the tasks to participants, or worker nodes, as they request work units. To simplify network communication and bypass any NAT problems that might arise with bidirectional communication, the centralized server never initiates communication with worker nodes; rather all communication is instantiated from the worker when more work is needed or results are ready for submission. In the current implementation of BOINC, data distribution and scaling is achieved though the use of multiple centralized and mirrored HTTP servers that share data with the entire network.

The centralized architecture of BOINC not only creates a single, or in the case of mirrored servers, small number of failure points and potential bottlenecks, but also it fails to take advantage of the client-side network bandwidth and capabilities. If client-side network bandwidth could be utilized successfully to distribute data sets, not only would it allow for larger data files to be distributed, but it would also minimize the needed network capabilities of BOINC projects, thereby substantially lowering operation costs. To decentralize the current model as it relates to data, we propose using a Peer-to-Peer data distribution approach.

When considering the practical application of P2P technologies to the "production" BOINC environment, several concerns must be adequately addressed if the solution is to be successful. For the purposes of this paper, we have chosen to focus on the following four:

- **Router Configuration** — A Peer-to-Peer infrastructure should have a way to automatically configure routers or somehow bypass NAT issues through use of relaying severs,

- **Data Integrity** — A mechanism for identifying hosts that supply bad data, and subsequently banning them from the network or having ways to avoid using them must be included.
- **Adaptable Network Topology** — Ability not only to adapt on the wide area network, but also to detect and exploit local area network topologies and relative proximity would be necessary.
- **BOINC Integration** — Any new technology must be easy to integrate with current BOINC client software, in practice this means a C++ implementation or binding.

4.1   Case Study of Two Selected P2P Approaches

Applying a P2P data distribution approach could be achieved in a variety of forms. In this paper, we discuss two implementations: one that uses a centralized tracker, as in *BitTorrent* where worker-nodes each share data, discussed in section 5; and the other that employs the use of *decentralized data servers*, built using a super-peer topology that could be configured to limit data sharing participants based upon project defined security constraints, presented in section 6. In the latter case, these policies could be implemented to have the data layer mimic the currently used system of a few known and trusted peers, yet would scale as the network size or data loads increase (by requesting more trusted peers to become data centers). Either of these types of systems would be especially beneficial to projects that: have large input files; use the same input file for several work units; and/or, have limited or slow outbound connections from the central project server. In the rest of the paper, we will present these two different approaches in more detail and outline what they would require to be applied to a BOINC application.

5.   Approach 1: Adapted BitTorrent for Data Distribution

In order to integrate BitTorrent in BOINC, the main BOINC server code remains relatively unchanged but a tracker is needed to co-ordinate the downloads. The tracker manages the .torrent file once it is created and acts as the first seed in the network. On the client side, not only is a BitTorrent client needed to download and share the file, but changes to the BOINC client code would be required. This is due to several reasons, but mainly concerned with the starting and stopping of the BitTorrent client, as well as handling its errors and managing its execution requirements, such as downloading and rebuilding files, verifying signatures, and removing obsolete .torrents.

There are some advantages and disadvantages to implementing a pure Bit-Torrent solution. The advantages are many, for example, BitTorrent has proven itself to be an efficient and low-overhead means of distributing data; can scale easily to large numbers of participants; and has built-in functionality to ensure relatively equal sharing ratios [10]. Some of these advantages, however, turn into disadvantages when trying to apply BitTorrent to a volunteer computing platform. Due to its flat topology, BitTorrent works only if enough nodes in its network are listening for incoming connections, which can prove problematic when confronted with firewalls and NAT systems. Another potential disadvantage when applying BitTorrent to the volunteering computing platform is its "tit-for-tat" sharing requirements, which forces most participants to share on a relatively equal scale with what they are receiving. Although this proves quite effective for preventing selfish file-sharing on traditional home networking systems, it is not necessarily a requirement when applying P2P technologies to volunteer computing. For example, in the volunteer computing case, not everyone may wish to be a BitTorrent node but they may wish to offer their CPU time to a project. Therefore, in the pure tit-for-tat BitTorrent world, this would not be possible.

In the following, the four target issues identified earlier in section 4 are discussed, with a brief overview of how they relate to BitTorrent integration.

Firewall & Router Configuration — BitTorrent, as other P2P protocols, is based on a two-way communication between peers. Every peer, seed or not, is supposed to accept requests for chunks from other peers and therefore must allow incoming connections, by opening the BitTorrent port (usually in the 6881– 6889 range) in their routers/firewalls. In a BitTorrent swarm, should no peer accept incoming connections (including the initial seed), the system would not work.

There is no easy answer for this problem, faced by most P2P protocols. If both clients are behind symmetric NATs, the only solution is to use a relay server, possibly a node with a public IP that would act as an intermediary between two clients. This methodology is used by Skype, but it would prove disastrous in this case, given the size of the shared files, causing an excessive overhead on the relay. For non-symmetric NATs, hole punching techniques could be used, but it would involve changes in the BitTorrent core software layer, which is beyond the scope of this paper.

Malicious Users — The integration of BitTorrent would bring new security issues to BOINC and create more possibilities for malicious users to exploit the system. The BitTorrent protocol itself does not strictly enforce fairness and exploits are possible, but the use of a central tracker decreases the danger of malicious attacks. Hashing prevents bad data from being propagated across the network and small chunk sizes can be used to avoid downloading too much corrupted data. An additional level of security is provided by certain BitTorrent clients like Azureus [23], that bans peers who share bad data. The "original" BitTorrent client by Bram Cohen [7] also incorporates a similar mechanism by default, with the tag: *retaliate-to-garbled-data*, which refuses further connections from addresses with broken or intentionally hostile peers.

Therefore, the main problem with BitTorrent is not in the protocol itself, but rather in the peer swarms which allow BOINC users to obtain a list of other users who are downloading the same file (and possibly executing the same work unit). A client could send consecutive requests for peer lists to the tracker and build a comprehensive database of peers sharing a file. Should a user from the list answer the attacker and agree to cooperate with him, or become compromised, several negative scenarios would be possible. For example, both users could report bad results that would be marked as correct if there were not enough replication. In practice, this number is not higher than three, so two users would build a quorum. Alternatively, they could report a much higher computation time/value than they had to use in an attempt to obtain more credits. A possible solution for this problem would be a trust-based system, in which peers would have a reputation based on their past actions.

Exploiting Network Topology — Another possible benefit of the BitTorrent protocol would be to take advantage of the network topology. Clients could give a higher priority to peers on the same Local Area Network, reducing the traffic generated to the outside. Bram Cohen's BitTorrent client has an option turned on by default, *–use-local-discovery*, that scans the local network for other clients with the desired content. An additional possibility would be to use an approach similar to that in the Julia Content Distribution Network [5], in which nodes gather statistics about the network conditions as the download progresses, and then contact closer nodes (in terms of latency and bandwidth).

Integration with BOINC — To allow for an easy integration with BOINC, the current prototype implementation has been completed in the same language as BOINC, C++. This minimized the conflicts and number of additional software packages needed. Additionally, a failure in the BitTorrent data distribution would simply cause a fallback to the standard centralized nature that BOINC currently implements.

5.1   Proposed Scenario

In this new architecture a BitTorrent tracker is installed on the central server and a port is defined to receive client requests (normally 6881). We decided to use a centralized tracker because the decentralized alternative is very recent. Also, the maintenance and construction of the DHT requires each peer to maintain an orthogonal set of neighbors within the DHT and pay the communication costs of maintaining the DHT in the face of high rates of churn [13]. A .torrent file is created for every input file that should be downloaded through BitTorrent, pointing to the tracker in the central server: file.data -> file.data.torrent. The original file and its torrent counterpart are hosted on a project data server. To start sharing the file, the BOINC server must run a BitTorrent client to act as a seed and announce itself to the tracker.

The .torrent file is related to the data file through the work unit. When creating work, a tag <bittorrent/> is added to the file info of the data file in the work unit template and the .torrent file itself is added as an input file.

Figure 1 shows the architecture and highlights the steps of a file transfer: *(1)* The client contacts the scheduler and asks for work. The scheduler then replies with a given work unit and a reference to a .torrent file that represents an input file made available via BitTorrent. The client then downloads the .torrent file through normal HTTP; *(2)* After downloading the .torrent file, the BOINC client initiates the local BitTorrent client with the .torrent as an argument. The

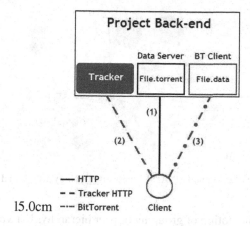

Figure 1. BT BOINC file transfer

BitTorrent library then contacts the tracker defined on the file and receives list of peers. *(3)* Finally, the client contacts the chosen peers and the BitTorrent protocol is used to download the subsequent file chunks and re-assemble the input file for processing by the local BOINC client.

This architecture can help reduce the load on the server and possibly improve transfer times for projects where input files are large and shared by many work units. It can provide new opportunities for projects that were previously limited by bandwidth issues on their server and, by improving the data distribution, speed up the scientific research behind the projects. On the other hand, this approach is likely to be received with skepticism, if not resistance, for three main reasons: *(i)* users are not willing to share their bandwidth when there is no direct benefit - network utilization is not a contributing factor to the credit ratings - and the alternative works; *(ii)* BitTorrent, like other P2P systems, is normally associated with piracy and illegal downloads, which taints its reputation; and, *(iii)* besides motivation, security can also be an issue since, to operate in good conditions, ports must be opened which increases users' vulnerabilities (not necessarily because of the BitTorrent protocol).

Recent experiments on the XtremWeb platform using BitTorrent showed promise [20] and should be an indicator of what to expect in this case. It is important to run experiments on a medium to large scale to ascertain the impact of the BitTorrent protocol on BOINC, as well as to determine the scenarios on which it will have the best performance. We expect to find a crossover point in performance in terms of file size and number of nodes sharing the file between the original BOINC and this version.

6. Approach 2: Super-Peers and Secure Data Centers

BitTorrent can fairly effectively solve the data needs of BOINC as they relate strictly to distribution. However, it has limited security beyond ensuring file

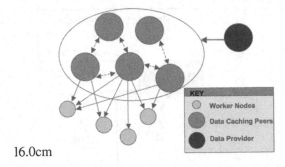

16.0cm

Figure 2.   Snapshot of example P2P-ADICS network topology after initial discovery phase.

integrity and has no notion of grouping or peer hierarchy. For volunteer computing communities, security can be a much larger issue than simply guaranteeing
data validity. Due to the sensitive and vulnerable nature of Desktop Grids,
and in particular volunteer networks used for research purposes, whose user
community is volatile, it is critical not only for data integrity and reliability to
be ensured, but also that peer nodes are secure from malicious attacks. This
requires a number of steps and can be implemented in a variety of fashions, each
with its own benefits and tradeoffs. The easiest, and perhaps most susceptible to
attacks, is a pure P2P network, in which any node is allowed to receive and share
information with any other node on the network, as BitTorrent does. Although
this is perhaps the most efficient use of a P2P network and could potentially
reap the largest rewards so far as potential disk space capacity and network
bandwidth utilization, it is also the most dangerous, given its requirements for
opening ports and generalized policy that all nodes participate on an equal level.
Since any node in this scenario has the capability to flood the network with false
information, regardless of whether it is later discarded as invalid, the probability
that this will happen is much greater than in a restricted network, where only
"trusted" peers are allowed to act as data providers and message relaying, or
rendezvous, nodes.

Secure data centers are a way of implementing a super-peer topology for
data sharing that would restrict the set of peers that are allowed to propagate
data. In this scenario, policies could be set by each BOINC project as to which
participants, if any, are allowed to host and redistribute data. Beyond simply
restricting data center membership, policies could also be introduced to govern
the relative sensitivity of data and retention policies. Adding these new types
of functionality would allow for more advanced scenarios, although with the
additional costs of software and network complexity.

The Secure Data Center ideas discussed here are currently in the process of
being implemented in the form of a software middleware entitled "Peer-to-Peer
Architecture for Data-Intensive Cycle Sharing" (P2P-ADICS) [16], which was
briefly introduced in section 2. P2P-ADICS is building a super-peer architecture
for data sharing that focuses on allowing for the dynamic configuration of group
membership. This facilitates creating secured data-caching overlay networks

that coexist with the conventional super-peer discovery overlay for bootstrapping purposes.

In this scenario, to implement the data sharing aspects of BOINC, a new overlay network would be created that contains only those nodes that have been promoted to data-centers. Within this overlay, data centers propagate data amongst themselves and serve requests to the underlying worker layer.

Figure 2 gives a visual representation of how the different components in this network relate to one another after the initial discovery process has taken place. In this discovery phase (not pictured), a worker node sends a request to known access points on the data center overlay, which responds with an updated list of data centers that the worker node can use to harvest data. Failing to discover anyone, the worker node will directly contact the data provider to request a data center reference.

In the following, the four target issues identified earlier in Section 4 are discussed, with a brief overview of how they relate to Secure Data Center integration and the preliminary implementation states of P2P-ADICS.

Firewall & Router Configuration — Depending on an individual projects configuration, firewall and router issues could be a potential problem, or a complete non-issue. In a free-for-all system where any member node permitted to be a data center, there could obviously be problems with that node's being behind a NAT. In this instance the tradeoff between "punching holes" in the firewall and the potential benefit of the node's available network bandwidth would have to be determined. For more restricted systems, in which pre-specified static or semi-dynamic nodes are dynamically promoted to be data centers as the network requires, firewall and router issues could be minimized, for example, through enforcing eligibility criteria for data centers to only those nodes that have a publicly addressable network space. In this instance, *semi-dynamic*, is referring to nodes that have gone through some pre-screening that verifies them as good candidates for data-centers, such as obtaining a specific certificate or accumulated substantial project credits. However, when they actually perform as data centers is determined dynamically, based upon network properties.

Current design of P2P-ADICS is working with the assumption that a more secured sharing will be desired and enforced. This requires data center peers to be publicly accessible machines, thereby for the moment forgoing the potential pitfalls of attempting to implement automatic firewall configuration, leaving this as a future implementation issue.

Malicious Users — As with *Firewall & Router Configuration*, the issue of how much relative freedom network participants have to manipulate the network will depend on the individual policies of each hosting project. In the most restrictive case, the only nodes that would be allowed to propagate data would be well known and trusted, thereby affording the same level of security currently available in the centralized network. In looser security configurations, which are configured to harvest more participant network resources, the security issues would be roughly equivalent to

BitTorrent as discussed in section 5. The advantage of the system proposed here is that there are middle-ground options lying between these two extreme alternatives that could be exploited.

P2P-ADICS relies on the data signing and validation procedures currently utilized by BOINC, which essentially guarantee that requested data will be what is ultimately retrieved. However, to effectively distribute a single data file from multiple data centers to an individual host, BitTorrent-style file-swarming techniques are being investigated. This requires two-level hashing of data, once on the individual chunks, and once on the entire file. Therefore, this additional chunk-level hashing is in the process of being implemented in an attempt to prevent malicious users from propagating "bad chunks," to the network.

Exploiting Network Topology — Similar to the mechanisms employed by BitTorrent and the Julia Content Distribution Network [5], network proximity would have to be determined to adequately map nodes and decide if any are on a local network. However, if the network parameters are set to limit the participants to known hosts, then the likelihood of internal LAN nodes being available to a given peer as a data center is significantly diminished. In these cases, a two-tier system of data servers is envisioned: one, in the traditional case, which meets certain selection criteria, but is available on the larger network via a public address; and another which has also met the selection criteria for a "trusted node," yet is unavailable to the larger network, but still is available to distribute files to local peers. Alternatively, LAN data centers could have lower security requirements placed upon them, as the data is digital signed to verify integrity. However, this could allow for malicious exploits involving the reporting of false results should multiple recipients on the same LAN be given identical tasks to compute.

P2P-ADICS, through its underlying reliance on P2PS, currently uses UDP multicasting for LAN discovery of data servers, and KaZaA-style "known peers" for WAN discovery. As the project progresses, technologies such as those employed by the Julia Content Distribution Network will be explored for more advanced network topology exploitation.

Integration with BOINC — The Secure Data Center approaches outlined here, in the form of P2P-ADICS, would demand more radical changes and a larger software stack than the BitTorrent implementation proposed in the previous section. This is primarily due to two distinct areas: internal integration with BOINC and external library dependencies. Regarding internal integration, the BitTorrent solutions are fairly straightforward: the centralized HTTP server contact address is simply replaced with the corresponding tracker. In the off-chance case where no peers are mirroring the data, the client simply downloads from the centralized server, as it would have under the current implementation. For P2P-ADICS, to ensure a comparable level of certainty, an if/else statement would have to be injected into the client code, whereby if a lookup on the P2P network failed, clients could resort to traditional download means.

Although this solution adequately manages the problem, it could incur severe latencies if not implemented correctly.

Regarding external library dependencies, BitTorrent solutions could only require the addition of a single C++ BitTorrent library, which could be used to broker BitTorrent downloads. P2P-ADICS is currently being built atop P2PS, which is implemented in Java. This creates a client dependency on a JRE. There are two possible solutions to this problem: *(1)* add a JRE to the required software to run BOINC, which could potentially limit adoption of P2P-ADICS; and, *(2)* create a light-weight client-side C++ implementation of the P2P-ADICS client download capabilities, thereby limiting the JRE requirement to nodes that wish to operate as data centers. The current design and plans for P2P-ADICS is pursuing option *1* in an attempt to build a working system. It will later reassess the necessity of option *2* based upon feedback from the BOINC user-community.

In [8] a more general cycle-sharing paradigm utilizing Peer-to-Peer systems to distribute work units was presented (authors Kelley and Taylor are in the overall design of this system, which is led by ICAR-CNR). Although the work presented there is more generalized, the fundamental "dynamic caching" and data distribution aspects are consistent with the ones presented here, and the results and arguments therein can be directly applied to the scenario proposed here. Specifically, [8] presents an argument that using dynamic data caching, while knowing the network and data properties, can allow for a more efficient configuration of data server replication, as opposed to the current static-sized set used by BOINC projects.

Based upon the preliminary results of [8] and the arguments presented here, it is our belief that decentralized data centers can prove to be both valid and useful solutions to distributing data in Desktop Grid environments. There is, however, a tradeoff between functionality and complexity that needs to be adequately addressed and balanced if such technologies are to be adopted by production environments such as BOINC. P2P-ADICS is an ongoing research project attempting to build a system that can address the needs of scientific users, while maintaining the benefits of a decentralized network that utilizes available network properties at much as possible.

7.   Conclusions

In this paper we have argued that the current centralized client/server architecture applied by BOINC and other Desktop Grid systems for data distribution is limiting and costly; these projects would benefit from P2P data distribution technologies. Specifically, we have presented two approaches for large-scale data management in Desktop Grid domains: one, based directly upon the BitTorrent protocol, and another employing a decentralized unstructured P2P network. For both of these potential solutions, we have provided the reader with arguments for and against, weighing the relative costs and benefits of uptake, as well as giving the current status and directions we are undertaking in our work in these areas. It is hoped that the ideas presented here will promote the discussion of Peer-to-Peer data distribution not only in the BOINC and Desktop Grid groups, but also to the wider scientific community, encouraging others to explore P2P as a valid and useful approach for data distribution.

Acknowledgments

The authors wish to thank Pasquale Cozza and Domenico Talia of DEIS University of Calabria, and Carlo Mastroianni at ICAR-CNR for their contributions and help. This work was supported by the CoreGRID Network of Excellence, the Center for Computation & Technology at Louisiana State University, and EPSRC grant EP/C006291/1.

References

[1] David Anderson. BOINC: A System for Public-Resource Computing and Storage. In *Proceedings of the 5th IEEE/ACM International Workshop on Grid Computing*, Pittsburgh, USA, November 2004.

[2] David Anderson. Volunteer Computing: Planting the Flag. *PCGrid 2007 Workshop*, Long Beach, March 30 2007.

[3] H. Balakrishnan, F. Dabek, M.F. Kaashoek, D.R. Karger, D. Liben-Nowell, R. Morris, and I. Stoica. Chord: a scalable peer-to-peer lookup protocol for Internet applications. *Networking, IEEE/ACM Transactions on*, 11.

[4] Berkeley Open Infrastructure for Network Computing (BOINC). See web site at: http://boinc.berkeley.edu/.

[5] Danny Bickson and Dahlia Malkhi. The Julia Content Distribution Network. *2nd Usenix Workshop on Real, Large Distributed Systems (WORLDS '05)*, San Francisco, USA, December 2005.

[6] F. Cappello, S.Djilali, G.Fedak, T.Herault. F.Magniette, V.Neri, and O.Lodygensky. Computing on large-scale distributed systems: XtremWeb architecture, programming models, security, tests and convergence with Grid. *FGCS Future Generation Computer Science*, 2004.

[7] Bram Cohen. Incentives build robustness in BitTorrent. Proceedings of IPTPS, 2003

[8] Pasquale Cozza, Ian Kelley, Carlo Mastroianni, Domenico Talia, and Ian Taylor. Cache-Enabled Super-Peer Overlays for Multiple Job Submission on Grids. To be published *ISC 2007 CoreGrid Workshop*, 2007.

[9] Gnutella Project. See web site at: http://www.gnutella.com/ .

[10] M. Izal, G. Urvoy-Keller, E. W. Biersack, P. A. Felber, A. A. Hamra, and L. Garces-Erice. Dissecting BitTorrent: Five Months in a Torrent's Lifetime. In *Proceedings of Passive and Active Measurements (PAM)*, 2004.

[11] P. Kacsuk, N. Podhorszki, and T. Kiss. Scalable Desktop Grid System. CoreGRID Technical Report TR-0006, MTA SZTAKI, University of Westminster, 2005.

[12] J. Kubiatowicz, D. Bindel, Y. Chen, S. Czerwinski, P. Eaton, D. Geels, R. Gummadi, S. Rhea, H. Weatherspoon, W. Weimer, C. Wells and B. Zhao Oceanstore: An architecture for global-scale persistent storage. *In the 9th International Conference on Architectural Support for Programming Languages and Operating Systems*, 2000.

[13] J. Li, J. Stribling, R. Morris, M. F. Kaashoek, and T. M. Gil. A performance vs. cost framework for evaluating DHT design tradeoffs under churn. *IEEE Conference on Computer Communications (INFOCOM)*, 2005.

[14] J. Liang, R. Kumar, K. W. Ross. *The KaZaA Overlay: A Measurement Study.* Computer Networks Journal, Oct. 2005.

[15] M. Litzkow, M.Luvby, and M.Mutka. Condor - A Hunter of Idle Workstations. Pages 104-111. *8th International Conference on Distributed Computing Systems (ICDCS).* Washington, DC, 1988.

[16] Peer-to-Peer Architecture for Data-Intensive Cycle Sharing (P2P-ADICS). See web site at: http://www.p2p-adics.org/.

[17] Sudharshan S. Vazhkudai, Xiaosong Ma, Vincent W. Freeh, Jonathan W. Strickland, Nandan Tammineedi, Stephen L. Scott. FreeLoader: Scavenging Desktop Storage Resources for Scientific Data. sc, p. 56,Ê *ACM/IEEE SC 2005 Conference (SC'05),*Ê 2005.

[18] J. Verbeke, N. Nadgir, G. Ruetsch, and I. Sharapov. Framework for Peer-to-Peer Distribution Computing in a Heterogeneous, Decentralized Environment. *Proceedings of the Third International Workshop on Grid Computing,* 2002.

[19] Ian Wang. P2PS (Peer-to-Peer Simplified). In *Proceedings of 13th Annual Mardi Gras Conference - Frontiers of Grid Applications and Technologies,* pages 54–59. Louisiana State University, February 2005.

[20] Baohua Wei, G. Fedak, and F. Cappello. Scheduling independent tasks sharing large data distributed with BitTorrent. pages 219-226. Grid Computing, 2005. The 6thIEEE/ACM International Workshop on, IEEE ComputerSociety, 2005.

[21] B. Y. Zhao, J. Kubiatowicz, and A. Joseph. Tapestry: An Infrastructure for Fault-tolerant Wide-area Location and Routing. UCB Tech Report UCB/CSD-01-1141, University of California, Berkeley, 2001.

[22] List of BOINC projects at: http://boinc.berkeley.edu/projects.php.

[23] Azureus BitTorrent client. See web site at: http://azureus.sourceforge.net/.

TACKLING THE COLLUSION THREAT IN P2P-ENHANCED INTERNET DESKTOP GRIDS

Gheorghe Silaghi, Luis Silva
University of Coimbra, Department of Informatics Engineering
Polo II, 3030-290, Coimbra, Portugal
{gsilaghi, luis}@dei.uc.pt

Patricio Domingues
School of Technology and Management
Polytechnic Institute of Leiria, Portugal
patricio@estg.ipleiria.pt

Alvaro E. Arenas
STFC, Rutherford Appleton Laboratory
Chilton, Didcot, OX11 0QX, UK
a.e.arenas@rl.ac.uk

Abstract   As Internet Desktop Grids become more and more popular in the success story of @Home projects, it is important to provide support for other more demanding applications that make use of large amounts of data to be computed. We have been investigating P2P techniques to facilitate the distribution of large chunks of shared data among an increasing set of workers. When we start using P2P techniques the workers will connect among them and, having a mean of communication, they can develop malicious coalitions. Classical sabotage tolerance techniques adopted by Internet Desktop Grid platforms assume the isolation of workers and do not tackle the collusion threat. In this paper we propose some sabotage tolerance techniques that can be used by a middleware like BOINC if enhanced with a P2P infrastructure for data distribution. The master will build the reputation of all the workers, by observing their trustworthiness from their previous results and the compliance with the P2P data delivery protocols. Reputation information can be incorporated in the result-validation process by using a weighted voting algorithm.

Keywords: desktop grids, collusion, weighted voting, reputation, BitTorrent

1.   Introduction

Internet Desktop Grids [1, 3] aggregate huge distributed resources over the Internet and make them available for running various applications.

BOINC [1], the most popular desktop grid platform, runs about 40 projects and collects together more than 400,000 volunteer computers performing on average over 400 TeraFLOPS [2]. BOINC is organized on a reverse master-worker computational model. The master takes care of all job distribution to workers, including data delivery. A meaningful number of applications that run on top of such distributed environments require various experiments to be performed on the same big amount of shared data. If the number of workers to distribute these shared data is also big, a lot of burden is put on the master. Thus, servers running the master need to have large bandwidth capabilities to scale the data delivery to this increased number of users.

Peer-to-peer content distribution becomes very popular in the last years, due to their scalability and robustness properties. Recent advances [19–20] proved that collaborative file distribution solutions enhances desktop grids by alleviating the bandwidth needs at the server side. With respect to BOINC, Costa et al. [5] proposes the usage BitTorrent [4] as a P2P data sharing technique to tackle the data distribution problem. By adopting this solution, workers will become peers and will acquire a technical mean of collaboration. But, this technical infrastructure can also be used to raise a collective malicious behavior, while we can not assume that peers are trustworthy and they do not pursue to sabotage the computation.

In its classical topology, BOINC volunteers are independent and isolated entities. The master guarantees the dependability of the system by implementing sabotage tolerance techniques [6] to cope with malicious volunteers. Among other techniques, BOINC uses replication with majority voting [1, 17]. But, if the workers are networked, small-sized malicious controlling coalitions can emerge and undermine the result outcome of voting processes, even in the presence of a majority of honestly-behaving workers. In the volunteer computing community, Zhao et al. [21] acknowledge the collusion threat for volunteers that can communicate to each other, using, for example, a DHT.

To face the new collision threat, this paper proposes to combine weighted voting with reputation for determining whether to accept a result or not. The master will possess a trust table with entries for each worker containing the reputation values. Before accepting the results, based on the reputation of the workers which have already computed the task, the master can decide on-the-fly if further replication is required. For building the reputation, we adapt the quizzes technique of Zhao et al. [21] to the requirements of BOINC.

Further, the behavior of workers in the BitTorrent P2P network could constitute valuable information to adjust the reputation values of socially-connected workers. We consider that a peer who did not comply with the BitTorrent protocol during data distribution is more likely to sabotage in the volunteer computing. In the BitTorrent network, we ask peers to assess the effectiveness of the collaboration received from other peers and to build local trust. The master will collect these local trust values, and applying the EigenTrust algorithm [11] can assess the global peers' trustworthiness in the BitTorrent distribution.

The paper is organized as follows. In section 2 we describe related work in the area of sabotage tolerance for volunteer computing. Section 3 presents the weighted voting decision criteria. Section 4 talks about reputation, presenting how the master builds the direct reputation of workers with the quizzes approach and the inference process for the indirect reputation assessing the trustworthiness of peers in the data distribution protocol. Section 5 concludes the paper.

2. Related work

Various schemes were proposed for sabotage tolerance. Sander and Tschudin [16] propose the usage of encryption techniques. When the master assigns a task, it includes two functions: specifically $f(x)$, representing the target of the computation, and an encrypted function $E(f)(x)$. At the end of the computation, the master verifies the received results $y = f(x)$ and $y' = E(f)(x)$. If $y = P(f)(y')$, where P is the decryption of E, the participant is considered trustworthy. The difficulty of this approach resides in generating the encrypted function $E(f)$ for a given function f.

If the volunteer computing platform has to solve a search problem over some space D, each worker will be responsible for searching a subspace D_i. According with Golle and Mironov [9], the master can plant ringers in each subspace to be sure the workers indeed carry out the full search. Similar to ringers is chaff injection proposed by Du et al. [8], which addresses the problem of 'hoarding cheaters'. Hoarding cheaters discover rare results in their search space but avoid reporting them, as they believe they can valorize these results in another better way.

BOINC uses replication for result validation [1]. For each work unit, more than one result replicas are created. If M is the replication factor, the master accepts a result only if at it collects least M responses that agree on the same result. This method gives impressive results for the case when the total number of saboteurs is very small. But it is very computation-demanding requesting each task to be computed at least twice and can not be used in volunteer environments with low resources [21].

A complement to replication is sampling. Instead of verifying all received results, the master perform sampling and verifies only a subset of them - named probes [7]. If probes verification succeeds, then the master accepts the results received from the verified worker. This technique can be easily compromised by malicious workers if they are able to distinguish the probes from the real applications.

Sarmenta [17] introduces probing by spot checking. Probes - named now spotters, are tasks with known results. If a worker fails to compute correctly a spotter, it will get blacklisted and all its results will be invalidated. Based on spot-checking, Sarmenta defines the credibility of a worker and a result. The credibility of a worker is an estimate of the probability the worker will return a correct result. The credibility of a result is the conditional probability that the result originating from a worker will be accepted as correct. Workers build credibility by passing spot checking. Specifically, if f is the proportion of malicious nodes, the credibility of a worker which correctly computed k spotters will be $1 - \frac{f}{1-f} \frac{1}{ke}$. If the master receives a result from a worker with a credibility less than some threshold ϑ, it will ask for a new result replica for that work unit. After workers pass enough spotters, they succeed to secure a high-enough credibility for their results.

Quizzes proposed by Zhao et al. [21] are very similar with the above-mentioned spotters. The probes are short questions with easy-to-compute responses. The master sends batches of jobs to workers and inserts such quizzes in each batch. If the worker responds correctly to quizzes, the results are accepted without additional verification. Workers gain reputation by passing quizzes. The master decides how many quizzes to administrate to a worker according with its reputation. Thus, a reputed worker get less verified. This is a trap for malicious volunteers which can behave well for a long period of time and then, start cheating, as they get enough reputation. Because the quizzes are usually short questions, the workers can easily distinguish them from the real tasks. Thus, a cheating strategy could be to compute correctly every medium-to-short length tasks and cheat only for long duration tasks, which have a small probability to be probes. The master should posses an efficient method for generating quizzes [6] and make the quizzes indistinguishable for the worker.

All the above-mentioned approaches do not directly tackle the collusion threat.

3.   Replication: Weighted Voting

In this section, we describe the weighted voting decision criteria for selecting the correct result for work unit.

Let assume a work unit was replicated n times to workers w_i, $i = \overline{1, n}$ and we collected m distinct results r_j, $j = \overline{1, m}$. The master holds a trust table $\mathscr{T}$ containing the reputation value t_i for each worker w_i. The reputation value t_i is a real number from interval $[0, 1]$, assessing how trustable is user i. In section 4 we will show how the master builds the trust table.

If $m = 1$ and $n = 1$ (i.e. only one result supplied by only one worker), we will directly accept this result if the reputation of the worker is 1. Otherwise, to decide which result r_j to accept, the master employs a weighted voting tournament [14], each result collecting the weighted votes of the workers that produced the result. Reputation values t_i constitute the weights.

Formally, we denote $\varphi_{i,j} = 1$ if the worker w_i computed the result r_j and $\varphi_{i,j} = 0$ otherwise. Thus, each result r_j yields a relative score s_j of eq. (1):

$$s_j = \frac{\sum_i \varphi_{i,j} t_i}{\sum_i t_i} \tag{1}$$

If $s_{j^*} = \max_j s_j$, the weighted voting decision criteria accepts result r_{j^*} if $s_{j^*} > \theta$, where θ is the required quorum (i.e. the result that scored maximum and this score is higher than the required quorum).

The quorum θ need to be selected after experiments such that

- $\theta > 0.5$, i.e. no minority can win

- to guarantee a good fitness of the results in the presence of low reputation workers.

In addition to the classical decision criteria presented above, we impose another restriction. Formally, if w_l is the lower reputed worker in set $\{w_i \mid \varphi_{i,j^*} = 1\}$ of winning workers and the result r_{j^*} would loose the voting contest without the contribution of w_l, then we require $t_l > 0.5$. According with Shapley and Shubik [18], the worker w_l is named *pivotal*.

By imposing this condition we remove the possibility that a low reputed worker to turn the voting balance toward a particular result and it protects the master against the possibility that a coalition of low reputed workers to undermine the result submitted by a high reputed worker. E.g., in the absence of condition this condition, 3 workers with reputation of 0.4 submitting the same result could overturn the result submitted by a worker with reputation 0.9. More, if two contradicting results are claimed by high reputed workers, the restriction over the reputation of the pivotal worker would forbid a low reputation worker to become decisive in the weighted voting tournament.

4. Reputation

In this section, we present the way the master builds the reputation value for each worker.

Reputation is what is generally said or believed about a persons' or things' character or standing, being a mean of building trust, as one can trust another based on a good reputation [10]. Therefore, reputation is a measure of trustworthiness.With regard to our problem, the master builds the reputation of workers by assessing their behavior in the volunteer computing pool. Each worker plays two roles: *workers* (i.e. computing tasks on the behalf of the master) and *peers* (i.e. helping the data distribution by participating in the BitTorrent protocol). The master is able to observe only the behavior or the participants as workers, while it needs to interrogate the community to find out the participants' behavior as peers. Reputation collected by assessing the behavior as a worker will represent the *direct reputation*. Reputation collected from the community will represent the *indirect reputation* and will potentially affect the direct reputation. The master will store the reputation values in its trust table, used for the weighted voting decision criteria.

4.1 Direct reputation

The master builds the direct reputation of a worker adapting the quizzes technique [21] for BOINC.

Using quizzes, the reputation of a worker is directly proportional to the number of quizzes successfully passed by the worker. Zhao et al. [21] proved that, if the worker passed v quizzes, in the case that 50% of the workers are malicious and each worker defects with a probability uniformly distributed between 0 and 1, then, the number m' of additional quizzes the worker should pass to obtain the error rate Err of a result is given by eq. (2):

$$m' = \sqrt{\frac{1}{Err}} - v - 2 \tag{2}$$

Thus, the amount $m_{max} = \sqrt{\frac{1}{Err}} - 2$ represents the maximum number of quizzes a worker should pass to acquire enough reputation for guaranteeing that its results are correct given the error rate Err. Therefore, each quiz passed successfully by a worker increases its reputation with $\frac{1}{m_{max}}$. Figure 1 show how many quizzes a worker should pass in order to obtain different demanded error rates.

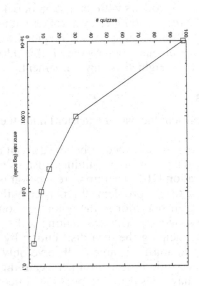

Figure 1.   Number of quizzes a worker should pass to obtain different demanded error rates

Adapting quizzes to BOINC platform is a difficult step. If by a quiz we refer to an indistinguishable task with an easy verifiable response, then, the master would have to embed quizzes together with real applications in one work unit, i.e. one executable. Thus, the master would have to append the quizzes at the end of the real application and to expect the response for quizzes in a particular position of the output file. But, this implies run-time generation of the application executable for work units. We consider that this is difficult to achieve in BOINC, because BOINC applications are compiled independent of the sabotage tolerance method used for result validation.

Instead, we propose to consider as a passed quiz each work unit successfully validated by the master, using the weighted voting replication. First, the master selects some acceptable error rate Err. When a new worker joins the computing environment, this host will get an initial reputation of 0. Each result produced by the worker will enter the weighted voting tournament. If the result is accepted, reputation of the worker will increase by the amount $\frac{1}{m_{max}}$.

We can note that after worker's reputation reaches 1, its results will be validated without any replication. To avoid the attack of a worker which behaves correctly for a long period of time and starts cheating only after a while, the master will register the time stamp t_e of every correctly computed result that contributed to the reputation of the worker. The master keeps the results together with their time stamps in a database and discards these results after a time period δ_t (which can be 1 week, 1 month etc.). When discarding a result from the results database, the master will update the worker's reputation by subtracting the value $\frac{1}{m_{max}}$. With this scheme, if a worker does not contribute to the volunteer environment for a while, its reputation will decrease gradually, as its results are dropped out of the master's database. If a result gets invalidated by the decision of the weighted replication, as advised in [21], the master will halve the reputation of the originating worker.

4.2   Indirect reputation

In subsection 4.1 we described the way a worker can collect reputation by correctly computing the work units. Although [21] reports very good results by applying the quizzes, we still did not consider the possibility of collusion. Now, workers have the means of communicating, because they are peers in the BitTorrent distribution. We consider that observing the workers behavior in BitTorrent is meaningful, because it can give an indication about the character of the peer. If a peer exploits or tries to sabotage the BitTorrent data distribution protocol, it would be much likely for that peer to attempt sabotage the BOINC computations.

To discover the above-mentioned behavior, we will let each peer to locally build the reputation of partners in the BitTorrent protocol. Before entering the weighted voting tournament, the master will ask the workers to deliver their information regarding another worker which produced a particular result. This information will allow the master to infer on the worker's trustworthiness and adjust the direct reputation values accordingly.

Although BitTorrent [4] has some incentive-based design mechanisms that emphasizes peer collaboration, it was proved that exploits are possible [15]. Peers free ride on BitTorrent, by downloading without uploading. Therefore, from the point of view of a peer i, another peer j has a good reputation if it lets i to download and the amount of data downloaded from peer j is higher than the amount i uploaded to j. If we denote by $d_{j \to i}$ the amount of data peer i downloaded from j, then, the download-upload factor d_{ij} is the report between $d_{j \to i}$ and $d_{i \to j}$. Higher the download-upload factor is, more reputed peer j is in the view of peer i. d_{ij} is the local reputation of peer i concerning peer j.

Regarding the download-upload factor of peers, a concern might relate peers that runs BOINC from home and have a slow Internet connection or their Internet Service Providers shape their traffic. Experiments [13] with the BitTorrent protocol shows that peers with similar bandwidth capabilities cluster themselves, i.e. a peer exchanges most of the data chunks with other peers with a similar bandwidth profile. Slow peers stay longer in the torrent and end up downloading from the seed, as the faster peers finish downloading earlier and leave the torrent. Therefore, we expect that bandwidth capabilities of peers to have a minor influence over the download-upload factor.

Further, we equip each peer i with a blacklist containing peers which tried to sabotage the data distribution. Peer i bans all peers j on its blacklist from further interactions within the BitTorrent distribution. A peer can get banned because it uploaded corrupted chunks of data or because it tried to abuse the connection it has with another peer in other ways. We can assume that if a peer is malicious and abuses its partners, it will do so it with majority of the peers in the pool.

Suppose the master coordinates n peers $p_1, \ldots, p_n$ in the BitTorrent distribution. The master performs the weighted voting decision criteria in order to accept a result. Decision criteria tournament runs over results submitted back by m workers $w_1, \ldots, w_m$ out of the n peers. Regarding each worker w_j, the master will ask each peer p_i ($p_i \neq w_j$) to report if w_j is on its blacklist or if not, to deliver the value d_{ij}.

Under the assumption that at most $\lceil n/3 \rceil$ peers are malicious, if we obtain at least $\lceil n/3 \rceil$ blacklists responses for a worker j, we can classify that w_j is malicious, invalidate its result and blacklist it from the volunteer environment. The value $\lceil n/3 \rceil$ is the maximum number of malicious peers a Byzantine agreement protocol can accommodate [12].

If no workers were classified as malicious after the verification of the blacklist information, the master possesses a matrix $D = \{d_{ij}\}$ ($d_{ii} = 0$) with the download-upload factors, which in fact are local trust values. The master can build this matrix as it coordinates the BitTorrent distribution and has all contribution values of all peers. Starting with this matrix, the master can apply the EigenTrust algorithm [11] to obtain the global trust value for each peer. This algorithm proceeds as follows:

- first, normalize matrix D to matrix $C = \{c_{ij}\}$ such as $c_{ij} = \frac{d_{ij}}{\sum_j d_{ij}}$

- initialize a vector $\vec{t}^{(0)} = (t_i^{(0)})$ with $t_i^{(0)} = \frac{1}{n}$ for every $1 \leq i \leq n$

- compute iteratively the vector $\vec{t}^{(k+1)} = C^T \vec{t}^{(k)}$, until the difference $\left\| \vec{t}^{(k+1)} - \vec{t}^{(k)} \right\|$ is less than a small value ϵ

- the values of vector $\vec{t}^{(k+1)}$ are the eigen values of matrix C and represent the global (indirect) trust values of each peer, as emerged from the peer compliance with the BitTorrent protocol.

Kamvar et al. [11] demonstrated that this algorithm converges and this scheme of computing the trust values is resistant against various attacks, including the one with collective malicious peers that supplies good reputation to each other while supplying a bad reputation to other peers.

Therefore, we can use them as a substitute for the indirect reputation, in order to adjust the direct reputation values of section 4.1. The reputation that will represent the weight of a vote will therefore be the direct reputation multiplied with the indirect global reputation value.

5. Conclusion

This paper describes sabotage tolerance techniques for tackling the workers' collusion problem in Internet Desktop Grids. Our methods address the BOINC platform, equipped with the BitTorrent data distribution facilities. Workers, now being involved in a P2P data distribution protocol, have the means of communicating each other and they can develop malicious coalitions to undermine the BOINC computations. We track the workers' behavior by the mean of reputation. To incorporate reputation in the result validation decision criteria, we adopted the weighted voting procedure. Reputation is collected from two sources. First, we assess the volunteers' previous behavior using the quizzes technique, adapted for BOINC. Second, using the EigenTrust algorithm, we compute the global reputation that emerges out of the local trust each peer develops regarding its partners in the BitTorrent data distribution.

As a further research, we plan to experiment our proposed sabotage tolerance methods. More, if the research in enhancing Internet Desktop Grids with P2P capabilities goes further, we plan to investigate new techniques for addressing data security issues and for restricting the possibility that a clique of malicious peers to get control over some part of the new created P2P network.

Acknowledgments

This research work is supported by the European Network of Excellence CoreGRID (project reference number 004265).

References

[1] David P. Anderson. BOINC: A system for public-resource computing and storage. In Rajkumar Buyya, editor, *5th International Workshop on Grid Computing (GRID 2004), Proceedings*, pages 4–10. IEEE Computer Society, 2004.

[2] David P. Anderson, and John McLeod VII. Local Scheduling for Volunteer Computing In *Large-Scale, Volatile Desktop Grids (PCGrid 2007)* 30 March 2007, Long Beach, USA.

[3] F. Cappello, S. Djilali, G. Fedak, T. Herault, F. Magniette, V. Neri, and O. Lodygensky. Computing on large-scale distributed systems: XtremWeb architecture, programming models, security, tests and convergence with grid. *Future Generation Computing Systems*, 21(3):417–437, 2005.

[4] B. Cohen. Incentives build robustness in BitTorrent. In *Proceedings of the Workshop on Economics of Peer-to-Peer Systems*, Berkeley, CA, USA, 2003.

[5] Fernando Costa, Luis M. Silva, Ian Kelley, Ian Taylor, Peert-to-Peer Techniques for Data Distribution in Desktop Ggrid Computing Platforms. In *CoreGrid Workshop on Grid and P2P System Architectures*, Heraklion, Grece, 2007

[6] Patricio Domingues, Bruno Sousa, and Luis Moura Silva. Sabotage-tolerance and trust management in desktop grid computing. *Future Generation Computer Systems*, 23(7):904–912, 2007.

[7] Wenliang Du, Jing Jia, Manish Mangal, and Mummoorthy Murugesan. Uncheatable grid computing. In *24th International Conference on Distributed Computing Systems (ICDCS 2004)*, pages 4–11. IEEE Computer Society, 2004.

[8] Wenliang Du and Michael T. Goodrich. Searching for high-value rare events with uncheatable grid computing. In *Applied Cryptography and Network Security, Third International Conference, ACNS 2005, Proceedings*, volume 3531 of *LNCS*, pages 122–137. Springer, 2005.

[9] Philippe Golle and Ilya Mironov. Uncheatable distributed computations. In *Topics in Cryptology - CT-RSA 2001, The Cryptographer's Track at RSA Conference 2001, Proceedings*, volume 2020 of *LNCS*, pages 425–440. Springer, 2001.

[10] A. Jfisang, R. Ismail, and C. Boyd. A Survey of Trust and Reputation Systems for Online Service Provision *Decision Support Systems*, 43(2):618–644, 2007.

[11] S.D. Kamvar, M.T. Schlosser, and H. Garcia-Molina. The Eigentrust algorithm for reputation management in P2P networks In *WWW '03: Proceedings of the 12th Intl. Conference on World Wide Web*, pages 640–651, ACM Press, 2003.

[12] Leslie Lamport, Robert Shostak, and Marshall Pease. The Byzantine General Problem *ACM Transactions on Programming Languages and Systems*, 4(3):382–401, 1982.

[13] Arnaud Legout, Nikitas Liogkas, Eddie Kohler, Lixia Zhang. Clustering and Sharing Incentives in BitTorrent Systems *ACM SIGMETRICS Performance Evaluation Review*, 35(1):301–312, 2007

[14] Jonathan Levin and Barry Nalebuff. An Introduction to Vote-Counting Schemes *The Journal of Economic Perspectives*, 9(1):3–26, 1995.

[15] Nikitas Liogkas, Robert Nelson, Eddie Kohler, and Lixia Zhang. Exploring the robustness of BitTorrent peer-to-peer content distribution systems. *Concurrency and Computation: Practice and Experience*, In Press, 2007.

[16] Tomas Sander and Christian F. Tschudin. Protecting mobile agents against malicious hosts. In Giovanni Vigna, editor, *Mobile Agents and Security*, volume 1419 of *LNCS*, pages 44–60. Springer, 1998.

[17] Luis F. G. Sarmenta. Sabotage-tolerance mechanisms for volunteer computing systems. *Future Gener. Comput. Syst.*, 18(4):561–572, 2002.

[18] L. S. Shapley and Martin Shubik. A Method for Evaluating the Distribution of Power in a Committee System. *The American Political Science Review*, 48(3):787–792, 1954

[19] Baohua Wei, G. Fedak, and F. Cappello. Scheduling independent tasks sharing large data distributed with BitTorrent. In *Grid Computing, 2005. The 6th IEEE/ACM International Workshop on*, pages 219–226, 2005. IEEE Computer Society.

[20] Baohua Wei, Gilles Fedak, and Franck Cappello. Collaborative data distribution with bittorrent for computational desktop grids. In *ISPDC '05: Proceedings of the The 4th Intl. Symposium on Parallel and Distributed Computing (ISPDC'05)*, pages 250–257, 2005. IEEE Computer Society.

[21] Shanyu Zhao and Virginia Lo and Chris GauthierDickey. Result Verification and Trust-Based Scheduling in Peer-to-Peer Grids. In *P2P '05: Proceedings of the 5th IEEE Intl. Conference on Peer-to-Peer Computing (P2P'05)*, pages 31–38, 2005. IEEE Computer Society.

Index